THE ROYALIST REVOLUTION

THE ROYALIST REVOLUTION

MONARCHY AND THE AMERICAN FOUNDING

ERIC NELSON

THE BELKNAP PRESS *of* HARVARD UNIVERSITY PRESS
Cambridge, Massachusetts
London, England
2014

Library of Congress Cataloging-in-Publication Data

Nelson, Eric, 1977–

    The royalist revolution : monarchy and the American founding / Eric Nelson.

        pages cm.

    Includes bibliographical references and index.

    ISBN 978-0-674-73534-7 (alk. paper)

  1. Political science—United States—History—18th century. 2. United States—Politics and government—18th century. 3. Constitutional history—United States—18th century. 4. Monarchy. I. Title.

  JA84.U5N35 2014

  320.47309'033—dc23   2014008415

For Quentin Skinner,
friend and teacher

Contents

The Rebels have erected the Standard at Cambridge; they call themselves the King's Troops and us the Parliaments. Pretty Burlesque!

—Lieutenant John Barker, 4th (King's Own) Regiment,
  May 1, 1775

"The War of Parliament"

On June 1, 1787, James Wilson of Pennsylvania rose in the Constitutional Convention to offer the motion that would create the American presidency. The new federal executive, he proposed, should "consist of a single person," and this chief magistrate should be vested with sweeping prerogative powers.[1] His colleague Edmund Randolph of Virginia immediately objected, declaring that "a unity in the Executive magistracy" would amount to "the foetus of monarchy" and insisting that Americans, having just rebelled against the British Crown, had "no motive to be governed by the British Government as our prototype."[2] Wilson, as reported by Rufus King of Massachusetts, responded as follows: "The people of America did not oppose the British King but the parliament—the opposition was not against an Unity but a corrupt multitude."[3] With this remark, Wilson grounded his constitutional program in a particular understanding of the character and purposes of the American Revolution. The colonists, on this view, had rebelled against a "corrupt multitude," not a monarch. They had sought protection for their liberties in the prerogatives of the Crown, not in the wisdom of popular assemblies. Those who would keep faith with "Revolution principles" ought therefore to favor the creation of a strong, independent chief magistrate—one wielding an "absolute negative" on legislation, plenary power of appointment to executive and judicial offices, the prerogative of clemency, and the dazzling authority of commander-in-chief. Only such a figure could truly represent the people as a whole and tame the tyrannical proclivities and partialities of the legislature. Wilson's remarks clearly resonated with the man who transcribed them. Years later, Thomas Hart

I

Benton of Missouri recalled a conversation with the aged Rufus King "upon the formation of the constitution in the federal convention of 1787." On this occasion, he explained, King "said some things to me which, I think ought to be remembered by future generations, to enable them to appreciate justly those founders of our government who were in favor of a stronger organization than was adopted."

> He said: "You young men who have been born since the Revolution, look with horror upon the name of a King, and upon all propositions for a strong government. It was not so with us. We were born the subjects of a King, and were accustomed to subscribe ourselves 'His Majesty's most faithful subjects'; and we began the quarrel which ended in the Revolution, not against the King, but against his parliament."[4]

This book is, in effect, an extended attempt to take the claims of Wilson and King seriously. The American Revolution, unlike the two seventeenth-century English revolutions and the French Revolution, was—for a great many of its protagonists—a revolution against a legislature, not against a king. It was, indeed, a rebellion in favor of royal power. Colonial whigs who had long been "slumbering under the old prejudices in favour of Parliamentary power" suddenly found themselves confronted in the 1760s and 1770s with a parliament that claimed the right to legislate for them "in all cases whatsoever."[5] Those we call "patriots" eventually responded to this challenge by developing the view that Parliament possessed no jurisdiction whatsoever over British North America. The colonies, they insisted, were connected to Britain solely through "the person and prerogative of the king."[6] But the late eighteenth-century British monarchy was in no position to function as the "pervading" and "superintending" power of the empire. The constitutional settlement that followed the Glorious Revolution had definitively subjected the king to Parliament, drastically curtailing his prerogatives and recasting him as a pure "executive."[7] The powers of state that legally remained with the Crown were no longer in fact wielded by the person of the king, but rather by ministers who were required to command a parliamentary majority (and who themselves sat in one of the two houses). Patriots of the late 1760s and 1770s were effectively proposing to turn back the clock on the English constitution by over a hundred years—to separate the king from his Parliament and his British ministers and to restore ancient prerogatives of the Crown that had been extinguished by the whig ascendancy. These theorists wanted more monarchy, not less.[8] Their complaint, as summarized by Benjamin Franklin, was that the Lords and Commons "seem to have been long encroaching on the Rights of their and our Sovereign, assuming too much of his Authority, and betraying his Interests."[9] Defenders of the British administration during the revolutionary period did not accuse patriots of being crypto-republicans, but rather of being de facto Jacobites and absolutists. As we shall see, the patriots were neither, but the charge reflected an awareness of the extraordinary degree to which American opposition writers had left the whig tradition behind them.

Indeed, as patriots attempted to make ideological sense of their new position, a great many gravitated toward the political and constitutional theory of those who had waged the last great campaign against the "usurpations" and "encroachments" of Parliament: the reviled Stuart monarchs of the seventeenth century. These patriots came to recognize that the very same questions about prerogative power and the theory of representation that had divided king and Parliament in the 1620s, 1630s, and 1640s were now dividing Britain's Atlantic empire. But, despite their impeccably whig upbringing, they found themselves taking the Royalist side in these disputes. For James I and Charles I had never permitted their parliaments to meddle in colonial affairs. They had regarded the colonies as private dominions of the Crown to be governed by the royal prerogative and had emphatically denied that such an arrangement was incompatible with the liberty of their subjects. Patriots consequently traced the origins of the imperial crisis of the 1760s to the defeat of the seventeenth-century Royalist cause. The first parliamentary bill that legislated for America, the Navigation Act of 1651, had been passed in the wake of the regicide by the Long Parliament—the very same body that had first declared "all the Dominions and Territories" of the Crown to be under "the Supreme Authority of this Nation, The Representatives of the People in Parliament."[10] In the words of one American pamphleteer, it was only "after the death of King *Charles* the First" that "the Commonwealth Parliament, which usurped the rights of the Crown, naturally concluded, that by those rights they had acquired some kind of supremacy over the Colonies of *America*."[11] This first act of legislative "usurpation" had been allowed to stand even after the Restoration of 1660, thus establishing a nefarious precedent that had been used to justify increasingly brazen encroachments by Parliament on the king's prerogative to govern his possessions in America. In the great constitutional crisis of the seventeenth century, so patriots came to believe, the Royalists had gotten it right after all.

When the rupture with Britain finally arrived in the early months of 1776, it was because George III refused the invitation of his American subjects to revive the defunct prerogatives of the House of Stuart. He was determined, as he put it, to continue "fighting the Battle of the Legislature," to be a parliamentary king or none at all.[12] But patriots no longer had any use for a parliamentary king; they sought instead the independent government of a transcendent, revivified sovereign. As the young Alexander Hamilton stated the case in 1775, the king "is the only Sovereign of the empire," such that "the part which the people have in the legislature, may more justly be considered as a limitation of the Sovereign authority."[13] Such an arrangement, on this account, was uniquely favorable to liberty because a monarch "is under no temptation to purchase the favour of one part of his dominions, at the expense of another; but, it is his interest to treat them all, upon the same footing. Very different is the case with regard to the Parliament. The Lords and Commons both, have a private and separate interest to pursue."[14] It was for the sake of this constitutional theory that a great many British Americans rebelled. As the king's prime minister, Lord North, would later reflect, "the American war, with all its horrors and misfortunes" was emphatically not a "war of the crown"; it was, rather, "the war of parliament." Indeed, "it was the war of the people; for it was undertaken for the express purpose of maintaining the just rights of parliament, or in other words, of the people of Great Britain, over the dependencies of the empire."[15] The administration pamphleteer John Lind took precisely the same view, insisting that "in considering the present contest between Great Britain and America, it is a truth which deserves our particular attention, and which therefore cannot be too often repeated, nor too strongly inculcated, that the dispute is not, *nor ever has it been,* between his *Majesty* and the *whole,* or any *part,* of his subjects. The dispute is *clearly between one part of his subjects and another.* The blow given by the Congress [in July 1776] appears indeed to be leveled at his *Majesty;* but the wound was intended for *us.*"[16]

On this point, at least, Lind's patriot opponents were in complete agreement. A British officer stationed with General Thomas Gage recorded on May 1, 1775, that "the Rebels have erected the Standard at Cambridge; they call themselves the King's Troops and us the Parliaments. Pretty Burlesque!"[17] The following month, a second British officer likewise reported to his superiors that "in all the American papers they exult much at the victory which they say they have gained over the Parliament Troops, as they call us & themselves the King's loyal & faithful subjects."[18] As late as 1776, an influential Philadelphia pamphleteer could still write that "the present contest is a contest of Constitutions, and the war a war of Legislatures. The common wars of nations are the wars of one crowned head against another, in which the people have little share, and are as little consulted. . . . But this war is a war between the *British* Parliament and the Colonial Assemblies."[19] It was because the king so resolutely refused to take the American side in this "contest of Constitutions" that his colonial subjects eventually determined to cut him loose.

The story of "patriot Royalism" does not, however, end in 1776. Despite the coming of independence and the abolition of the kingly office in America, those patriots who had most aggressively developed and propagated the neo-Stuart defense of prerogative power during the imperial crisis—John Adams, James Wilson, Alexander Hamilton, James Iredell, Benjamin Rush, and their allies—never changed their minds.[20] In energetic defiance of whig orthodoxy, they continued to argue for the next two decades that sweeping prerogatives in a single chief magistrate were not only compatible with the liberties of citizens and subjects, but in fact necessary for the preservation of free states. They likewise kept faith with the narrative of English constitutional decline that they had embraced during the imperial crisis, according to which it was the *erosion* of monarchical power in the wake of the parliamentarian revolutions that had corrupted the balanced constitution of Great Britain. The patriot campaign of the 1760s and 1770s, they insisted, had been waged to restore this balance. They all agreed, in Wilson's words, that "the people of America did not oppose the British king but the parliament."[21]

These theorists, whose ideas had provided the basis for a broad continental consensus in the waning years of the imperial crisis, found themselves suddenly marginalized in the immediate aftermath of independence. They emerged as fierce critics of the overwhelmingly whig state constitutions adopted during the first year of the Revolutionary War, fighting doggedly for the radical vision of independent prerogative power on behalf of which they had rebelled. Their efforts, while initially unsuccessful, began to bear fruit in the later 1770s and laid the foundation for a broad resurgence of Royalist constitutionalism in the 1780s. It is, indeed, no coincidence that virtually every patriot pamphleteer who defended the neo-Stuart account of the royal

prerogative in the twilight of Britain's Atlantic empire emerged in the following decade as a leading advocate for the chief magistracy created in Philadelphia in 1787. The Constitution, we might say, upheld the spirit of '75.

The account offered here thus departs quite significantly from the standard historiography on the political thought of the Revolution. Since the
1960s, scholars have tended to portray the patriots as radical whigs, or
republicans-in-waiting, who were motivated by a terror of crown power and
executive corruption.[22] The colonists may have turned briefly to the king on
the eve of Revolution, but this, we are assured, was essentially a forensic
ploy designed to outflank the ministry. After all, countless rebels against
monarchy in European history had claimed to be resisting "wicked" counselors in the name of their king. Even the Long Parliament had done so. Patriots, on this view, never seriously wished to augment royal power in
America; they merely sought to vindicate the supremacy of their colonial
legislatures by asserting an exclusive and more or less nominal connection
to the Crown (along the lines of what would later emerge as the British
Commonwealth).[23] The patriot flirtation with this "dominion" model came
to a conclusive end in January 1776, when the radical whig political theory of
the imperial crisis gave way, more or less seamlessly, to the overt republicanism of the Revolution itself. The latter ideology, with its egalitarian vision of popular sovereignty and its deep suspicion of executive power, carried the newly independent United States through the 1770s, only to be
supplanted by a new and more "conservative" (or sometimes "liberal") science of politics that took shape during the confederation crisis in the 1780s.[24]

Like all students of the subject, I am deeply indebted to the pioneering
scholars who developed this narrative, but I have come to believe that it is
doubly mistaken. First, patriots did indeed take up the banner of the royal
prerogative in the final years of the imperial crisis, and their campaign reflected a sincere desire to rebalance the English constitution in favor of the
Crown. In taking this view, I am associating myself with a much older line
of scholarship. It was Charles Howard McIlwain who observed in 1923 that
"the struggle popularly called the American Revolution, up to its latest constitutional phase, was a contest solely between the Americans and Parliament. The Crown was not involved."[25] Seen from this perspective, it becomes wholly unsurprising that "America's final constitutional position was
not Whig at all: it was a position not merely non-Whig, but anti-Whig."[26]
McIlwain's insight, which has since been endorsed by a small but distin-

guished group of scholars, is the beginning of wisdom.[27] Yet as we shall see, American patriots of the 1770s did not simply take up a constitutional position that *we* might regard in retrospect as anti-whig. Rather, a great many of them quite self-consciously and momentously ceased to be whigs. Their turn to the royal prerogative did not leave their most basic political and philosophical commitments undisturbed; it instead provoked a thoroughgoing ideological realignment. Patriots who had long envisioned themselves as intellectual heirs to the parliamentarian struggle against Stuart tyranny now saw themselves as latter-day champions of the Royalist cause, locked in an epic struggle with the very same tyrannical legislature that had "usurped" the prerogatives of Charles I. Consistent with their new self-understanding, they set about developing a revisionist historical account of the seventeenth-century constitutional crisis; they rejected the standard whig theory of English constitutional corruption; and they revived the Royalist theory of representation, which alone was capable of explaining why the existence of Jacobean and Caroline prerogative powers in the Crown might be consistent with the liberty of subjects. For these patriots, the imperial crisis brought about a change in world view, not a shift in tactics.

But the more serious problem with the standard narrative—one that McIlwain and his disciples never addressed—is its supposition that the "prerogativism" of the early 1770s (to the extent that it existed at all) was an ideological dead end, an aberrant flight of fancy that ceased to have any purchase once the imperial crisis reached its violent conclusion.[28] In fact, the turn to the royal prerogative was *the* formative moment in the history of what would emerge as American constitutionalism.[29] The very same principles that had underwritten the patriot campaign to rebalance the imperial constitution in favor of the Crown demanded in 1787 the creation of a recognizably Royalist constitution for the new United States. This constitution would exclude the office of king—as we shall see, the particular brand of republican political theory that had been unleashed in the colonies in the early months of 1776 required as much—but it would assign its rechristened chief magistrate far more power than any English monarch had wielded since William of Orange landed at Torbay in 1688.

This formulation will strike some readers as surprising. We tend to suppose that a "chief magistrate" and a monarch are fundamentally different things. On this view, it makes no more sense to speak of a "Royalist constitution that excludes the office of king" than it does to speak of a "bachelor who happens to be married." Yet a great deal of confusion has resulted from our tendency to project this modern understanding back onto the eighteenth century. In early modern European political thought, the distinguishing feature of monarchy was neither the kingly title nor hereditary right. Europeans knew only too well that the most famous monarch in Western history, Augustus Caesar, had eschewed the title of king (*rex*) as well as its accompanying ceremonial, claiming only to be *princeps,* or the "first man." And they were equally aware that a great many European monarchies were elective rather than hereditary: examples included the Holy Roman Empire, Poland, and, most famously, the papacy. Early modern theorists accordingly tended to define as a "monarch" any single magistrate who was entrusted with the executive power—and, a fortiori, any chief magistrate who was assigned prerogative powers to make law or to govern subjects without law. The vast majority of those who opposed monarchy during this period did not object to regal pomp or lineal descent; they alleged instead that discretionary power in a "single person" was incompatible with the freedom of subjects. It became the life's work of patriot Royalists to refute this charge, first in the context of the imperial crisis and later in the context of the extended debates over the state and federal constitutions. Prerogative had to be rendered compatible with liberty, the rule of one with the sovereignty of the people.

It is this project that I dub "the Royalist Revolution." In taking this term for my title, I certainly do not mean to imply that all of those who rebelled against Britain in 1776 shared a single ideology that should be classified as "Royalist." Quite the contrary, it seems clear to me that the revolutionary movement was characterized from the outset by what contemporary philosophers would call an "overlapping consensus."[30] Those who became "patriots" during the imperial crisis could all agree on several basic propositions—that the British constitution had become dangerously corrupt, that British Americans were not represented in Parliament, and so on—but they disagreed seriously among themselves concerning exactly *why* or *in what sense* these claims were correct. Some patriots never relinquished their whig commitments. They continued to believe that the English constitution had atrophied as a result of the endlessly expanding power of the Crown, they loathed the royal prerogative, and they insisted, with their parliamentarian predecessors, that only a well-constituted assembly could represent the people, not a "single person." We shall be encountering these whiggish patriots frequently in the pages that follow. The Royalist Revolution, as I use the term, is not coterminous with the American Revolution as a whole. It refers to a particular understanding of the purposes and character of the Revolution— one shared by a number of the movement's chief protagonists—that achieved intellectual dominance in America on two fateful occasions: once in the early 1770s and a second time in the later 1780s. The understanding in question ought to be styled "Royalist," because it straightforwardly endorsed the political and constitutional theory of those who took up the King's cause during the English Revolution of 1642–1660.[31]

It should thus be clear that this book does not offer a general history of American political thought during the revolutionary period. Its aim is, instead, to trace the emergence and development among patriot theorists of a certain orientation on questions relating to monarchy, prerogative power, constitutional corruption, the theory of representation, and (later) the proper understanding of "republican" government. The story told here is therefore partial in at least two respects: it is concerned only with a fixed number of themes in early American political theory (important debates about sovereignty, federalism, and written constitutions, for example, figure only incidentally in the chapters that follow), and it focuses on a subset of those who led the patriot cause. The patriots in question did not constitute an organized "party" and they did not agree with each other on all points—nor, unsurprisingly, did any one of them exhibit perfect intellectual consistency across time. They were, however, recognizably engaged in a common enterprise, and, if their story has a particular claim to historical reclamation, it is because they succeeded.[32]

Mapping the Possibilities: Royalists, Parliamentarians, and Whigs

The claim that many American patriots found themselves in fundamental agreement with the English Royalists of the seventeenth century will appear perverse if we accept the whig conceit that Charles I and his allies were "divine right absolutists." The patriots, it is agreed, were committed contractarians. They never doubted that legitimate political authority originates in the consent of the governed, and they took themselves to be defending a genuine "mixed monarchy," not royal absolutism. But the vast majority of Royalists in fact shared both of these commitments, and patriots of the

late 1760s and 1770s came to recognize as much. In this sense, they anticipated by more than two centuries the revisionist historiography that has
arisen in recent years to challenge the whig account of Royalist political
thought.[33] To be sure, many Royalists invoked some version of "divine right"
theory in order to deny the right of *resistance* to established political authority, but this position was perfectly compatible with a contractarian account
of political origins.[34] Moreover, the question of the right of resistance was
orthogonal to the question of constitutional form. To argue that subjects
are entitled (or not) to use force against tyrannical rulers does not imply an
endorsement of any particular kind of political regime. A republican might
deny the right of resistance, as many did after 1649, while a strident monarchist might endorse it. To the extent that Royalists embraced nonresistance,
this commitment was therefore easily detachable from their constitutional
theory.

The canonical statement of Royalist constitutionalism appears in the *Answer to the XIX Propositions of Both Houses of Parliament*, a pamphlet that
Charles I ordered published in his name in 1642. Drafted by Viscount Falkland and Sir John Culpepper, the essay addressed the constitutional crisis
into which the monarchy had been plunged by the passage of the Militia
Ordinance, a measure assigning control of military appointments and mu-
nitions stores to the two houses of Parliament. Parliamentarians claimed
the status of valid law for this edict, despite the fact that it had not been
submitted to the king for the royal assent. Charles predictably denied its legitimacy. The monarch, he insisted, was a constituent part of the legislature, and as a result, Parliament could not properly be said to have "acted"
absent his approval. At issue, therefore, was the king's "negative voice," his
essential prerogative to reject parliamentary bills. The two houses were effectively claiming the right to constitute a "Parliament" without him, and
their leading members were arguing with increasing boldness that the royal
assent should simply be granted as a matter of course to any measure passed
by the Lords and Commons. Their program thus threatened to eliminate
Charles's legislative power, leaving him only the delegated authority to execute laws framed by an assembly. The king's opponents further demanded
the right to select his privy counselors and insisted that in the future, he
must agree to undertake "no publique Act concerning the Affairs of the
Kingdom" unless "it be done by the advice and consent of the major part" of
these approved ministers.[35]

Charles responded with a full-throated defense of his prerogatives. "We call God to witnesse, that as for Our Subjects' sake these Rights are vested in Us, so for their sakes, as well as for Our Own, We are resolved not to quit them, nor to subvert (though in a Parliamentary way) the ancient, equall, happy, well-poised, and never-enough commended Constitution of the Government of this Kingdom."[36] England, on Charles's account, was a "mixed" monarchy. He did not deny that the House of Commons was "solely instructed with . . . the Leavies of Moneys" and the right of impeachment, nor did he question the prerogative of the Lords to judge.[37] But the king too had his prerogatives—those "Flowers of our crown as are worth all the rest of the garland"—which "preserve that Authoritie, without which [monarchy] would be disabled to preserve the Laws in their Force, and the Subjects in their Liberties and Properties."[38] As Charles went on to explain, the royal prerogative secures the liberty of subjects because it generates for the Sovereign "such a Respect and Relation among the great Ones [i.e., the nobility], as may hinder the ills of Division and Faction, and such a Fear and Reverence from the people, as may hinder Tumults, Violence, and Licentiousnesse." Moreover, the king is the only safe repository of such power because his interest is uniquely bound up with the interest of the kingdom as a whole: "We being most of any injured in the least violation of that, by which Wee enjoy the highest Rights and greatest Benefits . . . are therefore obliged to defend no lesse by our interest then by our Duty."[39] Legislative majorities, in contrast, always serve partial and factional interests.

Yet the two houses of Parliament were proposing to strip Charles of his legislative power and his freedom of action in "government," thus making "Our Self of a King of *England* a Duke of *Venice*, and this of a Kingdom a Republique"—that is, transforming him into a pure executive, subject to the Lords and Commons.[40] The king's counterattack first addressed itself to the royal negative. His opponents, Charles announced, were asserting a "new Doctrine, *That We are obliged to passe all Laws that shall be offered to Us by both Houses* (however our own Judgement and Conscience shall be unsatisfied with them)." But such a principle was "destructive to all our rights of Parliament." Instead, Charles countered, "you must admit Us to be a part of the Parliament, you must not . . . deny the freedom of Our Answer, when We have as much right to reject what We think unreasonable, as you have to propose what you think convenient or necessary."[41] As for the selection of the king's councilors, Charles declared that "we will retain Our Power of admitting no more to any Councell than the Nature of the businesse requires, and of discoursing with whom We please, of what We please, and informing Our Understanding by debate with any Persons, who may be well able to Inform and Advise Us in some particular."[42] And "though we shall (with the proportionable Consideration due to them) always weigh the Advices both of our Great and Privie Councell, yet We shall also look upon their Advices, as Advices, not as Commands or Impositions; upon them as Our Counsellors, not as Our Tutors and Guardians, and upon Ourself as their King, not as their Pupill, or Ward." Deprived of the negative voice and denied both the right to appoint councilors at pleasure and the prerogative to act independently of their advice, "we may be waited on bareheaded; we may have Our hand kissed; The Stile of Majestie continued to Us; And the King's Authoritie, declared by both Houses of Parliament, may be still the Stile of your Commands . . . but as to true and reall Power, We should remain but the outside, but the Picture, but the signe of a King."[43] Such a servant king could never protect the liberties of his subjects from legislative tyranny—and these liberties Charles had sworn to defend. On the scaffold seven years later, he would accordingly insist that "I am the Martyr of the People."[44]

The parliamentarian tradition in political thought organized itself in fundamental opposition to these claims. The leading theorists of the English Revolution developed the view that only a well-constituted assembly could be said to represent the people. Parliament, in the influential formulation of Henry Parker, is "vertually the whole kingdome it selfe" (that is, possesses its full "virtue," or power) and is the "quintessence" of the people.[45] It follows that "that which is the sense of the whole Parliament, is the judgement of the whole Kingdom."[46] In contrast, "the King does not represent the people"; he speaks and acts only for himself.[47] The implications of this argument were momentous indeed. A free people, it was agreed on all sides, must be governed according to its own will. Since the people as a whole cannot assemble to govern themselves, the laws of the state must be made instead by those who are empowered to speak and act in the name of the people—that is, by their legitimate representatives. To be governed by a power that is not "representative" in this sense is to be ruled by an "alien will." It is, quite simply, to be a slave.[48] If the king cannot be said to represent the people, then his decisions do not reflect their will. If the people cannot act without his permission (that is, if he is licensed to "refuse his assent" to bills passed by their legitimate representatives), they will find themselves in a state of dependence on an alien will—and hence in the condition of slavery. Parliamentarians accordingly concluded that while a purely executive monarchy might be permissible, prerogative powers in "a single person" were incompatible with the liberty of subjects. "Where the King is sole Iudge, or hath a negative voyce," explained John Cook, "there he is unlimited, and consequently a Tirant that may do what he pleases."[49]

Royalists, as we shall see in detail, developed their own rival theory of representation, according to which a hereditary monarch could perfectly well count as the representative of the people. But it was the parliamentarian theory that became constitutive of whig political thought in the aftermath of the Glorious Revolution.[50] Although the Convention Parliament had left the royal negative undisturbed, the power quickly passed into disuse in Britain, and the whig theorists whose writings suffused North American political culture in the decades leading up to the Revolution eagerly reimagined their monarch as a simple executive, acting through ministers accountable to Parliament. This is not to say that the whig tradition was monolithic in this respect. Indeed, one of the canonical texts from which eighteenth-century whigs drew their political commitments, John Locke's *Two Treatises of Government* (1690), exhibited a notoriously ambivalent attitude toward the parliamentarian theory. On the one hand, Locke straightforwardly agreed with his parliamentarian predecessors that "there can be but *one Supream Power,* which is *the Legislative,* to which all the rest are and must be subordinate," and he further affirmed their view that this power ought to be placed "in collective Bodies of Men, call them Senate, Parliament, or what you please"—and that only under such circumstances could "every single person" regard himself as "subject, equally with other the meanest Men, to those Laws, which he himself, as part of the Legislative had established."[51] Locke thus made it clear that subjects must be governed by laws promulgated by an elected assembly in order to count as self-governing, and he likewise insisted that only the members of such an assembly should be designated "representatives" of the people.[52]

In light of these remarks, we would expect Locke to follow Parker in rejecting prerogative powers as incompatible with the liberty of subjects. But Locke's view of prerogative is instead surprisingly complicated. In chapter 13 of the *Second Treatise,* for example, he offers the following remarks about executive power "vested in a single person":

In some Commonwealths where the *Legislative* is not always in being, and the *Executive* is vested in a single Person, who has also a share in the Legislative; there that single Person in a very tolerable sense may also be called *Supream,* not that he has in himself all the Supream Power, which is that of Law-making; But because he has in him the *Supream Execution,* from whom all inferiour Magistrates derive all their several subordinate Powers, or at least the greatest part of them: having also no Legislative superiour to him, there being no Law to be made without his consent, which cannot be expected should ever subject him to the other part of the Legislative, *he* is properly enough in this sense *Supream.*[53]

Locke here explicitly contemplates a monarchical chief magistrate who possesses "a share in the Legislative," which is to say a "negative voice." But does he *commend* this arrangement, or is he merely describing the juridical reality in England? (Recall that Locke wrote most of the *Two Treatises* in the late 1670s and early 1680s, well before the Glorious Revolution, although he did not publish the text until 1690).[54] In the very next paragraph, he entertains a very different scenario: "The *Executive Power* placed any where but in a Person, that has also a share in the Legislative, is visibly subordinate and accountable to it, and may be at pleasure changed and displaced."[55] Is this latter arrangement to be preferred, or are we meant to regard it as inferior? Locke never returned to the question, and his eighteenth-century readers would accordingly argue at great length about where his allegiances truly lay.[56] On one point, however, there could be no dispute: Locke's famous chapter "Of Prerogative" unmistakably endorsed the claim that, in any well-regulated political society, the executive must enjoy a "Power to act according to discretion, for the publick good, without the prescription of the Law, and sometimes even against it."[57] This power, he explained, is "that which is called *Prerogative.*" However cautious and opaque his pronouncements on the negative voice, Locke thus clearly denied that discretionary power in the executive was incompatible with the liberty of subjects—at least in cases of emergency or during the recess of the legislature.[58] Whigs would spend the next century apologizing for these remarks. In the words of William Knox, writing in 1768 to answer the extravagant claims on behalf of the royal prerogative that were beginning to emerge from the American colonies, "there are some passages in [Locke's *Second Treatise*], which probably the temper and fashion of that age drew from him, in which I can by no means agree with him, especially when he defines prerogative to be 'a power in the prince to act according to *discretion* for the public good, without the prescription of the law, and sometimes even against it;' . . . I mean not by this to throw any blame upon Mr. Locke, but merely to shew, that in a work of this extent there must be some inaccuracies and errors, and that it is not an infallible guide in all cases."[59]

Indeed, the celebrated whig political theorists of the eighteenth century left Locke's "middle ground" far behind and unambiguously aligned themselves with the parliamentarian defense of a purely executive monarchy—declaring that the king was "only a sort of sheriff to execute [parliament's] orders," as the bishop of Derry put it in 1700.[60] Robert Molesworth, in his massively influential *Account of Denmark* (1694), thus commended to his readers an idyllic "ancient constitution" in which "the Representative Body of the People" would take upon itself "all Matters relating to good Government," including the making of "good Laws" and "all Affairs belonging to Peace or War, Alliances, disposal of great Offices, Contracts of Marriages for the Royal Family, etc."[61] All of these were prerogative powers that England's seventeenth-century monarchs had adamantly refused to surrender to Parliament, and, even after the Glorious Revolution, the right to declare war and enter into treaties (what Locke had called the "federative power") and the prerogative of appointment remained with the Crown, at least as a formal matter.[62] But the business of Molesworth's monarch was simply "to see a due and impartial Administration of Justice executed according to the Laws . . . to be watchful and vigilant for the welfare of his People, to Command in Person their Armies in time of War, to encourage Industry, Religion, Arts and Learning."[63] By the time John Trenchard and Thomas Gordon took up their pens as "Cato" in the early 1720s, the discourse had progressed still further. Not only was it right and proper that the king no longer enjoyed any legislative authority or discretionary powers, but for the sake of English liberty it was necessary that even his executive functions should be performed by others in his name:

> Such is the monarchy of England, where the sovereign performs every act of
> his regal office by his authority, without the fatigue and anxiety of executing
> the troublesome parts of it in his person. The laws are chosen and recom-
> mended to him by his Parliament; and afterwards executed by his judges,
> and other ministers of justice: His great seal is kept by his chancellor: His

naval power is under the direction of his high admiral: And all acts of state and discretion are presumed to be done by the advice of his council. All which officers are answerable for their misbehaviour, and for all actions done within their several provinces, which they have advised or could have prevented by giving their advice, or by making timely and humble remonstrances; which they are obliged to shew that they have done.[64]

The king of a free people will not "fatigue" himself with governing "in his person." "His high office," on Cato's account, "consists in approving laws chosen by common consent; in executing those laws, and in being the publick guardian of the publick safety."[65] Cato thus fully agreed with Parker that it was the king's duty simply to "approve" all laws passed by the representatives of the people (of which the king himself was emphatically not one); if the monarch were empowered to refuse his assent to those laws at will, his subjects would find themselves slaves.

Two Theories of Corruption

But did the British monarchs of the late eighteenth century *in fact* possess an effective negative voice? Were cabinet decisions *actually* insulated from the "private inclination" of the prince, as Cato had demanded? Here Hanoverian Britons confronted a classic case of what social scientists would refer to as an "observational equivalence"—a situation in which the same data can be explained equally well by two contrasting hypotheses. All recognized that no monarch had refused the royal assent to a parliamentary bill since the reign of Queen Anne. But this fact could be explained in two very different ways: (1) the monarchy had been weakened to such an extent that no sovereign would dare to wield this power, so that as a practical matter it had gone into abeyance; or (2) the monarchy had become so spectacularly powerful that it was now invariably able to get its way in the two houses of Parliament without having recourse to the negative. Likewise, it was clear to all concerned that the executive powers of the Crown in relation to war and peace, etc., were in fact exercised, not by the king himself, but rather by ministers who were required to maintain the support of a parliamentary majority. One might conclude from this fact that the will of the sovereign no longer held sway in these areas of government, but one could equally well believe that the king never felt it necessary to contradict his ministers because the parliament to which they answered was filled with his "creatures." These divergent interpretations of the political "facts on the ground" thus lent themselves to two rival theories of constitutional corruption: one according to which the executive had been co-opted by the legislature, and a second according to which the legislature had been captured by the executive.

Opposition whigs in the "Country" tradition—that is, those who resisted the fiscal-military program of the Williamite and Hanoverian "courts"[66]— stridently defended the second of these narratives. English politics, Molesworth assured his readers, was characterized by "the perpetual Contests between the Kings and the People," in which the former always "endeavour'd to acquire a greater Power than was legally due" and the latter fought valiantly "to preserve or recover their just Liberties."[67] This millennial campaign of royal usurpation, in turn, depended upon the allure of "Pageantry, Luxury, and Licentiousness"; the people's representatives were "bribed" into exchanging "their Bread for a glittering piece of Tinsel."[68] The promise of riches from the Crown led them to "prefer gilded *Slavery* to coarse domestick *Liberty*," just as the wretched Israelites in Milton's *Samson Agonistes* had come to "love bondage more than liberty, / Bondage with ease than strenuous liberty."[69] "Cato" fully agreed with this analysis, insisting that the Crown had surreptitiously purchased the allegiance of the legislature by means of patronage. The first step for the ministry in this nefarious scheme had been to "promote luxury, idleness, and expence, and a general depravation of manners, by their own example, as well as by connivance and publick encouragement" in order to "divert men's thoughts from examining their behaviour and politicks" and "let them loose from all the restraints of private and publick virtue."[70] "From immorality and excesses," these unfortunate dupes predictably fell "into necessity; and from thence into a servile dependence upon power." The Crown had thus managed to "bribe the electors in the choice of their representatives, and so to get a council of their own creatures." For good measure, it had gone on "to corrupt the deputies after they are chosen," thus recruiting for "the perpetration of their crimes those very men, from whom the betrayed people expect the redress of their grievances, and the punishment of those crimes."[71] James Burgh, in his influential *Political Disquisitions* (1774), similarly declared that "in former times the court and commons were generally opposite; in ours the constituents and representatives."[72] The reason, once again, was that "a parliament filled with placemen and pensioners is literally a tabernacle of bribery"—one through which the "court" is able to govern in a manner "completely opposite to the people's interest."[73] The people's representatives had become "slaves to ministers."[74] Indeed, Burgh went so far as to lament the passing of "the too short period of the republic," during which Parliament had governed "without hopes, from a bribing court, and free from the incumbrances of such kings, or house of peers, to negative, or at least to entangle and impede their measures for general advantage."[75]

But this "Country" or "real" whig narrative of constitutional decline had its committed opponents. Beginning in the 1730s, a series of theorists began to argue that in fact the British monarchy had been largely absorbed by the legislature—that it had become too weak, not too strong. One of the most influential and subtle statements of this view appeared in Montesquieu's *Spirit of the Laws* (1748). In Book 11 of that work, Montesquieu offered an analysis of the English constitution, praising it for delivering "political liberty" to its subjects. Yet what appeared to be a mere description of existing practice was in truth an implicit critique of how the constitution had evolved during the course of the eighteenth century. Montesquieu forcefully insisted on the need for an independent executive, declaring that "if the executive power does not have the right to check the enterprises of the legislative body, the latter will be despotic."[76] The check in question turned out to be the royal negative: the "executive power . . . should take part in legislation by its faculty of vetoing; otherwise it will soon be stripped of its prerogatives."[77] To be sure, Montesquieu's understanding of the scope and purposes of the negative was quite narrow; he regarded it as a purely defensive weapon, designed to prevent the legislature from usurping executive power, not as an affirmative prerogative of the Crown to shape the framing of law in general. He was therefore closer to endorsing an ideal of the "separation of powers" than he was to embracing the very different, and Royalist, ideal of "checks and balances."[78] But despite this caveat, Montesquieu unambiguously placed the negative voice at the center of his account of the balanced English constitution.

The problem, as he knew perfectly well, was that the negative had not in fact been used in nearly half a century. Montesquieu was depicting the constitution as it existed in theory, not in practice. Indeed, he barely mentioned the word "minister" in his account, thus taking no official notice of the fact that the various powers he claimed for the sovereign had been exercised for two generations by a composite, plural executive called "the Crown," the members of which were drawn from the two houses of Parliament.[79] This was precisely the sort of arrangement that he had denounced as incompatible with "liberty," on the grounds that "the two powers [i.e., the executive and the legislative] would be united, the same persons sometimes belonging and always able to belong to both."[80] Montesquieu ended his chapter by remarking coyly that "it is not for me to examine whether at present the English enjoy this liberty or not. It suffices for me to say that it is established by their laws, and I seek no further."[81]

Others, however, did indeed seek further, and among them was Henry St John, Viscount Bolingbroke, with whom Montesquieu had developed a personal acquaintance. An erstwhile Jacobite who became a leading spokesman for "Country" principles in the early 1730s, Bolingbroke pivoted later in the decade and began to worry a great deal about the growing subjection of the monarch to parliamentary "factions." "The Government of Britain," he now believed, had degenerated into an "oligarchy"; the "monarchy" was "rather weakened than strengthened, rather imposed upon than obeyed."[82] Addressing Frederick, Prince of Wales (the father of George III) in 1738, he defended the idea of what he called a "patriot king," one who would "reinfuse" the constitution with the spirit of liberty by chasing the money changers from the ministerial temple.[83] A single chief magistrate, being "more compact" than a legislature, could transform himself into "the most powerful of all reformers."[84] "Instead of abetting the divisions of his people," Bolingbroke explained, a patriot king "will endeavour to unite them, and to be himself the centre of their union: instead of putting himself at the head of one party in order to govern his people, he will put himself at the head of his people in order to govern, or more properly to subdue all parties."[85] But what exactly did all of this entail in practice? Bolingbroke's central suggestion is put forward with considerable delicacy: the king should call "into the administration such men as he can assure himself will serve on the same principles on which he intends to govern," and "he may and he ought to show his dislike or his favour, as he judges the constitution may be hurt or improved, by one side or the other."[86] Bolingbroke, in other words, was proposing (albeit rather obliquely) that the king should revive the prerogative insisted upon by Charles I to appoint his own ministers at pleasure, irrespective of the wishes of the parliamentary majority, and that he ought to reassert his independent political agency.[87] Bolingbroke, like Montesquieu, sought to separate "king" from "Crown" in order to rebalance the constitution. But his embrace of prerogative extended no further. He notably declined, for example, to urge the king to revive the negative voice.[88]

Writing several years after Bolingbroke, David Hume returned to the same quandary in his essay "Of the Independency of Parliament" (1742). Hume, however, shared none of his predecessor's lingering "Country" anxieties about crown power. "The share of power, allotted by our constitution to the house of commons," he declared, "is so great, that it absolutely commands all the other parts of the government."[89] In Hume's view, the practice of seeking the royal assent for parliamentary bills had become a mere pantomime: "The king's legislative power is plainly no proper check to [the House of Commons]. For though the king has a negative in framing laws; yet this, in fact, is esteemed of so little moment, that whatever is voted by the two houses, is always sure to pass into a law, and the royal assent is little better than a form."[90] As a sympathetic reader of Hume would later put the same point, "the weakness of the crown" had reached such proportions that "the negative on bills, which constitutes the sovereign one of the estates of this realm, is nearly, if not entirely taken from him, and he is in imminent danger of being reduced to a mere signing clerk."[91] This pathological arrangement, Hume went on to explain, derived its authority among the people from the pernicious doctrine that "the dependence of parliament, in every degree, is an infringement of BRITISH liberty"—that is, from the notion that since only an elected assembly can represent the people, the dependence of parliament on the Crown *just is* the dependence of the people.[92] But Hume's proposed solution to what he called "this paradox" was unexpected. He did not propose that the king should revive his negative voice and other defunct prerogatives. Rather, he focused his hopes on the patronage power of the Crown.[93] The unending crusade of the Commons to subjugate the executive could be "restrained," Hume believed, by the self-interested behavior of individual legislators seeking royal favor. "The crown has so many offices at its disposal, that, when assisted by the honest and disinterested part of the house, it will always command the resolutions of the whole, so far, at least, as to preserve the ancient constitution from danger." Others might call this "influence" by "the invidious appellations of *corruption* and *dependence*," but in truth "some degree and some kind of it are inseparable from the very nature of the constitution, and necessary to the preservation of our mixed government."[94] In a world of unbridled parliamentary supremacy, patronage would have to replace prerogative.

This constellation of writings, blaming the degeneration of the English constitution on the weakness of the monarchy— often classified, problematically, as "Tory"[95]—would come to play a surprising role in the political thought of the revolutionary period. Before the late 1760s, British North Americans had almost uniformly rejected the views of these authors, championing instead the rival theory of the "Country" whigs.[96] They had immersed themselves in the pamphlets of Molesworth, Walter Moyle, Trenchard and Gordon, Burgh, and their disciples. The great danger to the English constitution, they had agreed, was to be found in crown patronage, prerogative power, and the "popery" that went along with them hand in glove.[97] Indeed, British Americans had understood themselves to be confronting a greatly magnified version of this constitutional pathology, for the royal prerogative was in fact a good deal stronger in the colonies than it was in Britain itself.[98] As a disgruntled colonist from North Carolina explained in 1714, the king's "power is greater over [the colonies], then over any other of his Subjects":

> All appeals from thence are determined by his Majesty in Council, and not by the House of Lords, as they are from the rest of his Dominions. His Majesty has power to repeal any of the Plantation Laws, without the concurrence of the Plantation Assemblys by whom they were made, or of any other whatsoever. Which cannot be done in the rest of His Dominions. He has power to erect any new Courts of Justice, or to change those already established. And in most things the will of the Sovereign has hitherto bin the Law of the Plantations.[99]

This account was not inaccurate.[100] The negative voice had been dormant in the metropolis since 1707 (indeed, a great many British Americans believed, mistakenly, that it had not been wielded there since the Glorious Revolution),[101] but it had been used throughout the eighteenth century to disallow bills passed by a large subset of colonial legislatures.[102] In practice, colonists recognized that the negative was wielded in these instances not by the king himself, but rather (as one pamphleteer explained) "thro' the channel of the Board of Trade," acting with the formal approval of the Privy Council.[103] But these executive agencies indubitably acted under the aegis of the prerogative. The Crown likewise regularly dissolved or prorogued colonial assemblies, appointed both governors and members of the upper houses of colonial legislatures, established prerogative courts, issued "instructions" that were frequently accorded the status of law, and claimed the right to vacate colonial charters. It was also of considerable importance that judicial appeals from America lay with the king-in-council, not, as in Britain itself, with the House of Lords.[104] The major political crises that enveloped the colonies before 1763—from the revocation of the Massachusetts charter in 1684 to the attempted reforms of the newly established Board of Trade in the late 1690s, and from the dispute over the status of common law in Maryland in the 1720s to the so-called Parson's Cause in Virginia in the 1750s—tended to pit British North Americans against the exertion of prerogative and seemed to validate every article of the whig catechism.[105]

It is, therefore, wholly unsurprising that American critics of the administration initially gravitated toward this same discourse of corruption as the imperial crisis of the 1760s got under way. Numerous pamphleteers eagerly attributed the travails of the Atlantic empire to "ministers and favorites" of the king whose "power and interest is so great that they can, and do procure whatever laws they please; having, (by power, Interest, and the application of the people's money, to *placemen,* and *pensioners,*) the whole legislative authority at their command."[106] But as the crisis wore on, a remarkable shift began to occur. Increasingly convinced that their enemy was not the Crown but rather a tyrannical Parliament, a great many patriots of the late 1760s and early 1770s found themselves telling a very different but still familiar story about English constitutional decline. Thomson Mason, a Virginia pamphleteer, put the new case as follows: "the general opinion, that the great defect in the present Constitution of *Britain* is the enormous power of the Crown" ought to be dismissed as "a vulgar errour."[107] Quite the contrary, it was the failure of the British people to restore "the ancient independence of the Crown" after the two revolutions that had crippled the mixed monarchy. The great imperative was accordingly "to check the growing power of aristocracy [i.e., Parliament] in *Great Britain,* and to restore your Sovereign to that weight in the National Councils which he ought to possess."[108] Patriots would now take the side of those eighteenth-century theorists who had rejected the whig discourse of corruption, inveighing instead against parliamentary usurpations of royal power. But with the notable exception of Alexander Hamilton, they would categorically refuse to rely (even in part) on "influence" as a device for rebalancing the constitution. Rather, they would actively campaign to revive the defunct prerogatives of the Crown—the negative voice, the sovereign's right to govern imperial commerce, his authority to alienate territories from the realm at pleasure, and his authority to remove subjects from the jurisdiction of Parliament—and, just as crucially, they would argue that the king should wield these powers *in his person*, not through his British ministers. Their program thus moved well beyond anything contemplated by Bolingbroke or his fellow "Tories." Indeed, both Sir William Blackstone and Jean-Louis Delolme, the two most famous advocates for royal power in the 1760s and 1770s, dismissed the American position as constitutional heresy.[109] They recognized that patriots had taken up the Royalist banner, arraying themselves against the great whig heroes of the seventeenth century—those whom Charles I had accused of subverting "in a Parliamentary way" the "ancient, equall, happy, well-poised, and never-enough commended Constitution of the Government of this Kingdom." It is this fact, more than any other, that explains the subsequent trajectory of American constitutionalism.

A Revolution in Ideas

Any work in the history of political thought must begin from a set of assumptions about how ideas interact with transformative events, and this book is no exception. Indeed, the story offered here both reflects and recommends a particular understanding of the nature of that interaction, one that should appear in sharper relief if we contrast it with two rival accounts of the causal significance (or lack thereof) of our political beliefs. According to one established view, ideas play no causal role in the emergence of social and political change. The strongest version of this claim, defended, for example, by Sir Lewis Namier and his disciples, holds that ideas are to be regarded as strictly "epiphenomenal," by which is meant that they arise as a by-product or symptomatic reflection of more basic social, psychological, or economic realities and have no "downstream" effects independent of these broader realities.[110] What matters in political controversy, on Namier's account, "is the underlying emotions, the music, to which ideas are a mere libretto, often of a very inferior quality."[111] If agents merely adopt political principles as instrumental rationalizations for their (independently) chosen courses of action, then these principles cannot be said to motivate the agents in question—from which it is taken to follow that ideas possess no causal efficacy. They are simply along for the ride.

A second view about the relation between ideas and events assigns a more robust causal role to social and political theory by emphasizing the degree to which human agents must, in practice, "legitimate" their proposed courses of action. When rulers or subjects wish to do something—go to war, raise a tax, alter the ecclesiastical establishment, and so on—they must ordinarily justify their behavior to others. But the set of plausible justifications in any given society is finite. In order to persuade, one must draw on the existing beliefs, discourses, and textual authorities that command respect in that particular community. In some contexts, "Aristotle favors X" is a powerful argument in favor of X; in others it strongly suggests that X is false; and in still others it has no force whatsoever. Likewise, the argument that "Y is inconsistent with liberty," in order to produce the desired effect, must appeal to a shared understanding of what "liberty" means. This view therefore takes ideas to be causally significant in part because they impose *constraints* on what political actors can do.[112] Not all actions can be legitimated, given the intellectual resources available in any given place and time, and so not every action can be taken. But scholars drawn to this position also emphasize the degree to which political arguments, once formulated in order to legitimate a particular course of action, can take on a life of their own—motivating others to act in surprising and often revolutionary ways. What these historians share with defenders of the Namierite view is the conviction that, at least in the first instance, social and political actors (including the sort who write political theory) do not act as they do *because* they believe their own arguments.[113] To speak of "legitimation" in the relevant sense is to attribute to historical agents a two-part process of deliberation: in part one, the agent decides what he (pre-theoretically) wants to do; and, in part two, he generates a set of arguments designed to legitimate his chosen course of action to others. But this is to take what the agent wants as *given* in advance of any arguments. The agent might perhaps be driven by economic interest, a desire for power, or some other psychological disposition, but he is not motivated by the conviction that his course of action conforms to the principles that he will invoke in its defense. This view accordingly invites us to regard the majority of political actors as disingenuous and the arguments they deploy as instrumental. The question "Is theorist X sincere in making argument Y?" will appear to be badly posed because political debate is taken to be insincere as such.[114]

Each of these views has had distinguished advocates, and this is certainly not the place for an extended discussion of their merits. But we should at least be somewhat wary of endorsing any account of political agency that is so deeply at odds with our understanding of what is going on when we ourselves engage in political debate. When we vote for our preferred candidates, campaign on behalf of public causes, or pen works of political theory, we usually take ourselves to be acting in the service of true principles (or those principles that we judge to be most probably true). We do not regard our principles or arguments as instrumental rationalizations for what we pre-theoretically want. It seems to us that our beliefs very frequently determine what we want, not the other way around, and most of us have had the experience of coming to want different things in response to changes in our beliefs. We could of course be wrong about all of this: the conviction that our principles shape our preferences might be a delusion, a kind of "false consciousness" under which we labor.[115] Perhaps, although the burden of proof on those who would defend such a position must be quite heavy. But, in any event, the claim that we lack psychological access to the true source of our preferences is very different from the claim that we are disingenuously engaged in "legitimation." The latter assertion presupposes that we *knowingly* misrepresent the grounds for our conduct—that we pretend to be guided by a set of arguments in moral, political, and constitutional theory, whereas in fact these elaborate constructions are merely designed to mask our pursuit of other interests. If this picture seems implausible as an account of our own behavior, why should we suppose that it adequately explains the behavior of historical actors?

There is, however, another option, one that is rather old-fashioned but perhaps no less attractive for that. We might instead adopt the supposition that historical agents generally mean what they say and that their actions in the political realm do indeed tend to reflect their advertised commitments.[116] Those drawn to this approach need not deny that agents sometimes deploy arguments disingenuously in order to advance their interests. Certainly they do. The view in question simply suggests that we should begin by trying to take seriously the account that agents give of the content of their own beliefs and of the relation between those beliefs and their actions. Likewise, if we accept that the beliefs of historical actors often shape the course of political events in decisive ways, we do not thereby deny that events can just as easily shape beliefs. The causal arrow need not point in only one direction.

Political thought never develops in a vacuum; it is always highly responsive to the force of political events, even as it shapes those events in crucial ways. It is, for example, undoubtedly the case that the intensifying fury of the English Revolution and the ultimate execution of Charles I in 1649 prompted English republicans to consider radical new arguments about the proper form of political life—arguments they would never have seriously considered even five years earlier. One can admit as much without being at all drawn to the view that English republicanism was merely "epiphenomenal" or that English republicans were not sincere about the political arguments they made.

Political crises change how people look at the world. They put pressure on received commitments, realign affections, and focus attention on new and different dangers. More to the point, political *debates* have their own governing dynamics and their own momentum: arguments are made, countered, revised in light of forceful objections, countered again, and so on. Under these specialized circumstances, the internal properties, or deep structure, of ideas and arguments can have profoundly important consequences, for the conceptual scrutiny brought to bear by extensive debate might reveal that a particular position is incoherent, that a conclusion fails to follow from a given set of premises, or that a particular argument has unexpected and absurd implications. Such demonstrations in turn put pressure on participants to revise their positions—not merely because the forensic ground upon which they are standing has become unpalatably shaky but also because they are liable to conclude that they have not, in fact, been thinking properly about the subject matter in question. Debates change what people think and, as a result, they often change what people want.

The development of American political thought during the revolutionary period seems to me to offer very good evidence in support of this last conception of the history of ideas. The reductionist "economic interpretation" of the Revolution, which treats the political and constitutional arguments of the colonists as essentially beside the point—mere surface reflections of a more fundamental shift in the Atlantic economy that drove Americans to seek commercial independence from Britain—is now over a century old and still has its adherents.[117] But its great flaw has always been that it appears to make nonsense of thousands of pages of impassioned trans-Atlantic debate on a vast array of theoretical questions. Economic regulations may have provoked this debate, but it certainly does not follow that

the debate itself was about economics. Indeed, it was a commonplace on
both sides of the conflict that the purely economic significance of the taxes
and duties to which patriots initially objected was "trifling."[118] As Edmund
Burke explained to a somewhat bewildered House of Commons in 1770,
those defenders of the administration who marveled at the opposition generated in America by a relatively miniscule tax on stamps mistakenly "consider nothing in taxes but their weight as pecuniary impositions." For the
colonists, in contrast, the problem was one of principle: "men may be sorely
touched and deeply grieved in their privileges, as well as in their purses,"
Burke reminded his colleagues, and "when a man is robbed of a trifle on the
highway, it is not the Two-pence lost that constitutes the capital outrage."[119]
Moreover, patriots insisted throughout the crisis that they were prepared to
abide by the economically onerous Navigation Acts; they simply insisted
that their acquiescence should be understood as a voluntary "concession"
rather than an acknowledgement of parliamentary jurisdiction. This seems
an odd posture to encounter in political agents whose fundamental purpose
was to be rid of restrictions on trade.[120]

At first glance, the "legitimation" model might appear to be a better fit.
Colonial discourse, after all, changed quite significantly during the course
of the revolutionary period. By the time the imperial crisis reached its cli-
max in 1774–1775, patriots were making arguments in favor of the royal prerogative and the House of Stuart that would have appalled their former
selves—and a year later the vast majority of them had conclusively rejected
the kingly office (although not, as we shall see, kingly power). A natural
thought is, accordingly, that their various interventions were more or less
forensic. They knew what they wanted (effective independence from Britain) and simply deployed a variety of different strategies of legitimation in
order to secure it, picking up arguments and casting them aside as the circumstances required.[121] The chapters that follow constitute my response to
this claim. Colonial discourse changed in the later 1760s, I suggest, because
the debate provoked by the Stamp Act and the Townshend Duties changed
the way that many patriots thought about politics.[122] As John Adams famously observed, "The Revolution was in the Minds of the People, and this
was effected, from 1760 to 1775, in the course of fifteen Years before a drop of
blood was drawn at Lexington."[123] The imperial debate forced participants
to explore the deep tissue of their political and constitutional theories to an
unprecedented degree, and it was conducted in the technical vocabulary of

legal and philosophical disputation. Antagonists were accused of "begging the question" or falling victim to "non sequiturs," their analogies were shown to be "false," and their arguments were said to "prove too much," to be "pregnant with fatal consequences," or to issue in "absurdity." The patriots who emerged as Royalists in the late 1760s rejected their earlier constitutional position because they came to recognize that it was incoherent. But this recognition did not merely provoke a shift in their tactics; it prompted a thoroughgoing reexamination of their most basic political commitments. Indeed, if the patriots in question were truly arguing instrumentally and cynically, then surely they ought to have jettisoned their defense of prerogative once and for all when the events of 1776 put to rest the specifically imperial dilemma it was intended to address. But they did not. On the contrary, they proceeded to wage a decade-long campaign to realize their Royalist constitutional vision in the new United States. The consequences of that campaign continue to shape our world.

CHAPTER 1

Patriot Royalism

*The Stuart Monarchy and the Turn to
Prerogative, 1768–1775*

One of the more ironic moments in the decade-long conflict between Great Britain and her American colonies occurred on January 26,
1775. In the midst of an acrimonious debate over the wisdom of the Coercive
Acts, the House of Commons paused to consider a very different question:
whether to instruct its chaplain to preach a sermon on the occasion of "King
Charles's Martyrdom on the 30th of January."[1] Proponents of the motion argued that they were simply abiding by the terms of an act of Parliament that
required such an observance. They pointedly declined to offer a defense of
the observance itself. As for the eighty-three MPs who voted against the
motion, their sentiments seem to have been perfectly captured by the remarks of the radical whig John Wilkes, lord mayor of London and MP for
Middlesex:

> The Lord Mayor, Mr. *Wilkes,* said, that he was for the observance of the day,
> not in the usual manner by fasting and prayer to deprecate the pretended
> wrath of heaven, but in a very different way from what some other gentle-
> men had proposed; that it should be celebrated as a festival, as a day of tri-
> umph, not kept as a fast; that the death of the first Charles, a determined en-
> emy of the liberties of his country, who made war on his people, and
> murdered many thousands of his innocent subjects—an odious, hypocritical
> tyrant, who was, in the great Milton's words, *ipso Nerone neronior*—should be
> considered as a sacrifice to the public justice of the nation, as highly approved
> by heaven, and ought to be had in solemn remembrance as the most glorious
> deed ever done in this, or any country, without which we should at this hour
> have had no constitution, degenerated into the most abject slaves on the face

of the earth, not governed by the known and equal laws of a limited monarchy, but subject to the imperious will of an arbitrary sovereign.[2]

For Wilkes and the other whigs who voted with him, Charles Stuart was the embodiment of arbitrary and absolute monarchy, a latter-day Nero who had laid waste to his own country. Far from producing a "martyr," the regicide of 1649 had instead offered up "a sacrifice to the public justice of the nation."

Wilkes returned to this theme on October 26th of the same year, when he rose in the House to deliver his famous speech advocating conciliation with America. His primary argument on that occasion was that war should be avoided on pragmatic grounds, lest "the grandeur of the British Empire pass away."[3] But he also dwelt at length on the "injustice" of the campaign then being contemplated: "I call the war with our brethren in America an unjust, felonious war, because the primary cause and confessed origin of it is, to attempt to take their money from them without their consent, contrary to the common rights of all mankind, and those great fundamental principles of the English constitution, for which Hampden bled." John Hampden was the plaintiff in the ship money case—that great symbol of Caroline tyranny and the evil of prerogative powers—who had been mortally wounded while fighting the Stuarts on Charlgrove Field in 1643. In Wilkes's telling, the American colonists were straightforwardly defending the parliamentarian principles of the 1640s: the Petition of Right, the rejection of prerogative rule, and popular sovereignty.[4] And Wilkes found their specific demands eminently reasonable: "They justly expect to be put on an equal footing with the other subjects of the empire, and are willing to come into any fair agreement with you in commercial concerns."[5]

This last statement summarizes the position that scholars have come to know as "the dominion theory."[6] In the wake of the Townshend Acts, the patriots had jettisoned their previous insistence that Parliament possessed substantial jurisdiction over the colonies but simply lacked authority to legislate for them in particular respects and had come to argue instead that America was juridically "outside the realm" of Great Britain and that Parliament accordingly lacked any jurisdiction over it whatsoever. What connected the American colonies to Great Britain, on this account, was simply the person of the king, who served the same constitutional role in each part of his dominions and who had granted charters to the various colonizing companies and proprietors by his grace and at his pleasure. The king's prerogative crossed the ocean, but Parliament's authority ended at Britain's shore. The only issue open for discussion concerned the regulation of North American trade, which most patriots were prepared to entrust to Parliament as a concession, but not as a matter of right. It was, as we shall see, an extraordinary position, but it was not without precedent. Indeed, the argument that America was "outside the realm" and therefore to be governed by prerogative had famously been made once before in English constitutional history, by the Stuart monarchs, James I and Charles I, in their acrimonious disputes with Parliament over colonial affairs in the 1620s. The stunning irony of witnessing a radical whig such as Wilkes endorsing the Stuart position on the royal prerogative was not lost on the prime minister. Responding to Wilkes and to Charles Fox (who had likewise cast the Americans as defenders of "Whig" principles), Lord North replied that "if he understood the meaning of the words Whig and Tory, which the last speaker had mentioned, he conceived that it was characteristic of Whiggism to gain as much for the people as possible, while the aim of Toryism was to increase the prerogative. That in the present case, the administration contended for the right of parliament, while the Americans talked of their belonging to the crown. Their language therefore was that of Toryism."[7]

In fact, as numerous contemporaries observed, Lord North did not go far enough. The constitutional position embraced by most patriots between 1769 and 1775 was not "Tory" in any recognizable sense. No English tory had advocated anything like it for nearly a century. It represented instead a return to the Royalism of the Jacobean and Caroline courts and it accordingly forced patriots to develop a radical, revisionist account of seventeenth-century English history. Having spent the better part of the decade envisioning themselves as heirs to the parliamentary struggle against Stuart absolutism and popery, they now became the last Atlantic defenders of the Stuart monarchy and, as their critics noted, found themselves drifting perilously close to Jacobitism. Nor should we dismiss this volte-face as a mere display of forensic opportunism. Patriots of the period did not simply cite Stuart precedents "in passing," without addressing or acknowledging the ideological stakes involved. Quite the contrary, they were in most cases only too happy to emphasize the Stuart pedigree of their new commitments and to reconsider the legacy of the two English Revolutions accordingly. Only when we have recognized this fact will we be able to appreciate the true drama and character of the republican turn in 1776.

I

In his *Massachusettensis* letters of 1774, the loyalist Daniel Leonard offered a cogent, if partisan, account of the manner in which the patriot position had evolved during the course of the 1760s:

> When the stamp-act was made, the authority of parliament to impose inter-
> nal taxes was denied, but their right to impose external ones; or, in other
> words, to lay duties upon goods and merchandise was admitted. When the
> act was made imposing duties upon tea, &c. a new distinction was set up,
> that the parliament had a right to lay duties upon merchandise for the pur-
> pose of regulating trade, but not for the purpose of raising a revenue: That is,
> the parliament had good right and lawful authority, to lay the former duty of
> a shilling on the pound, but had none to lay the present duty of three pence.
> Having got thus far safe, it was only taking one step more to extricate our-
> selves entirely from their fangs, and become independent states; that our pa-
> triots most heroically resolved upon, and flatly denied that parliament had a
> right to make any laws whatsoever, that should be binding upon the colonies.[8]

Despite the sarcasm of the passage, Leonard's summary was fairly accurate. The position of most American whigs at the start of the crisis was indeed that Parliament possessed extensive jurisdiction over the colonies but lacked the authority to impose direct, internal taxes. It was on these grounds that patriots denied the legitimacy of the Stamp Act. Some explained the restric-tion by asserting that taxation was distinct from legislation and required the direct consent of all those concerned (delivered through their representa-tives), while others argued more broadly that Parliament should be accorded jurisdiction only over the "external" affairs of the colonies. Taxation, on this latter account, was merely one important example of an "internal" power reserved to the various colonial legislatures.[9] Once the Stamp Act was re-pealed and replaced with the Townshend Acts in 1767, however, the patriots found themselves in something of a quandary. From 1763 to 1766, they had explicitly conceded Parliament's right to regulate imperial commerce and to impose duties on commercial products for that purpose (these were undeni-ably instances of "external" legislation).[10] On what grounds, then, could they dispute the legitimacy of a parliamentary bill imposing duties on im-ports? As Leonard observed, patriots first attempted to address this chal-lenge by endorsing a distinction—proposed by John Dickinson of Pennsyl-

vania in his *Farmer's Letters* (1768)—between parliamentary duties designed
to regulate commerce and those designed to raise revenue. The former,
Dickinson argued, were legitimate, whereas the latter were not.[11] In the
course of the pamphlet wars of the late 1760s, however, it became clear that
this was not a tenable position. In the first place, it seemed to require an
impracticable degree of access to the intentions of those who imposed commercial duties, since both sorts of duties could look the same on paper. More
fundamentally, it invited precisely the same challenge that had been leveled
so effectively against patriot denials of a parliamentary right of taxation:
How could it be that Parliament had the authority to pass laws regulating
commerce, but lacked the authority to impose duties on trade? Was this not
a distinction without a difference? As William Drayton of South Carolina
put it, "I must confess, that it seems astonishing, at least to my very limited
understanding, that any man should say . . . that altho' *consent* by representation, is absolutely necessary to the taxation of America, yet, British legislation may legally operate over America, without, and even *against her consent.*"[12] The arguments offered on behalf of this "middle position," as another
commentator put it, had ended up "proving *too much.*"[13]

The patriots solved their dilemma by embracing the dominion theory,
according to which Parliament possessed no jurisdiction whatsoever over
the colonies.[14] North America was now understood to be "outside the realm,"
a separate dominion within the British Empire. It did not follow, *pace* Leonard, that the colonies were to be regarded as "independent states"; rather,
they were to be understood as "dependent" solely on the person of the
king, and not upon the "Legislature of Great Britain." The first intima-
tions of this revised view seem to have come from Benjamin Franklin in the
early months of 1766, a period during which he was actively seeking to replace
Pennsylvania's proprietary government with a royal one (to move from "the
chains of Proprietary Slavery to Royal Liberty," as his protégé Joseph Galloway had put it), much to the chagrin of many prominent Pennsylvania
whigs.[15] In an essay dated January 11, Franklin observed that, when considering the merits of the colonial case against the Stamp Act, "it may be of use
to recollect; that the colonies were planted in times when the powers of
parliament were not supposed so extensive, as they are become since the
Revolution." Indeed, they "were planted in lands and countries w[h]ere the
parliament had not then the least jurisdiction."[16] The first settlers launched
their ventures "by permission from the crown" and the territories in which

they settled "thus became *new* dominions *of the crown,* settled under royal charters, that formed their several governments and constitutions, on which the parliament was *never consulted*; or had the *least participation.*" But Franklin refused at this stage to argue that Parliament therefore possessed no legitimate jurisdiction over the colonies in the present day; he stated only that the colonies "have had, from their beginning, like Ireland, their separate parliaments, called modestly assemblies. . . . How far, and in what particulars, they are *subordinate* and *subject* to the British parliament; or whether they may not, if the King pleases, be governed as *domains of the crown,* without that parliament, are points newly agitated, never yet, but probably soon will be, thoroughly considered and settled."[17] He took precisely the same line in his celebrated testimony before the House of Commons on February 13 of that year. "The Colonies," he declared, "are not supposed to be within the realm," but they were nonetheless prepared to acknowledge the right of Parliament to legislate for them in external matters and to impose duties on trade.[18] When asked whether he regarded this middle position as theoretically coherent, Franklin replied coyly that "many arguments have been lately used to shew [the colonists] that there is no difference, and that if you have no right to tax them internally, you have none to tax them externally, or make any other law to bind them. At present they do not reason so, but in time they may possible be convinced by these arguments."[19]

Franklin went much further, however, in a set of marginalia that he composed in his copy of the "protest" written by dissenting members of the House of Lords in opposition to repeal of the Stamp Act. These comments, probably written in March 1766, were intended as notes for an eventual pamphlet that would have answered the case against repeal, but Franklin evidently set the project aside and his remarks were never published. In response to the charge that the colonists were denying their subjection to Great Britain, Franklin commented, "Neg[ative]. All acknowledge their Subjection to his Majesty."[20] As for the Lords' claim that repeal of the Stamp Act would "make the *authority of Great Britain contemptible* hereafter," Franklin likewise editorialized: "Not the King's."[21] To assert "the legislative authority" of Great Britain over the colonies, he wished to persuade Parliament, was to "thrust yourselves in with the Crown in the Government. Of the Colonies," thus "encroaching on the Royal power."[22] It was true, he now conceded, that his position suggested that America ought to be considered as "absolutely free from any obedience to the *power of the British Legislature,*" but not, he stressed, "to the Power of the Crown."[23] "We are different States," he proclaimed, "Subject to the King," and while "America [is] not in the Realm of England or G[reat] B[ritain], No Man in America thinks himself exempt from the Jurisdiction of the Crown and their own assemblies—or has any such private Judgment."[24] The "Dignity of the Crown" was therefore "not concern'd" in the dispute over the Stamp Act, but merely that of "the Laws of Parl[iamen]t."[25]

British Americans were denied the opportunity to read these radical reflections by Franklin, but they would later find an extraordinarily concise and explicit statement of his emerging position in James Wilson's *Considerations on the Nature and the Extent of the Legislative Authority of the British Parliament* (written in 1768, although not printed until 1774), mistakenly attributed by its first readers to Franklin himself.[26] Having concluded that "there can be no medium between acknowledging and denying" the authority of Parliament over the colonies "in all cases," Wilson insists that it must be denied, but that "a denial of the legislative authority of the British Parliament over America is by no means inconsistent with that connexion, which ought to subsist between the Mother Country and her Colonies."[27] This "connexion," rightly understood, was simply through the person and prerogative of the king:

> To the King is entrusted the direction and management of the great machine of government. He therefore is fittest to adjust the different wheels, and to regulate their motions in such a manner as to co-operate in the same general designs. He makes war: He concludes peace: He forms alliances: He regulates domestic trade by his prerogative; and directs foreign commerce by his treaties, with those nations, with whom it is carried on. He names the officers of government; so that he can check every jarring movement in the administration. He has a negative in the different legislatures throughout his dominions, so that he can prevent any repugnancy in their different laws. The connection and harmony between Great-Britain and us, which it is her interest and ours mutually to cultivate; and on which her prosperity, as well as ours, so materially depends; will be better preserved by the operation of the legal prerogatives of the Crown, than by the exertion of an unlimited authority by Parliament.[28]

This is a remarkable passage. It was not unusual for English or American whigs to express devotion to the king, to look upon him as a defender of their liberties, or to assign him what formally remained the constitutional executive powers of the Crown (the right to make war, treaties, etc.), but it was wholly unprecedented in whig discourse to flee from parliamentary authority and seek safety in the "prerogatives of the Crown."[29] It was equally stunning to include among those prerogatives the dreaded "negative voice"—which had not been exercised by a British monarch over a parliamentary bill since the reign of Anne,[30] and which the king did not even enjoy on paper in several of the American colonies—as well as the power to "regulate domestic trade" (that is, trade within the empire) and "foreign commerce."[31] Wilson was particularly conscious of the radicalism of this final claim, but he boldly defended it nonetheless: "if the Commerce of the British Empire must be regulated by a general superintending power, capable of exerting its influence over every part of it, why may not this power be entrusted to the King, as a part of the Royal prerogative?"[32] This expansive understanding of the prerogative, Wilson assures his readers, is attested in "many authorities."

Just what sort of "authorities" he has in mind becomes clearer as he proceeds to offer a striking account of the original colonization of America, quite reminiscent of Franklin's.

> Those who launched into the unknown deep, in quest of new countries and habitations, still considered themselves as subjects of the English Monarchs, and behaved suitably to that character; but it no where appears, that they still considered themselves as represented in an English Parliament, or that they thought the authority of the English Parliament extended over them. They took possession of the country in the King's name: They treated, or made war with the Indians by his authority: They held the lands under his grants, and paid him the rents received upon them: They established governments under the sanction of his prerogative, or by virtue of his charters.[33]

In this account, the colonial charters were granted by the person of the king, and lands "granted" in them were originally his and his alone. Colonial governments were established by the king's "prerogative"; Parliament had nothing to do with the matter. America was understood by the chartering monarchs to be outside the realm. Indeed, Wilson adds the crucial claim that "it was chiefly during the confusions of the republic, when the King was in exile, and unable to assert his rights, that the House of Commons began to interfere in Colony matters."[34]

It is worth underlining the drama of this last statement. Wilson's position is that the Stuart monarchs who granted colonial charters, James I and

Charles I, had *correctly* understood North America to be a private dominion of the Crown, to be dispensed with and governed according to the royal prerogative (and then according to the terms of those freely granted charters) and that this understanding was no less correct after the Glorious Revolution than it had been before. It was only "when the King [Charles II] was in exile," during the republican interregnum, that Parliament had been able to usurp his prerogative "rights" and "interfere in Colony matters" by passing the first Navigation Act in 1651. Here we find the beginnings of an extraordinary revision of the patriot historical imagination. Throughout the 1760s, patriot writers had understood the events of their own time as reenactments of the long seventeenth-century struggle against Stuart tyranny: Parliament's claim to tax Americans without their consent was equivalent to the Stuart claim to raise revenue without the consent of Parliament. Both constituted attempts to rule over subjects by prerogative, and to be governed by prerogative was to live at the mere "grace" and pleasure of a master. It was, as every patriot writer ritualistically declared, quite simply to be a slave.[35] Thus, James Otis chose the pseudonym "Hampden" and thundered in his *Rights of the British Colonies Asserted and Proved* (1764) against the "arbitrary and wicked proceedings of the Stuarts," claiming to defend instead "the present happy and most righteous establishment" that had been "justly built on the ruins which those princes brought on their family, and two of them on their own heads."[36] John Adams, writing in his *Dissertation on the Canon and Feudal Law* (1765), likewise styled himself as a latter-day champion of the parliamentarian struggle against "the execrable race of the Stuarts," explaining that America was first settled by lovers of "universal liberty" who fled to the New World to escape Stuart regal and ecclesiastical tyranny.[37] These sentiments were repeated endlessly.[38] Wilson, however, begins to gesture toward a very different story indeed: one according to which the great seventeenth-century constitutional crisis had pitted the virtuous defenders of royal prerogative against the illicit encroachments of rapacious parliamentarians.[39]

Perhaps the most striking affirmation of this new historical and constitutional narrative from 1768 is preserved in a letter from the Philadelphia physician and patriot Benjamin Rush to Ebenezer Howard, dated October 22. The letter contains a well-known passage in which Rush, then a tourist in London, rhapsodizes about his emotional visit to the House of Lords:

> I felt as if I walked on sacred ground. I gazed for some time at the Throne with emotions that I cannot describe. I asked our guide if it was common for

strangers to set down upon it. He told me no, but upon my importuning him a good deal I prevailed upon him to allow me the liberty. I accordingly advanced towards it and sat in it for a considerable time. When I first got into it, I was seized with a sense of horror which for some time interrupted my ordinary train of thinking. "This," said I (in the words of Dr. [Edward] Young), "is the golden period of the worldly man's wishes. His passions conceive, his hopes aspire after nothing beyond *this Throne*."[40]

Scholars have periodically cited these words in order to underscore the degree to which British North Americans in the 1760s, however whiggish they may have been, remained committed to the English constitution and the monarchy at its center.[41] But the crucial passage in fact comes several lines later, when Rush describes the next stop on his tour:

From this I went into the House of Commons. I cannot say I felt as if I walked on "sacred ground" here. This, thought I, is where the infernal scheme for enslaving America was first broached. Here the usurping Commons first endeavored to rob the King of his supremacy over the colonies and divide it among themselves! O! cursed haunt of venality, bribery, and corruption![42]

Here Rush offers a straightforward endorsement of the view that Wilson (a friend and ally) had recently sketched out. The moment when the Commons "first endeavored to rob the King of his supremacy over the colonies" was 1651, when the Rump Parliament passed the first Navigation Act in the aftermath of the regicide—thus "usurping" the royal prerogative and "dividing it among themselves." Then as now, on Rush's account, any attempt by Parliament to govern America should be regarded as an encroachment on the just prerogatives of the Crown.[43] Neither Rush nor Wilson was as yet prepared to take the next logical step and mount an affirmative defense of the Stuarts against Parliament,[44] but patriots after 1768 would waste little time in doing precisely this.

II

It is one of the great ironies in this richly ironic story that the raw materials of the patriot defense of the Stuarts were initially provided by allies of the British administration. The year 1742 had seen the first printing in London of the *Journals of the House of Commons* for the period of James I's final parliaments (1621 and 1624) and Charles I's first parliaments (1625, 1626, and 1628). Readers were reminded that the 1621 parliament—which featured the arrests of the great whig heroes Sir Edward Coke, Sir Edwin Sandys, and John Selden[45]—had foundered in no small measure on a debate over colonial affairs and that this debate had likewise bedeviled its successor in 1624.

At issue were two bills brought forward by Sandys and his allies on behalf of the moribund Virginia Company: the first sought to establish a British monopoly for Virginia tobacco (despite a free-trade treaty with Spain that the king had recently signed) while the second sought to eliminate a royal monopoly on North American fishing that the king had granted to Sir Ferdinando Gorges's Plymouth Colony in the so-called Great Charter of New England (1620).[46] James was incensed that these bills had been carried in the Commons, and his secretary of state, Sir George Calvert (shortly to be created Lord Baltimore), declared on the king's behalf that "if Regall Prerogative have power in any thinge it is in this. Newe Conquests are to be ordered by the Will of the Conqueror. Virginia is not annex't to the Crowne of England And therefore not subiect to the Lawes of this Howse."[47] Sandys, along with Coke and Christopher Brooke, denounced Calvert's defense of prerogative, arguing that the North American colonies were indeed "annexed to the Crown" and were therefore part of the realm and within the jurisdiction of Parliament.[48] The debate (which continued bitterly through the next four parliaments, as the fishing bill was constantly reintroduced[49]) thus pitted defenders of the royal prerogative against the proponents of parliamentary power and "popular sovereignty" and focused particularly on the issue of trade. The significance of this fact was underscored in David Hume's *History of England*—dutifully read by a great number of Americans who participated in the debates of the 1760s and 1770s[50]—which declared that from these "small beginnings" in the 1621 parliament there arose "a mutual coldness and disgust between the king and the commons," such that "a civil war must ensue."[51]

The first pamphlet of the 1760s to make use of this material seems to have been the fourth edition of Thomas Pownall's *The Administration of the Colonies* (1768).[52] Pownall, who had served as royal governor of Massachusetts from 1757 to 1760, put forward a plan to integrate the colonies and other dominions into one "grand marine dominion" under the direction of a central authority in Whitehall.[53] This was a very different scheme indeed from the one shortly to be embraced by patriots: Pownall's plan would have given the new "American Department" and Parliament itself vast powers over the colonies, including the power to regulate their trade. But the two schemes shared a central premise: namely, that America had not originally been annexed to the realm. In Pownall's account, this aberration had resulted from what he regarded as the legally bankrupt practices of early American colonization. Just like other European sovereigns, "so our Sovereigns also thus at first assumed against law, an exclusive property in these lands, to the preclusion of the jurisdiction of the state. They called them their foreign dominions: their demesne lands *in partibus exteris*, and held them as their own, the King's possessions, not parts or parcels of the realm, 'as not yet annexed to the crown.'"[54] Pownall makes the provenance of this last fragment perfectly clear:

> So that when the House of Commons, (in those reiterated attempts which they made, by passing a bill to get a law enacted for establishing a free right of fishery on the coasts of Virginia, New-England, and Newfoundland,) put in the claim of the state to this property, and of the parliament to jurisdiction over it; they were told in the House by the servants of the crown, "That it was not fit to make laws here for those countries which are not yet annexed to the crown." "That this bill was not proper for this house, as it concerneth America." Nay, it was doubted by others, "whether the house had jurisdiction to meddle with these matters." And when the house, in 1624, was about to proceed upon a petition from the settlers of Virginia, to take cognizance of the affairs of the plantations; "upon the Speaker's producing and reading to the house a letter from the king concerning the Virginia petition; the petition, by general resolution, was withdrawn" . . . the house from this time, took no further cognizance of the plantations, till the commencement of the civil wars."[55]

Pownall has taken this material from the *Journals of the House of Commons*, to which he refers the reader in a footnote. He correctly relates the details of the dispute over the royal prerogative in North America and underlines the point that the Stuarts understood America to lie outside the realm. For Pownall, to be sure, this was an aberration to be remedied rather than a sound basis upon which to construct a new imperial order. It was, after all, central to his argument that the Stuarts had asserted their colonial prerogatives "against law."[56] But he had nonetheless introduced into the debate a series of materials that others would put to far more radical use.

Pownall's argument was first taken up by an anonymous but extremely influential pro-government pamphlet published in London, *The Controversy between Great Britain and Her Colonies, Reviewed* (1769)—now known to have been written by William Knox. Deeply alarmed by the first stirrings of the dominion theory in the colonies,[57] Knox wished to remind the patriots that they had stumbled onto a dangerous and disreputable argument. These colonists, he warned, should be careful what they wished for. If the dominion theory were to carry the day, "they ought to reflect, that whatever may be their condition, they cannot apply to parliament to better it. If they reject the jurisdiction of parliament, they must not in any case sue for its interposition in their behalf." "Whatever grievances they may have to complain of," the pamphlet continues, "they must seek redress from the grace of the crown alone; for, should they petition parliament to do them right, they themselves have authorized the crown to tell parliament, as the secretary of state to James the First did the house of Commons, 'America is not annexed to the realm, nor within the jurisdiction of parliament, you have therefore no right to interfere.'"[58] Here Knox turns once again to the fateful debate between Calvert (whose later conversion to Catholicism became notorious among whigs[59]) and the great whig heroes, offering a paraphrase of the former's famous statement on behalf of the king—one that would be quoted incessantly over the next five years. Knox's intention is to isolate what he regards as a stunning reversal in the patriot position. After five years spent bemoaning the enslaving effects of prerogative rule, the patriots, in formulating the dominion theory, were now inadvertently (so Knox supposed) choosing to live in utter dependence on "the grace of the crown." Indeed, he goes on to note the important fact that the proponents of the two colonial bills in 1621 and 1624 had been the early settlers of Virginia themselves: "How would they be amazed at the madness of their descendants, whom parliament hath taken under its benign protection, and rescued from the cruel fangs of prerogative and arbitrary power, Did they see them labouring with all their might to throw off the jurisdiction of parliament, and return under the unlimited authority of the crown?"[60] Knox elaborates in a crucial passage, which deserves to be quoted at length:

> My countrymen will there see [i.e. in the *Journals*], that the doubts of *the right of parliament to make laws to bind the Colonies,* was raised by the *king's secretary.* . . . The majority of the commons were so far from doubting of their jurisdiction,

that they passed the bill [on freedom of fishing in North America]. . . . It is well worthy of remark, that the excluding parliament, from jurisdiction over the Colonies, was at *this time* a matter of pecuniary, as well as honorary consideration with the crown; for as there was then no settled revenue for the support of the king's civil government, the grant of charters and monopolies were the most important of the king's methods of raising money independent of parliament; and from the especial provisions in these charters to the Virginia companies, it is evident, that the king then looked to the new plantations in America, as a source for a considerable revenue to himself and his successors, which might, perhaps enable them to subsist their households in future, without the disagreeable aid of parliament. In these circumstances it is more easy to suppose, that the king or his ministers, would have restrained parliament in its rightful jurisdiction, than have suffered it to *assume* jurisdiction over America, if parliament had not a right to it; and the frequent rejection of the fishing bill is a proof, that such was really the intention of the crown, whereas its frequent renewal is a like proof of an early jealousy in the commons, and of their strict attention to the rights of parliaments, and the true interests of their country.[61]

Here Knox reminds his American readers that the conflict between the Stuarts and Parliament over prerogative and the colonies had been no isolated affair, but rather a central front in the great battle over constitutional principles that resulted in the Civil War. On this account, the tyrannical Stuarts insisted that America was outside the realm precisely so they could maintain an independent source of revenue and thereby enable themselves to rule without Parliament (as Charles I proceeded to do for eleven years after 1629). Fortunately, however, the Revolution had foiled their nefarious plot, and now "we hear no more of that prerogative language from the crown to parliament."[62]

Yet the patriots seemed to be associating themselves with precisely such language. They "have been deluded into the absurd and vain attempt of exchanging the mild and equal government of the laws of England, for prerogative mandates: of seeking to inlarge your liberties, by disenfranchising yourselves of the rights of British subjects."[63] Indeed, as Knox pointed out, the patriot embrace of the Stuart position threatened to point them in an even more perilous and unexpected direction: "I would ask these loyal subjects of the king, what king it is they profess themselves to be the loyal subjects of? It cannot be his present most gracious majesty George the Third,

King of Great Britain, for his title is founded on an act of parliament, and they will not surely acknowledge, that parliament can give them a king, which is of all others the highest act of sovereignty, when they deny it to have power to tax or bind them in any other case."[64] If the patriots were truly going to deny that they were within the realm and therefore bound by acts of Parliament, would they then find themselves supporting the Catholic Pretender? Knox answers coyly that he has no reason to doubt that the Americans recognized William and Mary after the Glorious Revolution: "I believe they did so, for I never suspected them of Jacobitism, altho' they must see, that if they reject parliamentary authority, they make themselves to be still the subjects of the abjured Stuart race. This however is too delicate a matter to say more upon."[65]

It is clear, then, that Knox wrote his pamphlet from a particular point of view. He assumed that patriots would not wish to associate themselves with the Stuart monarchs of the mid-seventeenth century, let alone with the cause of the Pretender, and that they would be embarrassed when they recognized the Jacobean and Caroline provenance of their seemingly novel constitutional theory. He must therefore have been shocked when his patriot opponents responded by explicitly taking up the defense of the Stuarts. The first to do so was Franklin's friend and ally, the itinerant physician (and subsequent British spy) Edward Bancroft, in an anonymous response to Knox, *Remarks on the Review of the Controversy between Great Britain and Her Colonies* (1769).[66] Despite its author's relative obscurity, this pamphlet, first published in London and then reprinted in New London in 1771, became the most influential patriot text of the early 1770s, and it supplied a definitive template for defenses of the dominion theory.[67] Bancroft's basic argument is clear: "Though the King's Prerogative extends, indiscriminately, to all States owing him Allegiance, yet the Legislative Power of each State, if the People have any Share therein, is necessarily confined within the State itself."[68] He defends this claim by offering a short synopsis of English colonial history, clearly indebted to Pownall's, but differing from it in some crucial respects. Elizabeth and the first two Stuarts had claimed North America as a personal dominion, "and no Person will affirm, that the Nation had any Claims thereto, or that that Part of *America,* situated between the 33rd and 40th Degrees of North Latitude, was then annexed to the Realm; and I believe it will be difficult to prove, that it has been since united thereto, or indeed, that any Power, after it had been legally granted to others, could annex it to the Realm without *their* Consent."[69] It follows that if "the Crown, by Discovery or otherwise, acquired a Title to any Part of *America*, it belonged to the Crown alone, and could be forever alienated from the Realm, either to Subjects or Foreigners, at the Pleasure of the Crown."[70]

It is worth noting the tension in this argument, as it became a recurring feature of patriot writing during the period. Unlike a number of his disciples, Bancroft does not actually wish to endorse a right of discovery or conquest as a source of title in the New World, and he does not actually wish to defend the notion that the kings owned North America as a private, feudal possession. What he argues is that the Crown's title is the only *possible* title that could have resulted from the early colonization of America. If that title is dubious, then a fortiori Britain's claim to have absorbed the territory is even more ludicrous. The key point, for Bancroft, is that the colonies were formed on the basis of private contracts between monarchs and the various companies and proprietors.[71] These charters, Bancroft tells us, had left the colonies dependent only upon the Crown, not upon Parliament. As for the famous caveat in the various charters stipulating that colonial laws must not be "repugnant to the laws and statutes of England,"[72] Bancroft argues that the Stuart monarchs clearly intended it to mean only that the colonies should be governed according to the basic principles of the English constitution, not that they were subject to acts of Parliament. As evidence, he returns to precisely the same incident that Knox had discussed so extensively, although he treats it in a strikingly different manner:

> The Charter which provides that the Laws of *Virginia* shall not be contrary to the Laws and Statutes of England, bears the Date the 12th of *March*, 1612; and on the 25th of *April*, 1621, soon after the Constitution of *Virginia* had received that Form it has ever since retained, when a Bill was proposed in the House of Commons for granting to the Subjects of *England* free Liberty of Fishing on the Coast of *America*, the House was told by the Secretary of State, from his Majesty, that *America* was not annexed to the Realm, and that it was not fitting that Parliament should make Laws for those Countries; and though the House was uncommonly sollicitous for this Bill, and often offered it for the Royal Assent, it was always refused by the Crown, for those very just and cogent Reasons. And the King's Successor, Charles the First, by whom the *Plymouth, Massachusetts,* and *Maryland* Charters were soon after granted, when the same Bill was again offered, refused it the Royal Assent, declaring, at the same time, that it was "unnecessary; that the Colonies were without

the Realm and Jurisdiction of Parliament, and that the Privy Council would take order in Matters relating to them;" though a little after, when the Maryland Charter was granted, he reserved to the Subjects of *England* the same Right of Fishing upon the Coast of that Province, which was intended to be secured by the Bill that was denied the Royal Assent; which abundantly proves, that the King did not refuse the Bill for any secret Reasons, but only because he thought it might afford a Precedent for an unwarrantable Extension of Parliamentary Jurisdiction.[73]

Two important things have happened here. First, Bancroft has introduced an error into the narrative: Charles never actually refused the royal assent to the fishery bill. He surely would have, but the bill died in the Lords in 1625, and although it eventually passed both houses in 1626, it was never presented to the king.[74] But Bancroft has also completely recharacterized the debate itself. Whereas Knox had offered this incident as evidence that the patriots were associating themselves with Stuart tyranny, Bancroft argues that James and Charles had offered "very just and cogent reasons" for prerogative rule in America and had rightly resisted an "unwarrantable" parliamentary assault upon the Crown. Indeed, Bancroft is at pains to emphasize that this truly was a debate over constitutional principles: it had nothing to do with the merits or demerits of the fishing monopoly, since Charles had been happy to establish a free fishery *by prerogative* in the Maryland charter. The Stuarts resisted the bill only (and correctly) because it would have represented an unacceptable "precedent," a usurpation of the royal prerogative. To be sure, Parliament had finally prevailed in the wake of the regicide and assumed control of American commerce, but this too had been mere usurpation. The Navigation Act, on Bancroft's account, was no more legitimate than the fishery bill had been: "However extensive the King's Prerogative may be over his foreign Subjects, the *English* Constitution has made no Provision for this Species of National, External Legislation, the Power of Parliament being originally confined to the Limits of the Realm."[75]

But Bancroft does not leave matters there. He proceeds to offer a striking, revisionist account of the flight of the Puritans to the New World. Jettisoning the traditional understanding that they had fled Stuart absolutism, Bancroft now informs us that the settlement of New England "was occasioned by a noble Disdain of civil and religious Tyranny, the very Object for which it was solely undertaken being an Emancipation from the Authority of Parliament, and those Grievances which they suffered under the Laws of *England*."[76] In this telling, the Puritans had fled the tyranny of *Parliament*, not the king. It was for this reason that they had insisted on the king's protection as patron and guarantor of their chartered rights, refusing to allow Parliament to encroach in any way on their new life in America. Even when charters were periodically vacated (as in the case of Massachusetts), the colonists insisted firmly that in such circumstances, "the King might, by his Prerogative, put the Inhabitants of that Colony under whatever Form of Government he pleased."[77] Did all of this make them de facto Jacobites, as Knox had suggested? Bancroft recognizes the force of the charge and attempts to refute it in a lawyerly manner: Americans owe their allegiance to the king of Great Britain, he argues, and it just so happens that the identity of this person is determined by an act of Parliament. Americans can therefore recognize Parliament as the arbiter of the succession without recognizing its jurisdiction over America.[78] It is a measure of exactly how far the argument had progressed that Bancroft felt it necessary to engage in these particular acrobatics.

In the wake of Bancroft's pamphlet, the defense of the Stuart position became basic to patriot discourse. The first settlers of New England, an anonymous pamphleteer declared later in the same year, "conveyed themselves to the wilds of America" under the king's protection, "in quest of that freedom which they were denied within the jurisdiction of parliament."[79] Franklin agreed, utterly rejecting the view that the puritans had "take[n] shelter in those distant climes, from the tyranny of prerogative." "Another misrepresentation," he fumed. In truth, "it was to enjoy Liberty of Conscience, and Freedom from tyrannical Acts of Parliament."[80] James Lovell, shortly to become a Massachusetts delegate to the Continental Congress, similarly challenged his Boston audience in 1771 to "once more look into the early history of this province": "We find that our *English* ancestors, disgusted in their native country at a *legislation*, which they saw was sacrificing all their rights, *left its jurisdiction*, and sought, like wandering birds of passage, some happier climate. Here at length they settled down. The king of *England* was said to be the royal landlord of this territory; with HIM they entered into mutual, sacred compact, by which the price of tenure, and the *rules of management*, were fairly stated. It is in this compact that we find OUR ONLY TRUE LEGISLATIVE AUTHORITY."[81] It followed, in Lovell's account, that "the claim of the British parliament over *us* is not only ILLEGAL IN ITSELF,

BUT A DOWN-RIGHT USURPATION OF HIS PREROGATIVE as king of *America*."[82] This position was developed further in the famous debate on constitutional principles between Thomas Hutchinson and the two houses of the Massachusetts General Court in 1773. Although the council (i.e., the upper house) continued to acknowledge Parliament's jurisdiction over North America, denying only its right to impose taxes and particular sorts of duties, the house fully endorsed the dominion theory.[83] Its "Answer" to the governor's brief was drafted (in all probability) by John Adams, with some assistance from Joseph Hawley and Samuel Adams.[84] The essay begins by retracing Bancroft's steps, analyzing the status of the first charters, and then offering the following observations:

> But further to show the Sense of the English Crown and Nation that the American Colonists and our Predecessors in particular, when they first took Possession of this Country by a Grant and Charter from the Crown, did not remain subject to the Supreme Authority of Parliament, we beg Leave to observe; that when a Bill was offered by the two Houses of Parliament to King Charles the First, granting to the Subjects of England the free Liberty of Fishing on the Coast of America, he refused his Royal Assent, declaring as a reason, that 'the Colonies were *without the Realm and Jurisdiction of Parliament*'. In like Manner, his Predecessor James the First, had before declared upon a similar Occasion, that America *was not annexed to the Realm,* and it was not fitting that Parliament should make Laws for those Countries. This Reason was, not secretly, but openly declared in Parliament. If then the Colonies were not annexed to the Realm, at the Time when their Charters were granted, they never could be afterwards, without their own special Consent, which has never since been had, or even asked.[85]

The story has become a bit muddled here: it was Calvert who had made the famous comment denying that America was "annexed to the realm," not James I himself. Nonetheless, this material is taken directly from Bancroft, complete with the endorsement of Stuart constitutional theory.[86]

Indeed, Bancroft himself registered this fact. Writing anonymously from London in the November 1774 issue of the *Monthly Review,* he reiterated his account of how "several attempts in favour of the bill for free liberty of fishing on the coast of that continent were all frustrated by King James the First, Charles his successor, and their ministers, who held America to be without the realm and jurisdiction of parliament" and lamented once again that "a

very different policy" was ruinously adopted "in the time of the Commonwealth, by the Long Parliament," which had "usurped the right of the crown."[87]
At the beginning of the imperial crisis, Bancroft went on to explain, a legislative right to regulate commerce "was hastily conceded to parliament by the
colonists," but now "the Assembly of Massachusetts Bay, in 1773, having considered their political history and several charters," had "retracted this concession, and (adopting a system before proposed by an American advocate
[i.e., Bancroft himself]) maintained the colonies to have been originally
constituted distinct states, subject to the King, but independent of the parliament."[88] Bancroft noted with evident satisfaction that "since that time
the claims and arguments of the colonists have been generally founded
upon this system, which therefore becomes an object of importance."

    None of this was lost on Hutchinson, who announced in his retort that
the authors had taken their arguments from "an anonimous Pamphlet by
which I fear you have too easily been misled."[89] Assuming that James I and
Charles I were in fact properly quoted in the house's reply (Hutchinson noticed the discrepancies between this account and the one in Bancroft and
the *Journals*), he posed the following question: "May not such Declarations
be accounted for by other Actions of those Princes who when they were sol-
liciting the Parliament to grant the Duties of Tonnage and Poundage with
other Aids and were, in this Way, acknowledging the Rights of Parliament,
at the same Time were requiring the Payment of those Duties with Ship
Money, &c. by Virtue of their Prerogative?"[90] Hutchinson, good whig that he
is, here expresses his shock that the patriots would take James and Charles
for their constitutional authorities. Did they not realize that the very same
view of the royal prerogative had emboldened Charles to circumvent Parliament by collecting ship money?[91] So much for those "great fundamental principles of the English constitution for which Hampden bled." And Hutchinson
reiterates the charge of de facto Jacobitism: "If you should disown that Authority which has Power even to change the Succession to the Crown, are you in
no Danger of denying the Authority of our most gracious Sovereign, which
I am sure none of you can have in your Thoughts?"[92]

    This section of Hutchinson's reply to the house simply rehearses argu-
ments he had first tried out in his unpublished "Dialogue between an American and a European Englishman."[93] There, he had the "American" (his
imagined patriot interlocutor) begin by complaining that "from the latter

part of the reign of King James the First down to this day, the prerogative of the sovereign has in many instances been lessened."[94] It has accordingly— and lamentably—been forgotten that "the disposal of new discovered countries hath been left to the prince" by the English constitution.[95] The "American" then cites his constitutional authorities: "I have no doubt that both James and Charles the First supposed they had a right to the part of America which had been discovered under commissions from preceding princes without any control from Parliament."[96] Answering this intemperate speech, Hutchinson's "European" insists indignantly that "there is no inferring from the acts of such princes as James or Charles what was the constitution of England."[97] "Whatever King James might imagine," a grant of land under his personal prerogative was not "worth one farthing."[98] British North America was always within the realm, and the colonists owed their allegiance to "the King in Parliament."[99]

A similarly outraged and incredulous response to the house's arguments came in a 1774 pamphlet by the English political economist John Gray, *The Right of the British Legislature to Tax the American Colonies Vindicated*. Reflecting on the invocation of the Stuarts in the "Answer," Gray asks, "Who would have expected to have found such very zealous advocates for royal prerogative among the puritannical inhabitants of New England; but it has happened to them as to Eve, when she first deserted her husband, 'They fell in love with the first devil they met, / And out of pique ev'n help'ed to damn themselves.'"[100] He then turns to address the specifics of the argument:

> The charters of the colonies, they say, are granted by the crown; and, for many years after their first establishment, the sovereigns of England governed them without the interference of parliament. What follows from all that? The sovereigns of England, at that time, were also endeavouring to govern Great Britain without the interference of parliament; and both were unconstitutional. . . . How absurd then is it to found the independency of any British colony upon the principles and actions of kings, subversive of the general liberty of the subject.[101]

Like Hutchinson, Gray argues that the Stuart position on royal prerogative in the colonies was fundamentally linked to the Stuart position on royal prerogative at home.[102] It was an outrage against whig principles to ground a constitutional theory on the tyrannical utterances of such enemies to liberty. This denunciation was echoed in the same year by the loyalist Jonathan Boucher, who thundered in his *Letter from a Virginian* that "from this parliamentary authority, they [i.e. the colonists] never wished, until of late, to be emancipated, but would rather have fled to it for protection, from the arbitrary encroachments of a James, or a Charles, armed with the usurpations, and abuses, of privy seals, benevolences, proclamations, star chambers and high commission courts, and from the enormities of the two succeeding reigns."[103] For Boucher, the only possible conclusion was "that such were the practices of the times, when our early charters bear their dates, that if they were not granted by parliamentary Kings, they were granted by tyrants, and we shall gain nothing by recurring to first principles."[104]

English pamphleteer John Lind agreed in his *Remarks on the Principal Acts of the Thirteenth Parliament of Great Britain,* declaring that "the *one great* condition on which the capitulation or the charter is granted is, that the conquered or acquired country becomes *subject* of the *realm* of Great Britain. The unconstitutional maxims adopted by the Stuart family, threw no small obscurity on this question. They were wont to consider all conquered or acquired countries as belonging to the king *alone*; as being part of his foreign dominions, in the same manner as Gascony or Normandy, and as subject to the authority of the king alone. Charles I asserted this exclusive authority in a letter to the speaker of the house of commons. After the Restoration, this idea was, in part at least, abandoned."[105] Lind then proceeded to offer a lengthy discussion of the fishery bill, as well as a pointed reminder that the parliamentarians of the 1640s and 1650s—"men whose names are delivered down to us with the endearing epithets of Champions of liberty, and defenders of the rights of mankind"—had "considered our colonies in America as subject in *all things* to the supreme power of England."[106] Hutchinson himself made precisely the same point in a pamphlet written the following year: "The great Patriots in the reign of King Charles the Second, Lord Russell, Hampden, Maynard, &c. whose memories they [the colonists] reverence, declared their opinions, that there were no bounds to the power of Parliament by any fundamentals whatever, and that even the hereditary succession to the Crown might be, as it since has been, altered by Act of Parliament."[107] Yet "those who call themselves Patriots in the present day" have unaccountably abandoned the views of these whig heroes.

Even the Genevan émigré Jean-Louis Delolme, an avowed friend to the independent executive power of the Crown, went out of his way in the second edition of his *Constitution of England* to denounce the American position as absolutist:

> It may be laid down as an undoubted maxim, that a Sovereign who depends, with regard to supplies, on several Assemblies, in fact depends upon none. An Agent for the American Colonies [Benjamin Franklin], in his examination before the House of Commons (A. 1766, p. 122) has even suggested in three words the whole substance of what I have endeavoured to prove on that subject, when he said, "the granting of aids to the Crown is the only means the Americans have of recommending themselves to their Sovereign." Nothing, therefore, could be more fatal to English liberty (and to American liberty in the issue) than the adoption of the idea, cherished by the Americans, of having distinct independent Assemblies of their own, who should treat immediately with the King, and grant him subsidies, to the utter annihilation of the power of those ancient, and hitherto successful assertors of general liberty, the British Parliament.[108]

For Delolme, as for Knox before him, the American proposal to "treat immediately with the king" and grant him supplies independently would hand the Stuarts a posthumous victory, guaranteeing "a considerable revenue" to British monarchs "which might, perhaps enable them to subsist their households in future, without the disagreeable aid of parliament."[109] Indeed, a notable but lonely English observer eagerly embraced the patriot position for precisely the same reason that Delolme deplored it. In a letter to Samuel Johnson, James Boswell wrote that "as I am a steady and a warm Tory, I regret that the King does not see it to be better for him to receive constitutional supplies from his American subjects by the voice of their own assemblies, where his Royal Person is represented, than through the medium of his British subjects. I am persuaded that the power of the Crown, which I wish to increase, would be greater when in contact with all its dominions, than if 'the rays of regal bounty' were to 'shine' upon America through that dense and troubled body, a modern British Parliament."[110]

The patriots, however, were undeterred. North Carolina lawyer (and future U.S. Supreme Court justice) James Iredell proceeded to argue in his 1774 essay *To the Inhabitants of Great Britain* that "the king had a right to all uninhabited countries that should be discovered and possessed by any of his subjects" and that the charters he freely granted to American companies had explicitly denied any "latent claims of a British Parliament."[111] As evidence,

Iredell offered the following observation: "King James, and King Charles the First, it is well known, both prohibited Parliament from interfering in our concerns upon the express principle *that they had no business with them.* In any contract can the nature of it be better ascertained than by certainly discovering the sense of the parties?"[112] In the current crisis, Parliament was thus straightforwardly attempting "to deny the king the constitutional right over this country," whereas the patriots were seeking to vindicate it.[113]

Iredell's "Bancroftian" argument was promptly reproduced in an anonymous public letter to Lord North, published in Williamsburg in May 1774 under the pseudonym "Edmund Burke." Its author begins by asserting that "at the discovery of *America,* no person imagined any part of that Continent to be within the Realm of England . . . and the Sovereign then had, and still has, an undoubted prerogative right, to alienate for ever from the Realm without consent of Parliament, any acquisition of foreign territory."[114] "Conformable to this prerogative right," he continues, "King James the First, and Charles the First, did alienate unto certain persons large territories in America, and by the most solemn compacts, did form them into separate civil States."[115] The "Royal intention" of the Stuart monarchs was that these newly created colonies would be "dependent on the Crown, but not on the Parliament of England."[116] The author then proceeds to offer a straightforward paraphrase of Bancroft:

> Conformable to this intention, we find that when a bill was several times brought into the House of Commons, to secure the people of England a liberty of fishing on the coasts of America, messages were sent to the Commons by those Monarchs, requiring them to proceed no further in the matter, and alleging that "America was without the Realm and jurisdiction of Parliament;" and on this principle the Royal assent was withheld, during all those reigns, from every bill affecting the Colonies. These and other facts, which appear on the journals of Parliament, joined to the charters of the Colonies, fully demonstrate that they were really and intentionally created distinct States, and exempted from the authority of Parliament.[117]

It was only "after the death of King Charles the First," the author explains, that "the Commonwealth Parliament, which usurped the rights of the Crown, naturally concluded, that by those rights they had acquired some kind of supremacy over the Colonies of America."[118] Once more, the assertion of Parliament's jurisdiction over America is rooted in a "usurpation" of the royal prerogative.[119]

Turning northward again, we find precisely the same account being offered by the Connecticut minister Moses Mather in his 1775 pamphlet, *America's Appeal to the Impartial World*. The various American charters, he insists,
"were entered into and granted by the King for himself only. . . . No mention is made in them of the parliament." For Mather, all of this is simply a
matter of understanding that, in addition to the king's rights in his private
capacity, "in his political capacity he also hath certain prerogatives, royal
rights and interests, which are his own, and not the kingdom's; and these he
may alienate by gift or sale, &c."[120] The Stuart kings had done so in the various charters and at no time was America annexed to the realm. Indeed, as
Mather insists, "It was declared by James the first and Charles [the] first,
when a bill was proposed in the House of Commons, and repeatedly and
strenuously urged, to give liberty to the subjects of England to fish on the
coast of America; 'that it was unnecessary, that the colonies were without
the realm and jurisdiction of parliament, and that the Privy Council would
take orders in matters relating to them.' And liberty of fishing in America, is
reserved in some of the charters that were afterwards made; which shews
that without such reservation, they would not have had a right to fish on the
coast of the colonies."[121] As to the objection that "the settlement of the crown
is by act of parliament; and the colonies do acknowledge him to be their
King, on whom the crown is thus settled, consequently in this they do recognize the power of parliament," Mather replies (as Bancroft had) that "the
colonies do and ever did acknowledge the power of parliament to settle and
determine who hath right, and who shall wear the crown of Great-Britain;
but it is by force of the constitutions of the colonies only, that he, who is thus
crowned King of Great-Britain, becomes King of the colonies. One desig-
nates him the King of the colonies, and the other makes him so."[122]

Alexander Hamilton, who was appalled when a borrowed copy of Bancroft's pamphlet mysteriously disappeared from his room at King's College
in 1775, likewise recapitulated Bancroft's arguments, and those of the Massachusetts house, in his pamphlet debate with the loyalist Samuel Seabury.[123]
The latter had made a point of stressing the absolutist implications of the
dominion theory in *A View of the Controversy between Great Britain and Her
Colonies* (1774). "To talk of being liege subjects to King George, while we
disavow the authority of parliament," he argued, "is another piece of whiggish nonsense. I love my King as much as any whig in America or England
either, and am as ready to yield him all lawful submission: But while I submit to the King, I submit to the authority of the laws of the state, whose

guardian the King is. . . . There is no medium without ascribing powers to the King which the constitution knows nothing of—without making him superior to the laws, and setting him above all restraint."[124] Hamilton, who fully embraced the dominion theory, took up the challenge in his *The Farmer Refuted* (1775). The king, on this account, "is the only Sovereign of the empire," such that "the part which the people have in the legislature, may more justly be considered as a limitation of the Sovereign authority. . . . Monarchy is universally allowed to predominate in the constitution."[125] As for the colonies, "It is an invariable maxim that every acquisition of foreign territory is at the absolute disposal of the king."[126] It follows that the king "must have been the original proprietor of all the lands in America, and was therefore authorized to dispose of them in what manner he thought proper." In agreement with this principle, the Stuart kings had voluntarily entered into contractual agreements with the first settlers, and these charters had not bestowed any jurisdiction on Parliament.[127] How do we know that the caveat in the charters stipulating that colonial laws may not be "repugnant to the Laws of England" did not mean to extend any such jurisdiction? Hamilton gives the by-now-familiar answer:

> But the true interpretation may be ascertained, beyond a doubt, by the conduct of those very princes, who granted the charters. . . . In April, 1621, about nine years after the third Virginia charter was issued, a bill was introduced into the house of commons, for indulging the subjects of England, with the privilege of fishing upon the coast of America; but the house was informed by the secretary of state, by order of his majesty King James, that *"America was not annexed to the realm, and that it was not fitting that parliament should make laws for those countries."* In the reign of his successor, Charles the first (who granted the Massachusetts and Maryland charters), the same bill was again proposed, in the house, and was, in the like manner, refused the royal assent, with a similar declaration that *"it was unnecessary, that the colonies were without the realm and jurisdiction of parliament."* Circumstances which evidently prove, that these clauses [in the charters] were not inserted to render the colonies dependent on the Parliament; but only (as I have observed) to mark out a model of government, for them.[128]

Hamilton then scrupulously paraphrases Bancroft's revisionist account of the settlement of New England: it "was instigated by a detestation of civil and ecclesiastical tyranny. The principal design of the enterprize was to be emancipated from their sufferings, under the authority of parliament and the laws of England."[129] Once again, the Puritans fled not from Charles Stuart (whom Hamilton calls merely "unfortunate"), but from the tyrannical Parliament.[130] Indeed, Hamilton adds that his account of the Puritan settlement "ought to silence the infamous calumnies of those, who represent the first settlers in New-England, as enemies to kingly government; and who are in their own opinions, wondrous witty, by retailing the idle and malicious stories that have been propagated concerning them; such as their having erased the words *King, Kingdom,* and the like, out of their bibles, and inserted in their stead, civil magistrate, parliament, and republic."[131]

At this point it is worth anticipating a possible confusion about the argument I have just been tracing. One could be forgiven for supposing that despite all of their talk about the Stuarts and the royal prerogative, the patriots in question had no real interest in augmenting the king's authority over the colonies. Their real purpose, it might be thought, was rather to establish the autonomy of the colonial legislatures.[132] To this end, certain patriots did indeed assert that, at the moment of first settlement, the king had enjoyed a prerogative right to dispose of North America at his pleasure (hence their defense of the Stuarts against Parliament), but they were far more interested in what happened next: the king entered into contractual agreements with the various chartering companies and proprietors, in which he guaranteed that the resulting colonies would be governed by laws of their own choosing. This right, once granted, was irrevocable, and the British government was therefore obliged to respect it. The dominion theory, on this view, merely sought to export the settlement of the Glorious Revolution to the colonies. Each colony was to be ruled by the king *in its legislature* in precisely the same manner that Britain was now governed by "the king-in-parliament."

As it happens, this is not an implausible characterization of Bancroft's own position: despite his embrace of the prerogative and his vigorous defense of the Stuarts, he actually left very little role for the Crown in his proposed revision of the imperial constitution.[133] But as we have seen, those patriots who took up Bancroft's arguments in 1774 and 1775 were emphatically *not* arguing that the king should play the same constitutional role in each of the colonies that he currently played in Great Britain itself. The king in Britain had not enjoyed the negative voice for seventy years, and virtually no one in Britain dreamed of assigning him a prerogative right to "alienate for ever from the Realm without consent of Parliament, any acquisition of foreign territory" or the authority to govern all of imperial commerce *without any legislature* (as Wilson and others had proposed), unrestrained by his English ministers.[134] These patriots were arguing instead that something strongly resembling the monarchy of James I and Charles I should be reestablished in Britain and then generalized to the colonies.[135] Both the metropolis and the periphery had been "slumbering under the old prejudices in favour of Parliamentary power" for far too long, as one pamphleteer explained.[136] Thus, Hamilton invoked the Stuart example in order to denounce his contemporaries for "losing sight of that share which the King has in the sovereignty, both of Great-Britain and America,"[137] and Franklin likewise complained that the Lords and Commons "seem to have been long encroaching on the Rights of their and our Sovereign, assuming too much of his Authority, and betraying his Interests."[138] Indeed, when Josiah Tucker pointed out that the Americans were either, in effect, oddly "pleading for the Extension of the Prerogative of the Crown . . . beyond all the Bounds of Law, Reason, and of Common Sense!" in Britain itself, or else adopting the even more "absurd" view that "though the King cannot do these strange things in England, yet he can do them all in America; because his Royal Prerogative, like Wire coiled up in a Box, can be stretched and drawn out to almost any Length, according to the Distance and Extent of his Dominions," Franklin placidly replied, "What Stuff! Why may not an American plead for the just Prerogatives of the Crown?"[139]

The Virginia lawyer and pamphleteer Thomson Mason (younger brother of George Mason and a future chief justice of the supreme court of Virginia) agreed, declaring (as we have seen) that "the general opinion, that the great defect in the present Constitution of *Britain* is the enormous power of the Crown" ought to be dismissed as "a vulgar errour."[140] Quite the contrary, it was the failure of the British people to restore "the ancient independence of the Crown" after the two revolutions that had crippled the mixed monarchy.[141] The Americans, unlike their brethren across the sea, recognized this defect, and they were accordingly in a unique position to rescue the constitution, both in the colonies and in Britain itself: "Was our Sovereign, even now, to place a little more confidence in his *American* subjects, there are many amongst them whose knowledge of their country would enable, and whose affectionate loyalty to him would impel, them to point out constitutional modes of placing him in a very different situation from what a corrupt, selfish, *British* aristocracy wish to see; for, however humiliating the reflection may be to a *Briton,* it is the virtue of *America* only that can preserve *Great Britain* from becoming the prey of the most despotick aristocracy that ever yet was elected."[142] Turning to his "countrymen," Mason exhorted them in ringing tones to come to the defense of the beleaguered British monarchy:

> If you think that your Sovereign ought to be considered as supreme Ruler of the whole Empire, providing for the welfare of his subjects within the Realm, at the head of his *British* Parliament, and of those without, at the head of his *American* Assemblies, by laws adapted to the local situation, and suited to the emergencies of each, and by that negative with which he is invested by the Constitution, restrain the different states of his extensive Dominions from enacting laws to destroy the freedom or to prejudice the interest of each other; if you are satisfied that the independence of *America* upon the *British* Parliament is essentially necessary to check the growing power of aristocracy in *Great Britain,* and to restore your Sovereign to that weight in the National Councils which he ought to possess . . . and if reposing your trust in the Supreme Being, to assist a just cause, you are determined to unite firmly in asserting your native rights, coolly consider the second question: "What mode of proceeding will you adopt as the most rational and effectual to shake off the jurisdiction usurped over you?"[143]

Indeed, it is a testimony to the power of this view that, although the first Continental Congress was initially prepared to "concede" Parliament a power (as opposed to a freestanding right) to regulate America's "external commerce," even this concession disappeared in its petition to the king of October 1774. The latter document closed instead with the insistence that "we wish not a diminution of the prerogative. . . . Your royal authority over us and our connexion with Great-Britain, we shall always carefully and zealously endeavour to support and maintain."[144] As John Phillip Reid observed long ago, these were perhaps "the most revolutionary statements made by the first Continental Congress."[145]

Patriots were drawn to this Royalist position for perfectly intelligible reasons. An empire governed according to the dominion theory *without* an enhanced royal prerogative would, they realized, be unable to secure even the most basic legislative coherence across its constituent parts. Each colonial legislature would make its own decisions about matters of common concern; there would be no "superintending power" to coordinate policy for the empire as a whole. One way out of the impasse was of course to assign this role to Parliament, but the whole point of the dominion theory had been to deny its jurisdiction over the colonies.[146] All that remained was the king. As Hamilton put it, "There must indeed be some connecting, pervading principle; but this is found in the person and prerogative of the King. . . . His power is equal to the purpose, and his interest binds him to the due prosecution of it."[147] Yet the king could not serve as a superintending power for the empire unless his Jacobean and Caroline prerogatives were restored to him. The patriots accordingly undertook to bring about this restoration— and in doing so, they left the whig inheritance far behind them.[148]

III

To be sure, some patriot pamphleteers declined to take up the cause of the Stuarts in the manner of Adams, Bancroft, Iredell, Hamilton, and the rest,[149] and here the exceptions are as revealing as the rule. One of these was Thomas Jefferson, whose *Summary View of the Rights of British America* (1774) is frequently cited as an archetypal defense of the dominion theory.[150] Yet, seen in the context of Bancroft's pronounced influence over patriot writing during this period, Jefferson's essay appears idiosyncratic rather than representative. The *Summary View* does indeed robustly defend several features of the Royalist constitutional position: the king, on Jefferson's account, should be regarded as "common sovereign" of a number of distinct states—a "central link connecting the several parts of the empire thus newly multiplied."[151] George III would be able to serve this function only if he revived the negative voice in Britain. Recent monarchs, Jefferson explained, "conscious of the impropriety of opposing their single opinion to the united wisdom of two houses of parliament, while their proceedings were unbiased by interested principles, for several ages past have modestly declined the exercise of this power in that part of his empire called Great Britain."[152] But times had changed. "Other principles than those of justice simply have obtained an influence" on the deliberations of the House of Commons, and "the addition of new states to the British empire has produced an addition of new, and sometimes opposite interests." In order to safeguard the interests and liberties of his subjects outside the realm, "it is now, therefore, the great office of his majesty, to resume the exercise of his negative power, and to prevent the passage of laws by any one legislature of the empire, which might bear injuriously on the rights and interests of another."[153] In this particular case, the offending legislature was Parliament—described by Jefferson, in language that would reappear in the Declaration of Independence two years later, as "a body of men, foreign to our constitutions and unacknowledged by our laws"—and the king was accordingly obliged to strike down their nefarious "acts of power."[154]

Moreover, Jefferson was explicit, in a way that most patriot Royalist writers of the 1770s were not, about the degree to which this new vision of empire implied a deeply significant change in the *character* of the negative voice, not merely in its scope. For while the royal negative had been deployed on numerous occasions in British America (if not in Britain itself) over the previous century, everyone understood that this power was not in fact wielded by the person of the king. It was the Privy Council, acting on advice from the Board of Trade, that vetoed colonial bills in the name of the Crown. The patriots, in contrast, were proposing that the king should separate himself from his British ministers (who were Parliament men) and personally "resume the exercise of his negative power" both at home and abroad. Jefferson made this commitment perfectly plain: addressing the king directly, he wrote that "you are surrounded by British counsellors, but remember that they are parties. You have no ministers for American affairs, because you have none taken from among us, nor amenable to the laws on which they are to give you advice. It behoves you, therefore, to think and to act for yourself and your people."[155] The king, in short, should wrest the independent powers of the monarchy away from his parliamentarian ministers in order to rescue the imperial constitution.[156]

So far, this argument appears more or less consistent with the ones offered by an array of patriot Royalist writers. But a closer look reveals that, in fact, the *Summary View* seeks to undermine several crucial features of the standard account we have been reconstructing. To begin with, Jefferson explicitly rejects the neo-Stuart narrative of colonial settlement that Bancroft and his disciples had been developing over the previous five years. On Jefferson's account, the Stuart monarchs—a "family of princes" whose "treasonable crimes against their people brought on them afterwards the exertion of those sacred and sovereign rights of punishment reserved in the hands of the people for cases of extreme necessity"[157]—had presumptuously "parted out and distributed" the lands of North America among their favorites "by an assumed right of the crown alone."[158] This practice, Jefferson argues, was wholly illicit. As a matter of law, the colonies did not emerge from freely granted charters given under the royal prerogative. Rather, free Englishmen had independently settled North America in precisely the same manner in which "their Saxon ancestors . . . had possessed themselves of the island of Britain."[159] The resulting colonies became commercially important to the mother country at a certain point, and, accordingly, parliament "was pleased to lend them assistance against an enemy [i.e. France], who would fain have drawn to herself the benefits of their commerce, to the great aggrandizement of herself, and danger of Great Britain."[160] This was the very same sort of assistance that Britain had previously given to "other allied states." The last phrase is important: for Jefferson, the colonies were never truly British dominions, but rather "allied states" which, for their own purposes, had opted to "continue their union" with the mother country "by submitting themselves to the same common sovereign."[161]

Thus, despite Jefferson's formal acceptance of the dominion model, his account of it was deeply heterodox. Even his impassioned defense of the negative voice is followed immediately by a direct attack on the king for his "wanton exercise of this power on the laws of the American legislatures"—chiefly in refusing his assent to bills designed to abolish the slave trade. Jefferson was happy to entertain the thought of the king vetoing parliamentary bills, but, in the case of the colonies, he concluded that the king's "shameful" abuse of the negative voice would "if not reformed" require "some legal restrictions."[162] He also pointedly denied what other dominion theorists had enthusiastically acknowledged to be the king's authority to dissolve the various imperial legislatures, including Parliament itself.[163] On issue after issue, Jefferson insisted, the king seemed to demand that Virginians, and Americans more broadly, should "submit themselves the absolute slaves of his sovereign will."[164] This attack on regal rather than parliamentary tyranny places Jefferson definitively outside the mainstream of patriot discourse in this period. His distinctive radicalism was already present for all to see.

The other great exception—John Dickinson—is equally illuminating.[165] It is worth recalling that Dickinson had been the great opponent of Franklin's design to convert Pennsylvania into a royal colony in the mid-1760s.[166] At that stage, he had expressed his horror at the thought that so many colonial worthies were evincing a "desire to come *more immediately* under the

King's command" and to "be consumed in the blaze of royal authority."[167]
He also fretted openly at the prospect that "the prerogative should be exercised with its full force in our American provinces, to restrain them within
due bounds and secure their dependance" on Great Britain.[168] What he had
opposed in Pennsylvania on the eve of the Stamp Act he now likewise opposed at the high-water mark of patriot Royalism. Like Jefferson, Dickinson
offered a tepid and somewhat convoluted defense of the dominion theory in
his *Essay on the Constitutional Power of Great Britain over the Colonies* (1774),
but, unlike Jefferson, his reservations about it were fundamentally conservative in character. He rejected the patriot embrace of the royal prerogative
not in order to reimagine the colonies as mere "allied states" of Britain but
rather to anchor the debate over their future in the "Revolution principles"
of 1688. Dickinson's pamphlet in fact embodies a plea to return to an orthodox whig understanding of seventeenth-century English history: one in
which both the Stuarts *and* the Long Parliament had been tyrants in turn
and only the settlement of the Glorious Revolution had established the
proper equipoise between king and Parliament. Thus, he first endorses the
understanding of the American crisis that had been so familiar in the 1760s,
and virtually absent thereafter: the colonists were simply struggling to
avoid the fate that "the people of *Great-Britain* would have been reduced to,
had *James* the first and his family succeeded in their scheme of arbitrary
power."[169] "Changing the word *Stuarts* for parliament, and *Britons* for Americans," Dickinson tells us, the analogy becomes clear.[170] But Dickinson likewise fumes against the "illegal" commonwealth Parliament, which had first
asserted "a boundless right" over the colonies.[171] A proper whig would hold
both of these thoughts in his head at the same time, just as he would recognize that although Parliament cannot be regarded as "the supreme legislature over these colonies," nonetheless the "power of regulating our trade"
is "legally vested in parliament" as the "full *representative* of the parent
state"[172]—not in the king's prerogative, as Wilson and others had claimed.[173]

In order to sustain his argument, Dickinson felt that he had to address
head on the patriot defense of the Stuarts and, in particular, the American
reception of the Stuart parliaments of the 1620s. Recall that both the patriots
and their opponents agreed that James I and Charles I had originated the
view that America was outside the realm—the crucial principle of the dominion theory—in the course of their great conflict with Parliament. Loyalist writers claimed that this pedigree revealed the argument to be tyrannical

and potentially Jacobite, whereas patriots argued that James and Charles had been quite right to defend their undoubted prerogatives against rapacious parliamentarians. It was vitally important for Dickinson to change the terms of this debate, to show that one did not need to defend the Stuarts in order to defend the dominion theory. He attempts this in a fascinating two-page footnote. The note begins by observing that "the author of 'the controversy'" (i.e., Knox) provides "a good many fragments of proceedings in the house of commons from the year 1614 to 1628. The amount is this, that the ministers of the crown insisted, that parliament could not make laws for *America*; that the commons doubted, but at length in 1724 [*sic*], came to an opinion, that the king's patent for 'a *monopoly* of fishing on the *coasts of America* was a *grievance*,'—that a '*clause of* FORFEITURE' against those who interfered in the fishery was void—and past a bill 'for a *free* liberty of *fishing*' &c."[174] But Dickinson proceeds to argue, *pace* Knox, that this debate has been badly misconstrued:

> It appears in the debates that the fishery was free *before the patent was granted*— These extracts do not shew, what became of the bill in the house of lords. One Mr. *Brooke* said in 1621—"We may make laws here for *Virginia,* for *if the king gives consent* to this bill past here and by the lords, this will controul the patent." It seems, as if the notion of the king's regulating power still prevailed, but, that "a clause of *forfeiture*" in such regulations was void. So much had the power of parliament grown since king *John's* reign. Nor does it appear to have been unreasonable, as commerce became of more consequence. The instance here mentioned, related to a regulation of trade; and however the king might have accommodated the point, with the other branches of the legislature, the whole proceeding is immaterial. If it was a right actually enjoyed by *Englishmen* to fish on the coasts of a plantation—and a grant by the crown on the fishery to the people of the plantation excluding the people of *England*, could not *divest them* of their right—or, "if by the king's giving his consent to a bill passed by lords and commons,"—"the patent might be controuled"—it does not follow, that the king, lords and commons could divest the people of the plantations of all *their* rights.[175]

The prose is rather opaque, but Dickinson is arguing that there was in fact *no dispute* between the Stuarts and Parliament over whether America was outside the realm. All agreed that it was. The bills in question concerned the "regulation of trade," which, on Dickinson's account, remained with the king-in-parliament, despite the fact that America was not annexed to Great Britain. James and Parliament were debating two much narrower questions: (1) whether the king possessed the power to "divest" *Englishmen* of a right "actually enjoyed by them" to fish off the coast of America; and (2) whether acts of Parliament could alter the terms of a patent if the king gave his assent. No one in this debate, according to Dickinson's rather fanciful reconstruction, asserted *either* that America was within the realm *or* that "king, lords, and commons" had complete jurisdiction over America.[176] Dickinson thus denied the Stuart pedigree of the dominion theory in order to render it respectable. His was the posture of a true whig.

IV

In the end, patriot Royalism proved incapable of furnishing a viable resolution to the constitutional crisis of the British Atlantic empire, for the simple reason that George III had no intention of remaking himself in the image of the early Stuarts. As the king wrote to Lord North in September of 1775, he was determined to continue "fighting the Battle of the Legislature," to be a parliamentary king or none at all.[177] He would not attempt to revive prerogatives of the Crown that had gone into abeyance generations earlier (and which he now regarded as straightforwardly unconstitutional) in order to install himself as the sort of king/emperor that the patriots had come to desire. George Grenville had cautioned him in 1765 "as he valued his own safety, not to suffer any one to advise him to separate or draw the line between his British and American dominions" (that is, to deny Parliament's jurisdiction over America, leaving only the Crown and its prerogatives to govern the colonies)— and this was advice that he intended to follow.[178] The king accordingly reassured members of Parliament in November 1774 of his "firm and steadfast resolution to withstand every attempt to weaken or impair the supreme authority of this legislature over all the dominions of my crown."[179] He spurned the final petitions of the second Continental Congress and, on August 23, 1775, proclaimed the colonies to be in a state of rebellion. "The authors and promoters of this desperate conspiracy," he declared in his speech to both houses on October 25, "meant only to amuse" by offering "the strongest protestations of loyalty to me, whilst they were preparing for a general revolt."[180]

The king's declaration provoked a flood of pamphlets and loyal addresses from his English subjects, congratulating him for refusing to augment his own power in order to placate the colonists. The city of Oxford, in an address published in the *London Gazette,* enthused that "we have observed with the most sincere and heart-felt Pleasure, that your Majesty has not been tempted to endanger the Constitution of Great Britain, by accepting the alluring Offers of an unconstitutional Increase of your Prerogative."[181] The mayor and burgesses of Maidenhead similarly thanked the king for his "paternal Care" and added that "as Friends to our excellent Constitution" they could not "but protest against the Principles of those Men, who by asserting the Dependence of America on the Crown, exclusively of the Parliament of Great-Britain, endeavour to point out a Distinction, that in future Times may be productive of the most fatal Consequences to both."[182] An anonymous pamphleteer likewise insisted that "since the Revolution" no English monarch had dreamed of claiming "such a dangerous Prerogative" as the Americans now championed, and he thanked God that "our present Sovereign has too much Wisdom and Goodness to suffer himself to be prevailed on by those, who strangely call themselves the Friends of Freedom, to dispose of the Property of his People, otherwise than in Conjunction with 'those ancient and hitherto successful Assertors of general Liberty, the *British* Parliament'."[183] William Markham, archbishop of York, was even more expansive. The Americans, he proclaimed, "have used their best endeavours, to throw the whole weight and power of the colonies into the scale of the crown" and have therefore plainly rejected the settlement of "the glorious revolution."[184] It was simply through "God's good providence, that we had a prince upon the throne, whose magnanimity and justice were superior to such temptations."[185]

The reception of the king's speech in British America was, of course, very different. Once word reached the colonies that George had definitively refused to assume the constitutional role marked out for him by so many patriot pamphleteers and legislatures, the phase of the American crisis sometimes known as "the flight to the king" ended abruptly.[186] Traumatized and disillusioned, the same patriot writers who had championed the Stuarts and the royal prerogative only a few months earlier now turned on the king and, in some cases, on monarchy itself.[187] But even as they rejected the king who had so momentously rejected them, they continued to insist that he was, by right, the legal bearer of the very same mighty prerogatives that the chartering monarchs had wielded before the parliamentarian revolutions of the seventeenth century. It is, after all, no accident that the Declaration of Independence denounced George III as a tyrant partly on the grounds that he "has combined with others to subject us to a Jurisdiction foreign to our Constitution, and unacknowledged by our Laws [that of Parliament]; giving his Assent to their Acts of pretended Legislation."[188] Only because patriots remained convinced that the king possessed a constitutional prerogative power to "refuse his assent" to parliamentary bills could they indict him for having refused to wield it on behalf of the colonies. George could only be styled a "tyrant" on the supposition that he was, as a juridical matter, far more powerful than any British monarch had claimed to be for over a hundred years. Indeed, the fact that Congress indicted the king alone in July of 1776—so often taken as clear evidence of patriot antimonarchism—reveals, to the contrary, their continuing attachment to the neo-Stuart theory of empire. The only "Allegiance" from which patriots claimed to be "Absolved" was that "to the British Crown," because they acknowledged no other. The word "Parliament" never so much as appears in the text.[189] In a sense, therefore, the Declaration stands as the final Royalist brief of the imperial crisis.

CHAPTER 2

"One Step Farther, and We Are Got Back to Where We Set Out From"

Patriots and the Royalist Theory
of Representation

John Adams's forbidding three-volume *Defence of the Constitutions of Government of the United States* (1787–1788) features a lengthy and blistering attack on an unlikely target: the seventeenth-century English parliamentarian and republican Marchamont Nedham.[1] Adams composed this massive work chiefly in order to refute the arguments of the French statesman Anne-Robert-Jacques Turgot, who had criticized the recently unveiled American state constitutions on the grounds that "instead of collecting all authority into one center, that of the nation, they have established different bodies, a body of representatives, a council, and a governor, because there is in England a house of commons, a house of lords, and a king."[2] But Adams suspected that Turgot's defense of government by a single representative assembly—and his corresponding rejection of the English mixed constitution—itself had an English rather than a French pedigree. Its roots, Adams believed, were in the parliamentarian Revolution of the 1640s and 1650s. The enemies of Charles I had "felt the necessity of leaving the monarchical and aristocratical orders out of their schemes of government, because all the friends of those orders were their enemies, and of addressing themselves wholly to the democratical party, because they alone were their friends, at least there appears no other hypothesis on which to account for the crude conceptions of Milton and Nedham."[3] More specifically, Adams observed that "Mr. Turgot's idea of a commonwealth, in which all authority is to be collected into one centre, and that centre the nation, is supposed to be precisely the project of Marchamont Nedham, and probably derived from his book . . . 'The Excellency of a 'free State,' " which, Adams tells us, has many "partisans" in both France and America.[4]

Having established the seventeenth-century English provenance of Turgot's view, Adams next offers a précis of Nedham's famous pamphlet, quoting directly from the original text. Nedham had insisted that a free state should be governed by a single representative assembly and "that the other forms [of government], as a standing power in the hands of a particular person, as a king, or of a set number of great ones, as in a senate," or indeed "a mixture of the three simple forms," are "beside the dictates of nature, and mere artificial devices of great men, squared only to serve the ends and interests of avarice, pride, and ambition of a few, to a vassallizing of the community."[5] In short, at the center of Nedham's parliamentarian theory was the crucial claim that only an assembly could truly be said to represent the people, and that government by anything other than an assembly constitutes "vassalage." Adams emphatically rejects this claim, insisting instead that "if the original and fountain of all power and government is in the people, as undoubtedly it is, the people have as clear a right to erect a simple monarchy, aristocracy, or democracy, or an equal mixture, or any other mixture of all three, if they judge it for their liberty, happiness, and prosperity, as they have to erect a democracy; and infinitely greater and better men than Marchamont Nedham, and the wisest nations that ever lived, have preferred such mixtures, and even with such standing powers, as ingredients in their compositions."[6] Moreover, "even those nations who choose to reserve in their own hands the periodical choice of the first magistrate, senate, and assembly, at certain stated periods, have as clear a right to appoint a first magistrate for life as for years, and for perpetuity in his descendants as for life."[7]

It follows, on Adams's account, that Nedham was badly mistaken about the nature of representation. He offers his own view of this fundamental idea in a remarkable passage:

> An hereditary limited monarch is the representative of the whole nation, for the management of the executive power, as much as an house of representatives is, as one branch of the legislature, and as guardian of the public purse; and a house of lords too, or a standing senate, represents the nation for other purposes, viz. as a watch set upon both the representatives and the executive power. The people are the fountain and original of the power of kings and

lords, governors and senates, as well as the house of commons, or assembly of representatives: and if the people are sufficiently enlightened to see all the dangers that surround them, they will always be represented by a distinct personage to manage the whole executive power.[8]

Whereas Nedham had supposed that only an assembly could represent the people, Adams insists that any agency authorized by the people to act on their behalf is properly called a "representative"—whether elected or not, whether unitary or composite. A single hereditary monarch might be the representative of the people, and, a fortiori, if the people are wise enough to parcel out political authority among several "standing powers as ingredients" in an overarching scheme, a single first magistrate, whether elected for life or "for years," is likewise to be considered as the representative of the people.

The significance of this aspect of Adams's argument was not lost on his critics. South Carolina lawyer and politician John Taylor, who published *An Inquiry into the Principles and Policy of the Government of the United States* years later in 1814, directed his considerable ire at the very passage of the *Defence* we have just been discussing. It was bad enough, for Taylor, that earlier in the text Adams had equated "republicanism" with mere "subjection to law," thereby allowing temperate monarchies to count as "republics." But Adams's claim about the character of legitimate representation was simply beyond the pale:

> By this definition of representation, hereditary power in every shape, is as much a representative power, as that elected by the people. . . . The distinguishing superiorities of our policy, are, the sovereignty of the people; a republican government, or a government producing publick or national good; and a thorough system of responsible representation. All these, Mr. Adams transplants into his system of monarchy and privileged orders, from the policy of the United States, as Mahomet transplanted several of the best principles of Christianity into his system of religion. . . . He asserts that, *an hereditary limited monarch and a house of lords are as much the representative of the nation as a house of representatives elected by the people.* Thus he seizes upon our principle of responsible representation, and bestows that also upon his system of king and lords.[9]

On Taylor's account, Adams was guilty of a particularly egregious form of political heresy. The twin pillars of the system of government that had been secured by the American Revolution were republicanism and representation, and one could not have the latter without the former. No hereditary monarch or nobility could be said to "represent" the people.[10] To be sure, Turgot had been mistaken to suppose that only an assembly could do so: Taylor insisted that anyone elected by the people might be said to be their representative, including the president of the United States.[11] But to suggest that an unelected, hereditary monarch might be the representative of the people was to reject the "Revolution principles" of 1776 and 1787 and to embrace a reactionary sort of monarchism.

Yet Adams understood something crucial about the debate over representation that Taylor did not. He recognized that one could not coherently reject Turgot's Nedhamite position without conceding that a hereditary monarch might be the legitimate representative of the people.[12] The English Revolution of the 1640s and 1650s had produced two rival, systematic theories of representative government. One of these was the parliamentarian theory to which Nedham (and, later, Turgot) subscribed.[13] It argued that a legitimate representative must be a good *representation,* or image, of those represented. Accordingly, this view insisted that only an assembly reflecting the complex composition of the "body of the people" could be said to represent them—and that such an assembly might represent the *entire* body of the people even if many citizens did not elect members to it. The theory thus conveniently established two vital propositions: that the king could not be the representative of the people and that the House of Commons could be the representative of the whole people, despite the fact that nine-tenths of the English population did not elect members to Parliament. Royalists developed their own systematic account of representative government in order to counter this parliamentarian position. They denied that being a good "representation," or image, of the people was either necessary or sufficient to establish the legitimacy of a representative and insisted instead that any person or agency *authorized* by the people to exercise political power over them could be said to be their representative, whether a single person or an assembly (or some combination of the two). This rival theory was explicitly designed to vindicate the claim that Charles I, a hereditary monarch, could count as the representative of the people.

In the imperial crisis of the 1760s and 1770s, the British administration and its North American supporters invoked the parliamentarian theory—or the theory of "virtual representation" (a term already in use among

parliamentarians in the 1640s)—in order to establish that the American colonists were represented in Parliament despite the fact that they elected no
members to it. Most patriots, in contrast, came to believe that their cause
depended upon the overthrow of this parliamentarian theory. Accordingly,
they revived the authorization theory, arguing that Parliament, whatever its
status as a "representation," or likeness, of the people of North America,
could not be said to represent the colonists because it had not been *authorized* to do so. But here they fatefully diverged. Some patriots began to insist
not only that authorization was a necessary condition of legitimate representation but also that *voting* was a necessary condition of authorization.
That is, they developed the view (rehearsed by Taylor in his reply to Adams)
that one could only be said to have authorized a representative for whom
one had voted: it was because Americans did not vote in parliamentary elections that they could not be said to have authorized members of the House
of Commons to act as their representatives. This view, to be sure, embodied
a substantial repudiation of the parliamentarian theory, insofar as it entailed
that a single person (or a small group of people) could represent the people,
so long as he (or they) were elected by the whole population of free men, and
that no institution or person could represent the people unless authorized
by them to do so. But it stopped well short of endorsing the Royalist claim that
an unelected monarch might be the representative of the people.

Other patriots, however, recognized almost immediately that this "election theory of authorization" was a nonstarter. As loyalists and administration spokesmen gleefully pointed out in the late 1760s and early 1770s, if
we take the view that an individual cannot be represented by anyone for whom
he himself has not voted, we will conclude that every citizen must be given
a veto over the election of representatives and that every representative
must be given a veto over acts of legislation. But this is simply to embrace
anarchy. The alternative is to argue that our authorization is conveyed not
by voting per se, but rather by our continuing, tacit consent to be bound by
whatever decisions emerge out of the institutional scheme under which we
live (a scheme perhaps initially authorized by our forebears at a moment
of original contract), whether we agree with these decisions or not—and
whether the particular magistrates for whom we ourselves voted happen
to support them or not. But if this is the case, then the argument delivers a
momentous result: namely, that an unelected monarch might be the representative of the people. For why, on this account, am I more thoroughly

"represented" by a majority of legislators for whom I have not voted than I am by a king for whom I have not voted? The Royalist provenance of the authorization argument becomes obvious and inescapable. The theory of representation to which American patriots gravitated during the imperial crisis had been designed in the seventeenth century to vindicate the representative character of hereditary monarchy, and, as Adams and other patriots recognized, any attempt to hold the argument apart from its Royalist conclusion was bound to end either in incoherence or absurdity.[14] One could not reject Turgot without rejecting Nedham, and one could not reject Nedham without embracing something very much like the constitutionalism of Charles I. For many patriots of the 1770s, this was not a conclusion to be resisted. Their constitutional position, after all, was that the king, not parliament, had been authorized through the colonial charters to govern British America. Only the Royalist theory of representation could explain why government by royal prerogative was not inconsistent with the liberty of American subjects.

I

The seventeenth-century English debate over the theory of representation derived its intensity from the fact that both parliamentarians and their Royalist opponents wished to describe their preferred form of government as a kind of *self*-government. The Digest of Roman law, as well as the canonical texts of the English common law, had taught them that a free man is governed according to his own will, whereas one who is dependent on the will of another is, by definition, a slave.[15] Virtually all participants in the pamphlet wars of the 1640s and 1650s were therefore exceedingly eager to characterize the laws of their favored regime as (to some extent) expressions of the will of the people. If these laws could not be so described, then Englishmen would not count as self-governing freemen but rather as slaves. Yet since it was abundantly clear that Englishmen in general were in no position to offer or refuse their explicit consent to the laws of the state, it became necessary to conceive of some sort of mechanism by which the consent of some could stand in for the consent of all. The theory of representation offered such a mechanism. To say that some person or agency represents me is to say that he or it acts and speaks in my name. If the people as a whole are truly represented by those who make laws for them, then the people in question can be said to be governed by their own will and, as a result, to be a free and "sovereign" people. But if those who make laws for a given people cannot be said to be their representatives, then the people in question must be regarded as subject to an alien will and, thus, in the condition of slavery. The parliamentarian case depended upon the assertion that the king could not be regarded as the representative of the English people and, as a result, that the existence and exercise of his various prerogative powers (particularly the "negative voice") placed Englishmen in a state of servile dependence upon an arbitrary and alien will.[16]

But why exactly was it, on the parliamentarian account, that only Parliament, and not the king, could count as the representative of the people? The most sophisticated and elaborate answer to this question was provided by Henry Parker in a series of influential pamphlets from the early 1640s, most notably *Observations upon Some of His Majesties Late Answers and Expresses* (1642). Parker begins the *Observations* by endorsing the contractarian piety that political power originates with the people themselves and is then conveyed by them to magistrates "by a speciall trust of safety and libertie expressly by the people limited."[17] This formulation might be taken to imply that the people may entrust their "safety and libertie" to any constellation of magistrates they desire, but Parker emphatically denies that this is the case. The people in such a situation must act in accordance with reason, and no rational people, he tells us, would entrust political power to any person or agency whose will was not identical to their own, for to do so would be to forfeit their status as free men. The only legitimate representative *for* the people is one who is *representative* of the people. A people must be represented by an "image" or "likeness" of themselves in miniature, one that reflects their unique composition with such exactitude that the interests (and therefore the will) of the "representative body of the people" will be identical to the interests and will of the "natural body of the people." Parker thus straightforwardly imports into political theory the technical vocabulary of the visual arts: a well-poised assembly represents the people in precisely the same sense that a good piece of what we still call "representational" art represents its subject.

Having defended this set of propositions about the character of political representation, Parker is now able to argue that Parliament has the exclusive right to represent the people—that it justly "claimes the entire rite of all the Gentry and Commonalty of *England*."[18] The king is one man and, as such, cannot be said to be a good "representation" of a large and manifold people. Parliament, in contrast, is to be regarded as "vertually the whole kingdome it selfe" (that is, possessing its full "virtue," or power) and as the "quintessence" of the people.[19] Indeed, Parker claims revealingly that "in truth, the whole Kingdome is not so properly the Author as the essence it-selfe of Parliaments."[20] The key point, in other words, is not that Parliament has been "authorized" by the people (i.e., that the kingdom is its "Author"), but rather that Parliament offers such a "geometrically proportionable" image of the people that the "essence" of the kingdom may be said to reside there. Parliament is "nothing else, but the very people it self artificially con-gregated" in a "Representative Body,"[21] one to which "all the States doe so orderly contribute their due parts therein, that no one can be of any ex-treame predominance."[22] The perfection of the resulting image produces a unique congruity of interests between the representative and those repre-sented: "That which is the sense of the whole Parliament, is the judgement of the whole Kingdom; and that which is the judgement of the whole King-dom, is more vigorous, and sacred, and unquestionable, and further beyond all appeal, then that which is the judgement of the King alone, without all Councell, or of the King, with any other inferiour Clandestine Councell."[23] Parliament, insofar as it simply *is* the people "by vertue of representation united in a more narrow roome,"[24] will never "counsell or consent to any thing, but what is publickely advantagious"; it "is indeed the State it self."[25] The case is entirely different with Charles I: "the King does not represent the people, but onely in such and such cases: viz. in pleas of a common nature betwixt Subject and Subject. Wherein he can have no particular ends; and at such or such times, viz. when there is not a more full and neer representa-tion by the Parliament."[26] The king, unlike Parliament, does not represent the people. He has "particular ends" of his own in most cases, and because his will is not identical to that of the people, government by his prerogative constitutes enslavement.

Parker's argument was immediately taken up by all of the major parlia-mentarian theorists of the early 1640s and quickly established itself as a cen-tral ideological pillar of the Revolution. John Goodwin, writing in his pam-phlet *Anti-Cavalierisme* (1642), denounced Royalists for endeavoring "to dissolve and ruine that Assembly, which is by interpretation, or representa-tion (which you will) the whole Nation" (the fact that Goodwin treats "in-terpretation" as equivalent to "representation" in this context is itself quite revealing).[27] John Herle agreed that the great constitutional conflict of the 1640s should be characterized as a battle between the person of the king and the *"Kingdome, or Parliament* its representative body."[28] Parliament, he explained, embodies "the common interest of the whole body of the Kingdome" and likewise constitutes the *"Reason or Wisedome of State."*[29] Although Herle balked at Parker's suggestion that Parliament's judgment was actually infallible—he had no interest in advancing what he called a *"Parliament Papacy"*[30]—he nonetheless agreed that it offered a uniquely powerful expression of the will of the people and that it should therefore be regarded as *"vertually* the *whole."*[31] Other parliamentarian theorists were rather less reticent. The author of *A Soveraigne Salve* (1643), for example, straightforwardly endorsed Parker's view that Parliament possesses "politique infallibilitie" and, accordingly, that one must not "question the wisdom, Justice and honour of Parliaments."[32] Unlike the king, who should be characterized as a mere repository of delegated executive power, Parliament *just is* "the whole kingdome (in which it is radically and fundamentally by representation)."[33]

Indeed, it is a testimony to the mighty influence of this view that even Levellers would continue to accept its basic contours in their campaign against Parliament at the end of the decade. Richard Overton, writing in his *Appeale from the Degenerate Representative Body* (1647), was happy to concede the point that "such as is the represented, such and no other must the figure or representation be, such as is the proportion, countenance and favour of the man, such and so must be the picture of the man, or else it cannot be the picture of that man, but of some other, or of something else."[34] What he denied was that the current Long Parliament could in fact be regarded as a good image, or "representation," of the people of England: "Certainly tyrants and oppressors cannot be the Representers of the Free-men of *England,* for freedom and tyranny are contraries, that which representeth the one, doth not represent the other; therefore such as are the representers of *Free-men,* must be substantial and reall *Actors* for *freedome* and *liberty."*[35] If Parliament wished to represent the people, it would have to replenish itself by admitting those who resembled the people in their zeal for liberty. Once again, a representative must *be* representative; not all assemblies will count as true representatives, but nothing other than an assembly can truly represent the people.

It is worth stressing that elections played a fraught and easily misunderstood role in this parliamentarian argument. Parker and his disciples routinely emphasized that, in Parliament, the people were "reduced by an orderly election, and representation, into . . . a Senate, or proportionable body."[36] That is, they presented the fact that members of the House of Commons were elected by the various boroughs and corporations of the realm as further evidence that Parliament would inevitably constitute a good image, or representation, of the people of England. Since the different orders, regions, and professions elected members by their "owne free choice,"[37] the resulting body would better reflect the composition of the "body of the people" than an assembly merely appointed by a single person or small group of grandees. As Herle put it, members of the Commons are those "whose *elections* as they are from us, so their *representations* are of us, and *interests* the same with us."[38] The author of *A Soveriagne Salve* argued similarly that since "the multitude of a Parliament . . . are selected out of the whole Kingdom by the people," they will be far less likely than either a prince or an appointed council to err "in point of Judgement" or "in point of will."[39] Again, the device of elections was important insofar as it helped to ensure that the will of the representative body would correspond to the will of the body politic. But at no point did Parker and his colleagues suggest that one could not be represented in Parliament if one had not voted in a parliamentary election. They wished to establish that members of Parliament were elected by a "representative sample" of the different estates of the realm, not that they were (or ought to be) elected *by each individual over whom they exercised political power.* Election did not operate in this theory as a mechanism of authorization but rather as a tool for creating the most faithful image possible of the body of the people. It was therefore entirely consistent for parliamentarian theorists to claim that (1) Parliament represented the people; (2) it did so in part because its members were chosen in elections throughout the realm; and (3) the nine-tenths of the English people who did not vote in parliamentary elections were nonetheless represented (i.e., adequately portrayed or depicted) in Parliament. Again, the parliamentarian theory of representation was designed to demonstrate that only an assembly could represent the people *and* that an assembly could be said to represent the *whole* people even if a substantial proportion of the citizenry did not participate in elections.

Royalists responded to this parliamentary onslaught by developing their own rival theory of political representation, one according to which it is authorization, not resemblance (or "representativeness"), that is both necessary and sufficient to establish the legitimacy of a representative. As early as

1643, Sir John Spelman offered an explicit refutation of the parliamentarian view. Parker, he explained, had built his entire theory around the claim that "the Houses [of Parliament], without the King, represent the Universall Realm" and that, accordingly, they *are above the King, by reason of their representing the whole Kingdom.*[40] But this had been a fatal error. "The truth is," Spelman explained, that "the King, Lords and Commons in conjunction are *vertually the whole Kingdome,* for that all the people did at first submit themselves to their determination. 25 H.8.21. *your royall Majestie and your Lords and Commons representing the whole Realme, in this your most high Court of Parliament, have power, &c.*"[41] On Spelman's account, the king is as much a representative of the people as the House of Commons because he, like them, had been authorized by the people to act on their behalf: the people "did at first submit themselves" to be bound by the "determination" of the king-in-parliament. It is this fact, and not some metaphysically bizarre view about shared "essences," that entitles king, lords, and commons jointly to claim the "virtue" of the "whole Kingdome."

Indeed, Spelman took particular delight in pointing out that once one focuses squarely on the issue of authorization, there is no reason at all to suppose that Parliament represents the people to a greater degree than does the king:

> The Lords Vote in respect of their Barronies derived from the Crowne, the Commons Vote in right of their electors whom they represent, at least nine parts of the Kingdome, neither doe nor may Vote in their election, the Clergie in respect of their spirituall livings, may not, nor the most substantiall Copy-holders, Farmours nor Lessees for yeers, not inheritrixes, Jointresses, nor reversioners, Heirs apparent, and men that live upon Interest are excluded; and all that have not 40. s. per annum free-hold Land, which I imagine, cannot be above a tenth part of the Kingdome. Tell me good Sir you that list to unsettle principles, power being (you say) nothing else but that might and vigour which a society of men containes in it selfe, why should the might and vigour of these being farre the major part, be over mastred, and concluded by the Votes of those that are deputed by a miner number of the people? or why should halfe the Kingdome in which there are but few Burroughes, be equalled and overborne in Voting by two Counties, out of which many Burgesses are chosen? *Old Sarum* shal have as many Votes in Parliament, as the City of *London,* or County of *Wiltes:* By which it seemes the Commons are not sent with equallity from all parts, nor sent by all: how doe they then rep-

resent all? what reason is there that all the Kingdome should sit downe with their Votes?[42]

If it is authorization and not "representativeness" or "likeness" that entitles one agent to act on behalf of another, then the only way to show that Parliament, and not the king, truly represents the people is to establish that the people have authorized the former more thoroughly or completely than they have the latter. But, for Spelman, this notion is absurd on its face. True, the commons are elected, whereas the king is a hereditary prince, but since "at least nine parts of the Kingdome" do not vote for members of Parliament, there is no plausible sense in which those individuals can be said to have authorized the House of Commons more completely or thoroughly than they have the king.[43] We are driven back once again to the conclusion that king, lords, and commons all represent the people to the same degree, because they have all been authorized to the same degree in a moment of original contract.

Royalist Dudley Digges promptly echoed and expanded upon Spelman's case in *The Unlawfulness of Subjects Taking Up Arms* (1643). Digges begins his pamphlet by offering what we might describe as an internal critique of the parliamentarian theory. Parker and his allies had claimed that only an assembly, as a good image or likeness of the people, could be expected to act in the public interest and, accordingly, that such an institution was the only legitimate repository of political power in a free state. Digges, granting purely for the sake of argument that resemblance (or congruity of will) is necessary for legitimate representation, counters that in fact it is the *king's* "owne Interest" that is "altogether the same with the publique." "The greatest security the Subject hath, that equall lawes shall be preserved," he tells us, "is from [the king's] negative voyce. The interests of the major part in the House of Commons may be opposite to the good of the Kingdome in generall."[44] On this account, it is the king whose interest is most closely aligned to the interests of the kingdom as a whole; parliamentary majorities, in contrast, are more likely to act on behalf of factional concerns. Indeed, Charles I himself had offered precisely the same argument in his *Answer to the XIX Propositions* (1642): "We will be as careful of preserving the Lawes in what is supposed to concerne wholly our Subjects, as in what most concerns Our Self: For indeed We professe to beleeve, that the preservation of every Law concerns Us, those of obedience being not secure, when those of protection are violated. And We being most of any injured in the least violation of that, by which Wee enjoy the highest Rights and greatest Benefits, and are therefore obliged to defend no lesse by our interest then by our Duty."[45] The king, unlike individual members of Parliament, cannot prosper unless the kingdom as a whole prospers. His interests are therefore inextricably linked to those of the nation, and he alone can truly be said to govern according to the will of the people.

But we soon learn that Digges's critique of Parker runs much deeper than this and ultimately rests, like Spelman's, on a thoroughgoing rejection of the "image" or "resemblance" view of representation. It is, for Digges, authorization alone that can establish the legitimacy of a representative, and any authorized agent, whether one man or many (and whether unitary or composite) can thus be considered as the representative of the people. As Digges announces, "He that hath supreame, that is all their [the people's] power, is the representative [of] all, he is legally the whole people."[46] Parker and his colleagues had insisted that "the two Houses (which they call the Parliament)[47] are the people in this consideration,"[48] but this was very far from the truth. In point of fact the Lords and Commons "are the people only to such purposes as the law nominates, *viz.*, for consenting to Lawes or Taxes upon the Subject. To all other purposes (wherein Regall power is not expresly limited) the King is the whole people, and what he does is legally their Act."[49] Notice how strikingly this paragraph anticipates Adams's language from the *Defence*: both king and Parliament represent the people when performing their authorized roles, and there is no sense in which one is more "representative" than the other. As Digges puts it, when the king wields his constitutional powers, he is *"Populus Anglicanus."*[50] Whereas the parliamentarians had argued that the two houses *were* the people because they constituted a good representation, or likeness, of them, Digges proclaims that the king *is* the people because he has been authorized to act on their behalf.

The most systematic and famous defense of this Royalist theory of representation was offered by Thomas Hobbes in his *Leviathan* (1651). Yet, as we have seen, it would be a mistake to regard Hobbes as the father of this theory; his account simply refined and developed a set of arguments that had featured prominently in Royalist polemic for almost a decade. Like Digges and Charles I, Hobbes first wishes to offer an internal critique of the parliamentarian theory. He declares that "in Monarchy, the private interest is the same with the publique. The riches, power, and honour of a Monarch arise only from the riches, strength and reputation of his Subjects. For no King can be rich, nor glorious, nor secure; whose Subjects are either poore, or contemptible, or too weak through want, or dissention, to maintain a war against their enemies."[51] When it comes to a democratic assembly, in contrast, "the publique prosperity conferres not so much to the private fortune of one that is corrupt, or ambitious, as doth many times a perfidious advice, a treacherous action, or a Civill warre." Hobbes argues, in short, that even if one (mistakenly) supposes that a people can be represented only by an agent whose interests are fundamentally aligned with their own, it does not follow that only an assembly can represent the people: the "congruity argument," rightly understood, actually favors a monarchical representative. But Hobbes has no interest in supplying a purely internal critique of the "resemblance" theory. Like Digges again, he wishes to dismantle it and put in its place the rival "authorization" view of political representation.[52]

Hobbes begins his celebrated discussion by offering a definition of the word "person": "A PERSON, is he, *whose words or actions are considered, either as his own, or as representing the words or actions of another man, or of any other thing to whom they are attributed, whether Truly or by Fiction.* When they are considered as his owne, then is he called a *Naturall Person*: And when they are considered as representing the words and actions of another, then is he a *Feigned* or *Artificiall person*."[53] Some of these "Persons Artificall" have "their words and actions *Owned* by those whom they represent"; in such cases, "the Person is the *Actor;* and he that owneth his words and actions, is the AUTHOR: In which case the Actor acteth by Authority. . . . So that by Authority, is alwayes understood a Right of doing any act: and *done* by *Authority,* done by Commission, or Licence from him whose right it is. From hence it followeth, that when the Actor maketh a Covenant by Authority, he bindeth thereby the Author, no lesse than if he had made it himselfe; and no less subjecteth him to all the consequences of the same." For Hobbes, to be a representative is simply to have one's words and deeds "owned" by an "author," such that one's actions count as the actions of another. In the political context, a representative is created when a number of individuals "conferre all their power and strength upon one Man, or upon one Assembly of men, that may reduce all their Wills, by plurality of voices, unto one Will: which is as much as to say, to appoint one Man, or Assembly of men, to beare their Person; and every one to owne, and acknowledge himselfe to be Author of whatsoever he that so beareth their Person, shall Act, or cause to be Acted, in those things which concern the Common Peace and Safetie."[54] Again, authorization is both necessary and sufficient to create a legitimate representative. It follows that a representative can come in any number of shapes and sizes: it can be one man, a few, or many. Hobbes utterly rejects the thought that a representative must resemble or constitute a good likeness of those represented—that the "representative body" must *re-present* the "body of the people."[55] Kings are no less capable of representing the people than parliaments; it is authorization through political covenant that allows magistrates, of whatever number or character, to act and speak in the name of the nation as a whole. A king's actions can therefore count as *our* actions and the subjects of a monarch may be regarded as self-governing.[56] Here, in full bloom, was the Royalist response to the parliamentarian conceit that only a "representative" assembly could represent the people.

II

It has perhaps not been sufficiently emphasized by modern scholars that the eighteenth-century British theory of "virtual representation" simply *was* the parliamentarian theory of the two English revolutions.[57] Contemporaries, in contrast, recognized this perfectly well. "I am well aware," wrote the parliamentarian and civil servant Soame Jenyns in 1765, "that I shall hear *Locke, Sidney, Selden,* and many other great Names quoted, to prove that every *Englishman,* whether he has a Right to vote for a Representative, or not, is still represented in the *British* Parliament; in which Opinion they all agree."[58] Patriot James Ingersoll likewise explained that in the British view, the House of Commons "is supposed to represent, or rather to stand in the place of, the Commons, that is, of the great body of the people. . . . when it is said they represent the Commons of England, it cannot mean that they do so because those Commons choose them, for in fact by far the greatest part do not, but because by their Constitution they must themselves be Commoners, and not Peers, and so the Equals, or of the same Class of Subjects, with the Commons of the Kingdom."[59] That is, the House of Commons represents all English commoners because its members resemble them; it constitutes a good "representation" of the body of the people. Edmund Burke agreed that "virtual representation is that in which there is a communion of interests, and a sympathy in feelings and desires between those who act in the name of any description of people, and the people in whose name they act, though the trustees are not actually chosen by them."[60] "Such a representation," he continued, "corrects the irregularities in the literal representation, when the shifting current of human affairs, or the acting of publick interests in different ways, carry it obliquely from its first line of direction. The people may err in their choice; but the common interest and common sentiment are rarely mistaken."[61] It is resemblance, not authorization, that secures the true interests of the body of the people.

The next step was simply to extend this argument to embrace all *British* commoners, whether residing in Great Britain itself or in British dominions overseas.[62] As the loyalist Martin Howard Jr. explained in 1765, "It is the opinion of the house of commons, and may be considered as a law of parliament, that they are the representatives of every *British* subject, wheresoever he be."[63] "The freedom and happiness of every *British* subject depends," Howard insisted, "not upon his share in elections, but upon the sense and virtue of the *British* parliament, and these depend reciprocally upon the sense and virtue of the whole nation."[64] Again, it simply could not be the case that members of Parliament represented all Englishmen and were accordingly permitted to tax them because they had been *authorized* by all Englishmen through the mechanism of elections, "for every *Englishman* is taxed, and not one in twenty represented [in this sense]: Copyholders, Leaseholders, and all Men possessed of personal Property only, chuse no Representatives; *Manchester, Birmingham,* and many more of our richest and most flourishing trading Towns send no Members to Parliament, consequently cannot consent by their Representatives, because they chuse none to represent them; yet are they not *Englishmen?* or are they not taxed?"[65] But if one conceded that English non-electors were in fact represented in Parliament, along with those of, say, Scotland—"which contains near two millions of people, and yet not more than three thousand have votes in the election of members of parliament"[66]—then why not those of North America as well? If the "virtue" of representation "can travel three hundred Miles, why not three thousand?"[67] As the English pamphleteer John Gray explained, "The essence of a freeman, that is of a free subject . . . consists not in his being absolute master of his own property; for that no man in a state of society can be; but in his being governed by known and established laws, formed by the consent of a popular assembly."[68] The notion that "in a free state there can be no taxation but by personal assent or actual representation" was mere folly: the "representatives in the house of commons are not the direct representatives of the people of Great Britain, or of the colonists. They are only the direct representatives of their own constituents, and the virtual representatives of every British commoner wherever he inhabits."[69]

This line of argument quickly emerged as the official position of the British administration during the Stamp Act crisis. The patriot complaint that Americans were not represented in Parliament, on this account, betrayed a straightforward conceptual confusion. Thomas Whately, the administration spokesman who authored the Stamp Act, put it like this:

> The Inhabitants of the colonies are represented in Parliament: they do not indeed chuse Members of that Assembly; neither are Nine Tenths of the people of *Britain* Electors; for the Right of Election is annexed to certain Species of Property, to particular Franchises, and to Inhabitancy in some particular Places; but these Descriptions comprehend only a very small Part of the Land, the Property, and the People of this Island. . . . all landed Property in short, that is not Freehold, and all monied Property whatsoever are excluded. . . . Women and Persons under Age, be their Property ever so large, and all of it Freehold, have none. . . . none of them chuse their Representatives; and yet are they not represented in Parliament? . . . The Colonies are in exactly the same Situation: All *British* Subjects are really in the same; none are actually, all are virtually represented in Parliament; for every Member of Parliament sits in the House, not as Representative of his own Constituents, but as one of that august Assembly by which all the Commons of *Great Britain* are represented.[70]

Here again we have an orthodox statement of Parker's parliamentarian theory, suitably adapted to the imperial context. Parliament represents the inhabitants of the empire by virtue of its status as a good representation of the body of the people. Because its interests are aligned with their interests, it can justly be regarded as "virtually" the whole people—that is, as possessing their "virtues," or powers. A second administration pamphleteer, John Lind, was even more emphatic on this point: "It is not essential to the character of a freeman who is to contribute a tax, that he have a right of voting for his representative. The greater part of the subjects of England, though they contribute to taxes, have no right of voting for their representatives."[71] Yet it by no means followed, on his account, that most Englishmen were governed by an alien will and were therefore to be regarded as slaves. One should not suppose that representatives, rightly understood, are agents who act by "the authority, of their constituents"—that is, by virtue of having been directly "authorized" in some fashion (e.g., through elections). Quite the contrary, to "represent" a people is simply to "display, set forth—'the *condition of their country,*'" and a legitimate representative is "a body of men chosen by a *part* of the community; but so circumstanced and related to the rest, that they cannot have or *think* they have any separate interests of their own to pursue, to the prejudice of the rest."[72] Parliament is plainly such a body: "It is the circumstances, it is the particular relation, *that* body stands in, to the whole community" which ensures that "they cannot have, they cannot think they have, a separate and distinct interest from the rest of the community."[73] Parker's familiar argument that Parliament (and only Parliament) *is* the English people had become the administration's argument that Parliament (and only Parliament) *is* the British people.

Patriots who wished to answer this parliamentarian argument had two basic avenues open to them. The first and more obvious of these was to *accept* the parliamentarian theory of representation while simply denying that Parliament was in fact a good image, or representation, of the people of British North America. That is, patriots could argue internally that (1) resemblance between the representative body and the natural body of the people was indeed both necessary and sufficient to ensure legitimate political representation; and (2) the British Parliament was perhaps a good representation, or image, of the people of Great Britain and could therefore justly claim to be the representative of the whole nation, despite the fact that most Britons did not participate in elections; but that (3) the British Parliament was *not* a good representation, or image, of the British population of North America, and therefore could not justly claim to represent the colonies. Several patriot spokesmen were drawn to this approach, particularly in the early stages of the imperial crisis. Daniel Dulany, answering Whately directly in his influential *Considerations on the Propriety of Imposing Taxes in the British Colonies* (1765), accepted that *"virtual or implied representation"* was the only plausible path to self-government, and further agreed that non-electors in England were duly represented in Parliament.[74] He merely denied that the same reasoning applied to American non-electors, that "the Commons of *Great Britain* are *virtually* the Representatives of the Commons of *America*":[75]

> [In Britain itself] the Interests therefore of the Non-Electors, the Electors, and the Representatives are individually the same; to say nothing of the Connection among Neighbours, Friends, and Relations. The Security of the

Non-Electors against Oppression, is that their Oppression will fall also upon the Electors and the Representatives. The one can't be injured, and the other indemnified. . . . Under this Constitution, then, a double or virtual Representation may be reasonably supposed.—The Electors, who are inseparably connected in their interests with the Non-Electors, may be justly deemed to be the Representatives of the Non-Electors, at the same Time They exercise their personal Privilege in their Right of Election, and the Members chosen, therefore, the Representatives of both.[76]

The English commoners who sit in Parliament have been elected by a representative sample of the nation; they will therefore resemble non-electing commoners to a sufficient degree to ensure legitimate virtual representation. But America is so distant from Great Britain and the needs and interests of Americans are so different from those of English commoners that a representative sample of Englishmen cannot possible constitute a good image of the American body politic: "There is not that intimate and inseparable Relation between the *Electors of* Great-Britain and the *Inhabitants of the Colonies,* which must inevitably involve both in the same Taxation. . . . Moreover, even Acts, oppressive and injurious to the Colonies in an extreme Degree, might become popular in *England,* from the Promise or Expectation, that the very Measures which depressed the Colonies would give Ease to the Inhabitants of *Great-Britain.*"[77] Dulany concludes that "the Connection between a Freeholder of *Great Britain,* and a *British American,*" while certainly evident upon careful reflection, "is a Knot too infirm to be relied on as a competent Security" for the interests of the colonies.[78] Because Parliament could not count as a legitimate virtual representative of the people of British North America, its government over them constituted enslavement.

This was a powerful and attractive argument, insofar as it promised to bring down the British case from within. It also proved quite difficult for administration spokesmen to answer. A characteristic attempt, made by the author of an anonymous pamphlet entitled *American Resistance Indefensible* (1776), demonstrates why this was the case. The author reasons as follows: "The Argument we frequently hear urged, and with much Shew of Triumph, that our Legislators will be under the strongest Temptations to abuse their Power [of governing the colonies], because in Proportion as they grant the Property of *America,* they will save their own; if admitted to be at all conclusive, would prove too much. It would prove that great Numbers in this Island must be perpetually oppressed: For a Variety of Cases might be instanced, in which a Majority of those who impose the public Burthens might relieve themselves in the same Degree, in which they loaded particular Parts of the Community, or Persons of a particular Description."[79] The author argues, in short, that the interests of Parliament and those of particular regions or professions within England itself are no better aligned than the interests of Parliament and those of the colonists in British North America. If we deny on these grounds that Americans are virtually represented in Parliament, we will end up having to deny that certain groups in Great Britain are virtually represented in Parliament. And that, he supposes, would be absurd. But the problem with this response is that it gives the game away. Recall that, in the parliamentarian theory, the House of Commons represents all Englishmen, whether electors or non-electors, because it constitutes a good "representation" of the people of England; its will is therefore aligned with the will of the "whole kingdom." Once we concede that there is no such thing as *the* will of the whole kingdom—that Parliament has a distinct and partial will that neglects the interests of large numbers of subjects—why should we regard it (or indeed, any conceivable legislature) as a legitimate virtual representative of all Englishmen?[80] If the will of Parliament diverges from the will of "particular Parts of the Community, or Persons of a particular Description," why should these parts or persons not be regarded as subjects to an alien will and hence as slaves? The conundrum for British spokesmen could thus be expressed as follows: it was difficult to argue that American interests and the interests of English electors were identical, but it was simply not a plausible option for them to acknowledge the divergence of interests between metropolitan and colonial Britons *and* to insist at the same time that Americans were virtually represented in Parliament. Their theory of representation could not accommodate this position.[81]

We see, then, that the internal critique of the British position had quite a lot to recommend it. Yet, despite its obvious attractions, most patriot writers of the late 1760s and early 1770s chose to jettison it in favor of an outright assault on the resemblance theory of representation. True representation, they argued with increasing fervor, required authorization—and the question of whether the authorized agency did or did not constitute a good "representation" of the body of the people was a tertiary one at best. For these patriots, the very distance between the colonies and Britain served to dramatize a crucial fact about the parliamentarian theory: namely, that it allowed people to be "represented" by agents over whom they had *no control whatsoever*. If A may claim the right to speak for B provided that he is (or supposes that he is) a good "representation" of B, then it is irrelevant to ask whether B has given A permission to speak for him or whether he retains any sort of control over A.[82] This uncomfortable feature of the argument could be glossed over to some degree in the domestic English context (where A and B might be residents of adjacent boroughs and the latter might be thought capable of influencing the former), but it seemed much more vividly objectionable when A and B were on opposite sides of the Atlantic. As William Drayton of South Carolina put it, *"virtual representation"* is everywhere and always a "fiction," but it "is much easier comprehended with respect to *Durham,* than *America.*"[83] Indeed, if Americans were to be governed by magistrates whom they did not select and over whom they had no control, would they not count as slaves?[84] And if they found themselves in the condition of slavery, why should they take consolation in the fact that their governors might share their interests or altruistically pursue their good? In such a case, they would simply count as the slaves of benign masters. Stephen Hopkins of Rhode Island offered an explicit and influential statement of this position as early as 1765 in *The Rights of Colonies Examined.* He began his discussion by listing the premises that he shared with his opponents: "British subjects are to be governed only agreeable to laws to which [they] themselves have some way consented, and are not to be compelled to part with their property, but as it is called for by the authority of such laws. The former is truly liberty; the latter is really to be possessed of property, and to have something that may be called one's own."[85] "On the contrary," he explained, "those who are governed at the will of another, or of others, and whose property may be taken from them by taxes, or otherwise, without their own consent, and against their will, are in the miserable condition of slaves. 'For liberty solely consists in an independency upon the will of another; and by the name of slave, we understand a man who can neither dispose of his person or goods, but enjoys all at the will of his master,' says *Sidney* on government."[86] The question was whether American subjects were duly represented in the House of Commons, such that the will of Parliament could be equated with the will of British Americans.

Hopkins was fully aware that most of his readers would be tempted to address this question by asking whether the will of Parliament and the will of the colonists were likely to be well aligned in practice (that is, whether

Parliament constituted a good "representation" of British Americans), but this, he insisted, was to miss the more fundamental point. If I have not *authorized* the agency by which I am ruled, it makes no difference to my *status* whether the agency in question happens to want what I want—or whether, if our interests are not perfectly aligned, the agency nonetheless happens to possess a sufficient degree of virtue and forbearance to act in my interests: "If we are told that those who lay these taxes upon the colonies, are men of the highest character for their wisdom, justice, and integrity, and therefore cannot be supposed to deal hardly, unjustly, or unequally by any; admitting, and really believing that all this is true, it will make no alteration in the nature of the case; for one who is bound to obey the will of another, is as really a slave, though he may have a good master, as if he had a bad one."[87] On Hopkins's account, the shopworn concern about the symmetry of interests between representative and represented was simply a red herring (although he was happy in passing to endorse the "internal" argument that "the colonies are at so great a distance from *England*, that the members of parliament can, generally, have but little knowledge of their business, connections and interest").[88] If I have authorized someone to act as my representative, then he acts in my name whether his interests and mine are intrinsically aligned or not; conversely, if I have not authorized someone to act as my representative, his government over me would constitute slavery no matter how perfect the alignment of our interests. The parliamentarian theory—which reasoned from the perfection of the "image" to the alignment of interests to the legitimacy of the representative—had to be pulled up root and branch.

This orientation on the question became ubiquitous among patriots during the Stamp Act crisis and its aftermath.[89] "Will any man's calling himself my agent, representative, or trustee make him so in fact?," demanded James Otis in his 1765 reply to Howard. "At this rate," he continued, "a House of Commons in one of the colonies have but to conceive an opinion that they represent all the common people of Great Britain, and according to our author they would in *fact* represent them and have a right to tax them."[90] The great parliamentarian jurist Sir Edward Coke may well have asserted "that the House of Commons represent all the commons of *England*, electors and non-electors," but this "fiction of the common law of England," Otis insisted, would never serve to convince Americans that they were represented by magistrates whom they had not authorized.[91] In a similar vein, John Adams, writing in his *Dissertation on the Canon and Feudal Law* (1765), proclaimed that "rulers are no more than attorneys, agents, and trustees, for the people," and as such they govern only by the "authority" that the people "themselves have deputed."[92] Without this authority, it matters not at all "if the Parliament of Great Britain had all the natural foundations of authority, wisdom, goodness, justice, power, in as great perfection as they ever existed in any body of men since Adam's fall; and if the English nation was the most virtuous, pure, and free that ever was." Even in such a case, parliamentary government over America would constitute "real slavery." "There are," Adams reminds his reader, "but two sorts of men in the world, freemen and slaves. The very definition of a freeman is one who is bound by no law to which he has not consented. Americans would have no way of giving or withholding their consent to the acts of parliament, therefore they would not be freemen."[93]

Patriot pamphleteer Maurice Moore agreed that "if being taxed only by their own consent" is a fundamental right of British North Americans as freemen, "they cannot, with the least degree of justice, be taxed by the British parliament, in which they are not represented, no person in that assembly being authorized to signify their consent."[94] Again, the crucial issue is not that Parliament constitutes a poor image, or "representation" of the people of British America but rather that members of the House of Commons have not been "authorized" to "signify their consent." To be sure, Moore is aware that "it hath indeed pleased some of the honourable members of that august assembly to say, that the Colonies are virtually represented in parliament."[95] "But this," he declares, "is a doctrine which only tends to allow the Colonists a shadow of that *substance* which they must never be slaves without. It cannot surely be consistent with British liberty, that any set of men should represent another, detached from them in situation and interest, without the privity and consent of the represented. The office of a representative is founded on choice, and is intended for the benefit of the constituents."[96] James Iredell of North Carolina stated the same objection with great clarity: "But had your Parliament to this day, in every instance, appeared the wisest and most virtuous body on earth, and had behaved with particular condescension to us, and they had passed a law enacting that every man in America should pay a shilling sterling per annum, in lieu of all other taxes, and that they would, in that case, be themselves at the expense of supporting our civil establishments; I would as strenuously have exerted myself against that small demand as I now do, and hope I ever shall do against the accumulated evils of taxes, arbitrary laws, and cruel orders of power, which we now feel, and which are but the natural consequences of the other."[97] Once again, the fact that I am governed in accordance with my own best interests— even in accordance with what I *myself* take to be my own best interests—is neither necessary nor sufficient to establish my status as a free man. I am only free if I have authorized those who govern me.

But patriots who rejected the parliamentarian view in favor of the authorization theory disagreed sharply amongst themselves concerning the *mechanism* by which the people might be said to authorize an agency to act in its name, and this disagreement would have profoundly important consequences. A number of patriot "authorization" theorists fatefully gravitated toward the view that authorization could be conveyed only through voting. Only a magistrate for whom I have voted is entitled to claim that he has been authorized to act in my name and that he is therefore my representative. We find a few patriot pamphleteers endorsing something like this position quite early on in the crisis. Thus, Connecticut governor Thomas Fitch insisted in a 1764 broadside against the Sugar Act that free subjects are "necessarily vested with the power of electing their representatives" and that "this right or power is a fundamental privilege and so essential a part of the constitution that without it the subject cannot be said to be free."[98] Fitch continued that "it is a clear point that the colonies may not, they cannot, be represented in Parliament; and if they are not vested with legislative authority within themselves where they may be represented by persons of their own electing, it is plain they will not be represented in any legislature at all, and consequently if they are subjected to any laws it must be to such as they have never consented to either by themselves or any representatives, which will be directly contrary to that before-mentioned fundamental principle of the British constitution."[99] A free man may be governed only by laws agreed to by his representatives; he may be represented only by an agent whom he has authorized; and his authorization must be expressed through his "power of election."

This argument, periodically advanced but underdeveloped in the first half of the 1760s, would be formulated with increasing sophistication as the conflict progressed. In 1769, John Joachim Zubly's *Humble Enquiry* made the case that "the people have not representatives assigned, but chuse them, and being so chosen, the rights of the people reside now in them."[100] "Every representative in Parliament," Zubly insisted, "is not a representative for the whole nation, but only for the particular place for which he hath been chosen. . . . The electors of *Middlesex* cannot chuse a representative but for *Middlesex,* and as the right of sitting depends entirely upon the election, it seems clear to demonstration, that no member can represent any but those by whom he hath been elected; if not elected he cannot represent them, and of course not consent to any thing in their behalf." The implications of this position were quite sweeping, as Zubly himself appreciated:

> If representation arises entirely from the free election of the people, it is plain that the elected are not representatives in their own right, but by virtue of their election; and it is no less so, that the electors cannot confer any right on those whom they elect but what is inherent in themselves; the electors of *London* cannot confer or give any right to their members to lay a tax on *Westminster,* but the election made of them doubtless empowers them to agree to or differ from any measures they think agreeable or disagreeable to their constituents, or the kingdom in general. If the representatives have no right but what they derive from their electors and election, and if the electors have no right to elect any representatives but for themselves, and if the right of sitting in the House of Commons arises only from the election of those designed to be representatives, it is undeniable, that the power of taxation in the House of Commons cannot extend any further than to those who have delegated them for that purpose; and if none of the electors in *England* could give a power to those whom they elected to represent or tax any other part of his Majesty's dominions except themselves, it must follow, that when the Commons are met, they represent no other place or part of his Majesty's dominions, and cannot give away the property but of those who have given them a power to do so by choosing them their representatives.[101]

This passage embodies the most complete possible rejection of the parliamentarian theory of virtual representation and perhaps the boldest single pre-revolutionary statement of the view that authorization requires voting. On Zubly's account, only a magistrate for whom I have voted can be said to represent me. Those elected by others do not represent me, although they may certainly take it upon themselves to act in my interests once in office. It is worth noting in this connection that Zubly avoids the error of conflating the debate between "virtual" and "actual" representation with the quite different debate over the degree to which representatives should take themselves to be bound by the expressed opinions of their constituents—that is, whether representatives should regard themselves as "delegates" who must vote in accordance with the preferences of those who elected them (and *only* their preferences) or as "trustees" who should vote in accordance with their own best judgment and with an eye toward the common good of the whole.[102] These two controversies, Zubly recognizes, are orthogonal to each other. An advocate of virtual representation could, with complete consistency, adopt either a "delegate" or "trustee" approach to the ethics of representation, as could an authorization theorist.[103] "Virtual" and "authorization" theorists disagreed with each other about *what makes a legitimate representative*; "delegate" and "trustee" theorists, in contrast, disagreed with each other about *how a representative ought to conduct himself in office*. Zubly offers an unqualified endorsement of both the authorization theory and the trustee theory, but he never supposes that the former commits him to the latter, or vice versa.[104]

The most influential elaboration of Zubly's view was offered by James Wilson in *Considerations on the Nature and the Extent of the Legislative Authority of the British Parliament* (1774[105]), a pamphlet that established the terms in which Wilson and his acolytes would discuss the theory of representation for the next twenty years. Wilson begins by endorsing both the authorization theory of representation and the election theory of authorization: he insists that a free man must be governed by magistrates whom he himself has authorized and that authorization must take the form of voting. It follows that the only citizens who may safely be deprived of the franchise are those who are not free men—that is, those persons who are dependent on the will of others for their livelihoods. "All those are excluded from voting," Wilson explains, "whose poverty is such, that they cannot live independant, and must therefore be subject to the undue influence of their superiors. Such are supposed to have no will of their own; and it is judged improper that they should vote in the representation of a free state."[106] But these are the only exceptions. All free men must be governed by laws to which their representatives have consented, and they may only be represented by agents for whom they have voted. Armed with these arguments, Wilson is prepared to offer a striking account of the English constitution and the character of the imperial crisis:

> Though the concurrence of all the branches of the Legislature [Parliament] is
> necessary to every law; yet the same laws bind different persons for different

reasons, and on different principles. The King is bound, because he assented to them. The Lords are bound, because they voted for them. The Representatives of the Commons, for the same reason, bind themselves, and those whom they represent. If the Americans are bound neither by the assent of the King, nor by the votes of the Lords to obey Acts of the British Parliament, the *sole* reason, why they are bound, is, because the representatives of the Commons of Great-Britain have given their suffrages in favor of those Acts. But are the Representatives of the commons of Great Britain the Representatives of the Americans? Are they elected by the Americans? Are they such as the Americans, if they had the power of election, would probably elect? Do they know the interest of the Americans? Does their own interest prompt them to pursue the interest of the Americans? If they do not pursue it, have the Americans power to punish them? Can the Americans remove unfaithful members at every new election? Can members, whom the Americans do not elect; with whom the Americans are not connected in interest; whom the Americans cannot remove; over whom the Americans have no influence— Can such members be styled, with any propriety, the magistrates of the Americans?"[107]

Wilson flirts with several different arguments in this passage (his statement that members of Parliament and British Americans "are not connected in interest" recalls the internal critique of the parliamentarian theory[108]), but its basic thrust is unmistakable. Wilson argues that the House of Commons is the only representative of the English people, not (as the parliamentarians had insisted) because it alone constitutes a good likeness or representation of the people but because only its members are elected and therefore *authorized* by the people.[109] The king and lords are unelected and therefore unauthorized to govern Englishmen without the consent of the House of Commons, and the House of Commons is unelected *by Americans* and therefore unauthorized to govern them. As Wilson explains, "Allegiance to the King and obedience to the Parliament are founded on very different principles. The former is founded on protection: The latter, on representation. An inattention to this difference has produced, I apprehend, much uncertainty and confusion in our ideas concerning the connexion, which ought to subsist between Great-Britain and the American Colonies."[110] Representation requires authorization, and authorization requires voting.[111]

Wilson remained faithful to this position for the rest of his life. In his "Lectures on Law," delivered in 1790 at the College of Philadelphia, he offered a comparison between the English constitution and the new Constitution of the United States. In England, he explained, the principle of representation extends only to the House of Commons, because only the Commons are elected (and only imperfectly at that, given the restrictions on the franchise that Wilson continued to bemoan).[112] But in the new United States, the case was entirely different: "The American States enjoy the glory and the happiness of diffusing this vital principle throughout all the different divisions and departments of the government."[113] In America, all "departments" of government (executive, legislative, and judicial) in all "divisions" (state and federal) may be said to represent the people because all magistrates are elected by the entire population of free men (or are chosen by those who have been so elected) and have therefore been authorized by the people. "The right of representing," Wilson, explained, "is conferred by the act of electing."[114] Here we see the stark dividing line between Wilson's authorization theory and the parliamentarian theory of virtual representation: for Wilson, a single first magistrate (the president) or a small deliberative body (the senate) may be said to represent the people so long as he or they have been elected by the entire population of free men (Wilson zealously advocated the direct election of both senators and the president). Wholly absent from this view is the thought that a representative must be a good "representation" of the "body of the people"—that is, a large assembly. Accordingly, Wilson insists that the president of the United States is "the man of the people"[115] and that the Senate is no less "representative" of the people than the House of Representatives. But the line of demarcation between Wilson's theory and the Royalist theory of representation is equally clear: if representation requires authorization and if authorization requires voting, than a hereditary monarch cannot be said to represent the people.

Yet, as both loyalists and the more circumspect patriots quickly realized, this election theory of authorization was a hopeless muddle. Howard gestured at the problem when he proposed the following thought experiment: "Suppose that this *Utopian* privilege of representation should take place [that is, that *Americans* were granted the right to elect members to Parliament], I question if it would answer any other purpose but to bring an expence upon the colonies, unless you can suppose that a few *American* members could bias the determinations of the whole *British* legislature. In short, this right of representation is but a phantom, and, if possessed in its full extent, would be of no real advantage to the colonies; they would, like *Ixion*, embrace a cloud in the shape of *Juno*."[116] Howard's point was the following: if one claims that (1) free men must be governed by laws agreed to by their legitimate representatives; and (2) representation requires authorization; and (3) authorization requires voting, then how would sending a proportional number of elected American members to Parliament make any difference to the alleged enslavement of the Americans? For even if the colonists sent fifty members to the House of Commons, those fifty could always be outvoted by the English members. As Thomas Whately put it, the colonists would be "bound by the Consent of the Majority of that House, whether their own particular Representatives consented to or opposed the Measures there taken."[117] Since the non-American majority could not be said to represent the colonists (because, *ex hypothesi*, one can be represented only by an agent for whom one has voted), laws passed by the majority of the House of Commons (i.e., without the support of the American members) could not be said to have the consent of the Americans. It followed that, even under a scheme allowing colonists to elect members to Parliament in proportion to their numbers, Americans would remain subject to an alien will—that is, to the will of the non-American majority of the House of Commons.

But as other loyalists soon pointed out, Howard had understated the implications of his own objection. The problem with the election theory of authorization was not simply that it failed to explain why the election of American members to Parliament would serve to secure the liberty of the colonies; it also failed to explain why the hypothetical American members would represent *all Americans* in the first place, or why the English members of Parliament (and the American members of colonial legislatures) could be said to represent all of their constituents. As John Lind explained, if it were true of free men "that their own personal consent, or the personal consent of their representative is necessary to render a tax *legal* . . . it would follow, that no *representative* could be chosen but by the *unanimous* consent of every *constituent,* that no *law* could pass without the *unanimous* consent of every *representative.* . . . Yet this principle, pregnant with such fatal consequences, have many of the friends of America chosen as a shield to protect the colonies against the power of the British legislature. This principle has the same extravagance laid down as the corner stone of British *freedom.*"[118] In other words, the Wilsonian view that representation requires authorization and that authorization requires voting is tantamount to a defense of anarchy, for in every election there are citizens who vote for the losing candidate and in almost every legislative controversy there are representatives who vote against the eventual law. If it is really the case that one cannot be represented by a magistrate for whom one has not voted, and that one cannot be said to have authorized a law for which one's representative has not voted, then it would appear that there are only two choices: to grant every citizen a veto over the election of representatives, and every representative a veto over the enactment of laws, or to accept the enslavement of large numbers of citizens.[119]

The administration pamphleteer William Knox developed this objection even further in 1768, and drew the obvious conclusion:

> But the most curious part of the [election] argument has not yet been considered; for it will follow from this doctrine, that the minority will in all cases controul the majority; nay, every individual member of parliament will have the power to stop the proceedings of all the others. For whoever says, *he is against any tax,* neither himself, nor the people whom he distinctly represents, can be liable to pay such tax; because they do not, either by themselves, or their distinct representatives, consent to it. . . . So that *almost half* the people of Great Britain may, it seems, be taxed without either their own or their distinct representatives consent. Now, why may not the people in the Colonies, who do not amount to near that number, be taxed also without their own consent, or the consent of distinct representatives elected by themselves?—One step farther, and we are got back to where we set out from. The consent, you will perhaps say, of the majority of the distinct representatives of the people, of *necessity* involves the consent of the whole. So then it is necessary that the people should submit to pay taxes, to which neither themselves nor their distinct representatives do consent; and the whole meaning of this ingenious argument may be summed up in these few plain words:—That a people may constitutionally be taxed by those whom the constitution has vested with the power to impose taxes, which is the supreme legislature; and that every man who consents to that constitution or government . . . consents to all taxes imposed by it, inasmuch as he *consents* to the authority by which they are imposed.[120]

Knox's argument is straightforward. In order to avoid the reductio according to which each citizen, in order to count as a free man, must be governed only by laws to which his own chosen representative has consented (i.e., anarchy), one must concede that citizens may be said to have "willed" the laws of the state no matter whether their chosen magistrates voted in favor or against. As Soame Jenyns put it, one must first replace the argument "that no *Englishman* can be taxed without the Consent of the persons he chuses to represent him" with the very different claim that "no *Englishman* can be taxed without the Consent of the Majority of all those, who are elected by himself and others of his Fellow Subjects to represent them"—and one must then modify the latter, since there seems to be no good reason for supposing that a non-elector could not be "represented" in Parliament in just the same way as an elector whose candidate is not elected or whose chosen member is outvoted.[121] But this, as Knox recognized, is to deny the election theory of representation. If "almost half of the people of Great Britain" (that is, those not responsible for choosing the "50 percent plus one" members necessary to carry a measure in the House of Commons) may be said to have assented to parliamentary laws opposed by their own chosen members, then it must be the case that Parliament as a whole "represents" them (i.e., acts in their name), despite the fact that they played no role in selecting the dispositive majority. If this is true, then it cannot be the case that Americans are not represented *by* Parliament simply because they do not elect members *to* Parliament.

This last sentence could, of course, read like an endorsement of the parliamentarian theory of virtual representation, and most loyalists and administration pamphleteers were only too happy to construe it in this manner.[122] But, as Knox himself observed, it was also perfectly consistent with a very different view. One could argue instead that (*pace* the parliamentarians) authorization is both necessary and sufficient to establish a legitimate representative but that (*pace* election theorists such as Wilson) authorization does not require voting—that "*King, Lords, and Commons are their representatives*" (i.e., the representatives of all "the subjects of Great Britain") simply because "to them it is that they have *delegated* their individual rights over their lives, liberties, and property; and so long as they approve of that form of government, and continue under it, so long do they consent to whatever is done by those they have intrusted with their rights."[123] This was the Royalist theory of representation. It understood "authorization" to consist in an original grant of authority to a specified institutional scheme—one to which each succeeding generation must tacitly consent—and it accordingly explained why citizens could be said to have authorized laws for which their chosen magistrates had not voted. Knox turned to this theory in order to offer a novel defense of the British position: on his account, Parliament represented British Americans not (as the vast majority of English pamphle-teers and American loyalists had supposed) because the House of Commons constituted a good "image" of the colonists but rather because it was part of the constitutional scheme to which the colonists had given their consent.[124] Yet patriots immediately recognized that Knox's theory could just as easily be deployed in the opposite direction. If one simply denied the historical claim that Parliament was *in fact* part of the constitutional scheme to which Americans had given their consent, the Royalist theory could instead un-derwrite the very different conclusion that Americans were represented not by Parliament, but rather by the king. Knox's understanding of authoriza-tion, unlike Wilson's, necessarily allowed a hereditary monarch to count as the representative of the people. If I can be said to have authorized whatever measures are agreed to by a legislative majority that I myself had no role in selecting—that is, if authorization simply consists in my agreement to abide by "the rules of the game"—then why not the decisions of a monarch whom I myself had no role in selecting? While some patriots were reluctant to em-brace this logic, others were quite prepared to do so. For those patriots of the early 1770s who were anxious to revive the prerogatives of the Crown as a means of checking the encroachments of Parliament, the Royalist theory promised to explain why government by the king's will did not constitute enslavement. The Royalist theory of representation and the prerogativism of "patriot Royalists" went hand in hand.

III

Patriots of the 1770s, as we have seen, had evolved the view that America was "outside the realm" of Great Britain and therefore beyond the jurisdic-tion of Parliament.[125] But they argued at the same time that George III re-mained king of America and that his royal prerogative—or rather, the bun-dle of defunct prerogative powers that patriots wished the king to revive for the first time in more than a century—extended fully and robustly to the colonies. This position sat quite uncomfortably alongside the election the-ory of authorization. (Needless to say, it was wholly incompatible with the parliamentarian theory of virtual representation.) If one can only be said to have authorized a representative for whom one has voted and if govern-ment by those who are not one's representatives constitutes enslavement, it becomes very difficult indeed to explain why government by an unelected monarch's prerogative would not render the colonists slaves. Loyalist Samuel Seabury recognized as much when he insisted that the election theory was "republican, in its very nature; and tends to the subversion of the English monarchy."[126] Wilson too had struggled with this question. Recall that he embraced both the authorization theory of representation and the election theory of authorization but tried to make room for an energetic monarchy by arguing that "allegiance to the King and obedience to the Parliament are founded on very different principles. The former is founded on protection: The latter, on representation."[127] In other words, we owe obedience to the king not because he represents us (he does not, because we have not elected him) but rather because he protects us, and "protection and obedience are the reciprocal bonds, which connect the Prince and his Subjects."[128] Here Wilson offers a straightforwardly Hobbesian characterization of the nature of political obligation—Hobbes famously declared that he had written *Leviathan* "without other designe, than to set before mens eyes the mutuall Relation between Protection and Obedience"[129]—but he refuses to endorse Hobbes's conclusion, namely that by accepting the protection of a sovereign *I thereby make him my representative*. It is for this reason that Wilson gets into trouble: if the king is not my representative, then it follows that he does not have the right to speak and act in my name (recall that, on the authorization theory, a representative *just is* someone who has this right). If I am constrained to obey him notwithstanding this fact, then, by definition, I am dependent on an alien will and am therefore unfree. The election theory of authorization accordingly proved to be a double liability for patriots: it seemed unable to furnish them with either a cogent defense of ordinary electoral politics (because it could not explain why a legislative majority might be "authorized" to act on my behalf, despite the opposition of my particular legislator) or a serviceable vindication of the royal prerogative (because it could not explain why I could be said to have authorized an unelected George III to act on my behalf).[130]

A small number of patriot pamphleteers tried to address this obvious problem by reviving the seventeenth-century discourse of the "ancient constitution," according to which the primeval Saxon monarchy had been elective in character. In a 1774 sermon, for example, the Massachusetts minister Peter Whitney declared that "history shows us that the greater part of the kings of England, have come to the throne, not so much by right of inheritance, as by the *election* of the people, and the resistance they have made to them who were heirs apparent to the crown, or actually on the throne."[131] Whitney thus attempted to square the existence of a prerogativist monarchy with the election theory by suggesting that most English kings had in fact been elected and might therefore be said to have been authorized by the people. But this attempt to salvage the election theory was inadequate on its face: even granting its fanciful reconstruction of English history, it could not explain why those who initially voted against the chosen monarch were nonetheless represented by him, still less why contemporary subjects were represented by his putative heirs. No doubt recognizing the vulnerabilities of this argument, an important group of patriot pamphleteers turned instead to the full-fledged Royalist theory of representation. On their rival account, Parliament did not represent the people of British America because it had not been *authorized* to speak and act in their name—not because Americans did not elect members to the House of Commons. At no point had the colonists entrusted political authority to the "legislature of Great Britain," although, counterfactually, they could certainly have done so. (Parliament would then have been their legitimate representative, whether or not Americans elected members to it.) In contrast, the people of British America *had* authorized the king and his successors to govern them in conjunction with the various colonial legislatures. This authorization had taken the form of colonial charters, to which succeeding generations of British Americans had tacitly consented.[132] The theory thus delivered the desired result: the king, and not Parliament, acted in the name of British Americans, and his government over them did not constitute enslavement.[133]

To be sure, this argument did not simply materialize in 1770. As early as 1764, we find James Otis offering a version of it in *The Rights of the British Colonies, Asserted and Proved*. Political authority, he explains, rests "ultimately in the people or whole community where GOD has placed it; but the inconveniences, not to say impossibility, attending the consultations and operations of a large body of people have made it necessary to transfer the power of the whole to a *few*."[134] This logistical imperative necessarily "gave rise to deputation, proxy, or a right of representation. . . . the difficulties attending an universal congress, especially when society became large, have brought men to consent to a delegation of the power of all."[135] Although, on Otis's account, it is certainly true that "the wiser and more virtuous states have always provided that the representation of the people should be *numerous*," this is merely a prudential matter, not a requirement of the theory: the people may legitimately be represented by any agency they choose to autho-rize. Accordingly, "most nations" have authorized "one or some few of their number" to govern them and have made political authority *"hereditary* in the families of despotic nobles and princes."[136] While regrettable from Otis's point of view, such arrangements are wholly legitimate and the agencies in question duly "represent" the people. As Otis would put it in his 1765 reply to Howard, "the supreme legislative indeed represents the whole society or community," whatever its form.[137]

But it is beyond question that a full and self-conscious articulation of the Royalist position would await the 1770s. Here again, it was the Connecticut physician and pamphleteer Edward Bancroft who led the way. His political priority in the *Remarks on the Review of the Controversy between Great Britain and her Colonies* (1769), unlike Otis's five years earlier, was to establish that Parliament had no jurisdiction of any kind over the American colonies but that Americans were nonetheless subject to the royal prerogative. He de-fended this explicitly Royalist position by arguing that the king, not Parlia-ment, had been authorized to govern America in the various colonial char-ters. On this account, the original settlers could certainly have chosen to make Parliament their representative had they wished to do so—this de-spite the impossibility of electing their own members to the House of Com-mons. But, as it happens, they did not enter into any such agreement: "Not the least Provision is made therein [in the charters] for their Dependance, either on the law or Legislature of *England,* which are not even named in the Patents."[138] Lacking any such authorization, Parliament now governs the colonists "without *their* Consent" and for this reason alone cannot be de-scribed as "their Constitutional Representative."[139] Allegiance to the Crown and its succession, in contrast, is "provided for by Clauses for that Purpose in their Charters."[140] The king has therefore been authorized to govern the colonies in conjunction with their legislatures, and this original authoriza-tion is constantly renewed by tacit consent (a Lockean argument that Ban-croft endorses unreservedly).[141]

Bancroft's various disciples in the 1770s repeated and refined this analy-sis. In 1773, the Massachusetts House of Representatives declared in its reply to Thomas Hutchinson that "our Charters reserve great Power to the Crown in its Representative, fully sufficient to balance, analogous to the En-glish Constitution, all the Liberties and Privileges granted to the People."[142] But "is any Reservation of Power and Authority to Parliament thus to bind us, expressed or implied in the Charter? It is evident, that king Charles the first, the very Prince who granted it, as well as his Predecessor, had no such idea."[143] In fact, the house concludes, the charters themselves "are repugnant to the Idea of Parliamentary Authority," and for this reason, "if then the Colonies were not annexed to the Realm, at the Time when their Charters were granted, they never could be afterwards, without their own special Consent, which has never since been had, or even asked."[144] Again, it is not the fact that Americans do not elect members to the House of Commons that disqualifies Parliament from governing them; it is rather that they have not, by means of their charters, assigned Parliament the "authority" to govern them (although they might have done so at any time by annexing themselves to the realm). The colonists had, however, authorized the king to govern them, and the "great power" exercised by the Crown in America is therefore not incompatible with their status as free men.[145] The Connecticut minister Moses Mather agreed that "the obligation of obedience to a law, arises wholly from the authority of the makers, over those on whom it is enjoined; so that if the Americans are naturally independant of the power of parliament, and by no concessions and civil constitutions of their own have submitted thereto, and put themselves under it; no acts of parliament can make them dependant."[146] The king, in contrast, has full and legitimate "authority" by virtue of the charters: "It is by force of the constitutions of the colonies only, that he, who is thus crowned King of Great-Britain, becomes King of the colonies."

By 1774, this view had become dominant among patriot pamphleteers. James Iredell cited various statements of James I and Charles I in order to establish that the charters had intentionally "prohibited Parliament from interfering in our concerns, upon the express principle *that they had no business with them.*"[147] In contrast, the charters had fully authorized the king to exercise his prerogative rights over British America. Iredell is thus able to conclude as follows: "We respect and reverence the rights of the king; we owe, and we pay him allegiance, and we will sacredly abide by the terms of our charters. These were purchased by the hard and severe labor of our ancestors, which procured for our Sovereign this fine country. But we will not submit to any alteration of the *original terms* of the contract, because they were the price for which the service was engaged, and in pleasing consideration of which it was alone performed."[148] An anonymous pamphlet from Virginia, issued in the same year under the pseudonym "Edmund Burke," likewise argued that "from these charters it manifestly appears to have been the Royal intention, to form these Colonies into distinct States . . . dependent on the Crown, but not on the Parliament of *England*."[149] It followed that since the charters had not authorized Parliament to govern the colonists, "nothing but an act of union, made with their own consent, can annex them to the Realms, or subject them to its Legislature."[150] As the Newburyport minister Oliver North put it succinctly in a 1775 sermon, since "the parliament of *Great Britain* . . . were no party in the Contract [between the colonists and the "the king of *England*,"] there exists not, nor ever did, any kind of Contract or Bargain between us and them; we never chose them to legislate for us, they do not, they *cannot* represent us." It is simply because Americans "never chose" Parliament to govern them that the House of Commons does not and cannot represent the colonies.[151]

The young Alexander Hamilton offered perhaps the most expansive version of this argument in his *The Farmer Refuted* (1775). George III, he declared, "is King of America, by virtue of a compact between us and the Kings of Great-Britain. These colonies were planted and settled by the Grants, and under the Protection of English Kings, who entered into covenants with us for themselves, their heirs and successors."[152] By means of these covenants, the king had been authorized to exercise his prerogative powers over British America, and these powers were therefore not incompatible with the liberty of American subjects. Parliamentary laws, in contrast, "are subversive of our natural liberty, because an authority is assumed over us, which we by no means assent to."[153] But *should* we assent to such a scheme? Hamilton answers by reviving the "internal" Royalist critique of the parliamentarian theory, familiar to us from the writings of Charles I, Digges, and Hobbes:

> I will go farther, and assert, that the authority of the British Parliament over America, would, in all probability, be a more intolerable and excessive species of despotism than an absolute monarchy. The power of an absolute prince is not temporary, but perpetual. He is under no temptation to purchase the favour of one part of his dominions, at the expense of another; but, it is his interest to treat them all, upon the same footing. Very different is the case with regard to the Parliament. The Lords and Commons both, have a private and separate interest to pursue.[154]

Parliamentarians had argued since the 1640s that a well-poised popular assembly could never tyrannize over its people, because it simply *was* the people. As Parker himself had put it, "A community can have no private ends to mislead it, and make it injurious to it selfe, and no age will furnish us with one story of any Parliament freely elected, and held, that ever did injure a whole Kingdome, or exercise any tyranny, nor is there any possibility how it should."[155] Hamilton, in contrast, rejects "the doctrine of parliamentary supremacy"[156]—grounded in what he would later describe as the "fancy" that members of a popular assembly "are the people themselves"[157]—and follows his Royalist predecessors in arguing that, if our aim is to align the interests of the governed with those of their governors, we ought to fear an unchecked assembly far more than an unchecked monarch. The king's interest is inextricably linked to the well-being of the kingdom (or empire) as a whole; parliamentary majorities, in contrast, will tend to pursue factional interests.[158]

Hamilton's language here recalls that of his fellow pamphleteer William Hicks of Philadelphia, whose influential *Considerations upon the Rights of the Colonists to the Privileges of British Subjects* had appeared several years earlier. Hicks too had straightforwardly embraced the Royalist "alignment" argument:

> I am very far from being an Enemy to Parliamentary Power. I revere the House of Commons as the Watchful Guardians presiding over the Liberty of their Constituents; but when I see Them grasping at a Power altogether foreign, and inconsistent with the Principles of their own Constitution; I could wish to see Them reduc'd within their natural Bounds, and would even shelter myself under the Wings of the Royal Prerogative. I would much more willingly see my Property arbitrarily dispos'd of by a privy Seal, than extorted from me by the unwarrantable Power of a Parliament; whose Members would naturally endeavour to lessen their own Burthens, and gratify the selfish Wishes of their Constituents by sacrificing to Them the Interests of the Colonies. As loyal and industrious Subjects We may expect impartial Favour from our Prince; who must reasonably regard with an equal Eye the Happiness and Welfare of all his Dominions.[159]

To be sure, it did not follow for either Hicks or Hamilton that we would be wise to establish an absolute monarchy. Hamilton, for one, regarded it as an unassailable prudential maxim that "moral security, for our lives and properties . . . can never exist, while we have no part in making the laws, that are to bind us; and while it may be in the interest of our uncontroled legislators to oppress us as much as possible."[160] While our status as free men may be secured so long as we are governed by an authorized agency, our "moral security" demands a coordinate, mixed regime in which subjects have some role in making law. The colonial charters accordingly divided political authority between a monarch invested with sweeping prerogative powers and the elected legislatures of each American dominion. These authoritative contracts provided the sound bedrock upon which Hamilton and his colleagues proposed to erect a new imperial constitution.[161]

Yet despite their insistence that the king had been authorized to govern British America (and that Parliament was not the "constitutional representative" of America, simply because it had not been authorized to act as such), these patriots of the early 1770s quite noticeably declined to call the king their "representative."[162] The reason is clear enough. In the context of the imperial crisis, to designate the king as the representative of the colonies would have exposed patriots to the argument that they had in fact never been taxed without their own consent. Since parliamentary bills could not become law without receiving the royal assent (recall that it was the patriots themselves who were arguing that the defunct royal veto remained a viable prerogative of the Crown), if the king truly represented the colonists, his agreement to these bills could be construed as embodying their consent. As one anonymous English pamphlet put it, "No Part of the Property of the People can be taken from them, but by laws which receive the assent of the Sovereign, who has no Interest distinct from the general Interest of all his Subjects."[163] The patriots, of course, had an answer to this objection: on their account, the king had indeed been authorized to exercise a number prerogative powers over British Americans, but not to tax them without the consent of their colonial legislatures. His assent to a parliamentary tax bill therefore did not express the consent of the colonists to be taxed. But patriot pamphleteers clearly preferred to avoid this discussion altogether by reserving the term "representative" for the members of their colonial legislatures.

This rhetorical sleight of hand, however, amounted to very little in substantive terms. If I can be said to have authorized the king to govern me, such that his actions are to count as my actions, then his government over me is fully compatible with my status as a free man. Once I have accepted this conclusion, it matters not at all that I decline, for semantic or tactical reasons, to call the king my "representative"—for, at this point, to say that the king is not my representative has no normative bite (it is no longer to say that his government over me constitutes rule by an alien will, and thus amounts to slavery).[164] The parliamentarian theory had insisted that the will of the people could only be instantiated in the laws of a "representative" popular assembly and that those governed by any other sort of agency were therefore slaves. The Wilsonian election theory had insisted that the will of the people could be instantiated only through the authorizing mechanism of voting and that those governed by unelected magistrates were therefore slaves. These otherwise very different theories converged in denying that an unelected, hereditary monarch could ever be said to represent the people. Most patriot pamphleteers of the 1770s, in contrast, turned their backs on both of these theories in order to argue that a hereditary monarch (George III) had been authorized to govern British America while Parliament had not, and that the king's prerogativist government over them therefore did not constitute slavery. To take this view, as John Adams recognized, was to concede that "an hereditary limited monarch is the representative of the whole nation." It was, quite simply, to embrace the Royalist theory of representation.

IV

We see, then, that the imperial crisis of the 1760s and 1770s provoked an extraordinary and fatefully inconclusive debate among patriots over the nature of political representation. Some (particularly in the early 1760s) remained attracted to the parliamentarian theory of virtual representation and simply argued that the House of Commons constituted a poor image of the "body politic" of British America. Others rejected the parliamentarian view in favor of an authorization theory but asserted (incoherently) that authorization could be conveyed only through voting. And still others embraced the full Royalist theory of representation, insisting that a hereditary monarch might legitimately represent the body of the people. Among pamphleteers of the 1770s, the first of these views quite understandably lost its appeal but never wholly vanished, and no consensus was reached as between the second and the third. The issue remained open, and, as we shall see, the various positions taken during the imperial crisis would come to organize the second great American debate over the nature of representation, the one that surrounded the ratification of the federal Constitution a decade later. The parliamentarian theory would find perhaps its last great defenders among Antifederalists.[165] The author of the *Brutus* letters in New York, for example, declared that

> the very term, representative, implies, that the person or body chosen for this purpose, should resemble those who appoint them—a representation of the people of America, if it be a true one, must be like the people. It ought to be so constituted, that a person, who is a stranger to the country, might be able to form a just idea of their character, by knowing that of their representatives. They are the sign—the people are the thing signified. It is absurd to speak of one thing being the representative of another, upon any other principle. . . . It is obvious, that for an assembly to be a true likeness of the people of any country, they must be considerably numerous.—One man, or a few men, cannot possibly represent the feelings, opinions, and characters of a great multitude. In this respect, the new constitution is radically defective. . . . The state of New-York, on the present apportionment, will send six members to the assembly: I will venture to affirm, that number cannot be found in the state, who will bear a just resemblance to the several classes of people who compose it.[166]

Henry Parker could not have put it better himself—nor could Thomas Whately or John Lind. The author of the Antifederalist *Letters from a Federal Farmer* likewise insisted that "we have forgot what the true meaning of representation is":[167] "a full and equal representation, is that which possesses the same interests, feelings, opinions, and views the people themselves would were they all assembled—a fair representation, therefore, should be so regulated, that every order of men in the community, according to the common course of elections, can have a share in it—in order to allow professional men, merchants, traders, farmers, mechanics, &c. to bring a just proportion of their best informed men respectively into the legislature, the representation must be considerably numerous."[168] Only a large assembly that constitutes a recognizable image of the natural body of the people can be styled a true representative.

Federalists—and particularly those Federalists who had defended prerogativism and the Royalist theory of representation during the imperial crisis—took a very different view. For them, the question of resemblance between the representative and the represented was a red herring; representation rested instead on authorization. Hamilton could thus declare that "the President of the United States will be himself the representative of the people."[169] Nathanial Chipman likewise insisted that "the Senators," though a very small body, "are to be the representatives of the people, no less, in fact, than members of the other house [the much larger House of Representatives]."[170] A Connecticut pamphleteer agreed that "in our republican government not only our Deputies, but our Governor and Council may in a good sense be esteemed our representatives,"[171] as did Thomas Tudor Tucker of South Carolina when he argued that "in a free State, every officer, from the Governor to the constable, is, in so far as the powers of his office extend, as truly representative of the people, as a member of the legislature; and his act, within the appointed limitation, is the act of the people: for he is their agent, and derives his authority from them."[172] Few Federalists troubled to make clear exactly *which* theory of authorization undergirded their claims— that is, whether, on their account, the president and senate would represent the people by virtue of being *elected by them* in some attenuated sense (Wilson's theory),[173] or by virtue of the fact that Americans would authorize all magistrates, however chosen, to act on their behalf by accepting the Constitution (Adams's theory). In the context of the ratification debates there was no need to address this question, since both theories of authorization delivered the desired result: each established that, *pace* the parliamentarian theory of the Antifederalists, a single man or a small group of men could be said to represent the body of the people. But this strategic ambiguity on the part of the framers would have serious consequences for the future of American political thought. It would efface the crucial fact recognized by Adams and the other veterans of the pamphlet wars of the 1770s: that if American constitutionalism does not rest on the Royalist theory of representation, it rests on nothing.

CHAPTER 3

"The Lord Alone Shall Be King of America"

1776, Common Sense, and the Republican Turn

"NEVER were a People more wrapped up in a King, than the Americans were in George the Third in the Year 1763," wrote William Drayton of South Carolina in 1776.[1] This comment is justly famous, but it is also potentially misleading. George's personal popularity among his American subjects may well have reached its zenith in the early 1760s, but, as a political and constitutional matter, leaders of the patriot cause were in fact far more wrapped up in their king in 1774 and 1775 than they were at the conclusion of the French-Indian War. Following the repeal of the Stamp Act, they began to theorize a radically reconfigured imperial constitution with a newly strengthened and independent monarch at its center. They justified this new vision of imperial politics historically by endorsing the Stuart conception of the royal prerogative, and they defended it philosophically by reviving the Royalist theory of representation. Their new political theory of empire sought, in Thomson Mason's words, to reestablish "the ancient independence of the Crown" and to "restore [the] Sovereign to that weight in the National Councils which he ought to possess," or, as an anonymous critic put it rather less flatteringly, "to pay compliments to the King's personal power at the expense of his authority."[2] The patriot position thus embodied the sharpest possible break with the whig tradition and an outright assault on the ideological apparatus of the two parliamentarian revolutions of the seventeenth century. Its proponents, as James Lovell of Massachusetts explained, regarded themselves as *"rebels against parliament"* who "adore the king."[3] Their endeavor was, quite simply, to convince George III that "the claim of the British parliament over *us* is not only ILLEGAL IN ITSELF,

BUT A DOWN-RIGHT USURPATION OF HIS PREROGATIVE as king of *America*."[4] Royalism of this kind had not been seen or heard in Britain itself for a hundred years.

Yet by the spring of 1776, a great rupture had occurred. Faced with what they regarded as George III's unaccountable silence in the face of increasingly punitive parliamentary legislation, his seeming indifference to numerous and frantic American petitions, and his own proclamation of August 1775 declaring the colonies to be in a state of rebellion, British North Americans turned on their king with unprecedented ferocity and began to pursue independence.[5] The suddenness of this shift was widely remarked upon by contemporaries. David Ramsay, one of the Revolution's first historians, observed in 1789 that "the change of the public mind of America respecting connexion with Great-Britain, is without parallel."[6] He reminded his readers that "it was not till some time in 1776, that the colonists began to take on other ground, and contend that it was for their interest to be forever separated from Great-Britain. . . . Though new weight was daily thrown into the scale, in which the advantages of independence were weighed, yet it did not preponderate till about that time in 1776, when intelligence reached the colonists of the act of parliament passed in December 1775, for throwing them out of British protection, and of hiring foreign troops to assist in effecting their conquest."[7] Drayton himself anticipated Ramsay's analysis, marveling in 1776 at the "unexpected, wonderful and rapid Movements"[8] that had marked the last six months of the crisis, and recalling that as late as the previous summer, "even with the Sword of the Murderer at their Breasts, the Americans thought only of new Petitions [to the king]. It is well known, there was not then even an Idea that the Independence of America would be the Work of this Generation: For People *yet* had a Confidence in the Integrity of the British Monarch."[9] "It was," Drayton insisted, "even so late as the latter End of the last Year, before that Confidence visibly declined," with *"the Royal Sword yet REEKING with American Blood,* and the King still deaf to the Prayers of the People for 'Peace, Liberty and Safety.'"" Up until the very end, "it was thought, the Monarch, from Motives of Policy, if not from Inclination, would heal our Wounds, and thereby prevent the Separation."[10]

In an ironic sense, this reaction was itself made possible by the high Royalism that the colonists had imbibed over the previous four years. It was only because patriots had developed the view that the king himself, and not his British ministers or his British Parliament, retained the ancient prerogatives of the crown (especially the negative voice) that they could indict him for failing to employ them in defense of America—for refusing to "heal our Wounds." The Massachusetts minister and pamphleteer John Cleaveland, writing as "Johannes in Eremo" in January of 1776, thus explicitly rejected the whig conceit that "the King does nothing, as King, but by his Ministers, and, therefore, whatever wrong is done by the Administration of the King, must be attributed to his Ministers, not to him." Cleaveland's own position was very different:

> But are there not some Royal acts, which are not properly Ministerial? What are the Royal Charters to the *American Colonies,* but such acts, seeing they contain the sacred compact between the King and them, by virtue of which he is their King, and they his subjects; and, also, the King's oath to protect them in the enjoyment of all the rights and privileges of *Englishmen,* and their oath of allegiance to obey him as King? What was the present King's coronation oath, to maintain the *British* Constitution of Government and the Protestant religion inviolate in his empire, but another such act? And what is the King's assent to acts of Parliament, but a Royal act, not Ministerial? . . . Or, what if he should give his Royal assent to an act to raise a revenue on the Colonies without their consent; to an act claiming supreme authority over the Colonies, to make laws binding on them, in all cases whatsoever; to an act to send ships-of-war to block up our harbours, restrain our trade, put a stop to our fishery, and destroy our seaport towns; and armed men, by fire and sword, to carry into execution a number of acts of Parliament, contrived and framed to deprive the Colonies of their essential and constitutional rights and liberty? Would he not break his compact with, and violate his Royal faith to, the Colonists? And would not this be doing wrong?[11]

Only if the king, apart from his ministers, retained the right to veto parliamentary bills could his "assent" to those bills be regarded as a cause of American suffering; only if he existed as an independent power, separate from his English parliament, could it be argued that the American charters invested him alone with authority over British America; only if he were truly "the most powerful prince on earth"[12]—or "the only Sovereign of the empire," such that "the part which the people have in the legislature, may more justly be considered as a limitation of the Sovereign authority"[13]— could he be held responsible for the depredations of the previous year. George III's great sin was to have insisted upon "the supreme authority of the legislature over all his dominions," thereby denying the existence of his own "ample and splendid prerogatives."[14]

But Americans did not simply turn against their own particular king in the early months of 1776. In shockingly large numbers, they turned against kingship itself. Contemporaries were equally quick to underline the drama and unexpectedness of this parallel development, and they uniformly attributed it to the extraordinary influence of a single pamphlet published in January 1776: Thomas Paine's *Common Sense*. In April of that year, George Washington observed in a letter to Joseph Reed that "my Countrymen, I know, from their form of Government, & steady Attachment heretofore to Royalty, will come reluctantly into the Idea of Independancy; but time, & persecution, brings many wonderful things to pass; & by private Letters which I have lately received from Virginia, I find common sense is working a powerful change there in the Minds of many Men."[15] The loyalist governor of New Jersey, William Franklin (son of Benjamin), likewise observed in a March 28 letter to Lord George Germain that "the minds of a great number of people have been much changed in that respect [i.e., concerning whether "to adopt an independency"] since the publication of a most inflammatory pamphlet in which this horrid measure is strongly and artfully recommended." Franklin enclosed a copy of *Common Sense* for Germain's perusal.[16] David Ramsay agreed with these early assessments, explaining in retrospect that "in union with the feelings and sentiments of the people, it [*Common Sense*] produced surprising effects. Many thousands were convinced, and were led to approve and long for a separation from the Mother Country. Though that measure, a few months before, was not only foreign from their wishes, but the object of their abhorrence, the current suddenly became so strong in its favour, that it bore down all opposition."[17] Ramsay went on to emphasize one particular aspect of Paine's performance in order to account for its transformative effect on the colonial debate: "With the view of operating on the sentiments of a religious people, scripture was pressed into his service, and the powers, and even the name of a king was rendered odious in the eyes of the numerous colonists who had read and studied the history of the Jews, as recorded in the Old Testament. The folly of that people in revolting from a government, instituted by Heaven itself, and the oppressions to which they were subjected in consequence of their lusting after kings to rule over them, afforded an excellent handle for prepossessing the colonists in favour of republican institutions, and prejudicing

them against kingly government."[18] Paine, on Ramsay's account, had provoked an unprecedented wave of antimonarchism throughout British America by "pressing scripture into his service" and convincing a "religious people"
conversant with "the history of the Jews" that God regarded the institution of
kingship as sinful and illicit.

Ramsay was not alone in offering this diagnosis, nor was his judgment
simply a matter of hindsight. In an extraordinary letter dated April 27, 1776,
the Virginia planter and jurist Richard Parker reported to his close friend
Richard Henry Lee on the character of the newspaper debate that had been
sparked by the release of Paine's pamphlet: "I observe the Pensylvania Papers are filled with the controversy about Independance and think the writers have rather left the Question[.] What matters it to us at present whether
Monarchy is reprobated by the Almighty or not[?]"[19] In other words, while
the controversy may have begun as a debate about "the Expediency or Inexpediency of Independence"—that is, about whether George III had ir-
reparably forfeited the allegiance of his American subjects—it had quickly
turned into a scriptural debate over the theological permissibility of monarchy itself. As Parker went on to explain, Paine had written extensively
about "Monarchical Government as established amongst the Jews" and had
argued that "god was displeased with their demanding a King and was determined that they should suffer for his Crimes."[20] In contrast, "Cato [the
Rev. William Smith of Philadelphia, one of Paine's chief critics] thinks he
has refuted Common Sense by—producing a few texts of Scripture to shew
God was no enemy to monarchical Government but rather approved of it."
Parker himself thought that this debate should be postponed until after "we
have determined our selves independant,"[21] but he nonetheless proceeded to
endorse and then elaborately defend Paine's conclusion that "God has expressly declared his displeasure with the Jews for asking a King." While this
position on Biblical monarchy was controversial, Parker's characterization
of the debate over Common Sense was not. Both Paine's friends and his enemies, patriots and loyalists alike, understood the incendiary claim that
monarchy is "reprobated by the Almighty" to be his most momentous contribution to the debate over independence. Massachusetts minister Peter
Whitney, discussing "that incomparable pamphlet called 'Common Sense'" in
September 1776, reflected that "new truths are often struck out by the collision of parties, in the eagerness of controversy, which otherwise would have
lain hid, The divine disapprobation of a form of government by kings, I take

to be one of this sort of truths."[22] A rather less admiring reader, John Adams, fumed in an April 1776 letter about Paine's pamphlet that "the old Testament Reasoning against Monarchy would never have come from me."[23] Years later, he elaborated in his *Autobiography*: "One third of the book was filled with Arguments from the old Testiment, to prove the Unlawfulness of Monarchy. . . . His Arguments from the old Testiment, were ridiculous, but whether they proceeded from honest Ignorance, or foolish Supersti[ti]on on the one hand, or from willfull Sophistry and knavish Hypocrisy on the other I know not. . . . I dreaded the Effect so popular a pamphlet might have, among the People, and determined to do all in my Power, to counter Act the Effect of it."[24] Writing from Virginia, Landon Carter complained to Washington that Paine had savagely distorted "the Scriptures about Society, Government, and what not."[25] Later the same year, the author of an anonymous reply to *Common Sense*, published in Dublin, blisteringly described how Paine "ransack[s] the holy scriptures, for texts against kingly government, and with a faculty of perverting sacred truths to the worst of purposes, peculiar to gentlemen of his disposition, quotes the example of the Jews."[26] This critic revealingly chose a line of Shakespeare for his pamphlet's epigraph: "The Devil can cite Scripture for his purpose."[27]

But there was yet a further point about which Paine's admirers and critics were in fundamental agreement: they shared a common recognition that, in deploying this dramatic set of arguments about the status of Biblical monarchy, Paine was in fact reopening a long-dormant seventeenth-century debate. One of his English respondents observed that "his scripture politics are obsolete and superannuated in these countries by an hundred years."[28] Good whigs, according to a prominent American critic, "desired to leave Scripture out of the institution of modern Governments. It might be well for the author of *Common Sense* to follow the example in his future works, without stirring up an old dispute, of which our fathers were long since wearied."[29] This "old dispute" concerning the divine acceptability of monarchy, the author continued, had animated the likes of Hugo Grotius and Algernon Sidney; it had concerned the proper interpretation of a crucial biblical text, Deuteronomy 17, and had sent seventeenth-century theorists in search of how "the *Jews* commonly understood this chapter."[30] A third critic likewise insisted on the seventeenth-century provenance of Paine's argument, dating it to "that period, to which the soul of our author yearns, the death of Charles I. England groaned under the most cruel tyranny of a government, truly military, neither existing by law, or the choice of the people, but erected by those who in *the name of the Lord,* committed crimes, till then unheard of."[31] "We have from English history," the author observed, "sufficient proof, that saints of his disposition, tho' more eager to grasp at power than any other set of men, have a thousand times recited the same texts, by which he attempts to level all distinctions. Oliver Cromwell, the father of them, knew so well their aversion to the name of king, that he would never assume it, tho' he exercised a power despotic as the Persian Sophi."[32] But the most precise genealogy of Paine's argument in *Common Sense* comes to us from the man himself. Late in life, John Adams recalled a conversation that he had with Paine in 1776: "I told him further, that his Reasoning from the Old Testament was ridiculous, and I could hardly think him sincere. At this he laughed, and said he had taken his Ideas in that part from John Milton: and then expressed a Contempt of the Old Testament and indeed of the Bible at large, which surprized me."[33]

However reluctant we might be to credit Adams's retrospective testimony about Paine's early religious views (the temptation to project Paine's later deism onto his younger self may well have proved irresistible), his claim about the Miltonic origins of Paine's scriptural argument against monarchy is worth taking seriously, not least because it is obviously correct. The section of *Common Sense* on "Monarchy and Hereditary Succession" is indeed a straightforward paraphrase of Milton's argument in the *Pro populo Anglicano defensio* of 1651. In this text, Milton had turned to a radical tradition of rabbinic biblical commentary in order to explain why God became angry with the Israelites when they requested a king in I Samuel 8. Rejecting the traditional view that God had disapproved only of the *sort* of king that his people had requested, Milton argued instead that the Israelites had sinned in asking for a king *of any sort,* because monarchy per se is an instance of the sin of idolatry. In making this argument, he ushered in a new kind of republican political theory, which quickly became ubiquitous among defenders of the English commonwealth in the 1650s but which was emphatically rejected by whigs in the later seventeenth century.[34]

This Hebraizing doctrine revived by Paine was very different indeed from the heavily Roman theory of free states that had animated parliamentarians such as Henry Parker in the 1640s, and that would in turn ground the whig persuasion throughout the long eighteenth century. For neo-

Roman theorists, the great worry was *discretionary power*. A free man, they argued, must be *sui iuris*, governed by his own right. He must not be dependent on the will of another, which these writers took to mean (based on a freestanding set of claims about representation) that he must be governed only by laws made by a popular assembly and not by the "arbitrary will" of a single person.[35] On this account, kingship is by no means a necessary institution (neo-Roman defenses of republican government were quite common throughout the early modern period), but it is an entirely permissible one, so long as the monarch is a pure "executive"—entrusted with the task of enforcing law but invested with no prerogative powers by which he may *make* law or govern subjects without law. For Hebraizing theorists such as Milton, who embraced what has been called an "exclusivist" commitment to republican government, the great worry was instead the *status of kingship*, not the particular powers traditionally wielded by kings. In assigning a human being the title and dignity of a king, they argued, we rebel against our heavenly King and bow down instead to an idol of flesh and blood; in Paine's words, we lose sight of the fact that it is "sinful to acknowledge any being under that title but the Lord of Hosts."[36] We can put the contrast between these two positions as follows: the neo-Roman theory anathematized prerogative while remaining agnostic about kings; the Hebraizing exclusivist theory anathematized kings while remaining agnostic about prerogative. It is therefore of crucial importance to recognize that the "republican turn" in America took the Hebraizing route, for the anti-whig ideology popularized by *Common Sense* in 1776 would prove surprisingly compatible with the other great anti-whig ideology that patriots had revived in the early 1770s. In an ironic sense, it was Paine who ensured that Royalism—understood as a defense of prerogative powers lodged in a "single person"—would be able to survive the death of the American monarchy.

I

Any satisfactory account of the republican turn in British North America must begin by acknowledging that "republicanism" in early modern Europe was no one, single thing. Several distinct traditions of thinking about the *respublica* had developed alongside one another during the three centuries preceding American independence, and these traditions often pulled in sharply divergent directions. Even the semantics of the term itself were

fiercely contested throughout this period. While European writers and
their classical authorities had traditionally understood *respublica* to denote
any correctly ordered state in which free men pursued the common good,
Italian humanists of the fifteenth century, influenced by Leonardo Bruni's
Ciceronian translation of Aristotle's *Politics,* began to use the term to refer
instead to a specific sort of constitutional arrangement: one without a king
or prince.[37] Thus Machiavelli could claim at the start of the *Prince* (1513) that
"all states, all powers, that have held and hold rule over men have been and
are either republics or principalities."[38] It was this latter sense of the term that
Charles I invoked in his *Answer to the XIX Propositions* (1642) when he accused
his opponents of attempting to "make Our Self of a King of *England* a Duke
of *Venice,* and this of a Kingdom a Republique,"[39] and it was the one that Philip
Livingston of New York had in mind over a century later when he announced
in 1774 that "as to the thought of establishing a republic in America. . . . I consider it the most vain, empty, shallow, and ridiculous project, that could possibly enter into the heart of man."[40] But the older usage remained firmly in
place throughout the eighteenth century, as whigs continued to insist that
England was "the best republick in the world, with a prince at the head of it."[41]
It was this earlier semantic tradition that John Adams invoked in 1775 when
he declared that "the British constitution is nothing more nor less than a
republic, in which the king is first magistrate."[42]

Of those who followed the civic humanists in defining "republic" as "a
commonwealth without a king,"[43] many (such as Charles I and Livingston)
were avowed enemies of this constitutional form. But others, who were
drawn to the model of the city-states of Greek and Roman antiquity, admired it greatly and even went so far as to suggest that it constituted the
best political regime. This was, for example, the view championed by Machiavelli in his *Discourses on Livy*—"it is not the particular good but the common good that makes cities great. And without doubt this common good is
not observed except in republics"[44]—and it was later echoed by English parliamentarians in the late 1640s and 1650s. A republic, Marchamont Nedham
declared in 1650, "is the most commodious and profitable way of government, conducing to the enlargement of a nation every way in wealth and
dominion."[45] For many (although certainly not all) of these theorists, republics were to be preferred chiefly on the grounds that they maximally pro-
moted both the glory and the independence of citizens.[46] Their Roman
sources had taught them that the greatest evil in civic life was to find oneself

dependent on the will of a master—that is, to be a slave. Republican government, shorn of kings and their servile courts, was held to minimize this danger by preventing the accumulation of excessive power in individual men.[47] Monarchy, in contrast, was taken to be an inferior constitution because, in the words of the parliamentary bill that abolished the English crown in 1649, "for the most part, use hath been made of the Regal power and prerogative to oppress, and impoverish and enslave the Subject; and that usually and naturally any one person in such power, makes it his interest to incroach upon the just freedom and liberty of the people, and to promote the setting up of their own will and power above the Laws, that so they might enslave these Kingdoms to their own Lust."[48]

The "neo-Roman" theory encapsulated in this passage thus attached the highest value to liberty, defined as a status of independence, and championed republican government as a bulwark against enslavement (defined as government by "will and power," rather than law). But, significantly, it was not an "exclusivist" position: republicans of the neo-Roman stripe did not regard monarchy per se as an illegitimate constitutional form. They utterly rejected *prerogative,* on the grounds that the mere existence of discretionary power in the sovereign converted subjects into slaves (if a parliamentary bill could not become law without the king's assent, then subjects would find themselves in a state of servile dependence upon his mere "grace" and "pleasure"[49]), and they argued that even a purely "executive" monarchy was likely in practice to degenerate into "arbitrary" rule. But the theory fully conceded the possibility, if not the robustness, of a monarchical "free state," in which the king did not possess enslaving prerogatives. On this view, republics (understood as kingless regimes) might well constitute the safest repositories for the liberties of free men, but kingship remains conceptually distinct from tyranny and, in itself, licit as a political institution. It is of the highest possible importance to understand that this sort of republicanism was *not* the republicanism unleashed by *Common Sense.*

Paine's republicanism had its roots instead in an extraordinary ideological transformation initiated by John Milton in 1651. At issue was the proper understanding of Biblical monarchy.[50] For more than a millennium, Christian exegetes had struggled to harmonize two seemingly divergent scriptural passages, Deuteronomy 17 and I Samuel 8. In the Deuteronomy passage, God instructs the Israelites as follows (in the King James version): "When thou art come unto the land which the LORD thy God giveth thee, and shalt possess it, and shalt dwell therein, and shalt say, I will set a king over me, like as all the nations that are about me; Thou shalt in any wise set him king over thee, whom the LORD thy God shall choose."[51] God then goes on to insist that the chosen king must be an Israelite and that he must not abuse his authority by accumulating too much wealth and power. In this passage, God seems to have no objection in principle to an Israelite monarchy: he predicts that, at a certain point, the Israelites will ask for a king, and he appears ready to grant their request, so long as their king is of the right sort. Yet when the people duly ask for a king in I Sam. 8, both God and Samuel get extremely angry:

> Then all the elders of Israel gathered themselves together, and came to Samuel unto Ramah, 5: And said unto him, Behold, thou art old, and thy sons walk not in thy ways: now make us a king to judge us like all the nations. 6: But the thing displeased Samuel, when they said, Give us a king to judge us. And Samuel prayed unto the LORD. 7: And the LORD said unto Samuel, Hearken unto the voice of the people in all that they say unto thee: for they have not rejected thee, but they have rejected me, that I should not reign over them. 8: According to all the works which they have done since the day that I brought them up out of Egypt even unto this day, wherewith they have forsaken me, and served other gods, so do they also unto thee. 9: Now therefore hearken unto their voice: howbeit yet protest solemnly unto them, and shew them the manner of the king that shall reign over them (I Sam. 8:4–9).

The question for Christian commentators was both simple and inescapable: why did God become angry with the people for "rejecting him" in asking for a king when he had (apparently) given them permission to do precisely this in Deuteronomy?

Medieval and Renaissance exegetes tended to pursue one of two strategies of harmonization. The first was to suggest that the Israelites sinned in selecting kings who did not meet the criteria established by God in the Deuteronomy passage: their sin was not to have requested a king per se, but to have requested a king "like all the other nations." That is, the kings they wished to institute over themselves were avaricious and tyrannical, quite unlike the virtuous monarchs described in God's instructions.[52] The second strategy of reconciliation was to argue in a Pauline vein that in asking for a change of government, the Israelites committed the sin of rebellion against God's established order. All kings rule by divine appointment, and insurrection against them accordingly constitutes a rejection of God's sovereignty. This reading was particularly popular among sixteenth-century Protestants.[53] The two established approaches thus converged in denying that God became angry with the Israelites because they had asked for a king per se. By the late sixteenth century, however, a new and more incendiary interpretation had appeared on the scene. Some radical writers began to read Deut. 17:14 and I Sam. 8 through the prism of a famous comment by the Jewish historian Josephus, taken from his attack on the Egyptian Apion:

> Some peoples have entrusted the supreme political power to monarchies, others to oligarchies, yet others to the masses. Our lawgiver, however, was attracted by none of these forms of polity, but gave to his constitution the form of what—if a forced expression be permitted—may be termed a "theocracy," placing all sovereignty and authority in the hands of God. To Him he persuaded them to look, as the author of all blessings, both those which are common to all mankind, and those which they had won for themselves by prayer in the crises of their history.[54]

This view of the ancient Hebrew commonwealth made it possible for Josephus to understand God's rejection in I Sam. 8 in the following terms: "They [the Israelites] deposed God from his kingly office."[55] God, not Samuel, had been king in Israel before the insurrection of I Sam. 8, and in asking for a mortal king, the Israelites had rebelled against God's sovereignty. This was indeed a radical reading and was understood to be: it argued that human kingship itself was inconsistent with God's plan for his chosen nation. But— and this is the crucial point—it continued to treat Israel as a special case.[56] It had been a sin for the Israelites to ask for a king because they found themselves in the unique position of having God as their civil sovereign. For all other nations, in contrast, monarchy remained a perfectly legitimate constitutional form.[57]

The European discovery of rabbinic sources dramatically reorganized this long-standing debate. To begin with, the central discussion of monarchy in the Talmud (Babylonian Talmud: Sanhedrin 20b)—also based on Deut. 17:14 and I Sam. 8—offered a powerful new perspective on the monarchist position. Glossing the crucial verse in Deut. 17 ("When thou art come unto the land which the LORD thy God giveth thee . . . and shalt say, I will set a king over me, like as all the nations that are about me"), the rabbis focused their attention on the phrase "and shalt say" (ve-amarta). Although the syntax of the Hebrew sentence makes clear that this is purely descriptive, several rabbis pointed out that the same form of the verb could express the imperative.[58] That is, instead of "you will say" (or, better, "if you say") they chose to read "you shall say." As a result, these rabbis were prepared to argue that Deut. 17 did not simply offer a prophecy of what would happen when the Israelites entered the land (as conventional Christian readings had assumed)[59] but rather expressed a positive commandment to establish monarchy. On this latter reading, the Israelites were actually *obliged* to ask for a king. The majority opinion in the Talmud, attributed to Rabbi Yehudah, reads as follows: "There were three commandments that Israel were obligated to fulfill once they had entered the land: appointing a king, exterminating the offspring of Amalek, and building the temple."[60] Christian commentators were quick to seize on these arguments as soon as they entered wide circulation during the second half of the sixteenth century. The German scholar and Hebraist Sebastian Münster, who taught Hebrew to John Calvin, simply reproduced the rabbinic discussion in his commentary on Deut. 17:14: "The Hebrews observed that there were three commandments for the Israelites when they were going to enter the promised land, namely to constitute a king over them, to wipe out the seed of Amalek, and to build a Temple for the Lord."[61] Claude de Saumaise (Salmasius), Milton's famous antagonist, likewise assigned great importance in his *Defensio regia* (1649) to the fact that "the rabbis of the Jews teach that there were three obligations for the Israelites which it was necessary for them to fulfill after they were brought to the Holy Land, to constitute a king over themselves, to eliminate the Amalekites, and to build the Temple."[62] And Hugo Grotius concurred that "the laws of the king, the temple, and the destruction of the Amalekites pertain to the time of possessing the Land."[63] The Talmud, then, exerted a powerful and radicalizing influence on numerous expositors of biblical kingship, leading them to the conclusion that God had commanded rather than simply permitted monarchy in Israel. Indeed, these developments make sense of John Locke's claim in *The Second Treatise of Government* that Europeans "never dream'd of Monarchy being *Iure Divino* . . . till it was revealed to us by the Divinity of this last Age."[64] Not until the proliferation of the Talmudic reading of Deut. 17:14 were Christian theologians prepared to argue that God commanded his chosen people to establish monarchy.

But that is only half of the story. There was, after all, another important rabbinic discussion of Deut. 17:14 and I Sam. 8, one found not in the Talmud but in *Devarim Rabbah,* a compendium of classical Midrashim (rabbinic exe-getical commentary) to Deuteronomy, most likely redacted at the end of the ninth century. This analysis took an entirely different view of biblical mon-archy. It appears as the gloss on Deut. 17:14:

> Put not your trust in princes (Ps. 146:3). R. Simon said in the name of R. Joshua b. Levi: Whosoever puts his trust in the Holy One, blessed be He, is privileged to become like unto Him. Whence this? As it is said, Blessed is the man that trusteth in the Lord, and whose trust the Lord is (Jer. 17:7). But whosoever puts his trust in idolatry condemns himself to become like [the idols]. Whence this? As it is written, They that make them shall be like unto them (Ps. 115:8). The Rabbis say: Whosoever puts his trust in flesh and blood passes away and his dignity also passes away, as it is said, Nor in the son of man in whom there is no help (Ps. 146:3). What follows on this verse? His breath goeth forth, he returneth to his dust. God said: "Although they know that man is nought, yet they forsake my Glory and say: 'Set a king over us.' Why do they ask for a king? By your life, in the end you will learn to your cost what you will have to suffer from your king." Whence this? As it is writ-ten, All their kings are fallen, there is none among them that calleth unto Me (Hos. 7:7).[65]

On this reading, monarchy itself is a sin; it is everywhere and always the act of bowing down to flesh and blood instead of God and is therefore tanta-mount to idolatry.[66] The Israelites chose to worship human kings in whom "there is no help," rather than the true, heavenly king, and their punish-ment has accordingly been great.

It was this tradition of rabbinic exegesis that John Milton absorbed and then deployed in his defense of the regicide in 1651. Turning sharply away from his earlier view that monarchy was an acceptable, if inferior, constitu-tional form—and that, in the case of the Israelites, "it was expressly allow'd them in the Law to set up a King if they pleas'd; and God himself joyn'd with them in the work; though in som sort it was at that time displeasing to him, in respect of old *Samuel* who had govern'd them uprightly"[67]—Milton insisted in his first *Defense* that "God was angry not only because they [the Israelites] wanted a king in imitation of the gentiles, and not in accordance with his law, but clearly because they desired a king at all."[68] In support of this view, Milton cites what he calls "the works of the Hebrews": "Some of their rabbis deny that their fathers should have recognized any king but

God, though such a king was given to punish them. I follow the opinion of these rabbis."[69] These were the rabbis of the Midrash. Milton was familiar with their explosive reading of I Sam. 8 because it had been excerpted and translated into Latin by a favorite author of his: the German Hebraist Wilhelm Schickard, whose influential *Mishpat ha-melekh, Jus regium hebraeorum* was published in 1625.[70] Armed with this rabbinic source, Milton proceeds to gloss I Sam. 8 in the midrashic manner. As far as I am aware, this is the first appearance of this reading in the history of Christian biblical exegesis[71]:

> God indeed gives evidence throughout of his great displeasure at their [the Israelites'] request for a king—thus in [I Sam. 8] verse 7: "They have not rejected thee, but they have rejected me, that I should not reign over them, according to all the works which they have done wherewith they have forsaken me, and served other gods." The meaning is that it is a form of idolatry to ask for a king, who demands that he be worshipped and granted honors like those of a god. Indeed he who sets an earthly master over him and above all the laws is near to establishing a strange god for himself, one seldom reasonable, usually a brute beast who has scattered reason to the winds. Thus in I Samuel 10:19 we read: "And ye have this day rejected your God, who himself saved you out of all your adversities and your tribulation, and ye have said unto him, Nay, but set a king over us" . . . just as if he had been teaching them that it was not for any man, but for God alone, to rule over men.[72]

Milton concludes with the obvious coda: "When at last the Jewish people came to their senses they complained in Isaiah 26:13 that it had been ruinous for them to have other lords than God. This evidence all proves that the Israelites were given a king by God in his wrath."[73] On this account, the history of the Jews teaches us that monarchy is sinful; true Christians must await instead "the coming of our true and rightfull and only to be expected King, only worthy as he is our only Saviour, the Messiah, the Christ, the only heir of his father."[74]

Milton's perspective was promptly taken up by a host of republican writers in the 1650s. John Cook, for example, argued in *Monarchy, No Creature of God's Making* (1651) that "I. Sam. 8. Is the Statute Law concerning Kings where it cleerely appeares that the first generation of Monarchs and the rise of Kings, was not from above, not begotten by the Word and Command of God but from the peoples pride & ardent importunity, they were mad for a King to be like unto the Heathens."[75] "Majesty," Cook explained, is "a terme not fit for any mortall man, because higher then that wee cannot give";[76] it is the idolatrous usurpation of a "God-like state."[77] "Whether the kings be good men or bad, I will punish the people sayes the Lord, so long as they have any kings; it is not a government of my ordination, kings are the peoples Idols, creatures of their own making."[78] Writing in 1664 in his *Court Maxims*, Algernon Sidney likewise concluded that "monarchy is in itself an irrational, evil government, unless over those who are naturally beasts and slaves."[79] His defense of this proposition was straightforward: "The Israelites sinned in desiring a king, let us be deterred by it. God foretold the misery that would follow if they persisted in their wickedness and guilt, and brought upon themselves the deserved punishment thereof. Let their guilt and punishment deter us, let us take warning though they would not. And if we have no communication with satan, let us have none with those thrones which uphold that which he endeavors to set up against God."[80] Sidney elaborated on this point later in his *Discourses Concerning Government,* interpreting I Sam. 8 to teach that monarchy "was purely the peoples' creature, the production of their own fancy, conceived in wickedness, and brought forth in iniquity, an idol set up by themselves to their own destruction, in imitation of their accursed neighbours."[81]

The exclusivist position elaborated by these English authors embodied a categorical rejection of the status of monarchy and the kingly office. Its central preoccupation was not discretionary power, but rather the idolatrous pretention of assigning royal dignity to a mere mortal who (in Milton's words) "pageant[s] himself up and down in progress among the perpetual bowings and cringings of an abject people, on either side deifying and adoring him."[82] It was therefore both more and less radical than its neo-Roman rival: more radical in that it denied the legitimacy of all monarchies, however limited; less radical in that it left open the possibility of an extremely powerful chief magistrate, so long as he was not called "king" (it did not, like the standard parliamentarian theory, require government by a "representative assembly.")[83] Indeed, it is worth recalling that Milton himself was surprisingly amenable to government by "a single person" under the Protectorate.[84] In the aftermath of the Restoration, however, whigs emphatically rejected this view as well as the biblical exegesis upon which it was based. They offered instead a straightforwardly neo-Roman reading of I Sam. 8, according to which the Israelites had sinned not in asking for a king but in asking for a king with sweeping prerogative powers. The anonymous author of *The Judgment of Whole Kingdoms and Nations* (1710), for example, celebrated the whigs who crafted the Revolution settlement of 1689 on the grounds that they "have left nothing to the King's private Discretion, much less than to his arbitrary Will, but have assign'd him the Laws as the Rules and Measures he is to Govern by."[85] It is not kingship per se, on this account, but government by prerogative that endangers liberty. The author then turns to the biblical narrative: God "suffered his own peculiar People, the *Jews,* to be under divers manner of Governments at divers times; at first under patriarchs, *Abraham, Isaac* and *Jacob,* then under captains, *Moses, Joshua,* &c. then under judges, *Othoniel, Ehud,* and *Gideon;* then under High-Priests, *Eli* and *Samuel;* then under Kings, *Saul, David* and the rest. . . . And that God does approve of, or permit such Magistrate or Magistrates, the Community thinks fit to appoint, is plain by The testimony of Holy Scriptures, when God said to *Solomon, By me Kings Rule, and Nobles, even all the Judges of the Earth,* Prov. 8. 16. that is, by his Permission they govern, tho' chosen by the people."[86] Why then did God become angry with the people when they requested a king? The author supplies a modified version of the traditional answer: God's instructions in Deuteronomy 17 reveal that the monarchs he intended for Israel "were not to govern by their own Will, but according to that Law from which they might not receed. This was the law of God, not to be abrogated by Man; a Law of Liberty; directly opposite to the Necessity of submitting to the Will of any one Man."[87] The Israelites, in contrast, asked for a king "like all the other nations"—that is, one who would govern them according to his will rather than according to law, thus rendering them slaves.

This whig reading was given its classic formulation in Roger Acherley's *The Britannic Constitution* (1727). Acherly begins by addressing those seventeenth-century authors whose "Notions are Confined to the *Jewish* OECONOMY, As if the Mode of the Monarchical Government, and the Succession of the Crown, instituted in that One Single Nation, was to be the *Pattern* for all other Kingdoms, And that all other Institutions which differ from it, are *Unwarrantable.*"[88] These writers, he reports, "have read the Nature and Manner of the *Original Constitution* of that Kingdom, which in the First Book of *Samuel* is Accurately Described [that is, in I. Sam. 8:11–19, where Samuel describes the abuses that will be committed by Israel's kings], and have concluded from it that monarchical government is inherently " 'arbitrary.' " But this, Acherley insists, is to commit a grave error. The Israelites could have chosen the free and limited monarchy that God desired for them, but instead they "rejected

God" by demanding arbitrary kings: "The STATE they were desiring to enter into, That appeared in this View, That if they would have a King like All the Nations (of which *Egypt* was one) Then they must be in the like Subjection and *Slavery*, as the People of those Nations were; which differed not from the *Bondage* that was *Egyptian*. Whereas if they had Desired a King to Protect and Defend their Liberties and Properties, the Request had been Commendable."[89] Samuel "was therefore Amaz'd at this People's Importunity, not only to reject the Greatest Blessings God could Give, or they Enjoy, *viz Liberty* and *Property*, but to return again unto *Slavery*," and he accordingly warned the Israelites "that the Power of such a King as they Desired, *viz* Of a King like all the Nations about them, would be *Arbitrary*, And that the Liberty of their Persons, and the Property of their Estates, would necessarily fall under his Absolute Will and Disposal, after the Manner they had formerly been in *Egypt* . . . such a King would have in him the whole *Legislative* and *Judicial Power*, and that his *Arbitrary* Will and Pleasure would be the *Law* or *Measure* by which his Government would be Administered."[90] For Acherley, the Israelites had sinned in asking for a monarch who would combine executive, legislative, and judicial power, one who would govern by his "Arbitrary Will and Pleasure." Once again, it was discretionary power, not the kingly office or title, that God was said to despise.

II

To the extent that British North Americans discussed biblical monarchy at all during the first twelve years of the imperial crisis, it was simply to affirm this traditional understanding. God permitted each people to choose its form of government, and he had no objection whatsoever to the institution of limited monarchy. All participants in the pamphlet wars leading up to the Revolution could endorse this formulation—even patriot Royalists of the early 1770s, who, after all, were claiming that the ancient prerogatives of the crown were fully "legal" and did not threaten enslavement to anyone's "arbitrary will" (although it must be stressed that their pamphlets tended to ignore Scripture altogether). Indeed, as the crisis escalated in 1775, the very small number of colonial writers who began to argue for republican government did so while continuing to insist upon the legitimacy and divine permissibility of monarchy. They followed their parliamentarian predecessors in arguing simply that republican government would offer the best protection against arbitrary, discretionary power, that it would rescue them once and for all from the dangers of encroaching prerogative. Their writings from this twelve-month period therefore provide a fascinating glimpse of a road not taken—of what the "republican turn" might have looked like had Paine not published his pamphlet.

In his *Short Essay on Civil Government* (1775), Connecticut minister Dan Foster offered the incendiary argument that "England was never more happy before, nor much more since, than after the head of the first [*sic*] Stuart was severed from his body, and while it was under the protectorship of Oliver Cromwell."[91] Yet for all of its radicalism, his defense of the English republic resolutely shunned exclusivism. "A people," he insisted, "have an inherent right to appoint and constitute a king supreme and all subordinate civil officers and rulers over them, for their civil good, liberty, protection, peace and safety."[92] Foster accepted the Roman conceit that men are born "*sui iuris*"—independent of the will of others—and that it is contrary to reason for them to surrender their liberty when establishing civil society.[93] Those who designed England's "ancient constitution" had understood this perfectly: "CAESAR and TACITUS describe the antient Britons to have been a fierce people; zealous of liberty: a free people; not like the Gauls, governed by laws made by great men; but by the people."[94] These ancient free men, like their German forbears, preferred political regimes in which "the people had the principle authority." Yet notwithstanding this fact, "they often elected a Prince or a King; sometimes a General whom we call Duke, from the Latin word *Dux*. But the power of these chiefs descended entirely on the community, or people; so that it was always a mixed democracy. In other parts . . . the Kings reigned with more power; yet not to the detriment of liberty; their royalty was limited by laws and the reason of things."[95] The chief requirement of good government is the preservation of liberty, which in turn requires the absence of arbitrary, discretionary power in the chief magistrate. For this reason, Foster insists on the total elimination of the royal prerogative: war, peace, and trade must all be governed by the "consenting voice and suffrage of the people personally, or by representation,"[96] and a king ought to be deposed immediately if he "will not give the royal assent to bills which have passed the states, or parliament."[97]

So long as these conditions are met, Foster is prepared to acknowledge the legitimacy (if not the desirability) of monarchy, and he grounds his view in a striking reading of I Sam. 8:

And now they [the Israelites] manifest their desire of a King, one who should rule according to right and equity; and pray his assistance to constitute and set one over them, to judge, rule and govern them, as was customary in all other nations. SAMUEL intimates his displeasure at their request of a King; fearing they did not pay that respect to Jehovah which they ought; and from the lord he shews them the manner of the King who should reign over them; how he would conduct with them, their families and inheritances, and what would be the maxims of that government which he would exercise over the people, in the course of his reign. Notwithstanding all this, the people persisted in their request of a King, and still continued their petition. And though perhaps the circumstances attending Israel's request at this time, and their obstinacy in it, after the prophets remonstrances against it, were not to be commended, the Lord so far overlooked this, that he commanded Samuel to hearken to, and gratify the people, by accomplishing their desire in constituting a King to rule and govern them.[98]

In Foster's interpretation, the Israelites had asked for the right sort of king after all: one who would "rule according to right and equity." What they failed to appreciate is that in practice, monarchs tend to become tyrannical: "the maxims of that government which [Saul] would exercise over the people" were, Samuel realized, to be very different indeed from the ones endorsed by the people themselves when they asked for a king. It would therefore have been far better for them to retain their republican constitution—the safest possible bulwark against enslavement.[99] Nonetheless, God acceded to their request because he regarded it as perfectly permissible for a people to institute monarchy.

Harvard's president, Samuel Langdon, offered more or less the same view in a 1775 sermon, *Government Corrupted by Vice*. "The Jewish government," he observed, "according to the original constitution which was divinely established, if considered merely in a civil view, was a perfect Republic," and "the civil Polity of Israel is doubtless an excellent general model, allowing for some peculiarities; at least some principal laws and orders of it may be copied, to great advantage, in more modern establishments."[100] Indeed, Langdon went so far as to adopt the more radical Josephan gloss on I. Sam. 8, according to which the Israelites had deposed God as their civil sovereign by asking for a king: "And let them who cry up *the divine right of Kings* consider, that the only form of government which had a proper claim to a divine establishment was so far from including the idea of a King, that it was a high crime for Israel to ask to be in this respect like other nations; and when they were gratified, it was rather as a just punishment of their folly . . . than as a divine recommendation of kingly authority."[101] Yet Langdon insisted at the same time that "every nation, when able and agreed, has a right to set up over themselves any form of government which to them may appear most conducive to their common welfare." Monarchy remains perfectly permissible, so long as one guards against "the many artifices to stretch the prerogatives of the crown beyond all constitutional bounds, and make the king an absolute monarch, while the people are deluded with a mere phantom of liberty."[102] While it may have been seditious for the Israelites to ask for a human king, it was no sin for anyone else to do so. The Salem minister Samuel Williams agreed in his own 1775 sermon, *A Discourse on the Love of Our Country,* declaring that "infinite wisdom had seen fit to put that people [Israel] under a more excellent form of government, than any nation has ever had. God himself was their King. And they might have been long happy under a government, in which, the Ruler of the world condescended himself to execute the office of Chief-Magistrate. But such was their impiety and folly, that in many instances they greatly abused and perverted the privileges they were favoured with."[103] As a result, they soon found themselves in Babylonian exile, under "the arbitrary will of a proud, cruel, despotic monarch."[104] For Williams, republican government might well be the most "excellent" known to man, but monarchy remains permissible so long as it is not "arbitrary" and "despotic."[105]

III

Seen in the context of these discussions, Paine's *Common Sense* emerges as a transformative intervention.[106] Rejecting over a century of whig biblical exegesis, Paine returned in January 1776 to Milton and the Hebraic exclusivists of the 1650s. His argument in the section "Of Monarchy and Hereditary Succession" reads as follows:

> Government by kings was first introduced into the world by the Heathens, from whom the children of Israel copied the custom. It was the most prosperous invention the Devil ever set on foot for the promotion of idolatry. The Heathens paid divine honours to their deceased kings, and the Christian world hath improved on the plan by doing the same to their living ones. How impious is the title of sacred majesty applied to a worm, who in the

midst of his splendor is crumbling into dust! As the exalting one man so greatly above the rest cannot be justified on the equal rights of nature, so neither can it be defended on the authority of scripture; for the will of the Almighty as declared by Gideon, and the prophet Samuel, expressly disapproves of government by kings. . . . Near three thousand years passed away, from the Mosaic account of the creation, till the Jews under a national delusion requested a king. Till then their form of government (except in extraordinary cases where the Almighty interposed) was a kind of republic, administered by a judge and the elders of the tribes. Kings they had none, and it was held sinful to acknowledge any being under that title but the Lord of Hosts. And when a man seriously reflects on the idolatrous homage which is paid to the persons of kings, he need not wonder that the Almighty, ever jealous of his honour, should disapprove a form of government which so impiously invades the prerogative of heaven.[107]

For Paine, as for Milton before him, the Israelites sinned in asking for a king per se: "Monarchy is ranked in scripture as one of the sins of the Jews, for which a curse in reserve is denounced against them." "These portions of scripture," he announces, "are direct and positive. They admit of no equivocal construction." The issue was not the *sort* of king for which the Israelites asked—an "arbitrary" king whose prerogatives would enslave them—or that they asked for one despite being under God's unique, providential government at the time. On the contrary, they sinned because it is inherently idolatrous to assign any human being the title and status of king. "The Almighty," on Paine's account, "hath here entered his protest against monarchical government," and when the Israelites later entreated Gideon to become their king, the judge and prophet "denieth their right" to establish a monarchy and accordingly "charges them with disaffection to their proper Sovereign, the King of Heaven."[108]

Paine's whig critics fully recognized the radicalism of this position, as well as its tendency to shift the focus of conversation away from potentially enslaving kingly *powers* and toward the alleged evils of the very *title* of "king." Paine himself, after all, had gone out of his way to insist that the English monarchy was illicit despite being virtually powerless: "If we inquire into the business of a king, we shall find that (in some countries they have none) and after sauntering away their lives without pleasure to themselves or advantage to the nation, withdraw from the scene, and leave their successors to tread the same idle round. In absolute monarchies the whole weight of business civil and military, lies on the king; the children of Israel in their request for a king, urged this plea 'that he may judge us, and go out before us and fight our battles.' But in countries where he is neither a judge nor a general, as in England, a man would be puzzled to know what is his business."[109] The anonymous author of the Dublin pamphlet *Reason in Answer to a Pamphlet Entituled, Common Sense* begins by summarizing this aspect of Paine's argument: "England is governed by a king, and this, he says, is a great enormity, offensive to the Deity and degrading to human nature. . . . He then proceeds to ransack the holy scriptures, for texts against kingly government, and with a faculty of perverting sacred truths to the worst of purposes, peculiar to gentlemen of his disposition, quotes the example of the Jews, when tired of Theocratic government, which they alone of the whole world enjoyed, they demanded a king."[110] But the very fact that the Israelites lived under a unique "theocracy" explains, for the author, why we ought not to generalize on the basis of their idiosyncratic political experience: "Are the Americans under any such government? is our author a judge or a prophet? To what purpose has he repeated the dissuasions of Samuel? have not the people of America, experienced the benign authority of Britain's king, and can he not say with Samuel, 'whose ox have I taken, or whom have I defrauded, or whom have I oppressed, or at whose hand have I received any bribe to blind mine eyes therewith?' " [I Sam. 12:3] For the author, it is despotic and arbitrary monarchy, not monarchy per se, that God despises, and if Paine would deign to "peruse his Bible again, and with more attention, he would find that . . . regal authority has been exercised by many persons approved by Heaven."[111]

The danger of Paine's position, the author goes on to explain, is that it encourages colonial readers to become anxious about precisely the wrong things—to pursue shadow over substance. So long as their chief magistrate is not called "king," they will feel that the appropriate political principles have been satisfied fully; they will not fret at all about the sweeping prerogative powers that their suitably re-christened governors might come to wield. In the case of the English, "Cromwell . . . knew so well their aversion to the name of king, that he would never assume it, tho' he exercised a power despotic as the Persian Sophi. He knew 'twou'd make him odious to those who had overturn'd the state, he knew they were acquainted with the extent of royal prerogative, tho' not of kingly power."[112] Englishmen of the 1650s were happy to suffer the evils of the "royal prerogative," so long as the putatively idolatrous "name of king" had been abolished. Likewise, "the prince of Orange tho' in Holland called Stadtholder, yet exercised royal authority in its full extent, but in England, where he was acknowledged King, his authority was more circumscribed, so that in other parts of Europe he was wittily call'd the King of Holland and Stadtholder of England."[113] The royal powers wielded by William III as stadtholder of the United Provinces were far more sweeping than any he enjoyed as king of Great Britain. Yet Paine and his ilk would have us believe that the God of freedom "reprobates" the latter office and not the former.

The author of a second anonymous reply to *Common Sense*—this one published in London by "a member of the Continental Congress" (possibly John Rutledge of South Carolina)—offered precisely the same objection to Paine's analysis. "As every Argument that has an Appearance of Scripture to support it, with many Persons, is decisive, the Author makes no small use of it against Kings and Kingly Government; it will be very easy to shew that his Remarks prove nothing less than what is intended."[114] True, "the rejection of the Theocracy, which had hitherto obtained, and the desire of having a King over them, like the Heathen Nations, was undoubtedly a very great Wickedness" in the Israelites, but Paine is terribly wrong when "he makes the Almighty enter his 'Protest against Monarchical Government,' and saith, 'this must be true, or the Scripture is false.' "[115] For evidence, the author turns back to Deuteronomy 17: "Now that Kings and Monarchy are not absolutely sinful, and that God Almighty has not protested against their Existence, I suppose will appear sufficiently clear from the following Passage: '*Thou shalt in any wise set him King over thee, whom the Lord thy God shall choose;*' and then, among other Rules prescribed, he cautions him, 'that his Heart may not be lifted up above his Brethren, and that he turn not aside from the Commandment, to the Right Hand or to the Left.' "[116] God objects to overbearing and tyrannical kings, not to kings per se, and Scripture demonstrates that "there have been very good Kings, and very wicked judges."[117] Once again, Paine is guilty of engaging in a perverse sort of misdirection: "It is trifling to find Fault with the Term ["king"]. One whose Authority possibly he would respect, (*Cromwell*) observed, the Harm lay not in the four Letters K,I,N,G."

The controversy over Paine's scriptural argument likewise came to dominate the extensive debate over *Common Sense* in the Philadelphia newspapers.[118] James Chalmers of Maryland, writing as "Candidus," attacked Paine in the *Pennsylvania Gazette* for "quoting the anti-philosophical story of the Jews, to debase Monarchy, and the best of Monarchs. Briefly examining the story of this contemptible race, more barbarous than our savages: We find their history a continued succession of miracles, astonishing our imaginations, and exercising our faith."[119] For Chalmers, the Jewish example is simply irrelevant to contemporary political theory, but he nonetheless hastens to "remind our Author, who so readily drags in the Old Testament to support his sinister measures; that we could draw from that source, many texts, favourable to Monarchy, were we not conscious, that the Mosaic Law, gives way to the Gospel Dispensation."[120] A second early respondent, writing under the pseudonym "Rationalis," likewise disavowed any intention to "follow him [Paine] through his scripture quotations, which he has so carefully garbled to answer his purpose"[121] but still troubled to reproduce the very passages from *The Judgment of Whole Kingdoms and Nations* discussed above in order to demonstrate that "monarchy (especially a limited one, such as that of England) is not inconsistent with the Holy Scriptures, as is set forth in said pamphlet [*Common Sense*], but that it is pleasing to the Almighty, if agreeable to the people, as any other form of government, even the author's beloved republic."[122]

A third respondent, Charles Inglis (writing as "An American"), recognized in contrast that Paine's scriptural argument had to be taken far more seriously, and undertook to answer it in detail. He begins his discussion in *The True Interest of America* by addressing Paine's account of the pagan origins of monarchy: "'Government by Kings,' this writer tells us, 'was first introduced by Heathens.' And so, say I, was Greek and Latin—so was smoking tobacco; and yet I can dip into Homer and Virgil, or enjoy my pipe, with great composure of conscience."[123] Even if monarchy were indeed a pagan invention, it does not follow that Christians commit any sort of sin by embracing it. "From Heathenism," Inglis continues, "our author next flies to scripture for arguments against monarchy. Were I a parson I should be better qualified to deal with them in this way." For Inglis, this entire discussion is out of place in a debate about contemporary politics, but he concedes that he must play in Paine's ballpark, "however unusual the employment."[124] "'The will of the Almighty, as declared by Gideon and Samuel (says our republican) expressly disapproves of government by King.' So it might on these particular occasions, and for some particular reasons; and yet our government by Kings at this time, may be as acceptable to the Almighty, as any other government." As for the alleged "anti-monarchical parts of scripture" to which Paine had alluded, Inglis simply denies that they exist: "The Jewish polity, in which the Almighty himself condescended to be King (and thence called a Theocracy) is rather in favour of monarchy than against it; though I am not clear that any one species of regular government is more acceptable to the Deity now than another; whatever preference may be due to one above another, in point of expediency and benefit."[125]

Inglis next turns to examine Deuteronomy 17 and I Sam. 8, "the passages of Scripture, in which our republican author triumphs most; which, he says, 'are direct and positive, and admit of no equivocal construction. That the Almighty has in them entered his protest against monarchical government, is true, or else Scripture is false.'"[126] Here again Paine is badly mistaken: "The Almighty has not there entered his protest against monarchical government, further than the Jews had departed from a former permission he had given them to chuse Kings." To be sure, the Israelite request for a king "in some measure was displeasing to the Almighty," but "that simply desiring a King, could not be a crime, is undeniably evident; because the Almighty had long before expressly permitted it, had directed the mode of chusing a King, and prescribed the line of conduct the king should observe, when chosen. This is done in Deuteronomy xvii.14–20."[127] What, then, was the Israelite sin? Inglis gives the traditional neo-Roman, whig answer: "Their error lay in the *manner* of their asking a King—in the *principles* on which they acted—in a *disregard* of the venerable old prophet—but chiefly, in a *neglect* of the *directions* above mentioned. . . . The people tumultuously assembled to desire a King, who would resemble the despotic Kings which surrounded them."[128]

The most substantial critique of Paine's Hebraic exclusivist position came, however, from the Reverend William Smith, Anglican provost of the College of Philadelphia. Writing as "Cato," Smith took it as self-evident that Paine had "pervert[ed] the Scripture" in claiming that "monarchy . . . (meaning, probably, the institution of Monarchy,) 'is ranked in Scripture as one of the sins of the *Jews,* for which a curse in reserve is denounced against them.'"[129] But he recognized that in "a country in which (*God* be thanked) the Scriptures are read, and regarded with that reverence which is due to a revelation from Heaven," the argument of *Common Sense* could not safely be ignored. Smith therefore resolved "to rescue out of our author's hands that portion of the sacred history which he has converted into a libel against the civil

Constitution of *Great Britain*; and show in what sense the passage has been universally received, as well by the *Jews* themselves as by commentators, venerable for their piety and learning, in every Christian country."[130] He begins by reminding his readers that "the *Jews* were long privileged with a peculiar form of Government, called a Theocracy, under which the 'Almighty either stirred up some person, by an immediate signification of his will, to be their Judge, or, when there was none, ruled their proceedings himself, by Urim and Thummim.'" When the Israelites requested a human king, they sinned first and foremost in "rejecting the divine Government" under which they had prospered. But they sinned further in desiring "a King to judge them like all the nations," since "all the nations which they knew, were ruled by Kings, whose arbitrary will stood in the place of law; and it appears also that the Jews, since the day that they were brought out of *Egypt,* had still retained a particular hankering after the customs of that country."[131] God therefore "not only signifies his displeasure against all such arbitrary rulers, but against every people who would impiously and foolishly prefer such a Government to one immediately under himself, where, in his providence, he might think fit to appoint such an one."[132]

Yet Paine dares to argue that "the Almighty hath here entered his protest against Monarchical Government." Smith answers firstly that "the Almighty would have as strongly expressed his displeasure against the *Jews,* had they rejected his Government for one of their own appointment, whether it had been monarchical or democratical—to be administered by one man or a thousand men."[133] But Paine errs most spectacularly in assuming that when Samuel described the horrors that would be perpetrated by Israelite kings, the prophet meant to "extend his protest against all future Monarchical Governments, such as were to subsist some thousands of years afterwards, however limited and mixed, particularly that of *Great Britain,* (which must certainly be our author's meaning, or he proves nothing to his purpose)."[134] This, for Smith, is patently absurd: citing "*Acherley,* in his *Britannick Constitutions,*" he insists that "the particular case of the *Jews* cannot be applied to any other nation in this instance, as none else were ever in similar circumstances."[135]

In order to buttress this conclusion, he turns to the Hebrew text itself and to the tradition of Jewish commentary upon it. First comes "the celebrated *Grotius,*" who "tells us that *Samuel,* in this passage, does not speak of what our author calls the 'general manner of Kings,' or the just and honest right of a King to do such things; because his right is otherwise described elsewhere, as shall be shown. The prophet only speaks of such a right as the Kings round about *Israel* had acquired, which was not a true, right; for such is not the signification of the original word *Mishpat*; but such an action as (being founded in might and violence) hath the *effectum juris,* or comes in the place of right."[136] Grotius, along with Sidney (who is here transfigured into a respectable whig) is then said to be "well warranted in this interpretation, not only by the *Hebrew* text, but other clear passages of Scripture, and particularly the seventeenth chapter of *Deuteronomy,* where, with the approbation of Heaven, the duty of a good King is described and limited." Smith proceeds to summarize the rabbinic debate over this passage, as it had inflected the seventeenth century controversy over monarchy:

> The *Jews* commonly understood this chapter as containing an absolute promise from Heaven of a Royal Government, and a sufficient authority for the request made to Samuel more than three hundred years afterwards. Others understood it conditionally,—that if they did reject the Divine Government, and set up one of their own appointment, *God* would permit them; but their King should be chosen in the manner, and with the qualifications in that chapter described. All this, however, they disregarded when they asked an arbitrary King, like those of their neighbouring nations; and therefore, it is demonstratively certain that Samuel, in entering his protest against such Kings, did not protest against Kings or Monarchical Governments generally. Either this remark is true, or one part of Scripture is a direct contradiction to the other.[137]

Here Smith offers a précis of the Talmudic account, according to which Deut. 17 embodies an "absolute promise" of monarchy, as well as the traditional Christian view, according to which it contains a "permission" to establish a virtuous and lawful monarchy. Both readings converge in insisting that the Israelites sinned only in asking for the wrong *sort* of king. Smith conveniently neglects to mention that another group of rabbis, along with their early modern expositors, had taken precisely Paine's view of the matter.

For Smith, as for the rest of Paine's critics in 1776, the Hebraizing argument of *Common Sense* was most dangerous because it allowed tyrannical wolves to masquerade as republican sheep. "The popular leaders who overturned the Monarchy in the last age," he reminds his readers, "were not

themselves friends to Republicks. They only made use of the name to procure the favour of the people; and whenever, by such means, they had
mounted to the proper height, each of them, in his turn, began to kick the
people from him as a ladder then useless."[138] Once again, the embodiment of
this danger is Oliver Cromwell:

> *Cromwell* exercised the power of a King, and of the most absolute King, under
> the specious name of a Protector. The instrument of Republican Govern-
> ment, which he had at first extolled as the most perfect work of human inven-
> tion, he began (as soon as he thought his authority sufficiently established) to
> represent as "a rotten plank, upon which no man could trust himself without
> sinking." He had his eyes fixed upon the Crown; but when he procured an
> offer of it, from a packed Parliament, his courage failed him. He had outwit-
> ted himself by his own hypocrisy, and, in his way to power, had thrown such
> an odium upon the name of the King, that his own family, apprehensive he
> would be murdered the moment the diadem should touch his brow, per-
> suaded him to decline that honour.[139]

The Miltonic argument revived by Paine threatened to make a fetish out of
"the name of the King," delivering the colonists instead into the arbitrary
power of a non-monarchical tyrant. True "republicks" are defined by the
absence of discretionary power in any single person, not by the lack of an
allegedly idolatrous title. The "great *Sydney*," Smith insists in closing, "was
as much a foe to *Cromwell* as to *Charles* the First, considering both as governing above the laws. But he did not write against Kings generally, more than
other rulers who might abuse their power."[140]

IV

None of these critics succeeded in blunting the impact of Paine's pamphlet.
It had sold over 100,000 copies by April 1776, making it by far the most frequently printed pamphlet of the revolutionary period.[141] The crucial section
"Of Monarchy and Hereditary Succession" was also reprinted in full in the
February 19 issue of the *Connecticut Courant* and excerpted in countless other
newspapers throughout the colonies. (As we have seen, it was also substantially reproduced in each of the many critical responses to Paine.)[142] The literary remains of 1776 amply confirm David Ramsay's recollection that
thanks to *Common Sense*, "the name of a king was rendered odious" to a vast

number of Americans.[143] Writing in April to his good friend Richard Henry Lee—described by Landon Carter as "a prodigeous Admirer, if not partly a writer in the pamphlet *Common Sense*"[144]—Richard Parker offered a detailed commentary on the exchange between "Cato" and Paine. "If you will give me leave," he began, "I will shew you my Sentiments of Monarchical Government as established amongst the Jews."[145] The heathen nations surrounding them had "paid divine honors to their Kings," and the Lord, "being a jealous God took every means to prevent them from falling into the same Error." Yet he was rebuffed, and the subsequent depredations of the Israelite kings provide evidence of his great anger: "Can it be thought that the Almighty would have been so unmerciful to his people if it had not have been to shew them the impropriety of having a King for whose Trespasses they were to suffer[?]"[146] After all, "God had expressly declared to them long before they asked a King that they would do it and that he would punish them with the Kings they should set over them see the 28th Cap Deuteronomy to the 37th verse. Hosea in the 13th Chapter 11th verse says 'I gave thee a King in mine Anger and took him away in my wrath.' In short god was displeased with their demanding a King and was determined that they should suffer for his Crimes."[147] To be sure, "Cato thinks he has refuted Common Sense—by producing a few texts of Scripture to shew God was no enemy to monarchical Government but rather approved of it." Does not Deuteronomy 17, Cato had asked, "smell strong of Monarchy and even of Hereditary Monarchy?" Parker answers that "God has expressly declared his displeasure with the Jews for asking a King; but he knew long before they did demand one that they would do it; and he only tells them if they should be so foolish as to do it what sort they should choose & declares how he ought to conduct himself by which Conduct he should obtain his favor." "It is [a] pity," Parker concludes, that "Cato has not the Candor to compare the Scriptures, a crime he accuses Common Sense of. Cato gives a plain proof that he has a good deal of Priest craft, Is he not a scotch clergyman?"[148] The fact that this analysis came from the pen of an Anglican Virginia planter, and was addressed to a fellow member of the tidewater gentry, suggests that the reach of Paine's scriptural argument was quite considerable.[149]

Indeed, a varied host of colonial writers and ministers echoed Parker's sentiments over the next six months.[150] A popular "Tragi-Comedy" entitled *The Fall of British Tyranny*, published in May and attributed to John Leacock, exhorted its readers in verse: "Cast off the idol god!—kings are but vain! / Let justice rule, and independence reign. / Are ye not men? Pray who made men but God? / Yet men make kings—to tremble at their nod! / . . . Adopt the language of sound COMMON SENSE / And with one voice proclaim INDEPENDENCE."[151] In a sermon preached on May 29, 1776, Samuel West of Boston took as his text Isaiah 4:26: "And I will restore thy judges as at the first, and thy counselors as at the beginning: afterward thou shalt be called the city of righteousness, the faithful city."[152] He begins innocuously enough by insisting that "it becomes me not to say, what particular form of government is best for a community, whether a pure democracy, aristocracy, monarchy, or a mixture of all the three simple forms,"[153] but, by the end of the sermon, he is simply paraphrasing Paine: "The worst princes have been most flattered and adored: And many such in the pagan world assumed the title of gods; and had divine honors paid them. This idolatrous reverence has ever been the inseparable concomitant of arbitrary power, and tyrannical government: For even Christian princes, if they have not been adored under the character of gods, yet the titles given them, strongly savor of blasphemy, and the reverence paid them is really idolatrous."[154] "What right," West continues, "has a poor sinful worm of dust to claim the title of his most sacred Majesty; most sacred certainly belongs only to GOD alone, for there is none as holy as the Lord; yet how common is it to see this title given to kings?"[155]

West's Massachusetts colleague, Peter Whitney, went even further in a sermon preached on September 12: "When the people of Israel foolishly and impiously asked God to give them a king, hereby rejecting the kingly government of the most high, God condescended to gratify their desire, after previously warning them of what would be the certain consequences of their unhappy choice; they would be such as, if they had any reason left, and would consult their own interest, they would withdraw their petition, and desire rather to continue as they were."[156] Yet "they notwithstanding, persisted in their demand, and God gave them a king, but in his anger, and as a great scourge and curse to them." Whitney's verdict on this episode is, once again, an extended paraphrase of Paine, interspersed with direct quotations from the pamphlet:

It is a natural inference from sacred story, and from what has been said above, that kingly government is not agreeable to the divine will, and is often a great evil. The will of God as made known by Gideon; and the prophet Samuel expressly disapproves of government by kings. 'Near three thousand

years passed away from the Mosaic account of the creation, *before* the Jews
under a national delusion, asked a king.—'Till then their form of government
(except in extraordinary cases where the Almighty interposed) was a kind of
republic administered by a judge, and the elders of the tribes. Kings they had
none, and it was held sinful to acknowledge any being under that title but the
Lord of hosts. And when a man seriously reflects on the idolatrous homage
which is paid to the persons of kings, he need not wonder that the Almighty,
ever jealous of his honor, should disapprove a form of government which so
impiously invades the prerogative of heaven.' No form of government but
kingly or monarchical, is an invasion of God's prerogative; this is.[157]

The fact that "we are commanded to *pray* for kings, and to *submit* unto
kings," Whitney continues, does not constitute evidence of "the divine approbation of kingly government." It simply demonstrates that "when in
their folly, and 'strong delusion,' a people fix upon kingly, monarchical government, they must make the best of it, *pray* that their king may reign in
righteousness and rule with judgment, and must submit to his rule and authority, *so long* as it can be done consistent with their duty to themselves,
posterity, to mankind and to God."[158] None of this alters the underlying
truth that "the most high over all the earth, gave kings at first, to the Jews
(as he sends war) in anger, and as a judgment, and it may be affirmed, that
upon the whole, they have been a scourge to the inhabitants of the earth
ever since." "We in these States," Whitney concludes, "are now evidently
under the frowns of heaven for our many and great transgressions: it is to be
hoped we shall not 'add to our sins, this evil to ask *us* a king.' " The "evil," of
course, was to "invade the prerogatives of heaven" by assigning to a mortal
man the title of "king."[159]

The anonymous author "Salus Populi" likewise agreed with Paine in his
address "To the People of North-America on the Different Forms of Government" (1776), insisting that "kings and nobles are artificial beings, for
whose emolument civil society was never intended; and notwithstanding
they have had the good fortune to escape general censure from the world,
yet I will boldly affirm that nine-tenths of all the publick calamities which
ever befell mankind, were brought on by their means."[160] Indeed, "the protest which the Almighty entered against Kings, when the Jews demanded
one, shows in what estimation they are held by the Divinity." Turning to
his reader, the author then exclaims: "Point me out the King that does not

verify the description, and I will begin to suspect the divinity of the Bible. Wicked Kings and Governours make up the history of the Old Testament, and the chief part of the labour of the Prophets was to keep them within bounds."[161] His view was echoed the following month in the "Instructions to Delegates" published by the Committee for Charlotte County, Virginia. Having renounced their allegiance to George III, the citizens of the county were now committed to "taking the *God* of Heaven to be our King."[162] A sermon preached in Boston by Benjamin Hichborn took the same line: "I am inclined to think, that the great FOUNDER of societies has caused the CURSE of infatuating ambition, and relentless cruelty, to be entailed on those whose vanity may lead them to assume *his* prerogative among any of his people as they are cantoned about in the world, and to prevent mankind from paying that adoration and respect to the most dignified mortal, which is due only to *infinite wisdom and goodness,* in the direction of *almighty power,* and therefore that he alone is fit to be a MONARCH."[163]

Nor did the passing of the years diminish Paine's grip on the political imagination of British Americans. In 1778, the poet Philip Freneau echoed *Common Sense* in verse:

> To recommend what monarchies have done,
> They bring, for witness, David and his son;
> How one was brave, the other just and wise:
> And hence our plain Republics they despise;
> But mark how oft, to gratify their pride,
> The people suffered, and the people died;
> Though one was wise, and one Goliath slew,
> *Kings are the choicest curse that man e'er knew!*[164]

In a 1780 sermon preached "Before His Excellency John Hancock" to mark the "commencement" of the new Massachusetts constitution, the Boston minister Samuel Cooper took as his text Jer. 30:20–21: "Their Congregation shall be established before me: and their Nobles shall be of themselves, and their Governor shall proceed from the midst of them."[165] He begins by pointing out that "in the happy restoration promised in our text [after the captivity] it is observable, that the royal part of their government was not renewed. No mention is made in this refreshing prediction of a King, but only of Nobles, men of principal character and influence, who were to *be of themselves,* and such as they would chuse to conduct their affairs."[166] The reason, Cooper explains, is straightforward. Initially, "the form of government originally established in the Hebrew nation by a charter from Heaven, was that of a free republic, over which God himself, in peculiar favour to that people, was pleased to preside. It consisted of three parts; a chief magistrate who was called judge or leader, such as Joshua and others, a council of seventy chosen men, and the general assemblies of the people."[167] The Israelites had preserved this "civil constitution of the Hebrew nation" inviolate, "till growing weary of the gift of heaven, they demanded a King. After being admonished by the Prophet Samuel of the ingratitude and folly of their request, they were punished in the grant of it. Impiety, corruption and disorder of every kind afterwards increasing among them, they grew ripe for the judgments of Heaven in their desolation and captivity." God did not intend this anti-monarchical lesson to be "peculiar to the Jews," Cooper insists, but rather to demonstrate "in general what kind of government infinite wisdom and goodness would establish among mankind."[168]

Cooper's Connecticut colleague Joseph Huntington offered much the same account the following year in *A Discourse, Adapted to the Present Day* (1781). "The infinitely wise and good Being," he begins, "has given us the sum and substance of the most perfect form of civil government in his word. . . . I mean that ancient plan of civil policy, delineated for the chosen tribes of Israel."[169] In that divinely authorized constitution, "we find no king, no despot, no emperor, no tyrant, no perpetual dictator allowed of."[170] Instead "we find the nation, by divine order, composed of a number of states, that is to say thirteen, called the tribes of the children of Israel.—Jacob had twelve sons, but then you know the tribe of Joseph was subdivided and became two tribes, i.e. the tribe of Ephraim and the tribe of Manasseh, which made thirteen *united, free and independent states*."[171] Having established the providential connection between the thirteen tribes of Israel and the thirteen American colonies, Huntington goes on to explain that "each of these managed their internal police within themselves," but "these Thirteen United States or tribes of Israel, had by divine appointment a general congress ['I mean the Sanhedrim or seventy elders'], with a president at their head; Moses was the first, Joshua succeeded him, so on till the days of Samuel, when the constitution was subverted."[172] Huntington insists that "here God has marked out that form of civil government which is agreeable to his own will, adapted to the nature and state of mankind which secures the privileges of the subject, and affords all that liberty and equality which it is possible mankind should enjoy." Each people is free to adapt this basic structure to its own needs and requirements, "but thus much in general God has plainly taught us, viz. that no king, no monarch, no tyrant, or despot, ought ever to be admitted to rule over his people, or any people under heaven; and hence, when Israel rejected that glorious form of government, and would have a king to govern them, God expressly declares *they rejected him.*"[173]

John Murray of Newburyport returned to this theme in his sermon celebrating the Peace of Paris and the birth of the new United States in 1784. "Now hail thy DELIVERER-GOD," he exhorts his audience, "worship without fear of man. This day, invite him to the crown of America—proclaim him KING of the land."[174] Such a coronation, he goes on to explain, has been made possible by the extraordinary virtue and piety of the Americans and their leaders. In the Hebrew republic of old, Gideon was invited to become king, but he recognized that "the reins of kingly authority become no other hands than those of the all-perfect Sovereign of the universe." Only God "is fit to sit Monarch on a throne—before him only every knee should bow—at his feet should sceptered mortals cast their crowns—there should they lay them down—to resume and wear them no more for ever—and he who refuses this rightful homage to the only Supreme, deserves to be treated as a tyrant among men, and a rebel against God."[175] Why should Americans expect any less of their own greatest general? "Are not we the children of Israel too—a professing covenant-people, in a land peculiarly privileged with gospel-light?"[176] Indeed we are, and though Washington was never offered a crown—because, for Americans, "the idea of a human monarchy is too absurd in itself"[177]—if he had been, he surely would have replied in ringing tones that "the LORD alone shall be king of AMERICA."[178]

V

The uniformly rapturous reception of *Common Sense* in the 1780s should not cause us to lose sight of the fierce debate that it provoked in the late 1770s. Paine's argument, as we have seen, was by no means greeted with universal acclaim. Loyalists fiercely resisted his conclusions and even many patriots found his reasoning deeply uncongenial, particularly the scriptural argument against monarchy. But even Paine's most dogged critics recognized the power and import of his intervention. One of them, a Philadelphia writer who published in the *Pennsylvania Ledger* under the pseudonym "Moderator," categorically rejected Paine's argument for independence, believing instead that "a reconciliation with Great Britain, upon constitutional principles, is the most certain foundation for American happiness."[179] As for forms of government, he was inclined to dismiss a priori judgments and to focus instead on the degree of liberty that he might be expected to enjoy under each: the issue, for him, was not whether we ought to have a king or not but whether "I am to enjoy a greater liberty of conscience, a greater degree of personal security, more natural freedom, to possess more largely the means of acquiring a comfortable subsistence, and not to have the expences of government call on me for taxes overproportioned to the additional benefits to be derived from the change—if these can be cleared up to my satisfaction— here's my hand and here's my heart." But "Moderator" also offered an extraordinary account of how Paine's antimonarchical rhetoric had quite literally captured his imagination. It is worth quoting at length:

> When the pamphlet called *Common Sense* first appeared, I found myself stagger'd with the high wrought declamations against Monarchy in general, and of Britain in particular; I view'd the "Royal Brute" with an indignant frown, and began to new-mould my monarchical sentiments, into those of a common-wealth, whose virtue should reign triumphant, and vice be expelled from the land. . . . I read it a second time with more deliberation, and uninfluenced by those impressions, which are generally made by novelty; for I am one of those, who have a wonderful aptitude to be smitten with any thing that is grand—a lake, a mountain, a temple, or a capacious thought that includes a thousand worlds, immediately captivate my fancy, it instantly gets upon the wing, ranges with delight through the extensive scene, and forgets for a moment the real objects around me: such had been my situation of mind, when I surrendered the reigns of my imagination to the guidance of the ingenious author of Common Sense—we soar'd aloft into the wilds of fancy, the dull beaten tracks of monarchy, we left far behind us, and found a republic amidst the stars; and though the Sun might seem, to admiring mortals below, the grand monarch of the heavenly bodies, yet we found other suns and other worlds innumerable, who might only be considered as *Presidents,* not *Monarchs,* of the vast system; every where shone a republic, the various constellations which enspangle the sky, united upon the principles of perfect equality; and gravitating towards each other with wonderful adjustment, mutually attracted and mutually repelled; thus, gentle reader, was my imagination led captive, with fiery velocity. . . .[180]

In due course, "Moderator" had returned, like Noah's dove, to "dry ground," but he nonetheless vividly recalled the sublimity of the journey on which Paine had taken him. He had been persuaded, however fleetingly, to leave behind the "dull, beaten tracks of monarchy"—to recognize that just as the sun itself is a mere "President" in the eyes of the Creator of the "vast system" of the universe and no "grand monarch of the heavenly bodies," so too there is no human being on earth who is fit to be styled "king." Whatever the delusions of "admiring mortals below," God is the only true monarch.

Unlike "Moderator," the majority of British North Americans never came back down to earth. They thoroughly absorbed Paine's Hebraizing exclusivist argument against kingship, rendering it virtually unthinkable that an American monarchy would be established at the conclusion of the Revolutionary War.[181] But it was precisely because Paine had so effectively altered the focus of political debate—from the enslaving effects of kingly powers to the idolatrous pretensions of the office of king—that it later became possible for Americans to reconcile republicanism with prerogative (a reconciliation that Paine himself deplored).[182] Looking back on the coming of independence, Jefferson mused regretfully in 1816 that the distinctive antimonarchism of 1776 "had so much filled all the space of political contemplation, that we imagined everything republican which was not monarchy."[183] John Adams reflected on the same development with considerably less regret. In 1814, he shared the following vignette with a correspondent:

> The Prince of Orange, William V., in a conversation with which he honored me in 1788, was pleased to say, that "he had read our new constitution," and he added, "Monsieur, vous allez avoir un roi, sous le titre de président," which may be translated, "Sir, you have given yourselves a king, under the title of president." Turgot, Rochefoucauld and Condorcet, Brissot and Robespierre and Mazzei were all offended, that we had given too much éclat to our governors and presidents. It is true, and I rejoice in it, that our presidents, limited as they are, have more power, that is, more executive power, than the stadtholders, the doges, the podestàs, the avoyers, or the archons, or the kings of Lacedaemon or of Poland.[184]

Indeed, Adams had observed as early as 1789 that "I know of no first magistrate in any republican government, excepting England and Neuchatel, who possesses a constitutional dignity, authority, and power comparable to [the president's]"—his "prerogatives and dignities, are so transcendent that they must naturally and necessarily excite in the nation all the jealousy, envy, fears, apprehension, and opposition, that are so constantly observed in England against the crown."[185] Once the title of king had been abolished in accordance with the demands of Scripture, Americans were eventually able to make their peace with kingly power. "Let us now consider what our constitution is," Adams wrote, "and see whether any other name can with propriety be given it, than that of a monarchical republic, or if you will, a limited monarchy."[186] Montesquieu had famously characterized England as "a republic, disguised under the form of monarchy."[187] Thanks in large part to the Hebraizing turn initiated by Paine, the new United States would become the reverse.

CHAPTER 4

"The Old Government, as Near as Possible"

Royalism in the Wilderness, 1776–1780

On March 5, 1778, John Rutledge of South Carolina rose to address the General Assembly and Legislative Council of his state for the last time as its president. He had served in the position for two years, following the adoption of South Carolina's first constitution in March of 1776. That initial frame of government, alone among the eight state constitutions written during the first year of the Revolutionary War, had assigned the executive a "negative voice," decreeing that "the legislative authority shall be vested in the president and commander-in-chief, the general assembly, and the legislative council."[1] For two full years the president of South Carolina had thus constituted one coequal branch of the legislature and all bills had required his "assent" in order to become law. But in March of 1778, the General Assembly drafted a new constitution for the state, rechristening the president as a "governor" and stripping him of his negative. The revised document, as historian David Ramsay explained in 1785, was then "presented . . . to president Rutledge for his assent." Yet at this point, "by virtue of the negative power delegated to him by the temporary constitution, he refused to pass it."[2] In a remarkable speech defending his decision and simultaneously tendering his resignation, Rutledge offered two reasons for refusing his "assent to this bill." First, he explained, "I have taken an oath to preside over the people of this state, according to the constitution or form of government agreed to and resolved upon by the representatives of South-Carolina in March 1776; it is therefore impossible for me, without breach of this solemn obligation, to give my sanction to the establishment of a different mode of government."[3] But Rutledge did not leave matters there. Even if he had not been "restrained by an oath," he continued, "I should nevertheless put a negative on the bill, because it annihilates one branch of the legislature."

> On the late dissolution of government, the people, being at liberty to choose what form they pleased, agreed to one vesting an authority for making the laws by which they were to be bound in three branches, and committed it to the care of the several branches, not to be violated or infringed, but to be preserved as a sacred deposite, as that security of their lives, liberties and properties, which, after mature deliberation, they deemed it wisest to provide. . . . If we have power to lop one branch of the legislature, we may cut off either of the other branches, and suffer the legislative authority to be exercised by the remaining branch only, or abolish the third also, and invest the whole authority in some other person or body. Nor is it chimerical to suppose that such infractions may be attempted by others, since violations similar to these have been committed. We know that one of the houses of parliament voted the other house useless and dangerous, and that it ought to be abolished.[4]

The General Assembly, on Rutledge's account, had recklessly presumed to alter the state constitution unilaterally, eliminating one full branch of the legislature—the president, insofar as he possessed a "negative voice" as absolute as the one that patriots of the early 1770s had petitioned the king to revive—and threatening to ape the behavior of that archetypal tyrannical legislature, the Long Parliament. As Rutledge reminded his audience, no sooner had the renegade House of Commons of the late 1640s safely disposed of the sovereign's negative than it had turned its jealous eye on the House of Lords, abolishing the upper chamber in 1649.

Rutledge was thus offering an impassioned defense of that cluster of commitments that we have come to know as patriot Royalism. Prerogative powers in the executive—among them, the negative voice—are, on this view, fully compatible with the "liberties" of subjects and citizens, so long as the magistrate wielding such powers has been "vested" with the relevant "authority" by the people (in which case he may be said to represent them and his actions may count as their actions). Indeed, such powers are not merely *consistent* with the liberties of subjects and citizens, but are in fact *necessary* to secure them from the overweening encroachments of legislatures. The tyrannical House of Commons of the 1640s and 1650s had "usurped" the just prerogatives of the Crown (and then the Lords), thus

introducing into the English constitution an imbalance that had never properly been rectified. This imbalance had eventually provoked the imperial
crisis of the 1760s and 1770s, and Rutledge believed that an identical one was
now threatening to destabilize the newly independent American states.

Yet Rutledge's was a lonely and beleaguered voice in the America of 1778.
The frenzied antimonarchism unleashed by *Common Sense* and the final rupture with Britain in 1776 had led to a widespread resurgence of whig principles throughout the former colonies. The majority of legislators who framed
the initial state constitutions now agreed fully with the sentiments of North
Carolina's William Hooper, who announced to the assembly of his state in
October of 1776 that due to "the abuses which power in the hands of an Individual is liable to, and the unreasonableness that an individual should abro-
gate at pleasure the acts of the Representatives of the people,"[5] there should
be no negative voice in the chief magistrate—no third branch of the legislature. For Hooper, as for the parliamentarians and whigs before him, only
members of a popular assembly could possibly count as "the Representatives of the people." A single magistrate could not, and to be governed by
prerogative was accordingly to be governed "at pleasure" by an alien will. It
was quite simply to be a slave.

Principles such as these had never lacked for adherents in British North
America, even in the inhospitable years of the early 1770s. As we have seen,
the ideology of the revolutionary movement is perhaps best described as the
product of an "overlapping consensus." All of its proponents were able to
agree on two basic propositions: (1) Parliament did not represent the colonies; and (2) the English constitution had become hopelessly corrupt. But
patriots had evolved very different understandings of precisely *why* these
claims were correct. Some had always glossed them in a straightforwardly
whig manner: Parliament, on this account, did not represent the colonies
because it did not constitute a proper "likeness" or "image" of the colonists—
although the theorists who took this view never doubted the whig piety that
only a legislature *of some kind* could be said to represent the people—and the
English constitution had atrophied as a result of the endlessly expanding
patronage power of the Crown. But most of those who defended the patriot
cause in print during the final six years of the crisis had instead understood
these two propositions in Royalist terms. For them, as we have seen, Parliament did not represent the colonies because it had never been *authorized* to
wield power over them. The king, in contrast, had been so authorized, and

his prerogative powers were therefore fully consistent with the liberty of his American subjects. The English constitution, in turn, had grown corrupt because the legitimate, independent powers of the sovereign had never properly been restored after the parliamentarian revolutions of the seventeenth century. The problem, from their point of view, was too little Crown, not too much.

During the late 1760s and early 1770s, those who adopted the patriot Royalist position clearly had the wind at their sails. All of the participants in the pamphlet war that followed the repeal of the Stamp Act simply took for granted that these spokesmen were offering *the* American position; few patriots publicly disputed their contentions. In the immediate aftermath of independence, however, the wind unmistakably shifted. As state after state embraced whig constitutions that placed the executive firmly under the control of the legislature, no one could be in any doubt that the prerogativism of the imperial crisis had become deeply passé. Yet the leading theorists of the Royalist Revolution—James Wilson, John Adams, James Iredell, Alexander Hamilton, and their allies—did not abandon or alter their theoretical commitments during their years in the political wilderness. Almost to a man, they spent the second half of the 1770s reaffirming their interpretation of the origins of the imperial crisis and applying its lessons to the debate over the proper form of the state constitutions and the confederation. Their project was not, as has so often been claimed, a "conservative" reaction against the principles of the Revolution; it was, rather, an attempt to realize, at long last, the radical, anti-whig vision of independent prerogative power on behalf of which so many Americans had rebelled. Their efforts, while unsuccessful in the short term, laid the foundation for a resurgence of Royalist constitutionalism in the 1780s.

I

Anyone inclined to suppose that the patriot Royalists of the early 1770s merely adopted their constitutional argument out of forensic necessity, without any serious investment in its merits, need only look to their writings in the years following the rupture to be disabused of the notion. Independence had been declared, a war with Britain was now being waged, and the debate over the proper understanding of the imperial constitution had been rendered otiose. Yet the patriots in question continued to produce ornate briefs in support of their earlier contentions, elaborating on their arguments and beginning to apply them to the new political and ideological environment in which they suddenly found themselves. James Iredell, for one, straightforwardly repeated the Royalist constitutional argument of the early 1770s in a series of official documents that he composed long after the commencement of hostilities. On June 19, 1776, for example, he penned the "Declaration by the Vestry of St. Paul's Church," which proclaimed that "we the subscribers professing our allegiance to the King and acknowledging the Constitutional executive power of government, do solemnly profess, testify and declare that we do absolutely believe that neither the Parliament of Great Britain, nor any member or constituent branch thereof have a right to impose taxes upon these Colonies, to regulate the internal policy thereof."[6] Only weeks before independence was declared, Iredell was still insisting on the colonial attachment to the "Constitutional executive power" of the Crown.

He returned to this argument in a North Carolina jury charge that he prepared in May 1778, defending the conduct of the colonists during the imperial crisis. "Our allegiance to our sovereign was perfect," he maintained, "on the conditions of our charter. He had a negative on our laws, and the whole executive department of the state. This was a power sufficient for every useful purpose; we had no disposition to compliment him with any that was dangerous."[7] It is indeed striking that two years into the war—long after what Iredell dubbed "the revolution in our government" had taken place[8]—he once again felt the need to answer the charges of absolutism and Jacobitism that administration supporters had leveled against patriots in the late 1760s and 1770s. The colonists, he insisted, had never intended to "compliment" the king with "dangerous" new prerogatives; those assigned to him under the proper form of the English constitution would have more than sufficed to preserve the coherence and harmony of the empire, without any interference from Parliament. The Americans, on Iredell's account, had been "happy in the enjoyment of liberty, in the formation of our own laws, in the grant of our own money (subject only to a restriction we submitted to with pleasure, the negative of our sovereign)."[9] "The authority of the sovereign," he repeated, ought to have been "sufficient to preserve the whole in due order, but not to invade the liberties of any," and the empire, as the colonists had conceived of it, would have embodied "the entire and cordial union of many distant people, descended from the same ancestors, possessed nearly of the same rights, endued with generous and noble minds, warm in their affection, and zealous in their attachment to each other, under the influence of one common sovereign."[10] As for the legislature of Great Britain, "we knew of no right they could have" to legislate for the colonies, for "our charters did not recognize it."[11] Again, the king had been authorized by the charters to govern America; Parliament had not, and it was for this reason alone that it could not be said to represent the colonies.

Iredell further developed his position in two unpublished manuscripts, both written after the final rupture had come. In the first, dated June 1776, he begins by reaffirming that while the colonists had thoroughly rejected the pretended authority of Parliament, they had always "looked up to the King of Great Britain as their Sovereign, and paid him the most sincere and faithful allegiance; even at times when the other dominions of the Crown were convulsed with plots and massacres and civil wars."[12] He then proceeds to address the argument of administration pamphleteers that Parliament had possessed "unlimited power" over the colonies and, in particular, the right to annul or amend colonial charters. "The Crown, which granted the charters," these English writers had claimed, "is only *one* branch of the Supreme Power, and consequently his Acts may be controuled by the whole: the *executive* Power is inferior to the *legislative*, and of course the acts of the former must be subordinate, and subject to the superintendency of the latter."[13] But this, Iredell insists, is straightforwardly false. The Crown was in fact "the *sole Agent* in the business of these Charters." Whatever assistance the initial settlers received from the mother country "was merely the assistance of the Crown, without any of their immediate participation [i.e., that of Parliament], and which was sufficiently compensated by the important rights the *Crown* acquired."[14] The question accordingly becomes: "Did the *Crown* entertain any notion that Parliament had a right to interfere?" Iredell's answer is familiar. "On the contrary, there is evidence that James and Charles the first both forbid them intermeddling in our concerns and *these orders were obeyed.* I have already, in another place, remarked upon this circumstance."[15] And if one were to inquire "what right had the Crown to these [territories], exclusively of the supreme power; I answer, that it was the general sentiment of that Age, *the Crown was so entitled,* and this is sufficient for our purpose. I do not know what extraordinary lights the present age has received to justify them in calling in question the most solemn opinions of their Forefathers."

But Iredell immediately proceeds to offer a very specific account of what characterized these "new lights":

The new opinion upon this subject, I conceive, is derived from the harmonious and convenient connexion which of late years has taken place between his Majesty and his Parliament. This has introduced many pretty compliments, and handsome references from his Majesty to his *faithful Subjects*; and these in their turn have been wonderfully condescending to him. This new System, as I take it, has occasioned some *new* and *mighty* opinion of all Rights being ultimately consolidated in the supreme power. But in the age when these Charters were granted very different was the state of affairs. The Crown and Parliament had continual struggles for power, and it was understood they had *separate rights,* and different objects severally to act upon.[16]

The whig ascendancy, on Iredell's account, had introduced into English constitutionalism the pernicious fiction that the king possessed no powers "outside" Parliament. Parliamentarians before the "troubles" of the seventeenth century had never dreamed of infringing on the prerogatives of the Crown; they had merely insisted that "the laws in being of the Kingdom should be observed, and no new ones enacted but with their consent. They thought themselves sufficiently fortunate if they could secure their own liberties from violation, without seeking for new subjects of their legislative Power." As for the 1650 Act that had declared the colonies to be subject to Parliament, "it is to be considered, that at that time [after the regicide of 1649] the *regal* powers were consolidated in the *democratical;* and that this ordinance was passed by the infamous Rump Parliament, 200 of whose Members had been forcibly excluded by the Army; who respected no rights that interfered with their own despotism; and who were guilty of such enormous inequities that it is scandalous for any Man to quote any part of their proceedings as *a precedent.*"[17] In the good old days, the mighty and acknowledged "prerogatives of the Crown" were held "sacred," and "the prerogative in question [that of granting charters], as appears from remarkable instances cited [i.e., the tobacco and fishery bills, about which we have had so much to say], was deemed *equally sacred.*"

Iredell offered an equally explicit defense of the patriot Royalist position and its accompanying theory of English constitutional decline in an extraordinary manuscript letter addressed to George III himself (although never sent to the king) dated February 1777. When the Sugar Act and the Stamp Act were first announced, Iredell explains, "we were startled for a moment at the novelty of these Encroachments, and had some Curiosity to know the ostensible Reasons upon which you pretended to justify them."[18] But the mystery did not last long: "We discovered the mighty principle that was to do such mischief. It was a convenient one enough for Your Majesty and Parliament (between whom so friendly an Alliance had been formed) but it was violative of every principle of the Constitution, and every idea of Justice." The principle in question "was merely (to give it its' [sic] due name) an impertinent confusion of two Rights, in their nature totally distinct." On the one hand stood the right of Parliament, which "had ever been considered the Parliament of *Great Britain* only. The Peers were Peers only of *Great Britain*. The Commons Representatives alone of that People."[19] On the other stood the right of the Crown: "Your Majesty alone had any pretence, of the three branches, to any Legislative Authority over America, and this (as in other parts of your Dominions) was shared with the People." These distinct rights had been illicitly confounded in the whig discourse of parliamentary sovereignty, with the result that the genuine English "mixed monarchy" had effectively ceased to exist. "The sacred [i.e., divine] Right of Kings," Iredell observed, "(which, Sir, to your happiness heretofore, has been so justly ridiculed) of late years has been transferred to Parliament."[20] Now the administration proposed to export this new and perverse arrangement to the colonies, insisting that the empire required "one superintending Legislature over all." But in truth, as Iredell wrote to the king, this was "a mere modern Chimera, spun out of the cobwebs of the Schools."[21] "Ireland and Scotland are Examples, that in fact there may be a King over several different Countries," without any need for a monstrous imperial legislature. If George had only dared to rule, rather than merely reign, the crisis could have been averted.

Iredell continued to insist upon this view well into the 1780s, most emphatically in a poignant exchange with his uncle, Thomas Iredell Sr. Thomas, a wealthy Jamaican planter, fully supported the administration's American policy and accordingly refused to have any intercourse with his rebel nephew in North Carolina, answering letter after letter with a stony silence. In 1786, however, a missive from James had so outraged him that he was finally moved to reply. The offending document stated that any Englishman must at least be prepared to concede the *possibility* of legitimate armed resistance to political authority or else he must deny the legitimacy of the revolution that had sent James II into exile in 1688. Thomas's fiery response has not survived, but we do have James's answer to this salvo, on the basis of which we can reconstruct its contents. Thomas had evidently accused his nephew of justifying American resistance to Britain by *equating* the conduct of James II with that of George III (whereas, in fact, he had merely used the case of James II to vindicate the *principle* of legitimate resistance). In reply, James wrote as follows: "I never meant, in respect to the two Revolutions (as you will find if you will condescend to look at my letters, in case you have preserved them) to compare the personal or political character of the 2 Kings [James II and George III]. God knows nothing was further from my heart."[22] James then offered a crucial observation: "In respect to the American Revolution I look upon it to have been much more brought about by the intemperate violence of the People of England themselves than from any other cause." On James's account, it had been the people of England and their Parliament, not the king, who had provoked the imperial crisis, and it was chiefly against them that the Revolutionary War had been waged. "The Effect however as to us was the same, and it would have been a poor consolation in viewing the miseries of our Country to have said, 'The People of England are much more to blame for this than the King.'"[23] A full decade after independence, the Royalist theory of the Revolution remained firmly intact.

Iredell's ally James Wilson likewise returned over and again in the period following the rupture to a defense of this position.[24] In his "Address to the Inhabitants of the Colonies" (February 1776), drafted on behalf of the Continental Congress, he insisted that "the Share of Power, which the King derives from the People, or, in other words, the Prerogative of the Crown, is well known and precisely ascertained. It is the same in *Great Britain* and in the Colonies," and it answers to every useful imperial purpose.[25] Instead, "we trace your Calamities to the House of Commons," which has usurped the prerogatives of the Crown and achieved such unbridled power that it has fundamentally disordered both the imperial constitution and the constitution of Britain itself.[26] "If one Part of the Constitution be pulled down," Wilson explained, "it is impossible to foretell whether the other Parts of it may not be shaken, and perhaps, overthrown." "It is," he continued, "a Part of our Constitution to be under Allegiance to the Crown, Limited and ascertained as the Prerogative is, the Position—*that a King can do no wrong*—may be founded in *Fact* as well as in *Law,* if you are not wanting to yourselves."[27] But the House of Commons has attempted to absorb these prerogatives and, even more brazenly, has "undertaken to *give* and *grant* your Money." "From a supposed virtual Representation in *their* House it is argued, that *you* ought to be bound by Acts of the British Parliament"—a notion that "is no Part of the Constitution." It is for this reason that Wilson could declare, like Thomson Mason and so many others before him, that "we verily believe that the Freedom, Happiness, and Glory of Great Britain, and the prosperity of his Majesty and his Family depend upon the success of your Resistance. You are now expending your Blood, and your Treasure in promoting the Welfare and the true Interests of your Sovereign and your fellow-Subjects in Britain, in Opposition to the most dangerous Attacks that have ever been made against them."[28] Only if the patriot movement succeeded in restoring the king's independence in imperial affairs could the constitutional infirmities of Britain itself begin to be healed.

Wilson's tune had not changed at all the following year, when he composed a further address "To the Inhabitants of the United States" (May 29, 1777). On this occasion, he began his remarks by reaffirming his interpretation of the Revolution's origins, examining "in Retrospect, the Scenes, which are already passed." Wilson recalled that while his American audience had long been accustomed to "being governed by yourselves, or by those, upon whom you devolved the Powers of Government, you saw others, avow a Claim of governing you, without your Consent in all Cases whatever [i.e., in the Declaratory Act]."[29] Since this presumptuous assertion by a tyrannical legislature could not be allowed to stand, "you did, what a free and temperate People ought to do,—you petitioned and remonstrated against your Grievances." But "the ill founded Claim of governing you was the Injury offered; and you could not be heard till that ill-founded Claim was admitted."[30] The conflict accordingly began, "though, at no Time, you had transgressed the Bounds of your Duty as subjects, and though your Resistance to illegal Government ought to have had peculiar Merit with a Prince whose Family Resistance had led to the Throne, yet this virtuous Principle was pronounced Rebellion, and you were excluded from the Protection of the British Crown." The Americans had always acknowledged and supported the prerogatives of the Crown and had merely wished that "a Reconciliation, on the Principles of the British Constitution, would take Place." But, having been rebuffed, "you took the only Course left—you separated."[31] Indeed, Wilson was still defending these convictions as late as 1790, when he meticulously copied out his defense of the royal prerogative and the patriot theory of empire from the 1774 *Considerations* for inclusion in his "Lectures on Law." Here again he insisted that "the dependence of the colonies in America on the parliament of England seems to have been a doctrine altogether unknown and even unsuspected by the colonists who emigrated, and by the princes with whose consent their emigrations were made."[32]

The striking degree to which these patriot Royalist writers in the late 1770s kept faith with their earlier commitments is, however, perhaps best captured by the elusive figure of Thomas Jefferson. From the beginning, Jefferson had been a deeply heterodox, conflicted proponent of the Royalist position. As we have seen, his *Summary View* (1774) had urged the King to revive the negative voice at home and to govern the empire without his English ministers.[33] To this degree, his position had been every bit as Royalist as that of Adams, Hamilton, or Wilson. Yet, unlike these other writers, Jefferson had also attacked the king directly, threatened to restrict his negative in the colonies, and emphatically rejected the notion that America had ever been a private dominion of the Crown.[34] We find precisely the same ambivalence about Royalist constitutionalism on display in Jefferson's writings after the rupture. On the one hand, the draft constitution that he prepared for the commonwealth of Virginia in 1776 was as robustly anti-Royalist as any of the state constitutions adopted that year. It condemned monarchy as "an office which all experience hath shewn to be inveterately inimical" to liberty and declared that the newly established governor "shall have no negative on bills" and "shall not have prerogative of [his own] . . . but these [prerogative] powers to be exercised by legislature alone."[35] But at the same time, Jefferson routinely and emphatically endorsed the patriot Royalist interpretation of the imperial crisis. The preamble to his draft constitution justified rebellion by insisting that the king "hath given his assent" by "his own free & voluntary act" to the offending parliamentary bills.[36] The king, in short, ought to have revived the negative voice by striking down the Stamp Act, the Coercive Acts, and the other measures to which the colonists had objected. The fact that the veto had gone into abeyance over the previous century was a disorder in the constitution that cried out to be remedied. As Jefferson had put it in 1774, "it is now . . . the great office of his majesty, to resume the exercise of his negative power, and to prevent the passage of laws by any one legislature of the empire, which might bear injuriously on the rights and interests of another."[37] This, as we have seen, was precisely the same charge that Jefferson had written into the Declaration of Independence.[38]

But the most extraordinary reaffirmation of Jefferson's constitutional position from 1774 appears in a strangely neglected passage in his *Notes on Virginia,* the first edition of which was completed in 1781 (although it was not published until 1785). Here Jefferson offers an account of the origins of the Revolution, focusing on a very familiar moment of "original sin."

> And in 1650 [*sic*] the parliament, considering itself as standing in the place of their deposed king, and as having succeeded to all his powers, without as well as within the realm, began to assume a right over the colonies, passing an act for inhibiting their trade with foreign nations. This succession to the exercise of the kingly authority gave the first colour for parliamentary interference with the colonies, and produced that fatal precedent which they continued to follow after they had retired, in other respects, within their proper functions.[39]

At this late date, five full years after independence had been declared, Jefferson offers as full-throated an endorsement of the patriot Royalist position as had any writer of the early 1770s. The imperial crisis and the revolution that followed, on this account, had its true origins in the regicide of 1649, when the House of Commons had usurped the "kingly authority" of their "deposed" sovereign—most importantly his prerogative right to govern British America without any interference from Parliament. The first fruit of their usurpation had been the Navigation Act of 1651, that "fatal precedent" that had given rise to the insidious view that Parliament possessed jurisdiction over America. This pretension had survived the Restoration, even after the House of Commons "had retired, in other respects, within their proper functions." It is worth underlining the significance of this final claim. Jefferson is not simply arguing that the king, and not Parliament, had *in fact* wielded authority over America before the regicide; he is arguing that the English constitution, rightly understood, had assigned this role to the king and that, in expropriating it from him, the House of Commons had exceeded its "proper" bounds. Once again, the roots of the American crisis are said to lie in the defeat of the seventeenth-century Royalist cause. Indeed, Jefferson notes with evident pride that even after the regicide, "this colony . . . still maintained its opposition to Cromwell and the parliament."[40]

Quite remarkably, Jefferson reiterated this argument as late as 1821, when he composed his *Autobiography*. Reflecting on the imperial crisis that had led to revolution, he recalled that "in this I took the ground which, from the beginning I had thought the only one orthodox or tenable, which was that the relation between Gr[eat] Br[itain] and these colonies was exactly the same as that of England & Scotland after the accession of James & until the Union, and the same as her present relations with Hanover, having the same Executive chief but no other necessary political connection."[41] "Our other [Virginia] patriots," Jefferson continued, "Randolph, the Lees, Nicholas, Pendleton stopped at the half-way house of John Dickinson who admitted that England had a right to regulate our commerce, and to lay duties on it for the purposes of regulation, but not of raising revenue." But he himself had concluded that "for this ground there was no foundation in compact, in any acknowledged principles of colonization, nor in reason."[42] Only the king, wielding his prerogatives throughout his distinct dominions, could claim any right to govern America.[43]

Jefferson thus represents something of a "limit case" in this story, an illustration of just how difficult it proved even for those who found themselves deeply attracted to whig political and constitutional theory after 1776 to set aside the Royalist intellectual furniture of the imperial crisis. Moreover, as idiosyncratic as Jefferson undoubtedly was, his case reminds us of a more general fact: it was perfectly possible, and not necessarily inconsistent, for patriots to argue *both* that a prerogative-wielding monarch represented the only acceptable solution to the imperial crisis *and* that such a figure should not be replicated in the newly independent American states. After all, the question "what is the proper understanding of the English constitution and its relation to Britain's empire?" is very different indeed from the question "what form of government should a free people ideally adopt when starting from scratch?" One could give a Royalist answer to the first while offering a far more "whiggish" answer to the second (although, as we have seen, one could not coherently accept both the patriot Royalist position and the whig theory of representation).

Benjamin Franklin, for one, seems to have done precisely this. While he had been an early and consistent champion of the Royalist position in the late 1760s and the first half of the 1770s—declaring, as we have seen, that British Americans were "Subject to the King" alone and that the Lords and Commons were "thrust[ing] yourselves in with the Crown in the Government of the Colonies," thus "encroaching on the Royal Power"[44]—he supported Pennsylvania's unicameral constitution in 1776 and remained extremely suspicious of prerogative power in the executive throughout the 1780s.[45] But Franklin's was an unusual case. The other leading theorists of the Royalist Revolution never doubted for a moment that the same political principles that had promised to resolve the imperial crisis now had to be marshaled to secure liberty in the new American governments. They accordingly became sharp critics of the first set of state constitutions, seeing in each newly formed legislature the embryo of an American Long Parliament. And they proposed to tame these new behemoths just as they had proposed to tame the tyrannical British legislature only months before: through the transcendent, "pervading" power of a prerogative-wielding chief magistrate.

II

It was, perhaps unsurprisingly, John Adams who made the most seamless transition from thinking about the imperial constitution to thinking about the new American constitutions in 1776. In his "Novanglus" letters, written at the end of 1775, Adams had offered an unqualified endorsement of the view that sweeping prerogative powers in the sovereign, including the negative voice, were fully compatible with the liberty of subjects. If, as he insisted, "a republic" is simply *a government of laws, and not of men,"* then "the British constitution is nothing more nor less than a republic, in which the king is first magistrate."[46] "This office being hereditary, and being possessed of such ample and splendid prerogatives," Adams explained, "is no objection to the government's being a republic, as long as it is bound by fixed laws, which the people have a voice in making, and a right to defend." Restoring these ancient prerogatives of the monarch to their full seventeenth-century extent was, in turn, the only way to solve the problem of the imperial constitution. For "the truth is, the authority of parliament was never generally acknowledged in America. More than a century since, the Massachusetts and Virginia, both protested against even the act of navigation and refused obedience, for this very reason, because they were not represented in parliament and were therefore not bound—and afterwards confirmed it by their own provincial authority."[47] Once again, the first Navigation Act is presented as the original sin, a straightforward usurpation of royal authority that spawned the myth of parliamentary jurisdiction in America. In fact, Adams argues, this law was never acknowledged in Massachusetts "until 17 years afterwards," when "it was not executed as an act of parliament, but as a law of the colony, to which the king agreed."[48]

Only the king, in his personal rather than "political" capacity, possessed any claim to govern America. For the land "was not any part of the English realm or dominions. And therefore, when the king granted it," he did so not as part of the legislature of England but as a private landowner.[49] "As to the 'territory being holden of the crown,'" Adams argues, "there is no such thing in nature or art. Lands are holden according to the original notion of feuds of the natural person of the lord. Holding lands, in feudal language, means no more than the relation between lord and tenant. The reciprocal duties of these are all personal," owed to the natural person of the feudal lord—who simply happens in this case to be the king of England.[50] This understanding of the prerogative, floating free from parliamentary control, allows Adams to argue that the colonies "must be distinct states, as compleatly so as England and Scotland were before the union, or as Great-Britain and Hanover are now."[51] Adams assures us that "there is no need of being startled at this consequence. It is very harmless. There is no absurdity at all in it. Distinct states may be united under one king. And those states may be further cemented and united together, by a treaty of commerce. This is the case."[52] But it could not possibly have been the case without the presence of an independent, prerogative-wielding sovereign standing above each legislature in his extensive, highly personal dominions.

It was several months later, in the midst of the final rupture, that Adams turned his attention to the proper form of the new American constitutions, composing his celebrated *Thoughts on Government*. The close relationship between the various drafts of this widely read text and the "Novanglus" letters is unmistakable. Indeed, Adams himself insisted upon the continuity between his constitutional position during the imperial crisis and his proposal for the new state governments: when asked by John Rutledge at the end of 1775 to offer his "Opinion of a proper form of Government for a State," he answered that he hoped the people would "preserve the English Constitution in its Spirit and Substance, as far as the Circumstances of this Country required or would Admit," and, in particular, that "the three Branches of a Legislature would be preserved."[53] Accordingly, in the version of *Thoughts on Government* that he sent to William Hooper on March 27, 1776,

Adams began with a straightforward reaffirmation of his earlier characterization of the English constitution: "The British Constitution itself is Republican, for I know of no better Definition of a Republic than this, that it is an
Empire of Laws and not of Men."[54] Moreover, "as I look upon Republics to
be the best of Governments So I think, that particular Form of Government, or in other Words, that particular Arrangement, and Combination of
the Powers of Society, which is best calculated to Secure an exact and impartial Execution of the Laws, is the best Republic."[55] Once again, Adams
insisted that any number of "particular Arrangements, and Combinations
of the Powers of Society" are consistent with the "republican" government
of free men, including of course a monarchy vested with sweeping prerogative powers—for Britain itself was a republic, and, on Adams's understanding of the English constitution, its king was entrusted with "ample and
splendid prerogatives."

Since all duly authorized power is representative power, and thus compatible with the liberty of those over whom it is exercised, the only question
that remains for those who would frame a government is prudential: which
arrangement of institutions would most effectively answer the needs and
wants of the people? Adams freely granted that any desirable constitutional
scheme would feature a genuinely popular assembly; he even conceded that
this "Representative Assembly, should be an exact Portrait, in Miniature, of
the People at large, as it should think, feel, reason, and act like them."[56]
What he emphatically denied was that *only* an assembly of this sort could be
said to represent the people. Despite his use of the language of "portraiture"
and "miniature," he was not remotely interested in endorsing the parliamentarian "imaging" theory of representation. His point was simply that an
assembly would not be able to play its proper institutional role within a
mixed constitutional scheme unless it reflected the composition of the body
of the people: his claim, in other words, was about what makes popular assemblies *effective,* not about what entitles them to claim that they represent
the people.[57] Adams's answer to this latter question was the same as ever:
any authorized agency represents the people, whether one man, a few, or
many. He accordingly went on to ask "whether it is wisest to leave all the
Powers of Legislation in this single Body, or to make your Legislature more
complex?" Adams answered first that "I think a People cannot be long happy
or free, whose Laws are made only by one Assembly," and so defended bicameralism against the arguments of Paine and his allies.[58] This fear of rule

by "one Assembly," as Adams would make clear in the second draft of the essay, was motivated by a very specific example: "A Single Assembly will become ambitious, and after Some Time will vote itself perpetual. This was found in the Case of the long Parliament."[59] But even after two legislative chambers have duly been established, "an Inquiry will arise, is the Legislature compleat?" Adams's answer is both clear and familiar: "I think not. There should be a third Branch, which for the Sake of preserving old Style and Titles, you may call a Governor whom I would invest with a Negative upon the other Branches of the Legislature and also with the whole Executive Power."[60] Adams's wording here is noteworthy: the absolute "negative" with which the governor is to be entrusted is distinct from "the whole Executive Power," which he is also to be given. It is only in virtue of possessing a negative voice that Adams's proposed chief magistrate would constitute "a third branch" of the legislature.

Adams knew perfectly well that his prerogativist constitutional theory would find few ready subscribers in the early months of 1776. Accordingly, even in this first draft of what became *Thoughts on Government,* he began to anticipate objections and add language intended to soften the Royalist tenor of the proposal: "I know," he wrote to Hooper, "that giving the Executive Power a Negative upon the Legislative, is liable to Objections, but it seems to be attended with more Advantages, than Dangers, especially if you make this Officer elected annually, and more especially if you establish a Rotation by which no Man shall be Governor for more than three years."[61] He further insisted that the chief magistrate he envisioned would be divested "of most of those Badges of Domination call'd Prerogatives"[62]—this despite the fact that he would continue to possess the single prerogative power that the parliamentarian tradition had most thoroughly stigmatized (i.e., the negative voice). By the time the pamphlet was finally published, Adams had softened his language yet further. Whereas in the first draft, as in the "Novanglus" letters, he had insisted that "the British Constitution itself is Republican"—thus reconciling liberty and prerogative—he amended the final text to read instead that "there is no good government but what is Republican. That the only valuable part of the British constitution is so."[63] Only *part* of the British constitution, presumably the House of Commons,[64] was now to be styled as "Republican" in character. And Adams's proposal to create a chief magistrate who would himself constitute a third branch of the legislature likewise reappeared in a milder form, hedged round about with apologies and concessions:

Let [the two legislative chambers] unite, and by joint ballot choose a Governor, who, after being stripped of most of those badges of domination, called prerogatives, should have a free and independent exercise of his judgment, and be made also an integral part of the legislature. This, I know, is liable to objections; and, if you please, you may make him only President of the Council, as in Connecticut. But as the Governor is to be invested with the executive power, with consent of Council, I think he ought to have a negative upon the legislative. If he is annually elective, as he ought to be, he will always have so much reverence and affection for the People, their Representatives and Counsellors, that, although you give him an independent exercise of his judgment, he will seldom use it in opposition to the two Houses, except in cases the public utility of which would be conspicuous; and some such cases would happen.[65]

Indeed, by May 1776, Adams was clearly ready to contemplate a tactical retreat in the face of the considerable opposition that his proposal had aroused in Massachusetts. He now wrote to James Warren that "I dont expect, nor indeed desire that it should be attempted to give the Governor a Negative, in our Colony. Make him President, with a casting Voice."[66] By August, he was even less sanguine. Writing of his "little pamphlet" to Francis Dana, he observed that "the Negative given in it to the first Magistrate will be adopted no Where but in S. Carolina."[67] The citizens of Massachusetts, he had learned, "will call their Government a Commonwealth. Let Us take the Name, manfully, and Let the first Executive Magistrate be the Head of the Council board, and no more." "Our people," he added resignedly, "will never Submit to more, and I am not clear that it is best they should."[68] It was time, he had evidently concluded, to cut his losses.

Adams had judged the mood of his countrymen correctly. Although *Thoughts on Government* was widely read, and although its defense of bicameralism proved extremely influential throughout the former colonies, its qualified endorsement of prerogative power in a third legislative branch found few early defenders. As predicted, of the states that adopted new constitutions in 1776, only South Carolina followed Adams's initial advice. New Hampshire, Virginia, New Jersey, Delaware, Maryland, and North Carolina instead entrusted their new governors only with the execution of laws passed by two legislative chambers—and Pennsylvania famously adopted its radical whig constitution, assigning "the supreme legislative power" to a single "house of representatives of the freemen of the Commonwealth or state" and creating a wholly subservient, plural executive.[69] Unsurprisingly, it was none other than James Wilson who mustered the opposition to Pennsylvania's experiment. On October 17, Wilson and his allies called a large meeting in Philadelphia's Philosophical Hall to "consider of a mode to set aside sundry improper and unconstitutional rules laid down by the late Convention, in what they call their Plan or Frame of Government."[70] The group adopted a series of thirty-one resolves, clearly drafted by Wilson himself, laying out its objections. First and foremost, they charged "that the said Constitution unnecessarily deviates from all resemblance to the former Government of this State, to which the people have been accustomed."[71] "The people," Wilson wrote, "did not desire such strange innovations, but only that the kingly, parliamentary, and proprietary powers should be totally abolished, and such alterations made as would thereby be rendered necessary, so that a well-formed Government might be established, solely on the authority of the people." In other words, the people had wanted only to eliminate those aspects of their constitution that provided for their connection to Great Britain, not to change the fundamental *structure* of their constitution. As Wilson (or a close ally) would put it in May of 1777, writing under the pseudonym "Associator" in the *Pennsylvania Journal*, "instead of giving us the old government, as near as possible, (after expunging all royal, parliamentary and proprietary authority) a government which suited the habits and inclinations of the People; they have given us one, full of whimsies—a government with only one legislative branch, which never yet failed to end in tyranny. . . . Suppose we had been prevailed upon to submit to the acts of Parliament? A submission to the present tyranny will be equally absurd and dangerous."[72] The Pennsylvania constitution was to be rejected because it threatened to create a new tyrannical Parliament with the power to legislate "in all cases whatsoever."[73]

Indeed, as Wilson argued in the "Resolves," Pennsylvania's folly was to have deviated from the constitutional principles that had animated Congress's "first petition to the King of Great Britain."[74] That petition, Wilson reminded his readers, had been lodged in opposition to unchecked legislative power and in defense of the independent prerogatives of the crown. Yet the Pennsylvania Constitution "establishes only a single Legislative body" and "renders the Executive dependent on that single Legislative body; by whom alone the Executive officers are to be paid for their services; and by whom, from the great disproportion between the numbers of the Assembly

and Council, the President and Vice President must always be annually chosen." "In truth," Wilson declared, "the Legislative, Executive, and Judicial
powers, may be said to be united in one body—the Assembly, though there
is a semblance, on a slight view, of their being separated."[75] All of this despite "the sentiments of the most distinguished writers on the subject of
Government," chiefly "the Baron De *Montesquieu*," who composed "a long
and much-admired chapter on the *English* constitution, wherein he greatly
commends its distribution of Legislative power into several branches, &c."
Correct constitutional principles, in short, demand the creation of "several"
branches of the legislature, not merely two. Here again we find Wilson defending the negative voice that he had championed so tirelessly during the
imperial crisis.

His trusted ally Benjamin Rush—who in 1768 had excoriated "the usurping Commons" for "endeavor[ing] to rob the King of his supremacy over
the colonies and divide it among themselves"[76]—elaborated on this defense
of prerogative power in a series of contributions to the same coordinated
newspaper campaign. As "Ludlow," he took up an argument frequently offered by advocates of the new constitution: "We are told that the state of
Pennsylvania has always been governed by a single legislature, and therefore, that part of our Constitution is not an innovation."[77] But this claim, he
countered, is "without any foundation." Under Pennsylvania's colonial constitution, "the Governor always had a negative power upon our laws, and
was a distinct branch of our legislature." To be sure, Rush added in a nod to
the anti-monarchical enthusiasms of the moment, "it is true, he sometimes
exercised his power to the disadvantage of the people; for he was the servant
of a King who possessed an interest distinct from that of his people, and in
some cases the Governor himself possessed an interest incompatible with
the rights of the people. God forbid that ever we should see a resurrection of
his power in Pennsylvania." But, Rush continued, "I am obliged to own,
that I have known instances in which the *whole* state have thanked him for,
the interposition of his negative amendments upon the acts of the Assembly. Even the Assembly-men themselves have acknowledged the justice of
his conduct upon these occasions, by condemning in their cooler hours,
their own hasty, and ill digested resolutions."[78] Yet the framers of the new
constitution had clearly forgotten this vital lesson. They ought to have
heeded the advice of the author of *Thoughts on Government*, whom Rush
identifies for the first time as John Adams,[79] but instead they denied their

president "a negative upon the laws of the Assembly," thus destroying his "authority and influence in the state."[80] Rush closes with an extraordinary observation:

> It has been said often, and I wish the saying was engraven over the doors of every State-House on the continent, that "all power is *derived* from the people," but it has never yet been said, that all power is *seated* in the people. . . . History shews us that the people soon grow weary of the folly and tyranny of one another. They prefer one to many masters, and stability to instability of slavery. They prefer a Julius Caesar to a Senate, and a Cromwell to a perpetual Parliament.[81]

Power, though derived from the people by authorization, may be "seated" in any constellation of magistrates, and, if the people are wise, they will entrust some of it to a single chief magistrate armed with a negative voice. The alternative is rule by a "perpetual Parliament," which will end in the tyranny of one. Indeed, there is no government more dangerous than one in which "the supreme, absolute, and uncontrolled power of the whole State is lodged in the hands of *one body* of men."[82] Echoing the writings of Hicks and Hamilton from the early 1770s, Rush insists that "had it been lodged in the hands of one man, it would have been less dangerous to the safety and liberties of the community."[83]

In 1777, the first signs arrived that the ideological winds were beginning to shift yet again. New York adopted a new constitution that provided for the popular election of its governor—thus securing his independence from the two houses of the legislature—and assigned him a "qualified" negative over legislation (i.e., one that could be overridden by a supermajority of legislators).[84] But, at the same time, the constitution imposed considerable constraints on the exercise of the negative by mandating that the governor could only wield it in conjunction with a "Council to Revise," composed of the state's supreme court judges and the chancellor. (It likewise created a four-member council of appointment, in which the governor was assigned merely "a casting voice, with no other vote."[85]) One New Yorker in particular welcomed the document as a significant advance over the previous state constitutions, while still lamenting that it had not gone much further in the Royalist direction. Alexander Hamilton had joined the New York Artillery only weeks after publishing *The Farmer Refuted* and later became Washington's aide-de-camp. He wrote from the front to the New York Committee of

Correspondence on May 7, 1777, to offer his observations on the state's new "form of government." "Without flattery," he began, "I consider [it] as far more judicious and digested than any thing of the kind, that has yet appeared among us; though I am not so unreserved in my approbation as to think it free from defects."[86] Indeed, "while I view it in the main, as a wise and excellent system, I freely confess it appears to me to have some faults, which I could wish did not exist. Were it not too late to discuss particulars for any useful end, or could my judgment have any weight in a matter, which is the work of so many far more able and discerning, than I can pretend to be, I should willingly descend to an exhibition of those parts I dislike, and my reasons for disapproving. But, in the present situation of things, it would be both useless and presumptuous."[87]

Hamilton did, however, eagerly "descend to an exhibition of those parts" that he disliked in a private letter to Gouverneur Morris of Pennsylvania, dated May 19. Morris had written to Hamilton that "I think it [the new constitution] deficient for the Want of Vigor in the executive unstable from the very Nature of popular elective Governments and dilatory from the Complexity of the Legislature. For the first I apologize by hinting the Spirit which now reigns in America suspiciously Cautious."[88] Hamilton too bemoaned the "suspiciously Cautious" attitude toward prerogative power that now reigned throughout the former colonies and wrote back to express his full agreement with Morris: "That there is a want of vigor in the executive, I believe will be found true."[89] Indeed, throughout the winter encampment of 1777, despite the frenzied antimonarchism of the moment and the whig resurgence that was taking place all around him, Hamilton threw himself into a careful study of the proper form and extent of prerogative power in the context of a well-poised mixed monarchy. His military "Pay Book" from this period contains an extensive set of annotations on passages from three of Plutarch's *Lives*—those of Lycurgus, Romulus, and Theseus (the last two of which are paired in one of Plutarch's "comparisons," or *synkriseis*). The selection was not haphazard. Each of these essays contains a lengthy analysis of monarchical constitutions, and Hamilton's notes focus almost exclusively on these discussions.[90] Moreover, in the hands of John Dryden (who had composed the translation that Hamilton was using), the passages in question were transformed into commentaries on the nature and extent of "prerogative"—a concept that, needless to say, is entirely foreign to Plutarch's Greek.[91]

Hamilton begins by commenting on a claim from the *Lycurgus*: "The having two Kings, the senate and the Ephori are considered by Aristotle [*sic*][92] as the causes of the duration of the Spartan government."[93] Here Hamilton bristles, editorializing that "the first circumstance would be in modern times a source of endless confusion and distraction."[94] Despite Plutarch's assurances, only a single chief magistrate would do. Hamilton then reproduces a slightly altered version of Plutarch's account of how the Spartan monarchy had achieved its proper balance (as translated by Dryden):

> However careful Lycurgus was to temper the constitution, it is said the power of the Kings and senate was found to be too great and sometimes oppressive, which induced Theopompus, one of their Kings, to establish the Ephori. These were five in number chosen among the people for a year. Their authority was very extensive. Theopompus, when his Queen upbraided him one way [day] that he would leave the regal power to his children less than he had received it from his ancestors, replied that he would have it greater because more durable. For the prerogative being thus kept within reasonable bounds were secured both from envy and dangers.[95]

In Plutarch's Greek, Theopompus is merely said to have "cast aside envy and danger."[96] But Dryden's version of the passage is about maintaining the "prerogative" within its "reasonable bounds," thus securing a balanced monarchical constitution. Hamilton likewise reproduces a similar passage from the Romulus/Theseus *synkrisis*:

> For a Prince's first concern ought to be the preservation of the government itself; and in order to do this, he should neither claim more authority than is his due, nor on the other hand give up any part of his prerogative. Whoever gives up his right, or extends his claim too far, is no more a king, but either a slave to the people or a tyrant, and so becomes odious or contemptible to his subjects. The one seems to be the fault of easiness and good nature, the other of pride and severity.[97]

But here Hamilton adds an interesting note of dissent: "A false sentiment; it would often be praise worthy in a prince to relinquish a part of an excessive prerogative to establish a more moderate government, better adapted to the happiness or temper of his people!"[98] It is false, in other words, to claim that the prerogative should be maintained and preserved *no matter its initial extent*. What Hamilton now wanted, and what he had defended in *The Farmer*

Refuted two years earlier, was a robust prerogative "within reasonable bounds" at the center of a true mixed monarchy.[99] It is for this reason that Hamilton was so drawn to the comparison between Theseus and Romulus: neither of these rulers, Dryden's Plutarch reports, "preserved the proper character of a King."[100] Theseus surrendered too much power to the people, thus converting the Athenian regime into an ignoble democracy; Romulus hoarded too much power for the Crown, thereby making of Rome a tyranny. Hamilton uses these texts to think through the sort of balanced monarchical government that he would propose for the American states and, eventually, for the United States.

As early as 1780, Hamilton found himself engaged in an extensive set of conversations about the infirmities of the Articles of Confederation, which had reposed all federal power in a single legislative chamber (the Congress). A major "defect of our system," he wrote to James Duane on September 3rd, "is want of method and energy in the administration."[101] This defect, he explained, resulted partly from a lack of sufficient federal power *tout court,* "but in a great degree from prejudice and the want of a proper executive. Congress have kept the power too much into their own hands and have meddled too much with details of every sort. Congress is properly a deliberative corps and it forgets itself when it attempts to play the executive. It is impossible such a body, numerous as it is, constantly fluctuating, can ever act with sufficient decision, or with system."[102] At this stage, Hamilton was merely endorsing the proposal, then under consideration in Congress, to appoint a "single man" to run "each department of the administration," in the manner of "ministers" (or "executive ministers," as he called them in a letter to a French correspondent dated February 7, 1781.)[103] But by the time he took up his pen as "The Continentalist" in July of the same year, his rhetoric had gone very much further. He began by confronting the widespread concern that any increase in federal power would threaten American liberty.

> In a single state, where the sovereign power is exercised by delegation, whether it be a limited monarchy or a republic, the danger most commonly is, that the sovereign will become too powerful for his constituents; in federal governments, where different states are represented in a general council, the danger is on the other side—that the members will be an overmatch for the common head, or in other words, that it will not have sufficient influences and authority to secure the obedience of the several parts of the confederacy.[104]

Unlike Adams, Hamilton makes clear that, on his account, a "limited monarchy" is to be contrasted with a "republic"; the former is not merely one possible species of the latter. Hamilton's chief purpose, however, is to assure his readers that, in federal structures, the great worry is that the "members will be an overmatch for the common head," introducing dangerous instability and indecision, not that the common head will "overmatch" the members.[105] Indeed, he continues, the only reason that the Dutch United Provinces have managed to avoid the chaotic "extremities" to which composite states so often fall prey is because "the authority of the Stadtholder [the chief magistrate of the union] pervades the whole frame of the republic, and is a kind of common link by which the provinces are bound together."[106] This, of course, is straightforwardly the patriot Royalist language of 1774–1775. Only "the person and prerogative of the King," Hamilton had insisted in The Farmer Refuted, could serve as "the connecting, pervading principle" for the various, distinct dominions of the British Empire, or, as Jefferson had put it, "the central link connecting the several parts of the empire thus newly multiplied."[107] The vision of a single chief magistrate wielding his prerogative at the center of a confederated set of dominions remained Hamilton's touchstone as he confronted the confederation crisis.

III

Despite the first stirrings of anti-whig sentiment in New York in 1777, it was undoubtedly the ratification of the new Massachusetts Constitution in 1780 that marked the end of the wilderness years for patriot Royalism. The Massachusetts Assembly had drafted a proposed constitution in 1778 and sent it to the various towns for ratification, only to suffer an embarrassing defeat. Much of the opposition to this initial draft—which had assigned no negative voice to the governor—had been impeccably whig in character. The town of Beverly, for example, explained in its official reply that "Representation, which is the very basis and support of freedom in a large society, is the most exceptionable article in this Constitution."[108] Any body claiming to "to represent the People" must "be a miniature of the whole, so it ought to be, in justice and good policy too, an exact one: and the difficulty of making it so, however great, must be surmounted." But the new assembly envisioned in the draft constitution was too small and badly configured: "The power thus placed in their hands, combined with the almost irresistible allurements of interest will offer such a violent temptation to them to do wrong . . . but on the other hand, if that Body be a fair and exact Epitome of the whole People, or, in other words, if the Representation be equal, it will be invariably for their interest to do strict justice; whatever is for the interest of the people at large will be for theirs too, so that the general good will be their object."[109] Only an assembly that constitutes a proper "miniature," or "epitome," of the people as a whole may be said to represent them. This was straightforwardly the whig, parliamentarian theory of representation.

But at least one major intervention in the debate over this first proposed constitution took a decidedly different view. The authors of the "Essex Result" argued that the draft constitution was, in fact, overly enthralled to whig principles and placed far too much power in the new assembly. Their written response, as John Adams recalled in later years, was "in general agreeable to the Principles" of his own *Thoughts on Government* and clearly proved influential, although, as Adams somewhat defensively added, "the Essex Junto . . . need not be so vain glorious as to arrogate to themselves the honor of being the Founders of the Massachusetts Constitution."[110] Here once again the greatest threat to liberty was said to be a renegade parliament:

> The legislative power must not be trusted with one assembly. A single assembly is frequently influenced by the vices, follies, passions, and prejudices of an individual. It is liable to be avaricious, and to exempt itself from the burdens it lays upon it's constituents. It is subject to ambition, and after a series of years, will be prompted to vote itself perpetual. The long parliament in England voted itself perpetual, and thereby, for a time, destroyed the political liberty of the subject. Holland was governed by one representative assembly annually elected. They afterwards voted themselves from annual to septennial; then for life; and finally exerted the power of filling up all vacancies, without application to their constituents. The government of Holland is now a tyranny *though a republic.*[111]

The final phrase of this passage is worth remarking upon. In the republican tradition, the terms "tyranny" and "republic" had always been mutually exclusive. A republic, by definition, was a regime in which arbitrary power had been abolished and all free citizens governed themselves through a representative assembly. To speak of a "tyrannical republic" was, accordingly, to speak nonsense. Here, in contrast, a "republic" is merely a kingless regime and, as such, may come in any number of forms—including the arbitrary, tyrannical rule of a Long Parliament.

This pronounced fear of legislative tyranny prompted the authors of the report to offer a crucial objection to the draft constitution: "We cannot discover . . . in any part of the constitution that the executive power is entrusted with a check upon the legislative power, sufficient to prevent the encroachment of the latter upon the former." The executive power, they announced (in terms that would echo in the 1780s), must be wielded "with union, vigour, and dispatch."[112] In order to secure this power, they proposed two significant amendments to the frame of government drafted by the convention. First, they rejected the provision empowering the Senate and House of Representatives to select as governor any of the three candidates who received the highest number of popular votes:[113] "Should the supreme executive officer be elected by the legislative body, there would be a dependence of the executive power upon the legislative. . . . The people at large must therefore designate the person, to whom they will delegate this power."[114] Only pure popular election could secure the independent power of the chief magistrate as representative of the people; if selected by the legislature, he would be a mere creature of factional interests. But the authors more stridently challenged the whig pieties of the moment by proposing that the governor, "with the consent of the privy council," should be authorized to "negative any law, proposed to be enacted by the legislative body." Their reason was both straightforward and familiar: "Where this check was wanting," the "legislative in all states" had invariably attempted to "encroach" on the executive power, "stripping it of all it's rights."[115] "The freedom of the state" was accordingly "destroyed." This brand of legislative usurpation, the authors explained, "hath resulted from that lust of domination, which in some degree influences all men, and all bodies of men." The absolute negative voice would tame this *libido dominandi,* ensuring that "the executive power will be preserved entire—the encroachments of the legislature will be repelled, and the powers of both be properly balanced." Moreover, "all the business of the legislative body will be brought into one point, and subject to an impartial consideration on a regular consistent plan." There was no danger to be feared from empowering the chief magistrate in this manner. Echoing Benjamin Rush, the authors observed that "this Governor is not appointed by a King, or his ministry, nor does he receive instructions from a party of men, who are pursuing an interest diametrically opposite to the good of the state. His interest is the same with that of every man in the state."[116] Indeed, the only danger is that "he will be too cautious of using his negative for the interest of the state." This was an extraordinary argument to be offering in 1778, but it was a harbinger of things to come.

After the first draft constitution went down to defeat in the towns, Adams, freshly returned from France, took charge of preparing a second proposal. He wrote to Elbridge Gerry in August 1779 to say that "I am about to assist in the Formation of a new Constitution—a Subject which has been, out of my Head, so long, that I have forgotten, most of the Reflections I ever had about it."[117] Gerry answered that he was "happy to find that the State of Massachusetts has your Assistance in forming a Constitution," but he immediately raised a serious concern.[118] He had been "informed, that You are clearly in Favour of giving to the Governor a negative Power, in legislative Matters." This, Gerry recognized, "is a great Question, and I am fully persuaded that You have traced it, to its original principles, compared it with Circumstances of the Times, weighed with Accuracy the Advantages and Disadvantages resulting from each Determination thereof, and finally decided in favour of the proposition." "But," he continued, "granting, that upon a general Scale, the Measure is wise, yet is there not too much Reason to apprehend from it, great Injuries, and that the Community will be endangered, thereby?"[119] Adams replied as follows:

> I am clear for Three Branches, in the Legislature, and the Committee have reported as much, tho aukwardly expressed. I have considered this Question in every Light in which my Understanding is capable of placing it, and my Opinion is decided in favour of Three Branches. And being, very unexpectedly called upon to give my Advice to my Countrymen, concerning a Form of Government, I could not answer it to myself, to them, or Posterity, if I concealed or disguised my real Sentiments. They have been received with candor, but perhaps will not be adopted. In such a State as this, however, I am perswaded, We never shall have any Stability, Dignity, Decision, or Liberty, without it. We have so many Men of Wealth, of ambitious Spirits, of Intrigue, of Luxury and Corruption, that incessant Factions will disturb our Peace, without it. And indeed there is too much reason to fear with it. The Execu-

tive, which ought to be the Reservoir of Wisdom, as the Legislature is of Liberty, without this Weapon of Defence will be run down like a Hare before the Hunters.[120]

Adams argues that the executive must be armed with the negative voice in order to tame the factional proclivities of oligarchic legislatures. The chief magistrate alone transcends such divisions and, in "wisdom," seeks the good of the whole.[121]

Adams's proposed draft of the constitution accordingly provided that there should be three branches of the legislature, one of which would be constituted by a governor armed with an absolute negative voice. His proposal was then amended in several crucial respects by the full drafting committee. The final text provided that "the department of legislation shall be formed by two branches, a *Senate* and a *House of Representatives*," not the three that Adams had desired.[122] He raised this issue in a November 4 letter to Benjamin Rush, acknowledging that "if the Committee had boldly made the Legislature consist of three Branches, I should have been better pleased."[123] The significance of the amendment, Adams recognized, was considerable. On his Royalist view, the chief magistrate was not to be regarded as a mere "executive," but as a co-equal branch of the legislature itself. Moreover, while the committee retained Adams's language providing that "the first magistrate shall have a negative upon all the laws—that he may have power to preserve the independence of the executive and judicial departments," the full convention attached an override provision, very much like the one adopted in New York.[124] Adams would later come to regret this alteration a great deal, but in October 1780 he wrote to Jonathan Jackson that "the substitute for the Governors Negative is generally thought an Amelioration: and I must confess it is So wisely guarded, that it has quite reconciled me."[125]

Notwithstanding these significant amendments, the second draft constitution presented to the freemen of Massachusetts for ratification was a document unlike any that had received serious consideration in the new United States since 1776. The "Address of the Convention," which introduced the text to the citizenry of the commonwealth, made perfectly clear that this was no whig frame of government. "The Power of Revising, and stating objections to any Bill or Resolve that shall be passed by the two Houses," they declared, "we were of opinion ought to be lodged in the hands of some *one* person; not only to preserve the Laws from being unsymmetrical and inaccurate, but that a due balance may be preserved in the three capital powers of Government. The Legislative, the Judicial and Executive Powers naturally exist in every Government." But the crucial claim was to follow: "The Governor is emphatically the Representative of the whole People, being chosen not by one Town or County, but by the People at large. We have therefore thought it safest to rest this Power in his hands."[126] With this statement, the Massachusetts Convention unmistakably repudiated the whig theory of representation and the form of constitutionalism that it had underwritten in the four years following independence. A single chief magistrate, they now declared, could perfectly well count as a representative of the people. Indeed, *only* a single chief magistrate could reliably speak for "the whole people," since he would be beholden to no single faction or segment of society. It was therefore no infringement on the liberty of citizens to grant him a (qualified) negative voice. The will of the governor was not an "alien will."

Once again, over 200 townships throughout Massachusetts submitted written responses to the draft constitution—a "Phenominon," Adams enthused from his second posting in Paris, that is "new and Singular" and "forms a Kind of Epocha, in the History of the Progress of Society"[127]—but this time around their comments were of a very different sort. The town of Groton, for example, incorporated a great deal of the language from the convention's "Address" into their reply, but criticized it, in effect, for having amended Adams's original constitutional design: they were "of opinion that the Legislative Power of the Common Wealth ought to Consist of three Branches the Governor being one Branch thereof and vested with the power of a Negative upon all Laws and Acts of Legislation passed by the Senate and House."[128] The convention did wrong, in other words, in depriving the governor of a full "negative voice," thereby leaving the legislature with only two proper branches. Placing a full negative "in the hands of the Governor will have a manifest Tendency to prevent the other Branches from making dangerous encroachments upon the Executive and Judicial Departments, preserve a proper Balance in the three Capital powers of Government and make the Acts of Legislation more systematical and Coherent." "The Governor," after all, "is the Representative of the whole People and the first Magistrate of the Common Wealth."[129]

But the most extraordinary response to the proposed constitution came from the town of Wells, far to the north of Massachusetts (in present-day Maine).[130] Like the Groton committee, the drafters of the Wells report began by proposing that "the Governor might have a [full] Negative on all Acts of the Legislature."[131] "We think it very necessary," they explained, "that the Independance of the Executive and Judicial Departments be well secured—Nor can We conceive how this can be done effectually unless there be a Power lodged somewhere of negativing such legislative Acts as tend to destroy or violate this Independancy—And We are clearly of opinion that the Governor will be the most fit person to be intrusted with this Power; he being the first Magistrate and the Sole Representative of the whole Commonwealth." But the authors then added an excursus that was entirely their own. The governor, they insisted, will constitute "the Center of the Union to all the several parts and members of the political Body; who is chosen and constituted by the whole Community to be in a peculiar manner the Guardian of the Constitution and of the Rights and Interests of the whole State—All the Individuals have a like Interest in him and stand in a like Relation to him as their common Representative."[132] With legislative assemblies, the case is very different: "We can not but think it would be extremely dangerous and impolitick to trust an incontroulable Power of Legislation in the Hands of those who are only the Representatives of particular and smaller Districts of the Commonwealth; who may often be disposed to act upon the private narrow Views and Interests of their particular Constituents to the prejudice of the publick Welfair and the Injury of other parts of the Community." Indeed, they continued, "when we consider that the several Members of the Legislative Body are to be chosen only by particular Districts as their special Representatives and may not improbably be often chosen for the very purpose of serving and promoting such Views and Designs of their Constituents as would be injurious to other parts of the State," the dangers of assembly government become perfectly clear. It follows that "we cannot but think that the Representatives of the Whole People who can have no reason to act under the Influence of such partial Biases and Respects should be furnished with ample and Sufficient Powers to prevent effectively the pernicious Consequences of such narrow Policy, as is calculated to serve the Interest of one part to the injury of another who may happen not to have an equal Interest in the Legislature."[133]

The authors went on to explain that their heightened sensitivity to the dangers of legislative power, and the corresponding need to invest the chief magistrate with sweeping prerogatives, arose chiefly out of their experience of life on the periphery of a political community. "The distant parts" of the commonwealth, such as Wells, "may Scarce have a single Member to Speak and act on their Behalf" in the legislature, and, accordingly, the two chambers "may be prevailed upon to pass Bills injurious, oppressive and pernicious to a great part of the people."[134] The authors continued by observing— in language that should sound very familiar—that "as We with divers other parts of the State are like to be always remote from the Seat of Government and can seldom if ever expect to be equally represented in the Legislature or to have an equal Interest in the same with those parts of the State that are near the Capital[,] We cannot think it safe that an uncontroulable power of disposing of our Persons and properties should be vested in a Legislature in which it may sometimes happen that we are not represented and by Reason of our distance are seldom likely to have an equal Interest in it with most of our fellow Citizens."[135] But however estranged they might be from the metropolitan legislature, "we shall always have a Representative in the Person of our Governor, we may claim an equal Interest in him with the other parts of the State. If a partial or misguided Legislature should bear hard upon us his Protection may be claimed his Justice may be appealed to his Interposition may reasonably be hoped for." The authors "therefore think it highly reasonable and necessary that the common Representative of the people, who may sometimes be our principal or only Representative in the general Court chosen by us to act on our behalf, may have his Hand at full Liberty and may be empowered to act effectually and with strong Arm for the Protection of all and every part of his Constituents as there may be occasion." Indeed, the citizens of Wells saw no "danger in deligating ample powers to the common Representative for the publick Service in Superintending the Affairs of the Commonwealth," in part because "we cannot learn that our governors under the late Constitution, though holding their Commissions intirely at the pleasure of the British Crown have been wont to abuse their negativing power to the injury and vexation of the subject unless when they have acted by special Instructions."[136]

It is striking that this explicit repurposing of the patriot Royalist argument draws so precise an analogy between the predicament of a town such as Wells in 1780 and that of the American colonies before independence.

Both were peripheral communities, distant from the metropolis and sparsely populated in relation to it. They would rarely, if ever, send representatives to the legislature that claimed the right to govern them—a "partial" legislature in which the powerful, sectarian interests of wealthy and densely populated areas would inevitably hold sway. They accordingly placed their faith in the chief magistrate, their "common representative," on the grounds that they could "claim an equal Interest in him with the other parts of the State." Only his "interposition" could safely be relied upon to defend their rights and liberties. The degree to which all of this recapitulates the patriot discourse of the imperial crisis is clear. Hamilton, we should recall, had defended his expansive vision of the royal prerogative in 1775 by arguing that the King "is under no temptation to purchase the favour of one part of his dominions, at the expense of another; but, it is his interest to treat them all, upon the same footing. Very different is the case with regard to the Parliament. The Lords and Commons both, have a private and separate interest to pursue."[137] This had likewise been the view of William Hicks, who had written as early as 1766 that he would willingly shelter himself "under the Wings of the Royal Prerogative"—for while members of Parliament "would naturally endeavour to lessen their own Burthens, and gratify the Wishes of their Constituents by sacrificing to Them the Interests of the Colonies," the Americans, "as loyal and industrious Subjects," may "expect impartial Favour from our Prince; who must reasonably regard with an equal Eye the Happiness and Welfare of all his Dominions."[138] With the ratification of the Massachusetts Constitution, patriot Royalism had unmistakably returned to prominence in the former colonies.

IV

Among the first to greet the newly ratified Massachusetts Constitution was James Wilson, who wrote in April of 1780 to inform Adams that he had "been favoured . . . with the Perusal of the Plan of a Constitution for Massachusetts, reported by a Committee of the Convention of that Commonwealth. From the masterly Strokes of profound Jurisprudence, and of refined and enlarged Policy, which distinguish that Performance, I can easily trace it to its Author."[139] "The Constitution of every State in the Union," Wilson observed, "is interesting to the Citizens of every other State; as each spreads, in some Degree, its Influence over all. For this Reason, I feel a very sensible Pleasure, when I see a Prospect that happy Governments will be established around me. This Sentiment has, in no Instance, been more highly gratified, than by the Plan reported for the Government of Massachusetts." Adams duly replied that "the approbation of So able a Judge, of the Report of a Constitution for Mass[achusetts] gives me great Consolation. I never Spent Six Weeks in a manner that I shall ever reflect upon with more Pleasure than with that Society of Wise men who composed that Convention. So much Caution, Moderation, Sagacity and Integrity, has not often been together in this World."[140] He conceded that "the Convention have made alterations in the Plan: but these are done with so much Prudence and fortified with so much ability that I dare not Say they are not for the better."

Wilson's hope that the Massachusetts Constitution would "spread its influence" to his home state was not in vain. The 1780s witnessed a fierce debate in Pennsylvania over the radical whig constitution of 1776, culminating (under Wilson's own leadership) in the adoption of a revised frame of government in 1790, which duly created a bicameral legislature and a governor vested with a qualified veto.[141] The relationship between this new document and the one composed by Adams was lost on no one. On June 30, 1784, "A Peace Maker" wrote in *The Pennsylvania Journal* that "I think it [the proposed revision of the Pennsylvania Constitution] bears the strongest resemblance to the constitution of Massachusetts-Bay."[142] "That constitution," he continued, "was composed by some of the wisest men, and greatest friends to democratical government, in the United States—by men who taught *us* and most of the states by their writings and examples to love liberty, and to oppose tyranny, whether it came from Kings, Lords, or the people." Indeed, "I am told that the Senate, and the powers of the Governor (which are so very great) in that constitution were supported in the convention and carried through chiefly by Mr. Samuel [*sic*] Adams."[143] The granting of these new powers, in turn, had signaled the maturation of American constitutional theory: "We have been so long habituated to a jealousy of tyranny from monarchy and aristocracy, that we have yet to learn the dangers of it from *democracy*. Trace the history of tyranny in most countries, and you will find that men have fled from the oppressions of one another, or of *many*, to the oppressions of a *few*—and from these, they have at last retreated to tyranny of *one*." Once again summoning the ghost of the Long Parliament, "A Peace Maker" reminded his readers that "it was to escape the tyranny of the independents that other sects of dissenters, joined with the cavaliers in placing Charles the 2nd upon the English Throne."[144]

The defenders of the 1776 constitution, of course, saw things very differently. Those who composed the "Dissent to the Revision of the Pennsylvania Constitution" declared that "the alterations proposed . . . tend to introduce among the citizens new and aristocratic ranks, with a chief magistrate at their head, vested with powers exceeding those which fall to the ordinary lot of kings. We are sufficiently assured, that the good people of Pennsylvania, most ardently love equal liberty, and that they abhor all attempts to lift one class of citizens above the heads of the reast [sic], and much more the elevating of any one citizen to the throne of royalty."[145] Indeed, since all recognized that the royal negative had gone into abeyance in Britain a century earlier, the claim that the powers granted to the governor under the proposed revision exceeded "those which fall to the ordinary lot of kings" was not an absurd one. The "Address of the Minority of the Council of Censors," published in *The Pennsylvania Gazette* on January 28, 1784, likewise encouraged citizens to "tremble at the enormous powers that are to be wrested out of your hands, and lodged in your future governor."[146] In addition to creating an "Upper House" of the legislature, stocked with "the better sort of people" and vested with "full power to prevent any law from passing, which a number of honest farmers from the country may judge to be salutary and beneficial to the state," the citizens of Pennsylvania are also "earnestly requested to invest your Governor or King (for it matters not by what name you may call him) with absolute power to put a negative on any bill, which both Houses may agree to enact, unless he be so poor, or avaricious as not to be able to bribe one third of either House to adhere to the alterations he may be pleased to make."[147] In other words, the new "Governor or King" would need only to secure the cooperation of one-third of the legislature in order to render his "negative voice" as absolute as the one that had been wielded by the Stuart monarchs before England's troubles.

But such voices were now becoming increasingly beleaguered themselves. The perceived shortcomings of the first state constitutions, as well as the abject failure of the Articles of Confederation and the single assembly at its head, had provoked yet another turning of the ideological tide. Even Jefferson had come around to some degree. His revised draft constitution for Virginia, composed in the late spring of 1783 (after he had served two terms as governor of the commonwealth), extended the proposed gubernatorial term of office from one year to five, placed the "whole military of the state" under the governor's control, and broadly assigned him "those powers . . . which are necessary to carry into execution the laws, and which are not in their nature [either legislative or] Judiciary." "The application of this idea," Jefferson was now prepared to concede, "must be left to reason."[148] Most importantly, his revised draft followed the model of the New York Constitution by entrusting the governor (in conjunction with a "Council of Revision") with a qualified veto over legislation.[149] The great worry was no longer prerogative power in the chief magistrate but rather the *elective despotism* threatened by the rule of an unchecked assembly.[150] As Jefferson would put the same point four years later, "the executive in our governments is not the sole, it is scarcely the principal object of my jealousy. The tyranny of the legislatures is the most formidable dread at present, and will be for long years."[151]

Indeed, as John Adams sat down to answer Turgot in 1786 with his *Defence of the Constitutions of Government of the United States,* he had every reason to hope that all the various states of the union, as well as the new United States itself, would shortly move to adopt Royalist constitutions in the image of the one that he had crafted for the commonwealth of Massachusetts— that they would come to recognize that "two thirds of our States have made Constitutions, in no respect better than those of the Italian Republicks, and as sure as there is an Heaven and an Earth, if they are not altered they will produce Disorders and Confusion."[152] On March 20 of that year, Abigail Adams wrote to her son John Quincy to announce that "before this reaches You, [JA's] Book will have arrived." "I should like to know its reception," she mused. "I tell him [JA] they will think in America that he is for setting up a King. He Says no, but he is for giving to the Governours of every state the same Authority which the British king has, under the true British constitution, balancing his power by the two other Branches."[153] From 1769 until the eve of the Philadelphia Convention, the theorists of the Royalist Revolution had wanted nothing more than to assign their chief magistrate those prerogatives "which the British king has, under the true British constitution."

But Adams was nonetheless being perfectly sincere when he told his wife that, despite his continuing allegiance to Royalist constitutionalism, he was not in fact "for setting up a King." None of the theorists of the Royalist Revolution—with the complicated exception of Hamilton—supported the creation of a hereditary American monarchy after the rupture of 1776. This was not merely because they recognized that, in Wilson's words, "the manners" of the former colonists were now irretrievably "against a King" and "purely republican,"[154] or, as Adams himself put it, that a formal monarchy was more "than the Circumstances of this Country required or would Admit."[155] Their abandonment of the kingly office surely reflected an awareness of these very real political constraints, but it would be wrong to dismiss it as purely tactical in character. For these theorists too had been shaped by the distinctive republican turn of 1776. They had acquired a genuine (although in some cases temporary) distaste for the pretensions of monarchical *culture,* if not for kingly power. As Adams explained in a letter to Mercy Otis Warren in 1776, "A Monarchy would probably, somehow or other make me rich, but it would produce So much Taste and Politeness, So much Elegance in Dress, Furniture, Equipage. So much Musick and Dancing, So much Fencing and Skaiting; So much Cards and Backgammon; so much Horse Racing and Cock fighting; so many Balls and Assemblies, so many Plays and Concerts that the very Imagination of them makes me feel vain, light, frivolous and insignificant."[156] Indeed, Adams at this stage eagerly anticipated that his countrymen would "e'er long renounce some of our Monarchical Corruptions, and become Republicans in Principle in Sentiment, in feeling and in Practice. . . . In Republican Governments the Majesty is all in the Laws. They only are to be adored."[157] The "corruptions" of Monarchy are, on this account, a matter of "sentiment," "feeling," and "practice," and are straightforwardly attributable to the misplaced "adoration" offered to monarchs—not insofar as they wield any specific powers, but insofar as they occupy a *status* that commands idolatrous homage and debasing pageantry.[158]

Benjamin Rush, who, after all, had provided the title for Paine's *Common Sense,* took precisely the same view. Even as he fiercely championed the negative voice in print during the debate over Pennsylvania's first constitution, he was simultaneously writing to Adams at the French court that "while you are *gazed* at for your American-manufactured principles, and *gazing* at the folly and pageantry of animals in the shape of men cringing at the feet of an animal called a king, I shall be secluded from the noise and corruption of the times."[159] The same man who, in 1768, had approached the throne in the House of Lords "as if I walked on sacred ground" now regarded the kingly office as inherently idolatrous and therefore illicit.[160] Jefferson made use of the same language. Opining in 1789 on the "inconsiderable" number of

Americans "who would now establish a monarchy," he explained that "we were educated in royalism: no wonder if some of us retain that idolatry still."[161] Fortunately, however, "our young people are educated in republicanism. An apostacy from that to royalism is unprecedented and impossible." In this, Jefferson was correct. The American defense of royal power had momentously and irretrievably become detached from a defense of the kingly office, an ideological maneuver made possible by the colonial reimagining of "republicanism" in the wake of Paine's pamphlet. The great project of the Royalist Revolution in the late 1780s would accordingly be to create, in the words of Mercy Otis Warren, a "Republican *form* of government, founded on the principles of monarchy."[162]

CHAPTER 5

"All Know That a Single Magistrate Is Not a King"

Royalism and the Constitution of 1787

Few historiographical orthodoxies have proven more resilient than the view that the Constitution of the United States embodied a fundamental repudiation of the principles of the American Revolution. According to this familiar story, the ostentatious impotence of Congress under the Articles of Confederation, together with the threat of financial ruin and anarchy made vivid in the outbreak of Shays's Rebellion in the winter of 1787, created a window of opportunity in which a "conservative" set of "aristocratic" men were able to persuade their countrymen to abandon the egalitarian and radical republican constitutional ideals that had motivated the break with Britain.[1] The adoption and ratification of the document that emerged from the Philadelphia Convention in September of 1787 should accordingly be regarded as a sort of Thermidorian Reaction *avant la lettre,* to be applauded or lamented, depending upon the predilections of the scholar telling the story. Like most orthodoxies, this one contains a kernel of truth. It is, after all, undoubtedly the case that the anarchic unraveling of the confederation prompted many Americans to question the political commitments that had undergirded the initial wave of state constitutions and encouraged them to consider, and eventually endorse, a very different set of constitutional principles. Yet it would be a grave error to equate the principles of the first state constitutions with the principles of the American Revolution. Indeed, as we have seen, it would be highly misleading to talk about *the* principles of the American Revolution in the first place.[2] The patriots who led the opposition to Britain and waged the Revolutionary War had agreed on a small number of central claims—that the British constitution had become hopelessly corrupt, that the colonists were not represented in Parliament, and so on—but they had disagreed sharply, and fatefully, among themselves as to precisely *why* or *in what sense* these claims were correct.

Some patriots remained conventional whigs throughout the crisis, inveighing against the encroaching power of the Crown and keeping faith with the parliamentary theory of representation. For these theorists, whose influence crested with the drafting of the eight state constitutions adopted in 1776, the Constitution of 1787 did indeed amount to a conclusive repudiation of their most basic commitments. But theirs is only part of the story. The theorists of the Royalist Revolution, in contrast, had opposed the British administration in the name of the Crown; they had waged a campaign against what they regarded as a tyrannical legislature, aiming to rebalance the English constitution by restoring to the king his ancient prerogatives. These theorists, whose ideas had dominated the patriot movement during the early 1770s, were not "conservative" in any meaningful sense. Quite the contrary, they had spent two decades attempting to overturn the established constitutional principles that English whigs and their American disciples had defended for over a century (and, as we shall see, they were no friends of aristocracy).[3] For these men, the new frame of government embodied the apotheosis of their Revolutionary commitments, not a repudiation of them, although they uniformly regretted that the final document adopted by the convention did not go even further in the direction of pure Royalism. The Constitution, we might say, upheld the spirit of '75.[4]

James Wilson made this very point on June 1, 1787, when the convention first took up the question of executive power.[5] Having (unsurprisingly) taken it upon himself to lead the floor fight for the creation of a strong, prerogative-wielding chief magistrate, Wilson offered an initial motion, seconded by Charles Pinckney of South Carolina, "that the Executive consist of a single person."[6] Legal and constitutional scholar that he was, Wilson can have been in no doubt as to the historical resonance of this famous phrase.[7] The Act Abolishing the Office of King, passed by the Long Parliament in March 1649, had decreed "that the office of a King in this nation shall not henceforth reside in or be exercised by any one single person; and that no one person whatsoever, shall or may have, or hold the Office, Style, Dignity, Power, or Authority of King of the said Kingdoms and Dominions"— and the Oath of Engagement to the English Commonwealth, as amended after the fall of the protectorate, required citizens to swear their allegiance to a "Free State, without a King, Single Person, or House of Lords."[8] The statement of constitutional principles drawn up by the General Council of Officers in December 1659 was even more emphatic: for "the conservation of this Commonwealth," the officers declared that "they will not have any single person to exercise the office of chief magistrate in these nations."[9] It was this discourse to which John Adams was unmistakably alluding when he wrote in his *Defence of the Constitutions* that "by kings, and kingly power, is meant . . . the executive power in a single person."[10] Wilson's motion thus represented the most direct possible rejection of the parliamentarian ideology of the English commonwealth; for him, government by "a single person" armed with prerogative powers was fully consistent with citizenship in a "free state." After "a considerable pause," Edmund Randolph of Virginia rose to object, declaring that "a unity in the Executive magistracy" would amount to "the foetus of monarchy" and insisting that Americans had "no motive to be governed by the British Government as our prototype."[11] Wilson responded by making a striking claim about the character and genesis of the American Revolution: "The people of America did not oppose the British King but the parliament—the opposition was not against an Unity but a corrupt multitude."[12]

With this remarkable statement, Wilson grounded the quest for a powerful, prerogative-wielding chief magistrate in "Revolution principles." The Revolution, on this account, had not been waged against kingly power but rather against legislative tyranny. The very same principles that had underwritten the patriot campaign to rebalance the imperial constitution in favor of the Crown demanded in 1787 the creation of a strong, independent chief magistrate who would represent the people as a whole and tame the tyrannical proclivities and partialities of the assembly. It was Randolph and his allies who were speaking the language of the British administration and its loyalist supporters, wishing to create a plural executive in the image of the ministry and to subject it utterly to the legislature. Wilson accordingly proceeded to offer a series of motions designed to construct the sort of chief magistrate that he and his allies had championed during the imperial crisis of the 1770s and again throughout the decade-long debate over the proper form of the state constitutions—one possessing the "energy dispatch and responsibility" that would render him "the best safeguard against tyranny."[13] The president should be a "single person," free from the encumbrance of a privy council;[14] he "ought to have an absolute negative" (although Wilson eventually proposed "varying the proposition in such a manner as to give the Executive & Judiciary jointly an absolute negative," in order to prevent legislative encroachments on "the constitutional rights" of judges and to embolden the executive to correct the "improper views of the Legislature");[15] there should be no limit on the number of terms for which he might serve;[16] he should have the undiluted authority to make all executive and judicial appointments, without the interference of the Senate or any other body, as well as the unchecked prerogative of clemency and the authority of commander-in-chief;[17] and he should be elected "by the people at large."[18]

This final proposal, perhaps more than any other, illustrates the fundamental continuity in Wilson's thought, from the *Considerations* of 1768 to the convention itself. While he fully recognized that the notion of a popularly elected chief magistrate "might appear chimerical" to his colleagues, he fought doggedly for it, ultimately proposing the device of the electoral college as a second-best approximation of what he regarded as the proper procedure.[19] In his remarks on the subject, he justified his advocacy of popular election on the grounds that it would provide for an executive "as independent as possible" of the legislature (the alternative was to entrust the president's selection to one or both houses of Congress or to the states).[20] This was undoubtedly one of his central preoccupations, but another clearly emerged from his long-standing position on the question of representation. Wilson had argued all along that only an elected magistrate could count as the representative of the people, because individuals could only be said to have authorized agents for whom they themselves had voted. It followed that a people could only be said to be "sovereign" if it were governed exclusively by elected magistrates.[21] Wilson's conviction in this respect likewise prompted him to advocate the popular election of senators in the convention (again, unsuccessfully).[22] When discussing the method of election to the national legislature on June 6, Wilson stated that "he wished for vigor in the Gov[ernment] but he wished that vigorous authority to flow immediately from the legitimate source of all authority," namely from "the people at large." Only a procedure of direct election could secure the "representation" that is "made necessary only because it is impossible for the people to act collectively."[23] He therefore regarded direct election "not only as the corner Stone, but as the foundation of the fabric" and insisted that "the difference between a mediate and immediate election was immense."[24] Indeed, Wilson never ceased to regard it as among the great imperfections of the

Constitution that the Senate and the president were only indirectly "derived" from the people, thereby undermining their claim to be representatives in the full, juridical sense marked out by what he called "the correct theory of freedom."[25]

Wilson thus pursued a coherent agenda throughout the long debates in the convention on executive power, prodding his colleagues, often successfully, to move ever further along the route to a recognizably Royalist constitutional framework. But Wilson was adamant in insisting that the powerful chief magistrate he sought to create ought not to be regarded as a king, or as a "foetus of monarchy," as Randolph had suggested. While the "extent" of the United States," he observed, "seems to require the vigour of Monarchy, the manners are ag[ains]t a King and are purely republican—Montesquieu is in favor of confederated Republicks—I am for such a confed[eratio]n. if we can take for its basis liberty, and can ensure a vigourous execution of the Laws."[26] American "manners" and sensibilities could be accommodated by republican government alone: indeed, it was Wilson who suggested the final wording of Article IV, section 4 of the Constitution, guaranteeing to each state "a Republican form of Governm[en]t."[27] His challenge, therefore, was to explain why the sort of chief magistrate he envisioned should be regarded as compatible with republican principles. A number of his fellow delegates were deeply skeptical of this proposition, including some of those who were relatively friendly to executive power. Thus, John Dickinson declared that while he considered "a limited Monarchy . . . as one of the best Governments in the world"—and while he was highly dubious "that the same blessings were derivable from any other form," particularly from "the republican form"—he recognized that "a limited monarchy however was out of the question. The spirit of the times—the state of our affairs, forbade the experiment, if it were desireable."[28] But it followed for Dickinson that Wilson's proposals for a prerogative-wielding chief magistrate should therefore be rejected: "Such an Executive as some seemed to have in contemplation was not consistant with a republic. . . . a firm Executive could only exist in a limited monarchy"—or, as King reports the claim, "A rig[orou]s. executive with checks &c can not be republican, it is peculiar to monarchy."[29] Benjamin Franklin, who had developed over the previous decade into a strident opponent of executive power, agreed, fretting that although "it will be said, that we don't propose to establish Kings," the sort of chief magistracy championed by Wilson would excite "a natural inclination in mankind to

Kingly Government" and hasten the inevitable "Catastrophe" whereby a king will "be set over us" (the reference is to Deuteronomy 17:14).[30] One wonders whether Dickinson smiled as he heard these words coming from the mouth of the same man whose zealous campaign for the expansion of prerogative power in the early 1760s had very nearly succeeded in converting Pennsylvania into a royal colony, and whose Royalist enthusiasms during the imperial crisis had provoked Dickinson's own impassioned defense of the whig tradition.[31]

Wilson offered two primary responses to this challenge. First, he took considerable pains to resist Randolph's claim that his proposals amounted to "taking the British Government as our prototype." Since virtually all of the delegates to the convention agreed that Britain was not to be classed as a republic, this was a very serious charge indeed. Wilson accordingly insisted that "he did not consider the Prerogatives of the British Monarch as a proper guide in defining the Executive powers. Some of these prerogatives were of a Legislative nature. Among others that of war & peace &c. The only powers he conceived strictly Executive were those of executing the laws, and appointing officers, not ‹appertaining to and› appointed by the Legislature."[32] Following a rejoinder by Randolph, he repeated that "he was not governed by the British Model which was inapplicable to the situation of this Country." As the debate moved on, however, Wilson clearly came to recognize that he had to do better than this. It was certainly true that he had not slavishly followed the British model in delineating the prerogatives of the president. Neither he nor his allies had ever wished to assign their chief magistrate a prerogative to establish legislative districts, appoint members to one branch of the legislature, or govern an established church, for example—and Wilson did indeed favor dividing between the legislature and the executive what in Britain remained (at least as a formal matter) prerogatives of the Crown to make war and enter into treaties. But despite the creative reallocation of these powers, Wilson's proposed single chief magistrate would still wield an unchecked prerogative of appointment to both executive and judicial offices, the power of pardon and the authority of commander-in-chief, as well as an absolute negative voice.[33] The last of these in particular had always been regarded within the neo-Roman and whig traditions as tantamount to government by the "arbitrary will" of a "single person" and hence as incompatible with the liberty of free states. Yet Wilson regarded it as absolutely vital. "The prejudices ag[ain]st the Executive," he explained, have "resulted from a misapplication of the adage that the parliament was the palladium of liberty."[34] "Where the Executive was really formidable, King and Tyrant, were naturally associated in the minds of people; not legislature and tyranny. But where the Executive was not formidable, the two last were most properly associated. After the destruction of the King in Great Britain [in 1649], a more pure and unmixed tyranny sprang up in the parliament than had been exercised by the monarch." The Long Parliament that had "usurped" the royal prerogative by attempting to legislate for the colonies in 1651 remained the great villain in Wilson's constitutional imagination, as it did for Gouverneur Morris, who similarly declared that "if the Executive be chosen by the Nat[iona]l. Legislature, he will not be independent on it; and if not independent, usurpation & tyranny on the part of the Legislature will be the consequence. This was the case in England in the last Century."[35] The question remained: How could this zealous defense of royal power against the ideology of the English "free state" be consistent with "republicanism" in any meaningful sense?

Wilson's answer came three days later, when the debate over the executive resumed on June 4. Returning to Randolph's intervention of June 1, in which the Virginian had disparaged the single executive as a "foetus of monarchy," Wilson simply announced that "all know that a single magistrate is not a King."[36] It was a breathtakingly deflationary move, made possible (as we have seen) by the distinctive, Hebraizing form of antimonarchism unleashed by Paine's *Common Sense*. On Wilson's revisionist account, a government is republican so long as it does not include the kingly office; the fact that it entrusts sweeping prerogative powers to a "single person" does not render it "monarchical."[37] Rome under Augustus was a republic, as was England under Cromwell. As Wilson would explain further in his 1790 "Lectures on Law," quoting from Blackstone, the distinguishing feature of monarchy is that it attributes to a mortal man a "great and transcendent nature," such that "the people will consider him in the light of a superiour being." Indeed, in Britain "the king satisfies the wish of eastern adulation: he lives for ever!"[38] The architects of the American chief magistracy, in contrast, had come to recognize that "power may be conferred without mystery; and may be exercised, for every wise and benevolent purpose, without challenging attributes, to which our frail and imperfect state of humanity stands in daily and marked contradiction."[39] Deprived of such idolatrous reverence, a single magistrate is no monarch. In the convention, Wilson continued by pointing out that "all the 13 States tho' agreeing in scarce any other instance, agree in placing a single magistrate at the head of the Governm[en]t. . . . The degree of power is indeed different: but there are no co-ordinate heads."[40] The proposed federal chief magistracy should be regarded as no less "republican" than the chief magistracy of, say, Maryland, despite the fact that the former would possess an absolute negative voice, while the latter possessed none at all. Here was the final consummation of the unlikely union between prerogative and republicanism.

Wilson's great ally in the convention debates over the executive was, again unsurprisingly, Alexander Hamilton, despite the fact that the latter left Philadelphia on June 29 and did not return until the very end of the proceedings. Hamilton joined Wilson's ill-fated motion to assign the executive "an absolute negative on the laws," and he sought to reassure his colleagues that "there was no danger . . . of such a power being too much exercised" by observing that "the King of G[reat] B[ritain]. had not exerted his negative since the Revolution [sic]."[41] For the Hamilton of 1787, as for the Hamilton of 1775, the royal negative remained a valid constitutional prerogative of the Crown that the English monarchs since 1688 had simply neglected to use—a fact that Hamilton exploited in this context to assuage the anxieties of his fellow delegates but one that he continued to lament bitterly (as we shall see).[42] Yet Hamilton also parted company with Wilson on several crucial and predictable points. He had never subscribed to Wilson's election theory of representation and so shared none of Wilson's worries about the degree to which a hereditary monarch or an unelected House of Lords could be said to speak and act in the name of the people. Hamilton had always endorsed the pure Royalist theory of representation, according to which any (tacitly) authorized constellation of magistrates could be said to represent the people, whether elected or not. He therefore announced in his famous (indeed, infamous) speech of June 18 that "in his private opinion he had no scruple in declaring, supported as he was by the opinions of so many of the wise & good, that the British Gov[ernmen]t. was the best in the world: and that he doubted much whether any thing short of it would do in America," and although he fully recognized that "it would be unwise" to propose anything other than a "Republican Gov[ernmen]t" at this particular moment, he looked forward to the "progress of the public mind" that would prompt "others as well as himself" to quit their "prejudices" and "join in the praise bestowed by Mr. Neckar [sic] on the British Constitution, namely, that it is the only Gov[ernment]. in the world 'which unites public strength with individual security.'"[43] Later in the convention, he added that while "he acknowledged himself not to think favorably of Republican Government," he nonetheless "professed himself to be as zealous an advocate for liberty as any man whatever, and trusted he should be as willing a martyr to it though he differed as to the form in which it was most eligible."[44] Hamilton could regard hereditary monarchy the "most eligible form" of free government only because he had never ceased to believe that a hereditary monarch could *represent* his people.

Hamilton thus agreed with Wilson that the British constitution could not be characterized as "republican." In this respect, both men disagreed with their ally John Adams, who continued to insist from his London posting that monarchy was simply a species of republican government. But unlike Wilson, Hamilton was fully prepared to endorse limited monarchy despite this fact. Moreover, he expressed serious doubts that the sort of nonhereditary executive proposed by Wilson was in fact compatible with "republican government." Like Randolph, he regarded the president as "a foetus of monarchy"; he simply welcomed what the Virginian had deplored. Hamilton began by observing that "as to the Executive, it seemed to be admitted that no good one could be established on Republican principles."[45] Dickinson, as we have seen, had made precisely the same point, but Hamilton had no interest in endorsing his colleague's conclusion that the presidency should be subjected to the legislature so as to be rendered appropriately "republican." Indeed, for Hamilton, to argue that there could be no proper executive in a republic amounted to "giving up the merits of the question; for can there be a good Gov[ernmen]t. without a good Executive [?]" "The English model," he explained, "was the only good one on this subject. The Hereditary interest of the King was so interwoven with that of the Nation, and his personal emoluments so great, that he was placed above the danger of being corrupted from abroad—and at the same time was both sufficiently independent and sufficiently controuled, to answer the purpose of the institution at home"—or, as Robert Yates reports Hamilton's remarks, the king of Great Britain "can have no distinct interests from the public welfare."[46] The argument that good government required the existence of a strong, independent chief magistrate whose interests were bound up with the welfare of the realm as a whole had been a staple of Hamilton's thought since the imperial crisis.

Did it follow, then, that republican government was incompatible with substantial executive power in "a single person"? Here Hamilton hesitated. On the one hand, he seemed to offer a way of squaring the circle. The "inference from all these observations," he argued, was that "we ought to go as far in order to attain stability and permanency, as republican principles will admit. Let one branch of the Legislature hold their places for life or at least during good-behaviour. Let the Executive also be for life."[47] Hamilton's proposed executive would be even more powerful than Wilson's, enjoying an absolute negative, complete power of appointment to executive offices and a life term (the "General Government" of the union would also appoint "the Governour or president of each state," who in turn would possess "a negative upon the laws about to be passed in the State of which he is Governour or President," thus replicating the system of colonial governors under the Crown).[48] "But is this a Republican Gov[ernment]. it will be asked? Yes, if all the Magistrates are appointed, and vacancies are filled, by the people, or a process of election originating with the people."[49] This, of course, was very close to the view that Madison and others would defend at length throughout the debates over ratification.[50] But Hamilton immediately qualified his remarks by entertaining the following objection to his "Executive for life": "It will be objected probably, that such an Executive will be an elective Monarch, and will give birth to the tumults which characterise that form of Gov[ernment]."[51] He answered that "Monarch is an indefinite term. It marks not either the degree or duration of power. If this Executive Magistrate w[oul]d. be a monarch for life—the other prop[ose]d. by the Report from the Committee of the whole, w[oul]d. be a monarch for seven years. The circumstance of being elective was also applicable to both." The president, in short, would be a "monarch" whether given an absolute negative or a qualified veto; whether elected for seven years or for life. He would therefore resemble the "Roman Emperors," the Holy Roman emperors, and the Polish kings, although his "mode of election" might rescue the United States from the "tumults" that were mistakenly regarded as "an inseparable evil" of "Elective Monarchies."[52]

The question is whether Hamilton actually intended in his convention speech to classify elective monarchy as a species of republican government. If he did not, he was contradicting his earlier claim that his proposed chief magistracy should be regarded as "republican" (i.e., because he was now conceding that the president would be an elected monarch). If he *did* intend to classify it in this manner, he was taking a very different view indeed from the one shortly to be defended by Madison, who emphatically denied *both* that elective monarchy was a species of republican government *and* that the Constitution established an elective monarchy.[53] The question of Hamilton's intention in this regard is extremely difficult to answer, in large part because three surviving sets of notes on the convention report significantly different versions of the relevant portions of his speech.[54] It is, however, of interest that Hamilton's own notes for his remarks contain no trace of the argument that his proposed form of government should be styled "republican."[55] They state simply that if "a republican government does not admit a vigorous execution, It is therefore bad; for the goodness of a government consists in a vigorous execution. The principle chiefly intended to be established is this that there must be a permanent will." One might infer from this fact that Hamilton's attempted domestication of elective monarchy was extemporized, perhaps reflecting a last-minute anxiety as to the wisdom of conceding that his proposed form of government could not be classified as republican.[56]

In any event, Hamilton, who had drafted one of the most strident patriot defenses of the royal prerogative in the 1770s, undoubtedly offered the convention's most emphatic defense of expansive prerogative power in the executive, and his call for a presidential life term (or at least an appointment "during good behavior") found a surprisingly receptive audience. It was supported in the convention by four state delegations (New Jersey, Pennsylvania, Delaware, and Virginia), and its advocates on the floor included Madison, Gouverneur Morris of Pennsylvania, James McClurg of Virginia, Rufus King of Massachusetts, and Jacob Broom of Delaware.[57] George Washington himself voted in favor of the proposal.[58] Outside the convention, it attracted the vocal support of John Adams, who wrote to Jefferson in December of 1787 that if each new president ended up ruling for "as long as he lives," then "so much the better as it appears to me."[59] In the long run, Adams was clear (as he wrote to Benjamin Rush) that the United States would need to go further and evolve a proper "hereditary Monarchy" and aristocracy "as an Asylum against Discord, Seditions and Civil War, and that at no very distant Period of time."[60] These institutions, far from amounting to "Rebellion against Nature," in fact constituted "the hope of our posterity." Interestingly, Adams's sentiments in this respect were very much in line with those of Washington, who had written to Madison on the eve of the convention that while he recognized that "the period is not yet arrived" for adopting "Monarchical governm[en]t" in America, he was nonetheless fully prepared to admit "the utility; nay the necessity of the form."[61]

But the zealous defense of Royalist constitutionalism mounted by Wilson, Hamilton, and their allies in the convention provoked an equally impassioned response by a set of delegates who remained unambiguously devoted to whig, parliamentarian principles—that is, to the principles enshrined in the first wave of state constitutions. These were the men Adams had in mind when he wrote in the *Defence* that "there has been, from the beginning of the revolution in America, a party in every state, who have entertained sentiments similar to those of Mr. Turgot" (recall that Adams regarded Turgot as a disciple of the parliamentarians, and of Marchamont Nedham in particular).[62] The most important spokesman for this set of views in Philadelphia was unquestionably Roger Sherman of Connecticut. [63] Sherman offered a clear and cogent statement of his position at the very opening of the debate on executive power, responding directly to Wilson's motion to vest the executive power in "a single person":

> Mr. Sherman said he considered the Executive magistracy as nothing more than an institution for carrying the will of the Legislature into effect, that the person or persons ought to be appointed by and accountable to the Legislature only, which was the despositary [*sic*] of the supreme will of the Society. As they were the best judges of the business which ought to be done by the Executive department, and consequently of the number necessary from time to time for doing it, he wished the number might ‹not› be fixed, but that the legislature should be at liberty to appoint one or more as experience might dictate.[64]

It is difficult to imagine a more orthodox statement of whig constitutionalism. Only a well-poised legislature, on Sherman's account, can be regarded as the "depositary of the supreme will of the Society," an "image" of the body of the people that can be said to represent them.[65] Like all orthodox theorists of "virtual representation," Sherman had no attachment whatsoever to direct elections or an expanded franchise; voting, on his view, was entirely beside the point. He accordingly opposed even the popular election of members of the House of Representatives, on the grounds that "the people . . . ‹immediately› should have as little to do as may be about the Government."[66] The executive, for Sherman, is not a branch of the legislature,

entitled to wield prerogative powers; it is merely a creature of the legislature, tasked with "carrying its will into effect." As such, the legislature
should remain "at liberty" to constitute the executive in whatever form it
chooses, whether one man or several. Sherman went on to insist that the
"National Legislature" ought to elect the members of the executive and
"should have power to remove the Executive at pleasure."[67]

Underlying all of these claims was the fundamental whig conviction that
the executive must be, in Sherman's phrase, "absolutely dependent" on the
legislature. If an assembly alone can represent the people, it follows that "a
single person" cannot speak and act in their name; to be governed by the
prerogatives of such a figure would accordingly amount to government by
an "alien will"—that is to say, slavery.[68] Thus, Gunning Bedford Jr. of Delaware, an ally of Sherman's, rose to declare that he "was opposed to every
check on the Legislative, even the Council of Revision first proposed," on
the grounds that "the Representatives of the People were the best judges of
what was for their interest, and ought to be under no external controul
whatever," and Sherman himself likewise announced that "an independence of the Executive on the supreme Legislative, was in his opinion the
very essence of tyranny if there was any such thing."[69] Whereas Wilson saw
a single chief magistrate possessed of "energy dispatch and responsibility"
as "the best safeguard against tyranny"—or, in Gouverneur Morris's formulation, as "the guardian of the people, even of the lower classes, ag[ain]st.
Legislative tyranny, against the Great & the wealthy who in the course of
things will necessarily compose—the Legislative body"[70]—Sherman and
his colleagues saw this figure as the very *embodiment* of tyranny.

Here, once again, was the great collision between Royalism and the parliamentarian tradition, and it rapidly evolved into a familiar debate about
the English constitution and its discontents. For the Royalists in the convention, the English constitution had become hopelessly corrupt because the
Crown had never regained its independent prerogative powers after the two
seventeenth-century revolutions; the executive had very nearly been absorbed by the legislature.[71] As Wilson insisted, the "multitude" in the House
of Commons was the source of corruption in eighteenth-century Britain,
not the king, and the monarch had long been far too weak to "to interpose
his negative ag[ains]t. the unanimous voice of both houses of Parliament."[72]
Hamilton, for his part, went so far as to endorse the opinion of "‹one› of
the ablest politicians (Mr Hume)," who "had pronounced all that influence

on the side of the crown, which went under the name of corruption, an essential part of the weight which maintained the equilibrium of the Constitution."[73] The Crown's prerogative control of the "many offices at its disposal," Hume had argued, constituted the last remaining bulwark against
abject legislative tyranny: "The share of power, allotted by our constitution
to the house of commons, is so great, that it absolutely commands all the
other parts of government. The king's legislative power is plainly no proper
check to it. For though the king has a negative in framing laws; yet this, in
fact, is esteemed of so little moment, that whatever is voted by the two
houses, is always sure to pass into a law, and the royal assent is little better
than a form."[74] As Hamilton put the same point several months later in the
New York ratifying convention, "notwithstanding the cry of corruption that
has been perpetually raised against the House of Commons, it has been
found that that house, sitting at first without any constitutional authority,
became, at length, an essential member of the legislature, and have since, by
regular gradations, acquired new and important accessions of privilege; that
they have, on numerous occasions, impaired the prerogative, and limited
the monarchy."[75] He added later in the Philadelphia convention, in complete
defiance of whig orthodoxy, that while "the British House of Commons
were elected septennially, yet the democratic spirit of ye Constitution had
not ceased."[76] The young Charles Pinckney clearly agreed with the thrust of
Hamilton's remarks, pointedly observing (as had Wilson) that "under the
British Government, notwithstanding we early and warmly resisted their
other attacks, no objection was ever made to the negative of the King."[77]

For the whigs, in contrast, the English constitution had degenerated as a
result of the endlessly expanding patronage power of the Crown; the legislature, in effect, had been absorbed by the executive. Pierce Butler of South
Carolina accordingly attacked the notion that the "Executive Magistrate"
ought to be assigned "a compleat negative on the laws" by reminding his
audience that "it had been observed that in all countries the Executive
power is in a constant course of increase. This was certainly the case in
G[reat]. B[ritain]."[78] George Mason of Virginia likewise fretted that "the Executive may refuse its assent to necessary measures till new appointments shall be referred to him; and having by degrees engrossed all these
into his own hands, the American Executive, like the British, will by
bribery & influence, save himself the trouble & odium of exerting his
negative afterwards."[79] Mason "hoped that nothing like a monarchy

would ever be attempted in this Country" and claimed that "a hatred to its oppressions had carried the people through the late Revolution"—thereby directly contradicting Wilson's assertion (seconded by Pinckney) that "the people of America Did not oppose the British King but the parliament."[80] The debate in the convention between Royalists and whigs over prerogative power and the English constitution simply extended a controversy over the character of the Revolution that had begun in the early 1770s.

Perhaps the most ironic intervention in this debate came from Franklin. In his remarks on June 2 (read out for him by James Wilson) assailing the notion of a single executive, he had already voiced the opinion that "there is scarce a king in a hundred who would not, if he could, follow the example of Pharaoh, get first all the peoples money, then all their lands, and then make them and their children servants forever."[81] But it was on June 4, in his comments opposing the motion offered by Wilson and Hamilton to give the executive an "absolute negative," that Franklin explicitly addressed the English constitution. He began by observing that "he had had some experience of this check [i.e., the negative voice] in the Executive on the Legislature, under the proprietary Government of Pen[nsylvani]a. The negative of the Governor was constantly made use of to extort money. No good law whatever could be passed without a private bargain with him."[82] Turning from the colonial case to the situation in Britain itself, he insisted again that the absolute negative was "a mischievous sort of check." "It was true," he conceded, that "the King of G[reat]. B[ritain]. had not, As was said [by Hamilton], exerted his negative since the Revolution: but that matter was easily explained. The bribes and emoluments now given to the members of parliament rendered it unnecessary, everything being done according to the will of the Ministers." Franklin accordingly worried that "if a negative should be given as proposed . . . more power and money would be demanded, till at last eno[ugh] would be gotten to influence & bribe the Legislature into a compleat subjection to the will of the Executive."[83]

It is of course no surprise to find Franklin still railing against the proprietary power in Pennsylvania: as we have seen, he had led the crusade to have it abolished in favor of royal government in the 1760s. But it is quite another matter to find the same man who had spent the 1770s relentlessly arguing that the House of Commons "seem to have been long encroaching on the Rights of their and our Sovereign, assuming too much of his Authority, and betraying his Interests"[84] now adopting the standard whig theory of

English constitutional decline. For the Franklin of 1787, the royal negative had not been used in a hundred years, not because the king had become lamentably weak, but rather because he had become so strong that he was reliably able to get his way without wielding it. The ideological distance that Franklin had traveled since the imperial crisis was vast indeed and without parallel in the founding generation.[85]

Strikingly absent from this extensive set of debates about the English constitution and prerogative power in the chief magistrate was the figure whom we have long been taught to regard as the convention's indispensable man: James Madison. While Wilson and Hamilton locked horns with Sherman and Franklin on these great matters, Madison remained largely passive.[86] Alone among the central actors in the constitutional drama, he was not particularly interested in the question of executive power. As he frankly conceded in a letter to Randolph, written on the eve of the convention, "A National Executive will also be necessary. I have scarc[ely] ventured to form my own opinion yet either of the manner in which it ought to be constituted or of the authorities with which it ought [to be] cloathed."[87] Immediately following the convention, Madison reported to Jefferson that he had found the extensive debates over the chief magistracy "tedious."[88] His preoccupation at the time was, instead, with the "federal negative" on state laws that he proposed to assign the national legislature.[89] The terms in which he described this proposal in a letter to George Washington, dated April 16, 1787, are highly revealing:

A negative *in all cases whatsoever* on the legislative acts of the States, as heretofore exercised by the Kingly prerogative, appears to me to be absolutely necessary, and to be the least possible encroachment on State jurisdictions. Without this defensive power, every positive power that can be given on paper will be evaded & defeated. The States will continue to invade the national jurisdiction, to violate treaties and the law of nations & to harrass each other with rival and spiteful measures dictated by mistaken views of interest. Another happy effect of this prerogative would be its controul on the internal vicisitudes of State policy; and the aggressions of interested majorities on the rights of minorities and of individuals. The great desideratum which has not yet been found for Republican Governments, seems to be some disinterested & dispassionate umpire in disputes between different passions & interests in the State. The majority who alone have the right of decision, have frequently an interest real or supposed in abusing it. In Monarchies the sovereign is more neutral to the interests and views of different parties; but unfortunately he too often forms interests of his own repugnant to those of the whole. Might not the national prerogative here suggested be found sufficiently disinterested for the decision of local questions of policy, whilst it would itself be sufficiently restrained from the pursuit of interests adverse to those of the whole Society?[90]

This passage reminds us of a central but surprisingly overlooked fact about Madison: he was the only major advocate of the new Constitution who had not participated in the debates of the imperial crisis.[91] This was in part a generational matter. While he and Hamilton were roughly the same age (Madison was 36 when he arrived in Philadelphia), the latter had been dazzlingly precocious: recall that he published *The Farmer Refuted* (1775) while still an undergraduate at King's College. Wilson, Adams, Franklin, and most of the others were far older. It is impossible to imagine a veteran of the pamphlet wars of the 1760s and 1770s using the notorious phrase "in all cases whatsoever,"[92] the hated language of the Declaratory Act, to describe a newly envisioned legislative power, still less to imagine the disciples of patriot Royalism seeking to replace "the Kingly prerogative" with a legislative "negative." (Wilson, for one, was perfectly happy to offer lukewarm support to Madison's federal negative, but he never regarded it as a substitute for the chief magistrate's prerogative to "stand the mediator between the intrigues & sinister views of the Representatives and the general liberties & interests of the people."[93] Hamilton and Gouverneur Morris opposed the measure outright.[94]) For Madison, it was the legislature, not the executive, that was to serve as the "disinterested & dispassionate umpire in disputes between different passions & interests in the State"—even those arising from "the aggressions of interested majorities" *within* states—and as champion of the interests of "the whole society."[95] On his account, a single chief magistrate, like a monarchical sovereign, would form pernicious "interests of his own."[96] This, of course, was precisely the argument that the British administration and its whig defenders had made throughout the period leading up to the Revolution.[97] For them, only Parliament, and not the king, could serve as the "superintending" and "pervading" power of the empire. Madison, in short, was considerably less interested in the shape of the executive than were his fellow "nationalists" because, in his political imagination, a supreme legislature was to play the role that theorists of the

Royalist Revolution had always assigned the monarch. It was Congress that would "superintend," "pervade," and "interpose."[98]

But Madison's federal negative went down to defeat in the convention, leaving its sponsor with an ambivalence about prerogative power in the executive that remained with him for the rest of his life. While he always insisted on the need for an independent chief magistrate, he never made his peace with the notion that the president, or indeed a governor, should summon "the splendor of prerogative" to assume the role of "superintending" power (although, as president three decades later, he did veto more bills than any of his predecessors, almost always on the grounds that he regarded the measures in question as unconstitutional).[99] In his "Helvidius" letters, written in 1790 to criticize Hamilton's expansive view of the president's authority over foreign affairs, Madison observed that "writers, such as Locke and Montesquieu . . . are evidently warped by a regard to the particular government of England, to which one of them owed allegiance; and the other professed an admiration bordering on idolatry."[100] He then added the crucial observation: "The chapter on prerogative [in Locke's *Second Treatise of Government*], shews how much the reason of the philosopher was clouded by the royalism of the Englishman."[101] Madison plainly had no idea that, in making this claim, he was virtually paraphrasing William Knox's influential attack on the patriot constitutional argument from 1768. Responding to the extravagant defenses of the royal prerogative that were beginning to appear in the colonies, Knox had written that "there are some passages in it [Locke's *Second Treatise*], which probably the temper and fashion of that age drew from him [Locke], in which I can by no means agree with him, especially when he defines prerogative to be 'a power in the prince to act according to *discretion* for the public good, without the prescription of the law, and sometimes even against it' [i.e., in Chapter 14, "Of Prerogative"]. . . . I mean not by this to throw any blame upon Mr. Locke, but merely to shew, that in a work of this extent there must be some inaccuracies and errors, and that it is not an infallible guide in all cases."[102]

It was presumably this same view of prerogative power, particularly in relation to treaties, that had prompted Madison to declare in the Virginia ratifying convention that "the king of Great Britain has the power of making peace, but he has no power of dismembering the empire, or alienating any part of it," thereby unwittingly rejecting the most essential patriot constitutional claim of the 1760s and 1770.[103] What, after all, had grounded the patriot case during the imperial crisis, if not the radical contention that (as Hamilton had put it in 1775) "every acquisition of foreign territory is at the absolute disposal of the king";[104] or (in Edward Bancroft's canonical formulation) that all overseas possessions "could be forever alienated from the Realm, either to Subjects or Foreigners, at the Pleasure of the Crown"?[105] Only if the Stuart monarchs had been at perfect liberty to grant lands in their American dominions to the various chartering companies and proprietors, thus creating new and distinct states without the consent of Parliament, could it be argued that the British legislature had no jurisdiction over America. This was the argument that Hutchinson and other defenders of the administration had been so eager to expose as constitutional heresy.[106] Madison, in short, emerged from the 1780s as something of an inadvertent loyalist.

Two related implications emerge from these observations. The first is that Madison was not a representative Federalist. His distinctive preoccupation with the question of federal legislative power and its capacity to prevent majoritarian tyranny within the various states, as well as his corresponding lack of interest in the form of the new executive—attributable in part, or so I have suggested, to his absence from the imperial debates of the 1760s and 1770s—distinguish him quite sharply from the majority of his fellow "nationalists" in the convention. It is, as Max Edling has argued, high time to move beyond "the Madisonian interpretation of Federalism."[107] The second, and related, implication is that Madison's influence in the convention, and the degree to which he shaped the Constitution itself, have been exaggerated. It is beyond question that he played a decisive role in the political maneuvering that led to the calling of the convention and that his "Virginia Plan" set the broad parameters for its agenda.[108] But Wilson and Morris came a good deal closer to getting their way in Philadelphia than did Madison.[109] Indeed, one could go further. It is not merely that Madison frequently found himself on the losing side of major debates within the convention, although he certainly did;[110] it is, rather, that he and his fellow delegates disagreed sharply about what the major debates were. Our tendency to see the convention and the Constitution through Madison's eyes explains the general consensus among scholars that the presidency emerged as something of an afterthought from the convention—that the question of executive power did not figure prominently in the set of concerns that brought delegates to Philadelphia in 1787. This issue was indeed tertiary for Madison, but, for the theorists of the Royalist Revolution, as for their alarmed whig opponents, the presidency stood at the very center of the new constitutional scheme (the debate over its form occupied the convention longer than any other subject[111]), and its creation marked the successful conclusion of a twenty-year campaign in favor of prerogative power.

I

Article II of the Constitution assumed its final form as a result of a series of compromises between the Royalist and whig constituencies in the convention.[112] None of the delegates was completely satisfied with it, although Royalists were undoubtedly far happier with the final product than were their opponents—not least because Wilson managed to exert a pronounced influence on the all-important "Committee of Detail," which was tasked with giving concrete form to the broad principles adopted by the convention.[113] Only three delegates present in September refused to sign the document, among them Edmund Randolph.[114] The president would serve a relatively short term of four years, but would be indefinitely re-eligible, simultaneously grieving those who had sought a life term and those who had argued on behalf of a fixed, unrenewable term. (Impeachment, it is worth recalling, was ultimately embraced by Royalists in the convention as a remedy for the defect of a short presidential term: "Our Executive," Gouverneur Morris argued, was "not like a Magistrate having a life interest, much less like one having an hereditary interest in his office. He may be bribed by a greater interest to betray his trust; and no one would say that we ought to expose ourselves to the danger of seeing the first Magistrate in foreign pay without being able to guard ag[ain]st it by displacing him."[115]) The president would wield a qualified negative voice, capable of being overridden by a vote of two-thirds of each house of Congress, alarming both whigs who opposed a negative of any sort and Royalists who remained firmly committed to the absolute negative (or, as a second best, a qualified negative that could only be overridden by a vote of three-fourths of each chamber.)[116] He would wield the undiluted prerogative of clemency, but his appointment power and his prerogative of making treaties would be constrained by a requirement to seek approval from the new Senate. He would be elected neither by the federal legislature (as Sherman and his colleagues had sought) nor by the people themselves (as Wilson and Morris had proposed), but rather through the hybrid scheme of the Electoral College.

Each element of this compromise would be scrutinized fiercely during the yearlong national debate over ratification—a debate that has been characterized for two centuries as a confrontation between "Federalists" and "Antifederalists." Indeed, so well-entrenched is this terminology that it would seem tedious and pedantic to use any other. But while I shall employ the established language throughout the remainder of this chapter, I do so with a deep sense of its inadequacy. To label opponents of the Constitution as "Antifederalists" is to beg the very question that the parties were debating: namely, whether the Constitution, in its unamended form, provided the only plausible route to an effective federal union of the states. Virtually all of the participants in the ratification debates accepted that the Articles of Confederation had shown themselves to be gravely deficient and that a series of new powers should accordingly be conferred on the federal government. All of them were "federalists" in this sense.[117] The vast majority of participants likewise accepted bicameralism in principle and endorsed the creation of a federal executive. Finally, they all concurred in regarding the text of the Constitution as fundamentally flawed in numerous respects. They disagreed about *which* elements of the proposal counted as flaws, *why* these elements counted as flaws, and whether the flaws that existed were sufficiently grievous to justify rejection of the plan.

This fact is particularly important to keep in mind when considering the shape of the debate over executive power. Although it is true that many Antifederalists regarded the chief magistrate created by the Constitution as "monarchical" and far too strong, a significant number complained instead that he was too *weak*—that it had been a serious mistake to force the executive to share his proper prerogatives with the Senate and that the qualified negative would prove inadequate to the task of restraining the tyrannical impulses of an aristocratic legislature. As Wilson observed in the Pennsylvania ratifying convention, "the objection against the powers of the President is not that they are too many or too great; but . . . they are so trifling, that the President is no more than a tool of the Senate."[118] How could the president's meager veto be expected to shield Americans from the machinations of the Senate, wondered the Antifederalist "Centinel," when even "the king of England," with all of his power, "enjoys but in *name* the prerogative of a negative upon the parliament" and "has not dared to exercise it for near a century past"?[119] The dissenting minority in the Pennsylvania convention similarly worried that "the president general is dangerously connected with the senate; his coincidence with the views of the ruling junto in that body, is made essential to his weight and importance in the government, which will destroy all independency and purity in the executive department."[120] The author of the "Cincinnatus" letters agreed, declaring that the delegates in Philadelphia had committed an "egregious error in constitutional principles" by "dividing the executive powers, between the senate and the president." The great defender of royal power "M. [Jean-Louis] de Lolme," the author reminded his readers, had taught that "for the tranquility of the state it is necessary that the executive power should be in one."[121] In the Virginia ratifying convention, Antifederalist William Grayson went so far as to endorse the substance of Hamilton's convention speech: rather than the comparatively enfeebled executive envisioned in the Constitution, he announced, "I would have a President for life, choosing his successor at the same time; a Senate for life, with the powers of the House of Lords; and a triennial House of Representatives, with the powers of the House of Commons in England."[122] "By having such a President," Grayson explained, "we should have more independence and energy in the executive, and not be encumbered with the expense, &c., of a court and an hereditary prince and family."[123]

The categories "Federalist" and "Antifederalist," in short, do not straightforwardly map on to the categories "Royalist" and "whig." Moreover, casting the debate over Article II as a debate between Federalists and Antifederalists occludes the degree to which Federalists argued fiercely and extensively *among themselves* about this subject, often straightforwardly continuing the discussions that had dominated the convention. Perhaps the most remarkable exchange of this kind is to be found in a series of letters between Roger Sherman and John Adams from the summer of 1788. Sherman, who (as we have seen) had led the whig assault on prerogative power in the convention, nonetheless eventually voted to adopt the Constitution and wrote a series of newspaper essays advocating ratification. In one of these, published in *The New Haven Gazette,* Sherman explained that he had made his peace with the qualified negative assigned to the president: "The executive in Great Britain is one branch of the legislature, and has a negative on all laws; perhaps that is an extreme not to be imitated by a republic, but the partial negative vested in the President by the new Constitution on the acts of Congress and the subsequent revision, may be very useful to prevent laws being passed without mature deliberation."[124]

Adams, a fellow Federalist, was predictably appalled. In his *Defence of the Constitutions,* which (despite its later reputation) was taken very seriously indeed by the delegates in Philadelphia,[125] Adams had argued unabashedly that "the English constitution is, in theory, the most stupendous fabrick of human invention, both for the adjustment of the balance, and the prevention of its vibrations; and that the Americans ought to be applauded instead of censured, for imitating it, as far as they have."[126] He lamented only that "the Americans [in their state constitutions] have not indeed imitated it in giving a negative, upon their legislature to the executive power; in this respect their balances are incompleat, very much I confess to my mortification."[127] From Adams's point of view, Sherman's comment was doubly confused: first because it supposed that Great Britain, unlike the United States, was not a republic, and, second, because it dismissed the absolute negative as incompatible with republican government. Adams accordingly wrote to Sherman to insist that "England is a republic, a monarchical republic it is true, but a republic still; because the sovereignty, which is the legislative power, is vested in more than one man; it is equally divided, indeed, between the one, the few, and the many, or in other words, between the natural division of mankind in society,—the monarchical, the aristocratical, and democratical."[128] Monarchy for Adams remained a species of republican government; he had no patience for the view, expressed in different forms in the convention, that a "republic" should be defined as a regime without the kingly office. He went on to explain that "it is essential to a monarchical republic, that the supreme executive should be a branch of the legislature, and have a negative on all laws. I say essential, because if monarchy were not an essential part of the sovereignty, the government would not be a monarchical republic." If the chief magistrate is not a co-equal branch of the legislature, then he is a pure executive—an agent of the legislative power—and therefore not a monarch.

The question that we need to ask, on Adams's account, is simply "whether the new constitution of the United States is or is not a monarchical republic, like that of Great Britain."[129] If it is, then the absolute negative is not only permissible but essential; if it is not, then Sherman might have a point. Adams accordingly began by considering the view that the Constitution is republican, and therefore not monarchical, because its chief magistrate and senate are elected rather than hereditary. "The monarchical and the aristocratical power in our constitution, it is true, are not hereditary," he conceded, "but this makes no difference in the nature of the power, in the nature of the balance, or in the name of the species of government. It would make no difference in the power of a judge or justice, or general or admiral, whether his commission were for life or years. His authority during the time it lasted, would be the same whether it were for one year or twenty, or for life, or descendible to his eldest son." Adams was thus offering an argument strikingly similar to the one deployed by Hamilton in the convention (the latter may well have borrowed it from the *Defence*): a chief magistrate is a monarch so long as he is a constitutive part of the legislative power, whether he holds his office for a fixed term of years or for life; whether he is elected or a hereditary prince.[130] The mistake, Adams suspected, derived from the conjunction of two crucial premises: (1) in a "republic," the people are governed by representatives; and (2) a hereditary monarch cannot be regarded as a representative of the people—either because only assemblies of a certain kind can be said to represent the people (the whig view) or because only elected magistrates can be said to do so (Wilson's view). Adams was of course happy to concede the truth of the first premise: he had no doubt that republican government was government by representation. But he had always completely rejected the second. "The people, the nation, in whom all power resides originally," he now insisted yet again to Sherman, "may delegate their power for one year or for ten years; for years, or for life; or may delegate it in fee simple or fee tail, if I may so express myself; or during good behavior, or at will, or till further orders."[131] It followed, as he had put it in the *Defence,* that "an hereditary limited monarch is the representative of the whole nation, for the management of the executive power, as much as an house of representatives is, as one branch of the legislature, and as guardian of the public purse."[132] To be a representative, as Royalists had always argued, is simply to be authorized (tacitly) to speak and act in the name of the people; the issue of election is a red herring. (Indeed, Adams himself observed in December 1787 that "elections to offices which are great objects of Ambition, I look at with terror. Experiments of this kind have been so often tryed, and so universally found productive of Horrors, that there is great reason to dread them.")[133] One could therefore not distinguish "republican" government from "monarchy" on the grounds that the latter does not constitute "government by representation."[134]

Adams was now prepared to draw his conclusion. If the people are at liberty to "create a simple monarchy for years, life, or perpetuity, and in either case the creature would be equally a simple monarch during the continuance of his power"—that is, if a chief magistrate does not become something other than a monarch simply because he is elected for a fixed term—then we should "now consider what our constitution is, and see whether any other name can with propriety be given it, than that of a monarchical republic, or if you will, a limited monarchy."[135] True, "the duration of our president is neither perpetual nor for life; it is only for four years; but his power during those four years is much greater than that of an avoyer, a consul, a podestà, a doge, a stadtholder; nay, than a king of Poland; nay, than a king of Sparta."

> I know of no first magistrate in any republican government, excepting England and Neuchatel, who possesses a constitutional dignity, authority, and power comparable to his. The power of sending and receiving ambassadors, of raising and commanding armies and navies, of nominating and appointing and commissioning all officers, of managing the treasures, the internal and external affairs of the nation; nay, the whole executive power, coextensive with the legislative power, is vested in him, and he has the right, and his is the duty, to take care that the laws be faithfully executed. These rights and duties, these prerogatives and dignities, are so transcendent that they must naturally and necessarily excite in the nation all the jealousy, envy, fears, apprehensions, and opposition, that are so constantly observed in England against the crown.[136]

The Constitution therefore indisputably created a monarchical republic, or a limited monarchy. As such, all of the powers given to the president were strictly "necessary," but, Adams continued, "it is equally certain, I think, that they ought to have been still greater, or much less. The limitations upon them in the cases of war, treaties, and appointments to office, and especially the limitation on the president's independence as a branch of the legislative, will be the destruction of this constitution, and involve us in anarchy, if not amended."[137] As a matter of theory, "in our constitution the sovereignty,—that is, the legislative power,—is divided into three branches," but in fact "the third branch, though essential, is not equal. The president must pass judgment upon every law; but in some cases his judgment may be overruled. These cases will be such as attack his constitutional power; it is, therefore, certain he has not equal power to defend himself, or the constitution, or the judicial power, as the senate and house have." Sherman's posi-

tion that the Constitution ought not to have assigned the president an absolute negative "is therefore clearly and certainly an error, because the practice
of Great Britain in making the supreme executive a branch of the legislature, and giving it a negative on all the laws, must be imitated by every
monarchical republic"—and the new United States was one of these.[138]

Sherman replied in a rather unexpected manner. In the convention itself,
he had rejected the negative voice on standard whig grounds: since only an
assembly could be said to represent the people, prerogative powers in the
chief magistrate would constitute government by an alien will (i.e., slavery).
The negative would render the executive "independent" of the assembly
and therefore inherently "tyrannical." One would accordingly have expected Sherman to respond to Adams by invoking the theory of "virtual
representation," the parliamentarian view that only an artificial body constituting an adequate "image" (or "representation") of the people can be said
to speak or act in its name. This standard whig argument had enjoyed a
great vogue among Antifederalists during the months following the convention; it undergirded their conviction that the House of Representatives
was simply too small to "represent" the people. (Needless to say, most denied a fortiori that the Senate or the president could count as representatives.) In the words of "Brutus," writing in New York, "the very term, representative, implies, that the person or body chosen for this purpose, should
resemble those who appoint them—a representation of the people of America, if it be a true one, must be like the people. It ought to be so constituted,
that a person, who is a stranger to the country, might be able to form a just
idea of their character, by knowing that of their representatives. They are
the sign—the people are the thing signified. It is absurd to speak of one
thing being the representative of another, upon any other principle."[139] The
"Federal Farmer" likewise complained that "we have forgot what the true
meaning of representation is," insisting that "a full and equal representation,
is that which possesses the same interests, feelings, opinions, and views the
people themselves would were they all assembled—a fair representation,
therefore, should be so regulated, that every order of men in the community, according to the common course of elections, can have a share in it—in
order to allow professional men, merchants, traders, farmers, mechanics,
&c. to bring a just proportion of their best informed men respectively into
the legislature, the representation must be considerably numerous."[140] In
the New York ratifying convention, Melanchthon Smith agreed that "the

idea that naturally suggests itself to our minds, when we speak of representatives, is, that they resemble those they represent. They should be a true picture of the people, possess a knowledge of their circumstances and their wants, sympathize in all their distresses, and be disposed to seek their true interests"—and, on these grounds, he rejected out of hand the view that the envisioned federal legislature (let alone the chief magistrate) could represent the people.[141]

But Sherman had clearly moved away from this position in the year since he had left Philadelphia. Indeed, he may well have formed doubts about it by the end of the convention itself, since he ultimately decided to sign the Constitution. In his answer to Adams's letter, he did not reprise his earlier argument that an absolute negative in the chief magistrate was inherently enslaving. Quite the contrary, he now assailed the absolute negative chiefly on the grounds that it would *limit* the ability of the executive to check the legislature: "Can it be expected that a chief magistrate of a free and enlightened people, on whom he depends for his election and continuance in office, would give his negative to a law passed by the other two branches of the legislature, if he had power? . . . On the whole, it appears to me that the *power* of a complete negative, if given, would be a dormant and useless one, and that the provision in the constitution is calculated to operate with proper weight, and will produce beneficial effects."[142] Sherman was arguing, in other words, that the absolute negative—while acceptable in principle and even salutary in monarchies, where the prince was hereditary and the "rights of the nobility" required protection—would be too politically costly for an elected chief magistrate to exercise and would therefore lie "dormant."[143] As Wilson would put the same point a year later, it would "remain, like a sword always in the scabbard, an instrument, sometimes of distant apprehension, but not of present or practical utility."[144] The qualified negative, on the other hand, would simply "produce a revision" and "would probably be exercised on proper occasions; and the legislature have the benefit of the president's reasons in their further deliberations on the subject, and if a sufficient number of the members of either house should be convinced by them to put a negative upon the bill, it would add weight to the president's opinion, and render it more satisfactory to the people."

Hamilton had recently offered precisely this defense of the qualified negative in *Federalist* 73, stressing the degree to which it would in fact *strengthen* the prerogative, and Sherman had undoubtedly read and absorbed his argument.[145] Indeed, Sherman now observed that "the negative vested in the crown of Great Britain has never been exercised since the Revolution, and the great influence of the crown in the legislature of that nation is derived from another source, that of appointment to all offices of honor and profit."[146] It is the prerogative of appointment, not the negative, "which has rendered the power of the crown nearly absolute; so that the nation is in fact governed by the cabinet council, who are the creatures of the crown." Sherman, in short, maintained his allegiance to the whig theory of English constitutional decline—according to which the Crown had become "absolute" as a result of its "influence"—and, as a result, he continued to resist Adams's view (shared by Wilson, Hamilton, and their allies) that the president should have been given the prerogative to "appoint to offices without control." But he had clearly jettisoned the whig denunciation of the negative voice. The explanation for this shift appears at the beginning of his reply to Adams, where he addressed their quarrel over the meaning of the term "republic." "Writers on government," he explained, "differ in their definition"; some, indeed, now define a republic simply as *a commonwealth without a king.*"[147] But "what I meant by it was, a government under the authority of the people, consisting of legislative, executive, and judiciary powers; the legislative powers vested in an assembly, consisting of one or more branches, who, together with the executive, are appointed by the people, and dependent on them for continuance, by periodical elections, agreeably to an established constitution; and that what especially denominates it a *republic* is its dependence on the *public* or *people at large,* without any hereditary powers."

Once again, Sherman's evolving position clearly reflected his encounter with *The Federalist.* His account of "republican" government is drawn almost verbatim from Madison's celebrated definition in *Federalist* 39: "we may define a republic to be, or at least may bestow that name on, a government which derives all its powers directly or indirectly from the great body of the people, and is administered by persons holding their offices during pleasure, for a limited period, or during good behavior."[148] Madison had made the same point in shorthand in *Federalist* 10, defining a republic simply as "a government in which the scheme of representation takes place"—or one in which "the delegation of the government" is "to a small number of citizens elected by the rest."[149] Just as Adams had suspected, Sherman was now denying that hereditary monarchy was compatible with republican government because he had come to accept the

view that "republican government" consisted of "government by representation," as well as the corollary that only elected magistrates could count as
"representatives." He had traded in his earlier whig position for a "Wilsonian" one, which, as far as Adams was concerned, was no progress at all.[150]
But precisely because Sherman was now prepared to acknowledge that *any*
elected magistrate should be regarded as a representative of the people (and
not only a "representative" assembly), he no longer viewed the chief magistrate as the bearer of an "alien will." The president too would speak and act
in the name of the people and to be governed in part by his prerogative was
accordingly consistent with the liberty of citizens.

The momentous conflict between the Royalist and Wilsonian theories of
representation underlying Adams's exchange with Sherman would not be
resolved during the ratification debates, largely because Federalists could
afford to "bracket" it. Both of these rival theories, after all, were "authorization" theories. They converged in insisting that, in Hamilton's words, "the
President of the United States will be himself the representative of the
people"[151] and likewise yielded the result that the Senate and the House of
Representatives would represent the people, despite the fact that the latter
would be a fraction of the size of the House of Commons (representation,
Federalists could all agree, had nothing to do with "considerations of number").[152] Consider a fairly standard formulation of what would emerge as the
Federalist position, offered by Thomas Tudor Tucker of South Carolina:

> In a free State, every officer, from the Governor to the constable, is, in so far
> as the powers of his office extend, as truly representative of the people, as a
> member of the legislature; and his act, within the appointed limitation, is the
> act of the people: for he is their agent, and derives his authority from them."[153]

Tucker's claim here is remarkably, and fruitfully, ambiguous. In what sense
is every officer of a "free state" a "representative" of the people, such that he
may be said to "derive his authority" from them? Is it because a "free state"
is one in which the institutions of government have been "authorized" by
the people in a moment of original contract and then tacitly approved
by each succeeding generation (in which case even a hereditary monarch
might be said to "be truly representative of the people")? Or is it because a
"free state" is one in which all officers are *elected* by the people and for this
reason alone to be regarded as their representatives? Orthodox Royalists

could gloss the claim in the first manner; Wilsonians could gloss it in the second.

The target of this "overlapping consensus" was, of course, the whig parliamentarian theory of representation that had been embraced by so many Antifederalists. The shared imperative for Federalists was to explain why the ambition to create an "image" of the people in "miniature" was both self-defeating and perverse. It was self-defeating, as Adams explained in the *Defence,* because no assembly could ever replicate the people to such a degree that it could, with propriety, "be virtually deemed the nation"—or, as he would elaborate some years later, because "no picture, great or small, no statue, no bust in brass or marble, gold or silver, ever yet perfectly resembled the original, so no representative government ever perfectly represented or resembled the original nation or people."[154] It was perverse, as Hamilton put the case in the New York ratifying convention, because "the true principle of a republic is, that the people should choose whom they please to govern them. Representation is imperfect in proportion as the current of popular favor is checked. This great source of free government, popular election, should be perfectly pure, and the most unbounded liberty allowed."[155] The requirement to constitute a perfect "image" of the people must inevitably constrain the freedom of the people to choose their agents (they might not *want* to be governed by a body that resembles them)—and therefore vitiates the "authorization" that elections are designed to secure.[156] Hamilton put the issue as follows in *Federalist* 35: "The idea of an actual representation of all classes of the people, by persons of each class, is altogether visionary. Unless it were expressly provided in the Constitution, that each different occupation should send one or more members, the thing would never take place in practice. Mechanics and manufacturers will always be inclined, with few exceptions, to give their votes to merchants, in preference to persons of their own professions or trades."[157] The ambitions of the whig theory of representation, in short, could never be realized "under any arrangement that leaves the votes of the people free," and any arrangement that deprives the people of their free votes cannot yield legitimate representation.

But defenders of the Constitution could not leave matters here. Their opponents, after all, were not simply claiming that the Constitution failed to establish proper representative institutions; the majority of them were also claiming, in Randolph's terms, that it embodied a "foetus of monarchy"—a sorry attempt to ape the Constitution of Great Britain, or even to outstrip the British original in its eager embrace of prerogative power. In other words, even if Antifederalists could be persuaded to concede that the president might count as the representative of the people, most would have remained extremely anxious about the set of powers that he would be entitled to wield. Thus, Mercy Otis Warren fumed that the Constitution established a "Republican *form* of government, founded on the principles of monarchy," investing "discretionary powers in the hands of man, which he may, or may not abuse."[158] Returning to the Scriptural language of the debate over *Common Sense,* she insisted that while the people of the United States assuredly "deprecate discord and civil convulsions," they "are not yet generally prepared, with the ungrateful Israelites, to ask a King, nor are their spirits sufficiently broken to yield the best of their olive grounds to his servants, and to see their sons appointed to run before his chariots."[159] Luther Martin of Maryland, one of the dissenting delegates to the convention, likewise declared that the new president "as here constituted, was a KING, in every thing but the name" and that he would be able "to become a *King* in *name,* as well as in *substance,* and establish himself in office not only for his own life, but even if he chooses, to have that authority perpetuated to his family"[160]—a point seconded by "Montezuma," who wrote in the *Independent Gazetteer* (posing satirically as a Federalist) that "president" was merely a name adopted "in conformity to the prejudices of a silly people who are so foolishly fond of a Republican government, that we were obliged to accommodate in names and forms to them, in order more effectually to secure the substance of our proposed plan; but we all know that Cromwell was a King, with the title of Protector."[161] Patrick Henry was similarly outraged, declaring in the Virginia ratifying convention that, under the new Constitution, "there is to be a great and mighty President, with very extensive powers—the powers of a king. He is to be supported in extravagant magnificence; so that the whole of our property may be taken by this American government, by laying what taxes they please, giving themselves what salaries they please, and suspending our laws at their pleasure."[162] Indeed, Henry exclaimed, "I would rather infinitely—and I am sure most of this Convention are of the same opinion—have a king, lords, and commons, than a government so replete with such insupportable evils. If we make a king, we may prescribe the rules by which he shall rule his people, and interpose such checks as shall prevent him from infringing them; but the President, in the field, at the head of his army, can prescribe the terms on which he shall reign master, so far that it will puzzle any American ever to get his neck from under the galling yoke."[163] The anonymous author of the "Tamony" letters agreed: in truth, he observed, "though not dignified with the magic name of King," the president "will possess more supreme power, that Great Britain allows her hereditary monarchs."[164]

For theorists of the Royalist Revolution, one possible response to this barrage was to offer an affirmative defense of the principles of the English constitution, "rightly understood"—to concede that the new frame of government moved far beyond the state constitutions in its embrace of prerogative power, but to treat this as a welcome and long-overdue development. Benjamin Rush took this approach when he announced that "the confederation, together with most of our state constitutions, were formed under very unfavourable circumstances."[165] At the time of their drafting, "we had just emerged from a corrupted monarchy. Although we understood perfectly the principles of liberty, yet most of us were ignorant of the forms and combinations of power in republics. . . . We detested the British name; and unfortunately refused to copy some things in the administration of justice and power, in the British government, which have made it the admiration and envy of the world." "In our opposition to monarchy," Rush explained, "we forgot that the temple of tyranny has two doors. We bolted one of them by proper restraints; but we left the other open, by neglecting to guard against the effects of our own ignorance and licentiousness."[166] James McClurg had reasoned similarly in the convention itself, explaining he "was not so much afraid of the shadow of monarchy as to be unwilling to approach it; nor so wedded to Republican Gov[ernmen]t. as not to be sensible of the tyrannies that had been & may be exercised under that form. It was an essential object with him to make the Executive independent of the Legislature."[167] James Iredell, leading the Federalist forces in North Carolina, predictably insisted that "the jealousies" which had "disabled the Executive authority" in the state constitutions "may more fairly be ascribed to the natural irritation of the public mind at the time when the constitutions were formed, than to an enlarged and full consideration of the subject."[168] "Indeed," he reflected, "it could scarcely be avoided, that when arms were first taken up in the cause of liberty, to save us from the immediate crush of arbitrary power, we should lean too much rather to the extreme of weakening than of strengthening the Executive power in our own government." The aversion to prerogative power that had gripped the former colonies in the later 1770s had simply been a pathological symptom of postrevolutionary frenzy. It was now, mercifully, being laid to rest at last.[169] In truth, Tench Coxe of Pennsylvania reminded his readers (echoing Wilson), during the Revolution the colonists had never objected to "the constitution of England as it stood on paper," still less to their connection "with the British crown."[170] The Revolution had emerged out of a "quarrel between the United States and the parliament of Great Britain," in which the latter had sought unconstitutional and tyrannical power.[171]

These theorists likewise exhibited a common understanding of the rationale for prerogative power within the British and American constitutional schemes. Reviving and expanding upon a standard Royalist argument that had been further developed by Rush and Adams in the late 1770s, they insisted that the crucial alliance in modern politics was that between the "one" and the "many" against the "few." It is in the nature of legislative bodies to be "filled in the course of a few years with a majority of rich men," Rush had explained in his "Ludlow" letters, and "their wealth will administer fuel to the love of arbitrary power that is common to all men"— eventually yielding "aristocracy," a noxious regime in which there are "only two sorts of animals, tyrants and slaves."[172] Only a prerogative-wielding chief magistrate, constituting a full third of the legislative power, could resist the forces of aristocratic despotism in the name of liberty. As Adams had put the point as early as 1779, "we have so many Men of Wealth, of ambitious Spirits, of Intrigue, of Luxury and Corruption, that incessant Factions will disturb our Peace, without [the chief magistrate's negative voice]."[173] Writing to Jefferson in December 1787, he repeated his basic conviction: "You are afraid of the one—I, of the few. We agree perfectly that the many should have a full fair and perfect Representation.—You are Apprehensive of Monarchy; I, of Aristocracy."[174] Adams accordingly insisted that the wealthy few should be quarantined in a legislative chamber of their own (ideally one possessing far less power than the Senate agreed to in Philadelphia), thus preventing them from coming to dominate the popular chamber.[175] The "many" would then find their crucial support against the encroachments of the aristocratic house in the prerogatives of the chief magistrate: "It is the true policy of the common people to place the whole executive power in one man, to make him a distinct order in the state, from whence arises an inevitable jealousy between him and the gentlemen; this forces him to become a father and protector of the common people, and to endeavor always to humble every proud, aspiring senator, or other officer in the state, who is in danger of acquiring an influence too great for the law, or the spirit of the constitution."[176] Wilson had likewise defended both an independent chief magistrate and a weak senate in the convention on the grounds that the president should be "the man of the people," their ally against the aristocratic few.[177]

Hamilton supplied a historical narrative to go along with this argument in a lengthy speech to the New York ratifying convention. "In the ancient *feudal governments* of Europe," he explained, "there were, in the first place a monarch; subordinate to him, a body of nobles; and subject to these, the vassals or the whole body of the people. The authority of the kings was limited, and that of the *barons* considerably independent." The result was a series of "contests between the king and his nobility," in which the latter had largely prevailed, to the extent that "the history of the feudal wars exhibits little more than a series of successful encroachments on the prerogatives of monarchy."[178] It was here that the trouble began. The nobles "took advantage of the depression of the royal authority, and the establishment of their own power, to oppress and tyrannise over their vassals." But the aristocrats had miscalculated badly: "As commerce enlarged, and as wealth and civilization encreased, the *people* began to feel their own weight and consequence: They grew tired of their oppressions; united their strength with that of the prince; and threw off the yoke of *aristocracy*."[179] European liberty, on this Federalist account, was the product of a victorious struggle of king and people against a tyrannical aristocracy. It followed that any proper scheme of free government should invest its chief magistrate with the prerogatives enjoyed by the monarch "under the true British constitution."[180]

But most defenders of the Constitution who wished to blunt the force of the "monarchist" charge instead followed the approach unveiled by Hamilton in *Federalist* 67–77. Hamilton's strategy in these justly famous essays was complex. He sought, on the one hand, to defend a strong executive vested with sweeping prerogative powers; but, at the same time, he attempted to assuage concerns about the monarchical tendencies of the Constitution by stressing the *weakness* of the president relative to the king of Great Britain. Rather than applauding the degree to which the new Constitution borrowed from the British original, Hamilton's tactic in this context was to accentuate its distance from that model. This approach required two highly rhetorical series of maneuvers. First, Hamilton had to defend as virtues of the Article II presidency all of the features he had assailed as its vices in the convention itself: the lack of a life term, the absence of an absolute negative voice, the partial character of the chief magistrate's appointment power, and so on. Second, and even more importantly, he had to paint a wholly outlandish picture of the powers of the British monarch as they actually existed in 1787. That is, in order to make the presidency look weak in relation to the British monarchy, he had to contrast the former to a radically idealized, parchment version of the latter.[181] Hamilton, who had been defending the Royalist cause since the imperial crisis, knew perfectly well that the prerogative powers that he attributed to the Crown in these essays had not in fact been wielded by English kings for generations; indeed, this had always been his great lament (recall his endorsement of Hume's account of English constitutional decline in the convention). His performance in *Federalist 67–77* was, therefore, disingenuous in the extreme, but it was not simply that. The rhetorical imperative to make the British monarchy seem stupendously powerful gave him a final, grand opportunity to reaffirm his own radical conception of the *proper* role of the British sovereign (as opposed to the one actually played by George III and his Hanoverian predecessors).[182] The result was perhaps the most stridently Royalist account of the English constitution to appear in the eighteenth century.

Hamilton began his performance by complaining that no aspect of the proposed Constitution "has been inveighed against with less candor or criticised with less judgment" than its vision of the chief magistrate. "Here the writers against the Constitution seem to have taken pains to signalize their talent of misrepresentation. Calculating upon the aversion of the people to monarchy, they have endeavored to enlist all their jealousies and apprehensions in opposition to the intended President of the United States; not merely as the embryo, but as the full-grown progeny, of that detested parent" (here Hamilton was clearly recalling Randolph's charge that the president would be a "foetus of monarchy").[183] He proceeded to offer an elaborate satire of Antifederalist anxieties:

> To establish the pretended affinity [with monarchy], they have not scrupled to draw resources even from the regions of fiction. The authorities of a magistrate, in few instances greater, in some instances less, than those of a governor of New York, have been magnified into more than royal prerogatives. He

has been decorated with attributes superior in dignity and splendor to those of a king of Great Britain. He has been shown to us with the diadem sparkling on his brow and the imperial purple flowing in his train. He has been seated on a throne surrounded with minions and mistresses, giving audience to the envoys of foreign potentates, in all the supercilious pomp of majesty. The images of Asiatic despotism and voluptuousness have scarcely been wanting to crown the exaggerated scene. We have been almost taught to tremble at the terrific visages of murdering janizaries, and to blush at the unveiled mysteries of a future seraglio.[184]

Drawing perhaps from the opening of Book II of *Paradise Lost*—where we encounter Satan seated "High on a throne of royal state, which far / Outshone the wealth or Ormuz and of Ind, / Or where the gorgeous East with richest hand / Showers on her kings barbaric pearl and gold" (II.1–4)[185]—Hamilton lampooned his opponents for imagining the new president as an Asiatic grand signor, "decorated with attributes superior in dignity and splendor to those of a king of Great Britain."

His refutation of the charge takes the form of a point-by-point comparison of the powers of the president and the British monarch, designed to show the relative weakness of the former.[186] The discussion begins innocently enough by stating the obvious: although both the British constitution and the proposed American one vest the "executive authority" in "a single magistrate," in the latter "that magistrate is to be elected for *four* years; and is to be re-eligible as often as the people of the United States shall think him worthy of their confidence," whereas the king of Great Britain serves for life and is a hereditary prince.[187] Hamilton, of course, had bemoaned this asymmetry in the convention, but here it serves his purpose. He continues by pointing out that the president can be removed by impeachment, whereas the king is immune from such proceedings and his person is deemed "sacred and inviolable."[188] Likewise, the king presides over an established church and may "confer titles of nobility," whereas the president enjoys neither of these prerogatives.[189] And whereas the "the President is to nominate, and, *with the advice and consent of the Senate,* to appoint ambassadors and other public ministers, judges of the Supreme Court, and in general all officers of the United States established by law," the king "appoints to all offices" without the formal consent of a legislative body.[190] Once again, Hamilton (along with Wilson, Adams, and their allies) had desperately sought to

220 THE ROYALIST REVOLUTION

assign the president an analogous prerogative of appointment, but their fail-ure is presented on this occasion as a virtue of the scheme.

So far, all of this is relatively unremarkable.[191] But Hamilton does not leave matters here. "The President of the United States," he continues, "is to have power to return a bill, which shall have passed the two branches of the legislature, for reconsideration; but the bill so returned is not to become a law, unless, upon that reconsideration, it be approved by two thirds of both houses. The king of Great Britain, on his part, has an absolute negative upon the acts of the two houses of Parliament."[192] The royal negative, as Hamil-ton well knew, had not been exercised for generations, but here he insists that "the disuse of that power for a considerable time past does not affect the reality of its existence; and is to be ascribed wholly to the Crown's having found the means of substituting influence to authority, or the art of gaining a majority in one or the other of the two houses, to the necessity of exerting a prerogative which could seldom be exerted without hazarding some de-gree of national agitation."[193] In order to make the British monarch appear as strong as possible (and the president correspondingly weak), Hamilton deploys the whig explanation for the "disuse" of the negative: the king has simply felt no need to wield the negative because he is powerful enough to control both houses of Parliament by means of corruption. This, of course, was a view of the British constitutional predicament that Hamilton had al-ways rejected; he had instead followed Hume in regarding "corruption" as a wholly inadequate, but still essential, *replacement* for prerogative powers (chiefly, the negative voice) that now, regrettably, existed only as a matter of form. Like "Centinel," he bemoaned the fact that "the king of England . . . enjoys but in *name* the prerogative of a negative upon the parliament" and "has not dared to exercise it for near a century past."[194]

Moreover, Hamilton would shortly argue in *Federalist* 73 that the quali-fied negative of the president should be preferred to the absolute negative because it would *strengthen* rather than weaken the prerogative: "in propor-tion as it would be less apt to offend, it would be more apt to be exercised; and for this very reason, it may in practice be found more effectual."[195] But, in this polemical context, Hamilton is happy to emphasize the weakness of the president's qualified negative in relation to what he had regarded for two decades as a lamentably defunct prerogative of the sovereign. As one Antifederalist complained, "touching on the *President*" ("more properly, our new KING"), Hamilton and his disciples were aiming "to conceal his immense powers, by representing the King of Great Britain as possessed of many hereditary prerogatives, rights and powers that he was not possessed of." In particular, the president, unlike the British monarch, is to have "a negative over the proceedings of both branches of the legislature: and to complete his uncontrouled sway, he is neither restrained nor assisted by a *privy council,* which is a novelty in government."[196]

Next, we read that "the President is to be the 'commander-in-chief' of the army and navy of the United States. In this respect his authority would be nominally the same with that of the king of Great Britain, but in substance much inferior to it," for "that of the British king extends to the *declaring* of war and to the *raising* and *regulating* of fleets and armies—all which, by the Constitution under consideration, would appertain to the legislature."[197] This was an extraordinary claim. Although the making of war and peace formally remained prerogatives of the Crown, in reality decisions of this kind had long been taken by cabinet ministers. These ministers were in turn required to maintain the support of a majority in the House of Commons, and they themselves sat in one of the two houses.[198] Indeed, George III had only recently shown himself powerless to assume any personal control over the waging of the Revolutionary War and in 1779 had nearly provoked a constitutional crisis simply by choosing to summon and address his own cabinet (no monarch since Queen Anne had done so).[199] Moreover, while it remained a prerogative of "the Crown" (read: ministers of the Crown) to raise and equip armies and fleets, monarchs since the Glorious Revolution had lacked the authority to do so in the absence of an annual "Mutiny Act" passed by Parliament—and, in any event, required supply from the Commons in order to pay their troops.[200]

Hamilton's Antifederalist critics duly pounced. George Mason, who could identify no important respects in which "this president, invested with his powers and prerogatives, essentially differ[s] from the king of Great Britain (save as to name, the creation of nobility, and some immaterial incidents, the offspring of absurdity and locality)," pointedly observed in his "Cato" letters that "though it may be asserted that the king of Great Britain has the express power of making peace or war, yet he never thinks it prudent to do so without the advice of his Parliament, from whom he is to derive his support—and therefore these powers, in both president and king, are substantially the same."[201] Mason, indeed, had pointed out in the convention itself that in Britain, "the whole movements of their Government . . . are

directed by their Cabinet Council, composed entirely of the principal officers of the great departments," such that "when a Privy Council is called, it
is scarcely ever for any other purpose than to give a formal sanction to the
previous determinations of the other, so much so that it is notorious that not
one time in a thousand one member of the Privy Council, except a known
adherent of administration, is summoned to it."[202] William Lancaster likewise rose in the North Carolina ratifying convention to insist that "a man of
any information knows that the king of Great Britain cannot raise and support armies. He may call for and raise men, but he has no money to support
them."[203] The author of the "Tamony" letters went even further, observing
that the new president "will possess more supreme power, than Great Britain allows her hereditary monarchs, who derive ability to support an army
from annual supplies, and owe the command of one to an annual mutiny
law. The American President may be granted supplies for two years, and his
command of a standing army is unrestrained by law."[204] Hamilton registered these objections, but replied in the language of a strident Royalist:
"TAMONY, has asserted that the king of Great Britain owes his prerogative
as commander-in-chief to an annual mutiny bill. The truth is, on the contrary, that his prerogative, in this respect, is immemorial, and was only disputed, 'contrary to all reason and precedent' . . . by the Long Parliament of
Charles I."[205] In truth, Hamilton declared (quoting Blackstone's *Commentaries* but badly misrepresenting the position of his source[206]), "the sole supreme government and command" of armies and navies "EVER WAS AND
IS the undoubted right of his Majesty and his royal predecessors, kings and
queens of England, and that both or either house of Parliament cannot nor
ought to pretend to the same."

Hamilton's argument in *Federalist* 69 proceeds in much the same vein.
"The President," he continues, "is to have power, with the advice and consent of the Senate, to make treaties, provided two thirds of the senators
present concur. The king of Great Britain is the sole and absolute representative of the nation in all foreign transactions. He can of his own accord
make treaties of peace, commerce, alliance, and of every other description."[207] Opponents of the Constitution scoffed once again. "It is contended,"
observed Patrick Henry in the Virginia ratifying convention, "that, if the
king of Great Britain makes a treaty within the line of his prerogative, it is
the law of the land." But "can the English monarch make a treaty which
shall subvert the common law of England, and the constitution? Dare he
make a treaty that shall violate Magna Charta, or the bill of rights? Dare he

do any thing derogatory to the honor, or subversive of the great privileges, of his people? No, sir. If he did, it would be nugatory, and the attempt would endanger his existence."[208] Even some Federalists were prompted to concede as much: Wilson Nicholas of Virginia mocked the notion that "the king of Great Britain can make what treaties he pleases." "But, sir," he countered, "do not the House of Commons influence them? Will he make a treaty manifestly repugnant to their interest? Will they not tell him he is mistaken in that respect, as in many others? Will they not bring the minister who advises a bad treaty to punishment? This gives them such influence that they can dictate in what manner they shall be made."[209] Francis Corbin added that "if the king were to make such a treaty himself, contrary to the advice of his ministry," a constitutional crisis would ensue.[210] Moreover, a number of Antifederalists pointed out that treaties in Britain were in fact frequently laid before Parliament—not least the Peace of Paris that had ended the Revolutionary War.[211]

Hamilton once again stuck to his Royalist guns. "It has been insinuated," he wrote, "that his authority [i.e., the king's] in this respect is not conclusive, and that his conventions with foreign powers are subject to the revision, and stand in need of the ratification, of Parliament." But, Hamilton insisted, "I believe this doctrine was never heard of, until it was broached upon the present occasion. Every jurist of that kingdom, and every other man acquainted with its Constitution, knows, as an established fact, that the prerogative of making treaties exists in the crown in its utmost plentitude; and that the compacts entered into by the royal authority have the most complete legal validity and perfection, independent of any other sanction."[212] James Iredell, who simply paraphrased Hamilton's comparative argument in the North Carolina convention, agreed: "A gentleman from New Hanover has asked whether it is not the practice, in Great Britain, to submit treaties to Parliament, before they are esteemed as valid. The king has the sole authority, by the laws of that country, to make treaties." To be sure, "after treaties are made, they are frequently discussed in the two houses, where, of late years, the most important matters of government have been narrowly examined." But "the constitutional power of making treaties is vested in the crown; and the power with whom the treaty is made considers it as binding, without any act of Parliament."[213]

Hamilton had no compunction about carrying his argument through to its logical conclusion. He confidently attributed to the person of the king an effective prerogative to "prorogue or even dissolve the Parliament," to select his ministers at pleasure, to "make denizens of aliens," to "erect corporations with all the rights incident to corporate bodies," to "serve as the arbiter of commerce," "establish markets and fairs," "regulate weights and measures," "lay embargoes for a limited time," "coin money," and "authorize or prohibit the circulation of foreign coin."[214] And although the sovereign was duty bound to seek advice from his ministers, Hamilton insisted that "the king is not bound by the resolutions of his council, though they are answerable for the advice they give. He is the absolute master of his own conduct in the exercise of his office, and may observe or disregard the counsel given to him at his sole discretion."[215] Again, as a description of the British monarchy as it actually functioned in the late eighteenth century, this was mere burlesque. But as a defense of a particular conception of what the monarchy *should* be like under the proper construal of the English constitution, it was perfectly continuous with what patriot Royalists such as Hamilton had been arguing since the imperial crisis. At that time, even Jefferson had implored the king to separate himself from his "British counsellors"— who were dismissed as intruding "parties"—and to "think and act for yourself and your people."[216] But this high Royalist understanding of the kingly office was as reactionary in 1787 as it had been in 1775.

In other contexts, it suited Hamilton's purpose to acknowledge this fact. In *Federalist* 71, he developed a subtle a fortiori argument designed to reassure critics who might remain anxious about the prerogatives assigned to the chief magistrate. In Great Britain, the argument goes, the king is vested with hereditary power and other "splendid attributes," but even these advantages of the Crown had spectacularly failed to prevent the House of Commons from achieving complete supremacy during the course of the previous century. How much less, then, should we fear that the far weaker president, as imagined in Article II, would come to dominate the legislature? This argument, in short, attempted to strike yet another delicate balance: it once again sought to emphasize the strengths of the British monarch relative to those of the president, but at the same time to demonstrate that the monarchy had been gradually but utterly subjected to the legislature despite them (thus directly contradicting the carefully wrought account of sweeping royal power in *Federalist* 69). "If a British House of Commons," Hamilton reasoned, "from the most feeble beginnings, *from the mere power of assenting or disagreeing to the imposition of a new tax,* have, by rapid strides, reduced the prerogatives of the Crown and the privileges of the nobility within the limits they conceived to be compatible with the principles of a free government, while they raised themselves to the rank and consequence of a co-equal branch of the legislature; if they have been able, in one instance, to abolish both the royalty and the aristocracy, and to overturn all the ancient establishments, as well in the Church as State; if they have been able, on a recent occasion, to make the monarch tremble at the prospect of an innovation attempted by them [Charles James Fox's India bill[217]], what would be to be feared from an elective magistrate of four years' duration, with the confined authorities of a President of the United States?"[218] Here the king of Great Britain, depicted in *Federalist* 69 as master of all he surveys, is shown "trembling" before an all-powerful legislature.

Hamilton's Federalist allies immediately picked up this argument and deployed it with great energy. Iredell, for one, repeated Hamilton's analysis almost verbatim in the North Carolina ratifying convention: the king of Great Britain, he noted, possessed an "influence" and a "power" far beyond any that would be enjoyed by the new president. "Under these circumstances," he continued, "one would suppose their influence [i.e., that of the House of Commons], compared to that of the king and the lords, was very inconsiderable. But the fact is, that they have, by degrees, increased their power to an astonishing degree, and when they think proper to exert it, can command almost anything they please."[219] In the Virginia convention, Wilson Nicholas likewise argued that although the Crown was initially strong and the Commons weak, the latter "have increased their powers, in succeeding reigns, to such a degree, that they entirely control the operation of government, even in those cases where the king's prerogative gave him, nominally, the sole direction."[220] Nicholas then proceeded to apply this analysis to the question of the negative voice in particular. Noting that "there is scarcely an instance, for a century past, of the crown's exercising its undoubted prerogative of rejecting a bill sent up to it by the two houses of Parliament," he recognized that many of his fellow delegates were eager to explain this fact in the classical whig manner: the English monarchs, on this standard account, had simply declined to use the negative because they were powerful enough to get their way in each legislative chamber by means of "influence" and "corruption." Nicholas regarded this explanation as straightforwardly false: "It is no answer to say, that the king's influence is sufficient to prevent any obnoxious bills passing the two houses; there are many instances, in that period, not only of bills passing the two houses, but even receiving the royal assent, contrary to the private wish and inclination of the prince."[221] The king might retain his prerogatives on paper, but, in reality, the Commons had brazenly ignored his "private wish and inclination" for over a hundred years. The American Revolution, on the Royalist account, had been waged for no other reason.

II

Nearly fifteen years after the Constitution was ratified, the Virginia jurist St. George Tucker would revisit Hamilton's influential comparison of the presidency and the British monarchy in his 1803 annotated edition of Blackstone's *Commentaries*. The occasion was apposite: Hamilton had festooned his analysis of royal power in *Federalist* 69 with references and direct quotations drawn from Blackstone, plainly hoping that the appearance of agreement with England's greatest constitutional authority would lend credibility to his account. Tucker, for his part, was no committed defender of the new American chief magistracy: he openly mused that the presidency might perhaps be replaced with a "numerous executive," on the model of the French Directory, and fretted in his commentary that "if a single executive do not exhibit all the features of monarchy at first, like the infant Hercules, it requires only time to mature it's strength, to evince the extent of it's powers."[222] But he was nonetheless fully prepared to explore and acknowledge the ways in which the American executive might be seen to perfect the British original. His project, however, required emphasizing the degree to which Hamilton had, in fact, deployed a caricature of Blackstone's constitutional analysis in 1788. For while Blackstone had admittedly been a Tory who was eager to minimize the extent of the century-long transition from royal to ministerial government, Tucker recognized that he had also been a lucid observer of British political reality. The great jurist had indeed supplied a list of what remained, as a matter of law, the prerogatives of the Crown (although he took a far narrower view of these than Hamilton suggested[223]), but he had also immediately reminded his readers that many of these powers were no longer at the effective disposal of the king.

"The powers of the crown are now to all appearance greatly curtailed and diminished since the reign of king James the first," Blackstone had observed, to the extent that "we may perhaps be led to think that, the balance is enclined pretty strongly to the popular scale, and that the executive magistrate has neither independence nor power enough left, to form that check upon the lords and commons, which the founders of our constitution intended."[224] Blackstone argued that this conclusion was overly hasty, but not because he had any illusions that British monarchs could exert their prerogative powers in government as they had before the parliamentarian revolutions. Instead, like Hume, he identified "influence" as a substitute for prerogative, although he was both far more confident in its efficacy than was Hume and far more anxious about the dangers of the substitution (in this respect, he came rather close to endorsing the standard whig theory of English constitutional corruption).[225] "The instruments of [royal] power are not perhaps so open and avowed as they formerly were," in Blackstone's telling, "but they are not the weaker on that account." The rise of the eighteenth-century fiscal-military state had placed the monarch in control of an extensive patronage network and thereby assigned the "executive power so persuasive an energy . . . as will amply make amends for the loss of external prerogative." "Whatever may have become of the *nominal,* the *real* power of the crown has not been too far weakened by any transactions of the last century. . . . the stern commands of prerogative have yielded to the milder voice of influence."[226] On Blackstone's account, if the king remained strong, it was *despite* the fact that he no longer wielded the legal powers of the Crown; the latter were now the effective possession of ministers accountable to parliament.

Armed with this recognition, Tucker concluded that although it is certainly true that "many of the most important prerogatives of the British crown, are transferred from the executive authority, in the United States, to the supreme national council, in congress assembled," in a very real sense the Constitution had assigned the American president powers far *greater* than any enjoyed by the king of Great Britain.[227] In the English constitution, the "unity of the executive" and its attendant "dispatch" were, in truth, illusory:

> If such are the real advantages of a single executive magistrate, we may contend that they are found in a much greater degree in the federal government, than in the English. In the latter it exists, only theoretically, in an individual; the practical exercise of it, being devolved upon ministers, councils, and boards. The king, according to the acknowledged principles of the constitution, not being responsible for any of his acts, the minister upon whom all responsibility devolves, to secure his indemnity acts by the advice of the

privy council to whom every measure of importance is submitted, before it is carried into effect. His plans are often digested and canvassed in a still more secret conclave, consisting of the principal officers of state, and stiled the cabinet-council, before they are communicated to the privy council: matters are frequently referred to the different boards, for their advice thereon, previously to their discussion, and final decision, in the council. Thus, in fact, the unity of the executive is merely ideal, existing only in the theory of the government; whatever is said of the unanimity, or dispatch arising from the unity of the executive power, is therefore without foundation.[228]

Here was the great fact about the eighteenth-century British monarchy that Hamilton had deplored for all of his adult life, the same fact that he had been forced to occlude in order to make his rhetorical case in *Federalist 69*. While the Crown retained its "prerogatives," the king enjoyed most of them only in name.[229] Under the Constitution of the United States, in contrast, "we find a single executive officer substituted for a numerous board, where responsibility is divided, till it is entirely lost, and where the chance of unanimity lessens in geometrical proportion to the number that compose it."[230] Moreover, "as every executive measure must originate in the breast of the president, his plans will have all the benefit of uniformity, that can be expected to flow from the operations of any individual mind."[231] The president of the United States does in reality what the king of Great Britain does only in theory. This was the great victory of the Royalist Revolution.[232] As for the anxiety that a "single person" entrusted with powers far beyond those of a British monarch might prove dangerous to the new republic, Tucker suggested that Americans might console themselves with a simple thought: "The very title of our first magistrate, in some measure exempts us from the danger of those calamities by which European nations are almost perpetually visited. The title of king, prince, emperor, or czar, without the smallest addition to his powers, would have rendered him a member of the fraternity of crowned heads: their common cause has more than once threatened the desolation of Europe. To have added a member to this sacred family in America, would have invited and perpetuated among us all the evils of Pandora's Box."[233] As Wilson had put the same point in the convention itself, "all know that a single magistrate is not a King."[234]

"A New Monarchy in America"

On May 1, 1789, the United States Senate convened to review the minutes of George Washington's inaugural address, delivered the previous day to a joint session of the first Congress. William Maclay of Pennsylvania, who would shortly emerge as one of the new administration's most incendiary critics, was appalled to discover that the formal record of proceedings referred to the president's remarks as *"His most gracious speech."* Concluding that "I must speak or nobody would," he rose in his chair and addressed the newly elected vice president, John Adams: "We have lately had a hard struggle for our liberty against kingly authority. The minds of men are still heated: everything related to that species of government is odious to the people. The words prefixed to the President's speech are the same that are usually placed before the speech of his Britannic Majesty. I know they will give offense. I consider them as improper."[1] Maclay was pointing out that the king of Great Britain delivered a "most gracious speech" from the throne at the opening of each session of Parliament; to style Washington's address as "most gracious" was accordingly to invest the new American president with pernicious "trappings and splendor of royalty."[2] Adams, who had been responsible for inserting the offending phrase, responded by "express[ing] the greatest surprise that anything should be objected to on account of its being taken from the practice of that Government under which we had lived so long and happily formerly." He added that "he was for a dignified and respectable government, and as far as he knew the sentiments of people they thought as he did; that for his part he was one of the first in the late contest [the Revolution], and, if *he could have thought of this, he never would have drawn his sword.*"[3] Maclay recorded that Adams approached him after the debate to explain his position further and promptly "got on the subject of checks to government and the balances of power." "His tale was long," Maclay observed drily, and "he seemed to expect some answer. I caught at the last word, and said undoubtedly without a balance there could be no equilibrium, and so left him hanging in geometry."[4]

Having made his escape, however, Maclay later found himself reflecting with considerable interest on Adams's observation about the nature of the Revolution:

> The unequivocal declaration that he would never have drawn his sword, etc., has drawn my mind to the following remarks: That the motives of the actors in the late Revolution were various cannot be doubted. The abolishing of royalty, the extinguishment of patronage and dependencies attached to that form of government, were the exalted motives of many revolutionists. . . . Yet there were not wanting a party whose motives were different. They wished for the loaves and fishes of government, and cared for nothing else but a translation of the diadem or scepter from London to Boston, New York, or Philadelphia; or, in other words, the creation of a new monarchy in America, and to form niches for themselves in the temple of royalty.[5]

This passage perfectly captures Maclay's distinctive blend of pettiness and keen insight.[6] The claim that Adams's "party" greedily sought the spoils of office and wished to be adored as idols "in the temple of royalty" is both ad hominem and uninteresting. But underneath the bombast, there is a shrewd and important observation. Maclay recognized that Adams was by no means the only patriot who "would never have drawn his sword" if he had regarded the American Revolution as a campaign against monarchy. A great many colonists—far more, indeed, than Maclay appears to credit—had rebelled against the British Parliament in the name of the Crown, desperate to transform and revivify "that Government under which we had lived so long and happily formerly." The members of this "party" had committed themselves to an expansive vision of prerogative power in "a single person" during the imperial crisis, and despite the rupture of 1776, they had kept faith with their Royalist principles throughout the long struggle to define the shape of American constitutionalism. In that sense, they had indeed sought "the creation of a new monarchy in America," but not because they were dazzled by the "trappings and splendor of royalty."

Indeed, if Maclay had not condescendingly left Adams "hanging in geometry" on that remarkable morning in May, he might have had occasion to take seriously his antagonist's rationale for attempting to buttress the "dignity" of the executive office. As Adams made clear, he was driven to do so by his long-standing views on "the subject of checks to government and the balances of power." The ambition of the Royalist Revolution had been to secure the liberty of subjects and citizens by entrusting their care to a transcendent chief magistrate, one who would stand above faction and resist the tyrannical encroachments and usurpations of legislatures. When George III refused to play this role, the theorists in question had set about creating his replacement, and Adams believed that they had succeeded, at least in the round. The presidency, as he wrote to Washington in the early months of 1789, "by its legal authority, defined in the constitution, has no equal in the world, excepting those only which are held by crowned heads; nor is the royal authority in all cases to be compared to it."[7] But as Adams went on to insist, this sweeping "legal authority" could not stand on its own: "Neither dignity nor authority can be supported in human minds, collected into nations or any great numbers, without a splendor and majesty in some degree proportioned to them."[8]

It was this final argument that Adams definitively lost. During Washington's term, his countrymen embarked on a brief and ill-fated flirtation with royal pageantry and ceremonial. The president hosted formal "levees" (the English term for receptions at court) and traveled with a cohort of liveried servants in a lavish carriage drawn by four or six horses. His birthday was publicly celebrated and he was routinely serenaded to the tune of "God Save the King." After he addressed both houses of Congress with his "most gracious speech," members of the legislature "attended" him at his residence, and his portrait was painted in fulsome monarchical style. His title and the manner in which he was to be addressed occasioned extensive national debate (the leading candidate in 1789, "His High Mightiness, the President of the United States and Protector of Their Liberties," mercifully passed into oblivion).[9] But, as Maclay predicted, the "sentiments of the people" soon showed themselves to be irretrievably hostile to "all the trappings and splendor of royalty."[10] Paine's Hebraizing attack on "the idolatrous homage which is paid to the persons of kings" had done its lasting work.[11] The former colonists may have made their peace with kingly power in 1787–1788, but they would never again be reconciled to the pomp of the kingly office.

The nature of this ambivalent settlement was brilliantly captured by Washington Irving in "Rip Van Winkle" (1819). Having fallen asleep in pre-revolutionary America, Rip awakens twenty years later and takes a bewildered stroll around his hometown. When he reaches the old "village inn," he receives quite a shock:

> Instead of the great tree that used to shelter the quiet little Dutch inn of yore, there now was reared a tall naked pole, with something on the top that looked like a red night-cap, and from it was fluttering a flag, on which was a singular assemblage of stars and stripes—all this was strange and incomprehensible. He recognized on the sign, however, the ruby face of King George, under which he had smoked so many a peaceful pipe; but even this was singularly metamorphosed. The red coat was changed for one of blue and buff, a sword was held in the hand instead of a sceptre, the head was decorated with a cocked hat, and underneath was painted in large characters, GENERAL WASHINGTON.[12]

Rip finds that, while Washington has quite literally taken the king's place, he has not inherited the accoutrements of royalty. He does not carry a scepter; his coat is republican blue, not regal red; he is, emphatically, "General Washington," not "King George." But Rip recognizes that this new creature is at once less and more than a king. George III's replacement may lack regal splendor, but he carries a sword. While the king reigns, this man seems to rule.

The imperial crisis of the late eighteenth century thus set in motion a profoundly ironic divergence between British and American political cultures. Great Britain, with its kings and queens, would consolidate the whig constitution against which patriots had rebelled, eventually placing supreme, unchecked political power in a single legislative chamber elected by the people. This process may be said to have reached its formal conclusion in 1911, when the negative of the House of Lords was rendered merely suspensive,[13] but it was already well under way by the time Parliament enacted the Stamp Act in 1765. The new American republic, in contrast, would evolve and perfect a recognizably Royalist constitution, investing its chief magistrate with the very same prerogative powers that Charles I had defended against the great whig heroes of the seventeenth century.[14] On one side of the Atlantic, there would be kings without monarchy; on the other, monarchy without kings. Which of the two sides got the better of the bargain is, of course, an open question—but at least it is the right one.

Abbreviations

Archives   *American Archives: Fourth Series,* ed. Peter Force, 6 vols. (Washington, DC, 1837)

Defence   John Adams, *A Defence of the Constitutions of Government of the United States of America,* 3 vols. (London, 1787–1788)

Farmer Refuted   [Alexander Hamilton], *The Farmer Refuted: or, A more impartial and Comprehensive View of the Dispute between Great-Britain and the Colonies* (New York, 1775)

Federalist   *The Federalist Papers,* ed. Clinton Rossiter (New York, 1961)

MHS   Massachusetts Historical Society

PAH   *The Papers of Alexander Hamilton,* ed. Harold C. Syrett et al., 27 vols. (New York, 1961–1979)

PBF   *The Papers of Benjamin Franklin,* ed. William B. Willcox, et al., 39 vols. (New Haven, 1977–2008)

PJA   *Papers of John Adams,* Series Three, ed. Robert J. Taylor, Mary-Jo Kline, and Gregg L. Lint, 15 vols. (Cambridge, MA, 1977)

PJI   *The Papers of James Iredell,* ed. Don Higginbotham, 3 vols. (Raleigh, NC, 1976)

Records   Max Farrand, ed., *The Records of the Federal Convention of 1787,* 3 vols. (New Haven, 1911)

Summary View   [Thomas Jefferson], *A Summary View of the Rights of British America* (Williamsburg, 1774)

WJA   *The Works of John Adams, Second President of the United States,* 10 vols. (Boston, 1850–1906)

WMQ   *William and Mary Quarterly*

Notes

Introduction

1 *Records*, 1:65.

2 Ibid., 66.

3 Ibid., 71 (King). This statement is absent from Madison's notes, but there is no reason to doubt that Wilson made it. Madison's account of Wilson's intervention is characteristically compressed (ibid., 66), consisting only of broad topic headings. King's account follows precisely the same outline but fleshes out the speech in a number of particulars. For example, where Madison simply has Wilson stating that "nothing but a great confederated republic would do" for the United States, King likewise has Wilson announce that he is "for such an confed[eratio]n," but attributes to him the further remark that "Montesquieu is in favor of confederated republics." This is both correct and exactly the sort of thing Wilson would have pointed out. For a very similar invocation of Montesquieu, see James Wilson to the Speaker of the House of Representatives, December [?] 1791, in "The Life and Writings of James Wilson," ed. Burton Alva Konkle, unpublished MS (1946), Box 2, Folder 2, Letter 275, Department of Rare Books and Special Collections, Princeton University Library. King's report of Wilson's claim about the nature of the Revolution seems similarly plausible. Note that King represented his native Massachusetts at the convention; he moved to New York after ratification.

4 Thomas Hart Benton, *Thirty Years' View; or, A History of the Working of the American Government for Thirty Years, from 1820–1850*, 2 vols. (New York, 1858), 1:58.

5 [Richard Wells], *A Few Political Reflections Submitted to the Consideration of the British Colonies, by a Citizen of Philadelphia* (Philadelphia, 1774), 31. The Declaratory Act of 1766 asserted Parliament's jurisdiction over the American colonies "in all cases whatsoever."

6 *Farmer Refuted*, 16. I shall use the terms "patriot" and "loyalist" to denote the two sides of the colonial debate with great reluctance, since the first is undeniably question-begging and the second is proleptic. I believe, however, that the popular alternatives ("whig" and "tory") are even less satisfactory and are far more likely to cause confusion in this context. It is one of my central contentions that most of those we call "opposition whigs" ceased to be whigs in any meaningful sense after 1768.

7 When I refer to "the constitutional settlement that followed the Glorious Revolution," I have in mind the distinctive understanding of the king-in-parliament that developed in the two decades following the accession of William and Mary in 1689.

8 As I explain below, I believe that it is perfectly appropriate to refer to those who developed the patriot case as "theorists."

9 Franklin to Samuel Cooper, June 8, 1770, in *PBF,* 17:163.

10 "An Act Declaring and Constituting the People of England to Be a Commonwealth" (1649), in *Acts and Ordinances of the Interregnum, 1642–1660,* ed. C. H. Firth and R. S. Rait, 3 vols. (London, 1911), 2:122. More technically, it was the Rump Parliament that passed this measure.

11 "Edmund Burke" [pseud.], "To the Right Honourable Lord North" (1774), in *Archives,* 1:339. As we shall see in Chapter 1, this claim was endlessly repeated in the late 1760s and 1770s.

12 George III to Lord North, Sept. 10, 1775, in *The Correspondence of King George the Third,* ed. Sir John Fortescue, 6 vols. (London, 1927), 3:256. The colonists had long been well aware of the king's position. Richard Henry Lee explained to John Dickinson in 1768 that "tis reported, we are to be informed, that his Majesty having seen, disapproves our objections to the duty Act, is determined to support the authority of the British Parliam[en]t"; Lee to Dickinson, Nov. 26, 1768, in *The Letters of Richard Henry Lee,* ed. James Curtis Ballagh, 2 vols. (New York, 1911), 1:31. For the phrase "parliamentary king," see [Jonathan Boucher], *A Letter from a Virginian* (Boston, 1774), 11. It is therefore a deep irony that George III was charged, from the beginning of his reign, with holding "high prerogative" notions, reflected particularly in his selection of Lord Bute as his first minister.

13 *Farmer Refuted,* 16. Compare "Marginalia in *An Inquiry,* an Anonymous Pamphlet," in *PBF,* 17:345 ("the King . . . alone is the Sovereign"). Hamilton and Franklin were thereby aligning themselves with the views of the more conservative Royalists of the 1640s, those, like Henry Ferne, who denied that England was a "mixed monarchy" on the grounds that the sovereign power belonged entirely to the monarch. (The fact that the king was required to seek the concurrence of the two houses of Parliament in order to make law was, in this view, merely a salutary restraint on that power.) See Henry Ferne, *Conscience Satisfied* (London, 1643), 14. More moderate Royalists argued that the sovereign power itself was shared among the three estates.

14 *Farmer Refuted,* 18.

15 *The Parliamentary History of England: From the Earliest Period to the Year 1803,* ed. Thomas C. Hansard, 36 vols. (London, 1806–1820), 23:849. (The first twelve volumes in the series initially appeared as *Cobbett's Parliamentary History.*) See also Willoughby Bertie, Lord Abingdon, *Thoughts on Mr. Burke's Letter to the Sheriffs of Bristol on the Affairs of America* (Dublin, 1777), 46 ("this War of Parliament"). Compare John Courtenay's remark in 1781 that "though he never was, nor never would be an advocate for the justice, wisdom and expediency of the American war, yet he owned it was a popular one;—the asserting an unlimited sovereignty over America . . . was a Whig principle, maintained by Whig statesmen, and confirmed by repeated acts of a Whig parliament"; *Parliamentary History of England,* 21:1281.

16 [John Lind], *An Answer to the Declaration of the American Congress* (London, 1776), 7.

17 John Barker, *The British in Boston: Being the Diary of Lieutenant John Barker of the King's Own Regiment from November 15, 1774, to May 31, 1776,* ed. Elizabeth Ellery Dana (Cambridge, MA, 1924), 40.

18 Lieutenant William Fielding to Major Generals William Howe, John Burgoyne, and Henry Clinton, June 1775, in *The Lost War: Letters from British Officers during the American Revolution,* ed. Marion Balderston and David Syrett (New York, 1975), 29–30. He is referring to the engagements at Lexington and Concord on April 19. Compare the "Extract of a Letter from the Camp at Cambridge" published in the *New-York Gazette* on July 24, 1775. For a similar incident in New York, see *Pennsylvania Evening Post,* Mar. 11, 1775.

19 "Cassandra" [James Cannon], Letter 2 (1776), in *Archives,* 5:922. For a wise and important set of reflections on this theme, see J. G. A. Pocock, "1776: The Revolution against Parliament," in *Three British Revolutions: 1641, 1688, 1776,* ed. J. G. A. Pocock (Princeton, 1980), 265–288. See also John Emerich Dalberg, Lord Acton, "Inaugural Lecture on the Study of History," in *Lectures on Modern History,* ed. J. N. Figgis and R. V. Laurence (London, 1906), 305.

20 The great exception, as we shall see, was Benjamin Franklin. Several of those who made the neo-Stuart case during the imperial crisis did not participate at all in the debates of the 1780s—in most cases because they did not survive—but Franklin was the only major proponent of the royal prerogative in 1760s and early 1770s who became an opponent of prerogative power in the executive in the 1780s.

21 *Records,* 1:71.

22 This so-called whig account of revolutionary ideology was developed in a series of classic works: Caroline Robbins, *The Eighteenth-Century Commonwealthmen: Studies in the Transmission, Development, and Circumstance of English Liberal Thought from the Restoration of Charles II until the War with the Thirteen Colonies* (Cambridge, MA, 1959); Bernard Bailyn, *The Ideological Origins of the American Revolution,* rev. ed. (Cambridge, MA, 1992), originally published in 1967; Gordon Wood, *The Creation of the American Republic, 1776–1787* (Chapel Hill, 1969); and J. G. A. Pocock, *The Machiavellian Moment: Florentine Political Thought and the Atlantic Republican Tradition* (Princeton, 1975). This body of scholarship is likewise associated with the turn to "classical republicanism" in the historiography of the Revolution, but Bailyn importantly (and, in my view, rightly) resisted this terminology. For a helpful summary of the debate, see Daniel T. Rodgers, "Republicanism: the Career of a Concept," *Journal of American History* 79 (1992): 11–38. For my own views on the controversy, see Eric Nelson, *The Greek Tradition in Republican Thought* (Cambridge, 2004), esp. 195–199.

23 For two important statements of this view, see Jack P. Greene, *The Constitutional Origins of the American Revolution* (Cambridge, 2010), esp. 134–139; and Barbara A. Black, "The Constitution of Empire: The Case for the Colonists,"

University of Pennsylvania Law Review 124 (1976): 1157–1211, esp. 1193. See also R. R. Palmer, *The Age of the Democratic Revolution: A Political History of Europe and America, 1760–1800: The Challenge* (Princeton, 1959), 160–161; Ernest Barker, "Natural Law and the American Revolution," in *Traditions of Civility: Eight Essays* (Cambridge, 1948), 263–355, esp. 305; Richard Bushman, *King and People in Provincial Massachusetts* (Chapel Hill, 1985), 251; and Pauline Maier, "Whigs against Whigs against Whigs: The Imperial Debates of 1765–1776 Reconsidered," *WMQ* 68 (2011): 578–582. This characterization of the patriot position seems to have originated with Lord Mansfield. The colonists, he declared, "would allow the king of Great Britain a nominal sovereignty over them, but nothing else. They would throw off the dependency on the crown of Great Britain, but not on the person of the king, whom they would render a cypher"; *Parliamentary History of England*, 18:958.

24 This is, of course, a brief and necessarily schematic summary of a vast, complicated literature. The most comprehensive statement of the standard account remains Wood, *Creation of the American Republic*, 483–499. See also Wood, *The Radicalism of the American Revolution* (New York, 1991), esp. 95–168; and Wood, "The Problem of Sovereignty," *WMQ* 68 (2011): 573–577.

25 Charles Howard McIlwain, *The American Revolution: A Constitutional Interpretation* (New York, 1923), 5–6.

26 Ibid., 159.

27 See William D. Liddle, "'A Patriot King, or None': Lord Bolingbroke and the American Renunciation of George III," *Journal of American History* 65 (1979): 951–970; Paul Langford, "New Whigs, Old Tories, and the American Revolution," *Journal of Imperial and Commonwealth History* 8 (1980): 106–130; Richard R. Johnson, "'Parliamentary Egotisms': The Clash of the Legislatures in the Making of the American Revolution," *Journal of American History* 74 (1987): 338–362; John Phillip Reid, *Constitutional History of the American Revolution: The Authority to Legislate* (Madison, 1991); Reid, *Constitutional History of the American Revolution: The Authority of Law* (Madison, 1993), esp. 151–173; Reid, *Constitutional History of the American Revolution*, abridged ed. (Madison, 1995), esp. 90–99; and Brendan McConville, *The King's Three Faces: The Rise and Fall of Royal America, 1688–1776* (Chapel Hill, 2006), esp. 249–266. Reid, however, regards the final patriot position as respectably "whig," despite its embrace of the prerogative (see, e.g., Reid, *Constitutional History of the American Revolution: The Authority of Law*, 302–306); indeed, he denies that the final patriot position differed substantially from the initial patriot position (see Reid, *Constitutional History of the American Revolution*, abridged ed., 79–84). On his account, the patriots were consistently appealing to a "seventeenth-century constitution" of customary right and checks on arbitrary power against an "eighteenth-century constitution" of uncontrolled parliamentary supremacy. They were, in effect, siding with the seventeenth-century whigs against the eighteenth-century whigs. This notion of a collision between the "two constitutions" is drawn from McIlwain

(see *American Revolution*, 3–5), but McIlwain, unlike Reid, was clear that the constitutional theory invoked by patriots in the 1770s was not remotely whig. The disagreement results, I think, from Reid's equation of the patriots' "seventeenth-century constitution" with "the constitution of Sir Edward Coke . . . the constitution that beheaded Charles I"—i.e., with the English constitution as understood by seventeenth-century parliamentarians (Reid, *Constitutional History of the American Revolution: The Authority of Law*, 5; compare Reid, *Constitutional History of the American Revolution: The Authority to Legislate*, 60). In fact, as McIlwain perhaps recognized, patriots of the early 1770s were explicitly *rejecting* that understanding of the constitution; they were instead defending the constitution on behalf of which Charles had gone to the scaffold. As we shall see in detail, patriots were fully aware that Coke and the other parliamentarians had opposed their most basic constitutional claims. The patriot position was instead straightforwardly Royalist.

28 See, however, the suggestive remark in Liddle, "'A Patriot King, or None': Lord Bolingbroke and the American Renunciation of George III," 970.

29 In a sense, my argument is the precise inverse of Brendan McConville's (see *King's Three Faces*). McConville rejects the claim that eighteenth-century colonial political thought should be regarded as essentially "whig." Instead, he argues that British political culture was consistently and enthusiastically monarchical "almost to the moment of American independence" (7). It was the Revolution that launched the career of radical whiggery in America, more or less overturning the consensual "royalist" constitutionalism of the previous century. I am arguing, in contrast, that eighteenth-century colonial political thought was indeed essentially whig, that the imperial crisis provoked an unprecedented turn toward the "prerogativism" of the Stuarts, and that the revolutionary period marked the beginning, not the end, of this ideology's American journey. At issue between us is the difference between "monarchism" (what McConville calls "royalism") and what I am calling "Royalism" (the political and constitutional theory of those who defended Charles I). McConville and I are in agreement that eighteenth-century British Americans generally felt great "devotion to the monarchy," but such devotion was not in itself a *constitutional* position. Orthodox whigs could feel it as well. I am unpersuaded that significant numbers of eighteenth-century British Americans subscribed to Royalist political and constitutional theory before the late 1760s or endorsed a Royalist understanding of England's great seventeenth-century crisis.

30 John Adams observed as much in response to Mercy Otis Warren's charge that he had "forgotten the principles of the American Revolution"; Warren, *History of the Rise, Progress, and Termination of the American Revolution*, 3 vols. (Boston, 1805), 3:392. "The principles of the American Revolution," Adams replied, "may be said to have been as various as the thirteen States that went through it, and in some sense almost as diversified as the individuals who acted in it. . . . I say again that resistance to innovation and the unlimited claims of Parliament,

and not any particular new form of government, was the object of the Revolution"; John Adams to Mercy Otis Warren, July 20, 1807, in *Correspondence between John Adams and Mercy Otis Warren Relating to Her* History of the American Revolution, ed. Charles Francis Adams (1878; repr., New York, 1972), 338, 352.

31 By "Royalism," I therefore do not mean either a sincere attachment to the monarch or a disposition to regard the "patriot king" as a defender of English liberties. Neither of these postures was remotely inconsistent with whig orthodoxy in the late eighteenth century. Rather, I use the term to denote the position of those who defended the Stuarts in their struggle against Parliament.

32 One might well worry that since American theorists of the 1770s and 1780s did not themselves use the term "Royalist" (or "neo-Stuart") to describe their position, the use of this label risks misrepresenting their views. I am in general quite sympathetic to this sort of anxiety, but in this case, I simply do not see a better alternative. The surviving labels from the period—"patriot," "Federalist," and so on—refer to broad coalitions of political actors engaged in a common enterprise (opposing the British administration, advocating ratification, etc.) and therefore occlude the degree to which these actors held profoundly different views about political theory and constitutionalism. Yet it is precisely these differences with which I am concerned. John Adams, for example, recorded that "there has been, from the beginning of the revolution in America, a party in every state, who have entertained sentiments similar to those of Mr. [Anne-Robert-Jacques] Turgot"—whom Adams identified in turn as a disciple of the English parliamentarians of the 1650s (*Defence,* 1:2). The fact that neither he nor his contemporaries evolved a label for theorists of this persuasion seems like a poor reason to deny that such a group existed. Likewise, I believe that the use of the term "Royalist" is licensed by the fact that the patriots in question explicitly equated their position with that of the Stuart monarchs of the seventeenth century and traced the origins of the imperial crisis of the 1760s to the defeat of the seventeenth-century Royalist cause.

33 See, most importantly, Glenn Burgess, *Absolute Monarchy and the Stuart Constitution* (New Haven, 1996); David L. Smith, *Constitutional Royalism and the Search for Settlement, c. 1640–1649* (Cambridge, 1994); and Kevin Sharpe, *The Personal Rule of Charles I* (New Haven, 1992).

34 Royalists argued that God imposes on every people a duty to institute government and, this being the case, any government that the people create can be said to exist "by divine right," such that it would be contrary to God's law to resist it. For a representative statement of this view, see [John Jones], *Christus Dei, The Lords Annoynted* (London, 1643), esp. 10. Two famous supporters of the Royalist cause, Sir Robert Filmer and Thomas Hobbes, did indeed defend absolute monarchy, but the latter rejected conventional arguments from divine right, while the former was a deeply idiosyncratic theorist whose most important work (*Patriarcha*) was written over a decade before the outbreak of civil war (and enjoyed its brief vogue only after being published in 1680). See Johann

Sommerville's introduction to *Filmer: Patriarcha and Other Writings,* ed. Johann P. Sommerville (Cambridge, 1991), xxxiii. Filmer himself recognized that even those "who have bravely vindicated the Right of Kings in most Points . . . when they come to the Argument drawn from the *Natural Liberty and Equality of Mankind,* do with one consent admit it for a Truth unquestionable, not so much as once denying or opposing it"; *Filmer: Patriarcha,* 3. Compare the characteristically shrewd remarks in Charles Howard McIlwain, *The High Court of Parliament and Its Supremacy: An Historical Essay on the Boundaries between Legislation and Adjudication in England* (New Haven, 1910), 347.

35 See *Nineteen Propositions Made by Both Houses of Parliament to the Kings Maiestie* (London, 1642), 2–3.

36 *His Maiesties Ansvver to the XIX Propositions of both Houses of Parliament* (London, 1642), 9. For the constitutional theory defended in the *Answer,* see Corinne Comstock Weston, "The Theory of Mixed Monarchy Under Charles I and After," *English Historical Review* 75 (1960): 426–443.

37 *His Maiesties Ansvver,* 10. Scholars in the whig tradition have tended to dismiss these statements as pragmatic concessions to parliamentarian constitutional theory offered by an increasingly desperate monarch. They point, for example, to Charles's insistence on the scaffold that the liberty of his subjects "consists in having of Government; those Laws, by which their Life and their Goods may be most their own. It is not for having share in government (Sir) that is nothing pertaining to them. A Subject and a Soveraign are clean different things," which is taken to constitute a straightforward affirmation of his true, absolutist convictions; *King Charls His Speech Made upon the Scaffold at Whitehall-Gate* (London, 1649). The problem is that by "government," Charles plainly meant in this context only what we would call "administration" or the "executive power." He had used precisely the same terminology in the *Answer* itself: "In this Kingdom," he explained in the pamphlet, "the *Lawes* are ioyntly made by a King, by a House of Peers, and by a House of Commons chosen by the People," but "the Government according to these Lawes is trusted to the King" (9). His contemporaries were perfectly aware of the relevant semantic point: when Charles speaks of "government," Richard Baxter reminded his readers in 1659, "he meaneth the executive part"; Baxter, *A Holy Commonwealth* (London, 1659), 465. Earlier in his scaffold speech, Charles had likewise repeated his previous acknowledgments of the legislative competence of the Lords and Commons: "I never did begin a War with the two Houses of Parliament. And I call God to witness, to whom I must shortly make an account, that I never did intend for to encroach upon their privileges." All of this is consistent with the claim that Charles probably did regret the *Answer*'s endorsement of "estates theory" (according to which the king is said to share *sovereignty* with the Lords and Commons). Other Royalists criticized this concession, and Charles's own view was probably that the king alone possessed sovereign power. The prerogative of the Lords and Commons to consent to the making of law, in this understanding,

simply provided a salutary constitutional "limit" on the exercise of that power. (It is this latter view that Hamilton and Franklin were endorsing in the passages referenced above.) For the significance of this debate, see Michael Mendle, *Dangerous Positions: Mixed Government, the Estates of the Realm, and the Making of the Answer to the XIX Propositions* (Tuscaloosa, 1985).

38 *His Maiesties Ansvver, 3, 9–10.*

39 Ibid., 11.

40 Ibid., 9.

41 Ibid., 2, 7.

42 Ibid.

43 Ibid., 6.

44 *King Charls His Speech.*

45 [Henry Parker], *Some Few Observations upon His Majesties Late Answer to the Declaration or Remonstrance of the Lords and Commons of the 19th of May, 1642* (London, 1642), 4; [Henry Parker], *Observations upon Some of His Majesties Late Answers and Expresses* (London, 1642), 28.

46 [Parker], *Some Few Observations, 9.*

47 [Henry Parker], *Ius Populi* (London, 1644), 19.

48 For the Roman provenance of this argument, see Quentin Skinner, *Liberty before Liberalism* (Cambridge, 1997).

49 Cook likewise posed and answered the following question: "But may not people live happily in a mixt Monarchy; where the King may have a prerogative in many things, and yet the people enjoy their Liberties; I say not"; Cook, *Monarchy No Creature of Gods Making* (Waterford, Ireland, 1652), 129–130.

50 "The whig saw in parliament the nation itself in miniature"; G. H. Guttridge, *English Whiggism and the American Revolution* (Berkeley, 1966), 7.

51 John Locke, *Two Treatises of Government*, ed. Peter Laslett, rev. ed. (Cambridge, 1967), 384, 347–348. Locke in fact stated that men could not *"think themselves in Civil Society,* till the Legislature was placed in collective Bodies of Men" (347). This passage is in obvious tension with Locke's remarks in chapter 10 (see 372).

52 See, for example, ibid., 343, 388.

53 Ibid., 386. Compare 426–428.

54 It was Peter Laslett's great achievement to have established this dating. See his introduction to ibid., esp. 45–66. The strongest suggestion that Locke did not in fact approve of the royal negative appears in chapter 19 (432).

55 Ibid., 386.

56 For the view that Locke opposed the royal negative, see Baptist Noel Turner, *The True Alarm* (London, 1783), 1–2, 10–21.

57 Locke, *Two Treatises, 393.* The literature on Locke and prerogative power is immense. Important contributions include John Dunn, *The Political Thought of John Locke: An Historical Account of the Argument of the 'Two Treatises of Government'* (Cambridge, 1969), 148–116; Harvey C. Mansfield, *Taming the Prince: The Ambivalence of Modern Executive Power* (New York, 1989), 181–211; and Quentin

Skinner, "On Trusting the Judgment of Our Rulers," in *Political Judgment: Essays for John Dunn,* ed. Richard Bourke and Raymond Geuss (Cambridge, 2009), 113–130.

58 See Locke, *Two Treatises,* 84–85.

59 [William Knox], *The Controversy between Great Britain and Her Colonies, Reviewed* (London, 1769), 78–80. See also [Anon.], *A Speech, in Behalf of the Constitution, Against the Suspending and dispensing Prerogative, &c.* (London, 1767), 7–9, 38–53. There has been a great deal of controversy concerning the precise extent of Locke's influence on the debates surrounding the American Revolution. Louis Hartz famously placed the Lockean discourse of natural rights at the center of patriot ideology; Hartz, *The Liberal Tradition in America: An Interpretation of American Political Thought since the Revolution* (New York, 1955). The "whig" historians of the 1960s and 1970s stressed instead the importance of "Country" opposition literature and (later) of "classical republicanism," and John Dunn offered an influential statement of the view that Locke's role in revolutionary thought was in fact exiguous; see Dunn, "The Politics of Locke in England and America in the Eighteenth Century," in *John Locke: Problems and Perspectives, A Collection of New Essays,* ed. John W. Yolton (Cambridge, 1969), 45–80. More recently, scholars seem to have reached a temperate (and, to me, congenial) compromise: Locke played an important role in structuring political debate during the 1760s and 1770s, but he was not remotely alone in doing so. See, for example, Yuhtaro Ohmori, "The Artillery of Mr. Locke: The Use of Locke's *Second Treatise* in Pre-Revolutionary America" (PhD diss., Johns Hopkins University, 1988). For a valuable summary of the debate, see Mark Goldie, introduction to *The Reception of Locke's Politics,* ed. Mark Goldie, 5 vols. (London, 1999), 1:xlix–lix.

60 Quoted in Mark Goldie, "The English System of Liberty," in *The Cambridge History of Eighteenth-Century Political Thought,* ed. Mark Goldie and Robert Wokler (Cambridge, 2006), 40.

61 Robert Molesworth, *An Account of Denmark, with Francogalia and Some Considerations for the Promoting of Agriculture and Employing the Poor,* ed. Justin Champion (Indianapolis, 2011), 50–51. The classic account of this discourse remains J. G. A. Pocock, *The Ancient Constitution and the Feudal Law: A Study of English Historical Thought in the Seventeenth Century* (Cambridge, 1957). For the reception of the idiom in colonial America, see Trevor Colbourn, *The Lamp of Experience: Whig History and the Intellectual Origins of the American Revolution,* 3rd ed. (Indianapolis, 1998), esp. 30–47.

62 See *His Maiesties Ansvver,* 3, 6, 8–9.

63 Molesworth, *An Account of Denmark,* 51.

64 John Trenchard and Thomas Gordon, *Cato's Letters, or Essays on Liberty, Civil, and Religious, and Other Important Subjects,* ed. Ronald Hamowy, 2 vols. (Indianapolis, 1995), 1:107 (no. 14).

65 Ibid., 108.

66 At issue were the rise of public credit, standing armies, and a muscular anti-French foreign policy, along with the consequences of the Septennial Act (1716), which allowed parliaments to maintain themselves for up to seven years without calling elections.

67 Molesworth, *An Account of Denmark*, 11.

68 Ibid., 9.

69 *John Milton*, ed. Stephen Orgel and Jonathan Goldberg (Oxford, 1991), 679, lines 270–271.

70 Trenchard and Gordon, *Cato's Letters*, 1:126 (no. 17).

71 Ibid.

72 James Burgh, *Political Disquisitions: Or, An Enquiry into Public Errors, Defects, and Abuses*, 3 vols. (London, 1774), 2:30.

73 Ibid., 37–38.

74 Ibid., 32.

75 Ibid., 18.

76 Montesquieu, *The Spirit of the Laws*, ed. and trans. Anne M. Cohler, Basia Carolyn Miller, and Harold Samuel Stone (Cambridge, 1989), 162 (11:6). *"Si la puissance exécutrice n'a pas le droit d'arrêter les enterprises du corps législatif, celui-ci sera despotique"*; Montesquieu, *Oeuvres Complètes*, ed. Daniel Oster (Paris, 1964), 588.

77 Montesquieu, *Spirit of the Laws*, 164. *"La puissance éxecutrice, comme nous avons dit, doit prendre part à la législation par sa faculté d'empêcher; sans quoi elle sera bientôt dépouillée de ses prérogatives"*; Montesquieu, *Oeuvres Complètes*, 589.

78 The latter conception presupposes that the relevant powers are very far from being "separated." The executive, on this account, should wield part of the legislative power and the legislature should wield part of the executive power (e.g., insofar as the latter's approval must be sought for treaties, appointments, etc.). The term "checks and balances"—which first appeared in a 1777 sermon by Hugh Blair—was popularized by John Adams's *Defense of the Constitutions of Government of the United States* (1787–1788), where it was presented as an alternative to the notion of "separation of powers." For Montesquieu's debt to Bolingbroke's ideas on these subjects, see Robert Shackleton, "Montesquieu, Bolingbroke, and the Separation of Powers," *French Studies* 3 (1949): 25–38. On the language of "checks and balances," see the provocative account in David Wootton, "Liberty, Metaphor, and Mechanism: 'Checks and Balances,'" in *Liberty and American Experience in the Eighteenth Century*, ed. David Womersley (Indianapolis, 2006), 209–274.

79 His one anodyne reference to "ministers" appears on page 162.

80 Montesquieu, *Spirit of the Laws*, 161. *"Que s'il n'y avait point de monarque, et que la puissance exécutrice fût confiée à un certain nombre de personnes tirées du corps législatif, il n'y aurait plus de liberté, parce que les deux puissances seraient unies; les mêmes personnes ayant quelquefois, et pouvant toujours avoir part à l'une et à l'autre"*; Montesquieu, *Oeuvres Complètes*, 588.

81 Montesquieu, *Spirit of the Laws*, 166. *"Ce n'est point à moi à examiner si les Anglais jouissent actuellement de cette liberté, ou non. Il me suffit de dire qu'elle est établie par*

leurs lois, et je n'en cherche pas davantage"; Montesquieu, *Oeuvres Complètes*, 590. Montesquieu expands on his critique of contemporary English politics in 19:26 and 20:7.

82 Henry St John, Viscount Bolingbroke, "On the Spirit of Patriotism" (1736), in *Political Writings*, ed. David Armitage (Cambridge, 1997), 206.

83 Bolingbroke, "The Idea of a Patriot King" (1738; published 1749), in ibid., 250. The text was reprinted in 1752, 1767, 1775, and 1783. For its complicated reception, see David Armitage, "A Patriot for Whom? The Afterlives of Bolingbroke's Patriot King," *Journal of British Studies* 36 (1997): 397–418.

84 Bolingbroke, "The Idea of a Patriot King," 250–251.

85 Ibid., 258.

86 Ibid., 253–254, 260.

87 Bolingbroke was notoriously ambiguous about whether the sovereign should do this as a matter of course or only in response to constitutional emergencies. See, for example, ibid., 260–261, 263.

88 It was this fact, along with the studied ambiguity of his various constitutional pronouncements, that allowed Bolingbroke to be read by some as a radical whig. See Armitage, "A Patriot for Whom?," 407.

89 David Hume, *Political Essays*, ed. Knud Haakonssen (Cambridge, 1994), 25.

90 Ibid., 25.

91 Turner, *True Alarm*, 5, 17–18.

92 Hume, *Political Essays*, 26.

93 For the views of the "Court whigs" whose thoughts prefigured Hume's, see, for example, Simon Targett, "Government and Ideology during the Age of the Whig Supremacy: The Political Arguments of Sir Robert Walpole's Newspaper Propagandists," *Historical Journal* 37 (1994): 289–317, esp. 307–313.

94 Hume, *Political Essays*, 26.

95 The problems with this terminology are legion. Among the most serious are: 1) the term misleadingly suggests an ideological continuity between the Tories of the late seventeenth century and the writers in question; and 2) the fissure between "Court" and "Country" had by this time largely supplanted the division between "whig" and "tory." For Hume's fraught relationship with "toryism," see J. G. A. Pocock, "Hume and the American Revolution: The dying thoughts of a North Briton," in *Virtue, Commerce, and History: Essays on Political Thought and History, Chiefly in the Eighteenth Century* (Cambridge, 1985), 125–141.

96 The classic defense of this claim remains Bernard Bailyn, *The Ideological Origins of the American Revolution*, rev. ed. (Cambridge, MA, 1992). Despite several decades of scrutiny and revision, I believe that his basic argument stands in this respect.

97 Jonathan Mayhew, for example, recalled that he had been "initiated, in youth, in the doctrine of civil liberty" by "such as Sidney, and Milton, Locke and Hoadley." See Mayhew, *The Snare Broken* (Boston, 1766), 35. See generally Colbourn, *The Lamp of Experience*.

98 See Bernard Bailyn, *The Origins of American Politics* (New York, 1965), 66–105.

99 "Of the American Plantations," in *The Colonial Records of North Carolina*, ed. William L. Saunders, 10 vols. (Raleigh, 1886–1890), 2:166. This report is dated October 18, 1714; it was forwarded by the secretary of state to the Board of Trade on February 23, 1715.

100 The final sentence is both hyperbolic and polemical. Note that the author refers to the negative voice as a power of "repeal," highlighting the fact that colonial laws disallowed by the Board of Trade had, for the most part, already gone into effect.

101 It was, for example, taken as an uncontroversial statement of fact in the Constitutional Convention that "the King of G[reat] B[ritain]. had not exerted his negative since the Revolution [i.e., 1688]." See *Records*, 1:98–99 (note that Hamilton and Franklin agreed on this point). British Americans were not alone in making this error. See, for example, Jean-Louis Delolme, *The Constitution of England* (London, 1775), 398–399.

102 The Crown lacked a negative voice in Rhode Island and Connecticut, which were charter colonies, and in proprietary Maryland. See Robert J. Spitzer, *The Presidential Veto: Touchstone of the American Presidency* (Albany, 1988), 8; and Charles M. Andrews, "The Royal Disallowance," *Proceedings of the American Antiquarian Society* 24 (1914): 342–362. As a technical matter, royal disallowance of colonial legislation differed from the royal negative "proper" in two respects: (1) it was the monarch him- or herself (in theory) who would "negative" parliamentary bills within Britain, whereas colonial legislation was "disallowed" by the Privy Council; and (2) colonial acts were usually (but not always) allowed to go into effect pending Privy Council review, and rights and duties arising under them were not retroactively negated by disallowance, whereas parliamentary bills did not become law until they had received the royal assent. I shall, however, follow the eighteenth-century practice of referring to the Crown's "negative" over colonial legislation.

103 See Maurice Moore, *The Justice and Policy of Taxing the American Colonies, in Great Britain, Considered* (Wilmington, NC, 1765), 12. For the mechanics of the sixteen-member Board of Trade and Privy Council review of colonial affairs, see Alison Gilbert Olson, *Making the Empire Work: London and American Interest Groups, 1690–1790* (Cambridge, MA, 1992). As Olson points out, colonial merchants and corporations enjoyed considerable success in influencing the determinations of these royal agencies during the middle decades of the century and accordingly worked hard to keep colonial matters off of the parliamentary docket during the 1750s and 1760s. It would therefore be a considerable oversimplification to state that eighteenth-century British Americans generically "opposed" the royal prerogative. The point is, rather, that (as Jack P. Greene explains) "colonial concern tended to fix not upon Parliament's efforts to turn the economies of the colonies into channels thought to be most profitable to the metropolis, efforts the colonies eventually came to accept, but upon the crown's claims to extensive authority over and within the colonies." Greene, *Peripheries and Center: Constitutional Development in the Extended Politics of the British Empire and the United States, 1607–1788* (Athens, GA, 1986), 20.

104 See Mary Sarah Bilder, *The Transatlantic Constitution: Colonial Legal Culture and the Empire* (Cambridge, MA, 2008); and Joseph Henry Smith, *Appeals to the Privy Council from the American Plantations* (New York, 1950).

105 On this, see, most recently, Craig Yirush, *Settlers, Liberty, and Empire: The Roots of Early American Political Theory, 1675–1775* (Cambridge, 2011). The defense of prerogative in these instances was left to crown officials. See, for example, Daniel J. Hulsebosch, "*Imperia in Imperio*: The Multiple Constitutions of Empire in New York, 1750–1777," *Law and History Review* 16 (1998): 319–379, esp. 328–329; and Greene, *Peripheries and Center*, 34–41.

106 John Allen, *The American Alarm* (Boston, 1773), 8–9.

107 "The British American" [Thomson Mason], Letter 6 (1774), in *Archives*, 1:519. See also William Strahan to David Hall, Apr. 7, 1766, in "Correspondence between William Strahan and David Hall, 1763–1777," *Pennsylvania Magazine of History and Biography* 10 (1886): 86–99, esp. 97–98. "The Crown, even upon the ablest Head, is now hardly able to retain its just and proper Weight in the Legislature."

108 "The British American" [Thomas Mason], Letter 7 (1774), in *Archives*, 1:543.

109 See, for example, Jean-Louis Delolme, *The Constitution of England, or An Account of the English Government*, 2nd ed., 2 vols. (London, 1778), 1:32n; and (for Blackstone's view of the patriot constitutional position) *Proceedings and Debates of the British Parliaments Respecting North America*, ed. Leo Francis Stock, 5 vols. (Washington, DC, 1924), 2:148.

110 Marx's historical materialism is frequently presented as an archetypal instance of this "strong programme." But in fact Marx's view is importantly different. An orthodox Marxist, to be sure, will insist that ideas emerge out of particular "modes of production" and lose their salience as soon as these fundamental conditions give way to others, a transition that is itself not caused by ideas but rather by predictable disruptions of the economic order. But the Marxist account of "ideology" crucially depends upon the conviction that although ideas may arise as by-products of economic arrangements, once in place they do indeed have significant effects, insofar as they serve to justify and thereby perpetuate the established order. They are therefore not properly "epiphenomenal." What Marx did believe, in common with "epiphenomenalists," is that ideas are never the true engines of social and political *change*. See Karl Marx, "Preface to *A Contribution to the Critique of Political Economy*," in *Karl Marx: Selected Writings*, ed. Lawrence K. Simon (Indianapolis, 1994), 209–213. For an influential reformulation, see G. A. Cohen, *Karl Marx's Theory of History: A Defence* (Oxford, 1978). My reflections on these matters have been greatly stimulated by conversations with Michael Rosen, as well as by his 2010 Isaiah Berlin Lectures.

111 Sir Lewis Namier, *Personalities and Powers* (London, 1955), 4. See also Namier, *England in the Age of the American Revolution* (London, 1930); and Namier, *The Structure of Politics at the Accession of George III*, 2nd ed. (London, 1957).

112 See, classically, Quentin Skinner, *The Foundations of Modern Political Thought*, 2 vols. (Cambridge, 1978), 1:xii–xiii. See also Skinner, *Liberty before Liberalism*,

104–105. Skinner has done more than any other scholar to shape my view of how the history of political thought should be written. As James Harrington said of Thomas Hobbes, if I disagree with him from time to time, it is "to show him what he taught me"; J. G. A. Pocock, ed., *The Political Works of James Harrington* (Cambridge, 1977), 423.

113   The Marxist position on this question is notoriously unclear. Many Marxists have endorsed a model according to which agents deploy ideas instrumentally in order to defend their class interests, but it is certainly open to a Marxist to claim that ideas (though generated in some sense by underlying economic realities) sincerely motivate the actions of those who come to hold them. The agents in question would simply be unaware of the true sources of their beliefs; they would find themselves in the grip of "false consciousness." Another way of putting this point is to observe that the question "should we adopt an 'internalist' or 'externalist' account of the formation of ideas?" is very different from the question "should we regard ideas as causally efficacious?" One could, like Marx, take a strongly externalist view of the formation of our ideas—according to which they are to be explained as arising out of economic relations or psychological states—while still believing that they motivate the actions of those who come to hold them. Conversely, one could defend the view that ideas emerge and develop through a purely "internal" process of ratiocination while denying (with perfect consistency) that ideas motivate action. I shall be defending both a broadly internalist account of the formation of ideas and a sanguine view of their causal efficacy, but neither of these positions entails the other.

114   Skinner occasionally suggests that he is merely *assuming* the legitimation view in order to offer an internal critique of the Namierite position. That is, he takes himself to be demonstrating that "even if your professed principles never operate as your motives, but only as rationalizations of your behaviour, they will nevertheless help to shape and limit what kinds of action you can successfully pursue" (Skinner, *Liberty before Liberalism,* 105)—so that even on the Namierite view ideas cannot be dismissed as epiphenomenal. This way of putting the case leaves open the possibility that your "professed principles" *do* frequently operate as your motives. Compare Skinner, "Moral Principles and Social Change," in *Visions of Politics,* 3 vols. (Cambridge, 2002), 1:145–157, esp. 146–148; and Skinner, "The Principles and Practice of Opposition: The Case of Bolingbroke versus Walpole," in *Historical Perspectives: Studies in English Thought and Society in Honour of J. H. Plumb,* ed. Neil McKendrick (London, 1974), 93–128, esp. 107–108.

115   Needless to say, there is a good deal of room in the middle here: we can certainly acknowledge that our emotions or interests sometimes draw us toward "serviceable" principles (because we feel a strong need to legitimate our actions to *ourselves*) without denying that the reverse is frequently true.

116 See, for example, Lord Acton, "Inaugural Lecture on the Study of History," 2–6, 310–311. See also Herbert Butterfield, *George III and the Historians* (London, 1957). We might refer to this view as "weak historical idealism." It is a form of idealism insofar as it assigns to ideas a significant causal role in the emergence of historical change; it is "weak" relative to the very strong form of idealism defended by Hegel, according to which all of human reality is to be understood as the organic unfolding of an "idea."

117 See, for example, Marc Egnal and Joseph A. Ernst, "An Economic Interpretation of the American Revolution," *WMQ* 29 (1972): 3–32. For a recent defense of this position that attempts to carve out more space for ideological concerns, see Staughton Lynd and David Waldstreicher, "Free Trade, Sovereignty, and Slavery: Toward an Economic Interpretation of American Independence," *WMQ* 68 (2011): 597–630. For a cogent and skeptical response, see (in the same issue) Jack Rakove, "Got Nexus?," 635–638.

118 See, for example, [Richard Wells], *A Few Political Reflections Submitted to the Consideration of the British Colonies, by a Citizen of Philadelphia* (Philadelphia, 1774), 7: "The present tax demanded of us is so trifling, that, for the mere *quantum*, it might not be an object of our attention; but all the horrid train of Parliamentary impositions, which would certainly follow, must rouse every man to acknowledge the necessity of our bleeding freely in this important contest." Compare *Life and Correspondence of James Iredell, One of the Associate Justices of the Supreme Court of the United States*, ed. Griffith John McRee, 2 vols. (New York, 18571858), 1:211.

119 Edmund Burke, "Conciliation with America," in *Pre-Revolutionary Writings*, ed. Ian Harris (Cambridge, 1993), 249. Burke likewise stressed the symbolic importance of taxation in the minds of British Americans (see 222).

120 For an eloquent statement of this point, see Albert B. Southwick, "The Molasses Act—Source of Precedents," *WMQ* 8 (1951): 389–405, esp. 399.

121 Scholars wishing to advance an "idealist" account of the Revolution have accordingly been eager to minimize the extent to which patriot argument changed in between 1763 and 1776—or even to deny that it changed at all. The notion is that shifts in argument over time constitute evidence of insincerity, whereas ideological stasis indicates genuine attachment to "principle." I see no reason to accept either of these suppositions. For a lucid discussion of the issue, see Gordon Wood, "Rhetoric and Reality in the American Revolution," *WMQ* 23 (1966): 3–32, esp. 10–12. For a classic defense of the "continuity" thesis, see Edmund S. Morgan, "Colonial Ideas of Parliamentary Power," *WMQ* 5 (1948): 311–341; and Edmund S. Morgan and Helen M. Morgan, *The Stamp Act Crisis: Prologue to Revolution* (Chapel Hill, 1953).

122 I take myself to be agreeing here with those who have defended an "ideological" or "idealist" account of the Revolution's origins (chief among them Bailyn and Wood), although of course I offer a different account of what the salient "ideology" looked like.

123 Adams to Thomas Jefferson, Aug. 24, 1815, in *The Adams-Jefferson Letters,* ed. Lester J. Cappon (1959; repr., Chapel Hill, NC, 1987), 455.

1. Patriot Royalism

 1 *The Parliamentary History of England: From the Earliest Period to the Year 1803,* ed. Thomas C. Hansard, 36 vols. (London, 1806–1820), 18:183.
 2 Ibid., 183–184.
 3 Ibid., 734–735.
 4 Wilkes, indeed, had been a great hero to the colonists in the middle 1760s, and the repeated attempts to deny him a seat in Parliament fueled American suspicions that the British government had become hopelessly corrupt. See Pauline Maier, "John Wilkes and American Disillusionment with Britain," *WMQ* 20 (1963): 373–395; and Maier, *From Resistance to Revolution: Colonial Radicals and the Development of American Opposition to Britain, 1775–1776* (New York and London, 1972), 163–169.
 5 *Parliamentary History of England,* 18:736.
 6 Sometimes referred to as the "dominion status theory" or, rather less satisfactorily, the "doctrine of allegiance."
 7 *Parliamentary History of England,* 18:771. Compare "A Revolution Whig," *Scots Magazine* 37 (1775): 646.
 8 "Massachusettensis" [Daniel Leonard], *The Origin of the American Contest with Great Britain* (New York, 1775), 62–63. *The Origin* was serialized in 1774.
 9 The archetypal statement of the second view is Richard Bland, *The Colonel Dismounted* (1764). See *Pamphlets of the American Revolution, 1750–1776,* ed. Bernard Bailyn, vol. 1 (Cambridge, MA, 1965), 320–321. Other notable proponents included Daniel Dulany, Thomas Fitch, John Dickinson, Jonathan Mayhew, Oxenbridge Thacher, and even Stephen Hopkins, who explicitly conceded in 1765 that the colonies "are dependant on the kingdom of *Great Britain*" and that it is "the indispensable duty of every good and loyal subject, chearfully to obey and patiently submit to all the acts, laws, orders, and regulations that may be made and passed by parliament for directing and governing" the colonies' external affairs, including trade; see Hopkins, *The Rights of Colonies Examined* (Providence, 1765), 5, 11. The relevant pamphlets by Dulany, Fitch, and Thacher are collected in *Pamphlets of the American Revolution.* Mayhew defends this position in *The Snare Broken* (Boston, 1766), 25–26. See also John Dickinson, *Letters from a Farmer in Pennsylvania to the Inhabitants of the British Colonies* (Boston, 1768), esp. 7–14. The internal/external distinction is likewise defended in virtually every address, petition, set of colonial resolves, and newspaper attack on the Stamp Act compiled in Edmund Morgan, ed., *Prologue to Revolution: Sources and Documents on the Stamp Act Crisis, 1764–1766* (Chapel Hill, 1959). An exception is [Stephen Hopkins?], "A Letter from a Plain Yeoman," *Providence Gazette,* May

11, 1765, which moves beyond this approach and gestures at what would become the "dominion theory" (see *Prologue to Revolution*, 71–77). This last source was brought to my attention by John Compton and Karen Orren, "Political Theory in Institutional Contex: The Case of Patriot Royalism," *American Political Thought* 3 (2014): 1–31 (see esp. 5–6). Compton and Orren's essay responds to the initial version of my argument that appeared as Eric Nelson, "Patriot Royalism: The Stuart Monarchy in American Political Thought, 1769–75" in *WMQ* 68 (2011): 533–577. As of the mid-1760s, however, the patriots did not have a coherent account of which laws should count as "internal" and which "external." See, for example, Benjamin Franklin, "On the Tenure of the Manor of East Greenwich," in *Benjamin Franklin's Letters to the Press, 1758–1775*, ed. Verner W. Crane (Williamsburg, VA, 1950), 48.

10 There has been a great deal of debate over the precise character of this initial patriot position. Edmund Morgan argued influentially that, *pace* Leonard and other "Tories," the colonists in fact made no distinction at this stage between internal taxes and duties on trade—although even Morgan conceded that they did distinguish between "internal" and "external" affairs more generally; Edmund S. Morgan and Helen M. Morgan, *The Stamp Act Crisis: Prologue to Revolution* (Chapel Hill, 1953), 119–121. For a prominent endorsement of this view, see John Phillip Reid, *Constitutional History of the American Revolution*, abridged version (Madison, 1995), 79–84. My sense, however, is that Morgan overstated the case. Although a small number of colonists may have intended to deny Parliament's authority to impose duties on trade (Morgan's two examples are ambiguous on this point), the vast majority clearly did not, particularly if by "duties on trade" we mean duties that did not have as their *purpose* the raising of a revenue. See, for example, James's Iredell's analysis of the evolving patriot position in his "Principles of an American Whig" (1775?), in *PJI*, 1:333–334, and the account in William Gordon, *The History of the Rise, Progress, and Establishment, of the Independence of the United States of America*, 4 vols. (London, 1788), 1:150–152, 220. In general, I accept Jack Greene's recent characterization of the patriot position during this phase of the controversy; Jack P. Greene, *The Constitutional Origins of the American Revolution* (Cambridge, 2010), 67–103.

11 Dickinson, *Letters from a Farmer*, esp. 7–14.

12 William Drayton, *A Letter from a Freeman of South-Carolina, to the Deputies of North-America, Assembled in the High Court of Congress at Philadelphia* (Charleston, 1774), 31. Compare James Wilson, *Considerations on the Nature and the Extent of the Legislative Authority of the British Parliament* (Philadelphia, 1774), 21.

13 John Cartwright, *American Independence the Interest and Glory of Great Britain* (London, 1774), 18. The dissenting minority of the House of Lords who voted against repeal of the Stamp Act made precisely the same point: "The reasons assigned in the public resolutions of the Provincial Assemblies, in the North

American Colonies, for their disobeying the Stamp Act, viz. 'that they are not represented in the Parliament of Great Britain,' extends to all other laws, of what nature soever"; "Protest against the Bill to Repeal the American Stamp Act, of Last Session," reprinted in *PBF,* 13:218–219.

14 The best account of the broad contours of the theory remains Charles Howard McIlwain, *The American Revolution: A Constitutional Interpretation* (New York, 1923), 114–147. McIlwain's analysis was anticipated in some respects by Randolph Greenfield Adams, *Political Ideas of the American Revolution: Britannic-American Contributions to the Problem of Imperial Organization, 1765–1775* (Durham, 1922). See also Alison Lacroix, *The Ideological Origins of American Federalism* (Cambridge, MA, 2010), chapters 2 and 3; Brendan McConville, *The King's Three Faces: The Rise and Fall of Royal America, 1688–1776* (Chapel Hill, 2006), 250–261; Martin S. Flaherty, "More Apparent than Real: The Revolutionary Commitment to Constitutional Federalism," *Kansas Law Review* 45 (1996–1997): 993–1014; J. C. D. Clark, *The Language of Liberty, 1660–1832: Political Discourse and Social Dynamics in the Anglo-American World* (Cambridge, 1994), 93–110; John Phillip Reid, *Constitutional History of the American Revolution: The Authority of Law* (Madison, 1993), 151–162; Jack Rakove, *The Beginnings of National Politics: An Interpretive History of the Continental Congress* (New York, 1979), 34–41; Gordon Wood, *The Creation of the American Republic, 1776–1787* (Chapel Hill, 1969), 344–354; and Bernard Bailyn, *The Ideological Origins of the American Revolution* (Cambridge, MA, 1967), 216–229.

15 See Benjamin Franklin, *Cool Thoughts on the Present Situation of Our Public Affairs* (Philadelphia, 1764), esp. 20–21. See also David L. Jacobson, *John Dickinson and the Revolution in Pennsylvania, 1764–1776* (Berkeley, 1965), 9–26; Robert Dennis Fiala, "George III in the Pennsylvania Press: A Study in Changing Opinions, 1760–1776" (PhD diss., Wayne State University, 1967), 37–45, 92–114; and Gordon Wood, *The Americanization of Benjamin Franklin* (New York and London, 2004), esp. 98–101. For Galloway's phrase, see John Penn to Thomas Penn, May 5, 1764, Penn MSS, Official Correspondence, IX, 220, Historical Society of Pennsylvania.

16 "On the Tenure of the Manor of East Greenwich," in *PBF,* 13:22. Franklin likewise endorsed this view in a well-known letter to his son, William (October 6, 1773, in *PBF,* 20:437), and in subsequent letters to Lord Kames, William Strahan, and Samuel Cooper; see *PBF,* 14:68 and 16:244; and *The Writings of Benjamin Franklin,* ed. Albert Henry Smyth, 10 vols. (London, 1907), 5:260–261. For a retrospective endorsement by James Madison, see *The Writings of James Madison,* ed. Gaillard Hunt, 9 vols. (New York, 1900–1910), 6:373–374.

17 *PBF,* 13:22.

18 "Examination before the Committee of the Whole of the House of Commons" (February 13, 1766), in ibid., 153. Franklin pointedly reminded his audience that "I came over here to solicit in Behalf of my Colony a closer Connection with the Crown" (225).

19 Ibid., 156.

20 "Marginalia in Protests of the Lords against Repeal of the Stamp Act," in ibid.,
    212.

21 Ibid., 213.

22 Ibid., 212, 214. Franklin would return to this language in a March 4, 1774 letter
    to *The Public Ledger* in London, accusing an opponent of proposing to "thrust
    [the English people] into the Throne cheek-by-Jole with Majesty" and "forget-
    ting that the Americans are Subjects of the King"; ibid., 21:137.

23 Ibid., 13:219.

24 Ibid., 215, 221.

25 Franklin reiterated all of these arguments in a second set of important margi-
    nalia dating (probably) to 1770. See "Marginalia in *An Inquiry*, an Anonymous
    Pamphlet," in ibid., 17:317–348.

26 See *The Works of Benjamin Franklin*, ed. Jared Sparks, 10 vols. (Boston, 1856),
    4:409n. The piece was first attributed to Franklin in the October 30, 1774, issue
    of *The New York Gazette*. Lord Mansfield and Josiah Tucker both subsequently
    directed their criticisms of Wilson's pamphlet at Franklin.

27 Wilson, *Considerations*, A2^r, 29.

28 Ibid., 33–34. Wilson's Scottish background may well have predisposed him to
    think in these terms: between 1603 (the accession of James I/VI) and 1707 (the
    Act of Union), Scotland and England had been distinct states sharing a com-
    mon monarch. On this, see LaCroix, *Ideological Origins of American Federalism*,
    24–29, 86–87. See also T. H. Breen, "Ideology and Nationalism on the Eve of
    the American Revolution: Revisions *Once More* in Need of Revising," *Journal of
    American History* 84 (1997): 13–39, esp. 23–28.

29 Wilson's language here echoes that of the Philadelphia pamphleteer William
    Hicks: "I am very far from being an Enemy to Parliamentary Power. I revere
    the House of Commons as the Watchful Guardians presiding over the Lib-
    erty of their Constituents; but when I see Them grasping at a Power alto-
    gether foreign, and inconsistent with the Principles of their own Constitu-
    tion; I could wish to see Them reduc'd within their natural Bounds, and
    would even shelter myself under the Wings of the Royal Prerogative. I would
    much more willingly see my Property arbitrarily dispos'd of by a privy Seal,
    than extorted from me by the unwarrantable Power of a Parliament; whose
    Members would naturally endeavour to lessen their own Burthens, and grat-
    ify the selfish Wishes of their Constituents by sacrificing to Them the Inter-
    ests of the Colonies. As loyal and industrious Subjects We may expect impar-
    tial Favour from our Prince; who must reasonably regard with an equal Eye
    the Happiness and Welfare of all his Dominions"; [William Hicks], *Consider-
    ations upon the Rights of the Colonists to the Privileges of British Subjects* (New
    York, 1766), 21. For the demonization of prerogative in pre-revolutionary
    America, see Greene, *Constitutional Origins of the American Revolution*, 32–33,
    60–61.

30 Anne vetoed the Scottish Militia Bill in 1707. The Hanoverian monarchs had of course used the negative to nullify acts of American colonial legislatures, a practice bitterly opposed by colonists of the earlier period.

31 The Crown lacked a negative voice in Rhode Island and Connecticut, which were charter colonies, as well as in proprietary Maryland; see Robert J. Spitzer, *The Presidential Veto: Touchstone of the American Presidency* (Albany, 1988), 8. For the centrality of prerogative in the dominion theory, see the insightful (albeit brief) discussion in Jerrilyn Greene Marston, *King and Congress: The Transfer of Political Legitimacy, 1774–1776* (Princeton, 1987), 36–39. See also Reid, *Constitutional History of the American Revolution: The Authority of Law*, 151–162, and the suggestive remarks in Edmund S. Morgan, *Inventing the People: The Rise of Popular Sovereignty in England and America* (New York, 1988), 244. Other scholars have associated the defense of prerogative instead with the class of imperial agents during the middle of the eighteenth century. See, for example, Daniel J. Hulsebosch, *"Imperia in Imperio:* The Multiple Constitutions of Empire in New York, 1750–1777," *Law and History Review* 16 (1998): 319–379, esp. 328–329.

32 Wilson, *Considerations,* 34. By 1774, most dominion theorists were prepared to argue pragmatically that although Parliament lacked the right to regulate American trade, such a power might be "conceded" to it by the colonies as a purely discretionary matter (although this power would *not* include a license to impose "external taxes," i.e. duties). This was, for example, the position taken by the First Continental Congress in article four of its Declaration of Rights, although even this concession disappeared in its petition to the king of October 1774. The latter document closed with the insistence that "we wish not a diminution of the prerogative" but rather only to be rescued from parliamentarian tyranny; *Journals of the Continental Congress: 1774–1789,* ed. Worthington Chauncey Ford, et al., 34 vols. (Washington, DC, 1904–1937), 1:119. Compare William Hicks, *The Nature and Extent of Parliamentary Power Considered* (New York, 1768), 8, 22; [Anon.], "America Solon," *Boston Gazette,* January 27, 1772; and [Richard Wells], *A Few Political Reflections Submitted to the Consideration of the British Colonies, by a Citizen of Philadelphia* (Philadelphia, 1774), 17. See also Rakove, *Beginnings of National Politics,* 58–62; and John Phillip Reid, *Constitutional History of the American Revolution: The Authority to Legislate* (Madison, 1991), 265–266. Reid astutely points out that the New York General Assembly's petition to the king of March 25, 1775, denied the legitimacy of the Currency Act on the grounds that it constituted "an abridgement of your Majesty's prerogative" to regulate trade.

33 Wilson, *Considerations,* 29, Wilson's italics.

34 Geoffrey Seed suggests that Wilson was being "less than sincere" in offering this defense of the royal prerogative, on the grounds that "in his speech to the Pennsylvania convention in 1775 he implied very clearly that he would not

even nominally allow [the king] any part in framing policy"; Seed, *James Wilson* (New York, 1978), 10. I see no evidence that Wilson's 1775 speech was meant to imply any such thing; see *The Works of James Wilson,* ed. Robert McCloskey, 2 vols. (Cambridge, MA, 1967), 2:747–758. To be sure, Wilson did deny in that address that the king had a prerogative right to "alter the charter or constitution" of Massachusetts Bay at pleasure (753), but this claim is wholly consistent with his position in *Considerations.* It is unfortunate that Wilson's meager correspondence from this period contains virtually no discussion of constitutional questions, but in July 1774 he reported to General Arthur St. Clair that "the public attention is much engrossed about the late conduct of the Parliament with regard to America." Once again, the enemy is Parliament, not the king. See James Wilson to General Arthur St. Clair, July 7, 1774, in "The Life and Writings of James Wilson," ed. Burton Alva Konkle, unpublished MS (1946), Box 2, Folder 1, Letter 30, Department of Rare Books and Special Collections, Princeton University Library.

35 The classic account of this aspect of the discourse remains Bailyn, *Ideological Origins of the American Revolution,* esp. 55–93. For a standard instance of the claim, see Hopkins, *Rights of Colonies,* 4: "Those who are governed at the will of another, or of others, and whose property may be taken from them by taxes or otherwise without their own consent and against their will, are in the miserable condition of slaves." Compare Richard Henry Lee to [anon.], May 31, 1764, in *The Letters of Richard Henry Lee,* ed. James Curtis Ballagh, 2 vols. (New York, 1911), 1:6. For the Roman provenance of this argument, see Quentin Skinner, *Liberty before Liberalism* (Cambridge, 1997). The notion that a parliament too might rule "by prerogative" and thereby enslave a people had been a staple of Leveller polemic during the mid-1640s. See, e.g., Richard Overton, "An Arrow against All Tyrants," in *The English Levellers,* ed. Andrew Sharp (Cambridge, 1988), esp. 56–57.

36 *Pamphlets of the American Revolution,* 441.

37 *The Political Writings of John Adams,* ed. George W. Carey (Washington, DC, 2000), 7. See also Adams, "The Earl of Clarendon to William Pym," Letters 1–2, *Boston Gazette,* January 13/20, 1766.

38 For several particularly noteworthy instances, see [Joseph Galloway?], "Letter to the People of Pennsylvania" (1760) in *Pamphlets of the American Revolution,* 264; Jonathan Mayhew, *Observations on the Charter and Conduct of the Society for the Propagation of the Gospel in Foreign Parts* (Boston, 1763), 157, 175; Oxenbridge Thacher, "The Sentiments of a British American" (1764), in *Pamphlets of the American Revolution,* 491; [Benjamin Franklin?], "Pacificus," *The Public Advertiser,* January 23, 1766; and Hicks, *The Nature and Extent of Parliamentary Power Considered,* 15–16, 37–38. Because of the dominance of this paradigm in the first five years of the crisis and its return to prominence in 1776, the usual assumption has been that the patriot identification with the Puritans and Parliamentarians was a consistent feature of revolutionary thought. See, for example,

Richard Bushman, *King and People in Provincial Massachusetts* (Chapel Hill, 1985), 5; Trevor Colbourn, *Lamp of Experience: Whig History and the Intellectual Origins of the American Revolution,* 3rd ed. (Indianapolis, 1998), 51–57, 71–162; James Spalding, "Loyalist as Royalist, Patriot as Puritan: The American Revolution as a Repetition of the English Civil Wars," *Church History* 45 (1976): 329–340; Reid, *Constitutional History of the American Revolution: The Authority of Law,* 52–63; and Wood, *Creation of the American Republic,* 200. For the American reception of the English Revolution after the rupture of 1775–1776, see McConville, *King's Three Faces,* 266–274.

39 Franklin himself had absorbed this new narrative by 1774. In a list of questions he compiled for a prospective meeting with Lord Camden, he included the following: "Was the Parliament advis'd with by the Crown concerning the Terms of Settlement [of the colonies]? Did it form any Regulations thereupon? Did it understand itself to have any Power over them? . . . Were [the colonies] not first reduc'd to any Submission to Parliament in the Time of the great Rebellion?"; "Queries for a Conversation with Lord Camden," in *PBF,* 21:406–407.

40 Rush to Ebenezer Howard, October 22, 1768, in *Letters of Benjamin Rush,* ed. L. H. Butterfield, 2 vols. (Princeton, 1951), 1:68.

41 See, for example, Gordon Wood, *The Radicalism of the American Revolution* (New York, 1991), 15–16; and Paul F. Lambert, "Benjamin Rush and American Independence," *Pennsylvania History* 39 (1972): 443–454, esp. 446–447.

42 *Letters of Benjamin Rush,* 1:68.

43 Compare also Silas Downer, *A Discourse, Delivered in Providence . . . at the Dedication of the Tree of Liberty* (Providence, 1768), 8. Downer declares the king "the supreme Lord of these dominions" and brands the measures adopted by Parliament as "an invasion of the rights of the King."

44 Wilson, for example, opines, tellingly, that "Kings are not the only tyrants: The conduct of the long Parliament will justify me in adding, that Kings are not the severest tyrants" and rejoices that "at the Restoration, care was taken to reduce the House of Commons to a proper dependence on the King," but still feels it necessary to endorse the "patriotic spirit" of the initial struggle against Charles I; Wilson, *Considerations,* 8–9. Wilson also accepts the standard narrative according to which the first settlers "fled from the oppression of regal and ministerial tyranny" (16). As we shall see, subsequent patriot writers would reject this account; compare Richard Henry Lee to Arthur Lee, December 20, 1766, in *Letters of Richard Henry Lee,* 1:21–22. Lee dates the disfigurement of Virginia's constitution to "the arbitrary reign of James [the] first, and the subsequent confusion that happened in that of his Son" but nonetheless takes pride in the fact that Virginians "have ever been remarkable for loyalty and firm attachment to their Sovereign. A celebrated instance of this they gave, in refusing as they always did to pay any obedience to the usurped power of Oliver Cromwell."

45 Selden, unlike the others, was not yet an MP at the time; he had been retained by the House of Lords as an expert on English legal history.

46 See Robert Zaller, *The Parliament of 1621: A Study in Constitutional Conflict* (Berkeley), esp. 101–104; David Berkowitz, *John Selden's Formative Years: Politics and Society in Early Seventeenth-Century England* (Washington, DC, 1988), 55–58; Theodore K. Rabb, *Jacobean Gentleman: Sir Edwin Sandys, 1561–1629* (Princeton, 1998), 227–240; John T. Juricek, "English Claims in North America to 1660: A Study in Legal and Constitutional History" (PhD diss., University of Chicago, 1970), chapter 9; and Ian K. Steele, "The British Parliament and the Atlantic Colonies to 1760: New Approaches to Enduring Questions," *Parliamentary History* 14 (2005): 29–46, esp. 34–35.

47 *Commons Debates 1621*, eds. Wallace Notestein, Frances Relf, and Hartley Simpson, 7 vols. (New Haven, 1935), 4:256. Compare *Proceedings and Debates of the British Parliaments Respecting North America*, ed. Leo Francis Stock, 5 vols. (Washington, DC, 1924), 1:30–36. Note that the transcription Notestein provided was not available in the eighteenth century; the published journals contained only a summary of the exchange; see *Journals of the House of Commons. From November the 8th 1547 . . . to March the 2d 1628 . . .* [London, 1742], 19 James, April 25, 1621, quoted below by Pownall and Knox. A second record of the debate, published in Edward Nicholas, comp., *Proceedings and Debates of the House of Commons, in 1620 and 1621*, 2 vols. (Oxford, 1766), 1:318–319, put the issue even more starkly: "Mr. Secretary saith, that *Virginia, New England, Newfoundland,* and those other foreign Parts of *America,* are not yet annexed to the Crown of *England,* but are the King's as gotten by Conquest; and therefore he thinketh it worthy the Consideration of the House, whether we shall here make Laws for the Government of those Parts; for he taketh it, that in such new Plantations the King is to govern it only by his Prerogative, and as his Majesty shall think fit." For Calvert's role in American colonization more broadly, see L. H. Roper, *The English Empire in America, 1602–1658: Beyond Jamestown* (London, 2009), 103–119. James's position found further expression in his preferred motto for Virginia: "*En dat Virginia quintum*" (Behold, Virginia gives a fifth [dominion of the crown], i.e., alongside those of England, Scotland, Ireland, and France). See Emily Rose, "The Reluctant Imperialist: King James I and the Surrender of Virginia," working paper no. 07-02, International Seminar on the History of the Atlantic World, 1500–1825 (2007), 18.

48 For a legal evaluation of the two positions, see Barbara A. Black, "The Constitution of Empire: The Case for the Colonists," *University of Pennsylvania Law Review* 124 (1976): 1157–1211, esp. 1188–1194.

49 *Proceedings and Debates*, ed. Stock, 1:58–61, 74–75, 77, 79–95. For Charles I's insistence in 1625 that Virginia must be considered "outside the realm," see R. M. Bliss, *Revolution and Empire: English Politics and the American Colonies in the Seventeenth Century* (Manchester, 1990), 18–23.

50 The old conceit that Hume's *History* was reviled and neglected in colonial America because it was understood to be "tory" has been laid to rest. See, for

example, Mark G. Spencer, *David Hume and Eighteenth-Century America* (Rochester, NY, 2005).

51 David Hume, *The History of England from the Invasion of Julius Caesar to the Revolution in 1688,* ed. William B. Todd, 6 vols. (Indianapolis, 1983), 5:88, 96. Compare the account of the 1621 Parliament in Laurence Echard, *History of England from Julius Caesar to 1689,* 3 vols. (London, 1707–1718), 3:955.

52 John Phillip Reid deserves a great deal of credit for having noticed the importance of the 1621 and 1624 precedents in constitutional debate during this phase of the revolutionary crisis. Although the conclusions I reach in what follows are different from his, I am indebted to his scholarship. See *The Briefs of the American Revolution: Constitutional Arguments between Thomas Hutchinson, Governor of Massachusetts Bay, and James Bowdoin for the Council and John Adams for the House of Representatives,* ed. John Phillip Reid (New York, 1981), 103–111. His analysis here is reprinted in Reid, *Constitutional History of the American Revolution: The Authority to Legislate,* 163–166. See also Juricek's wise remark that "legal-minded American like John Adams and James Wilson rediscovered the arcane constitutionalism of the early Stuarts"; Juricek, "English Claims to North America," 781.

53 On Pownall and his plan, see John A. Schutz, *Thomas Pownall, British Defender of American Liberty: A Study of Anglo-American Relations in the Eighteenth Century* (Glendale, CA, 1951).

54 Thomas Pownall, *The Administration of the Colonies,* 4th ed. (London, 1768), 48. The first edition, which was published in 1764, did not include this material.

55 Ibid., 48–50.

56 Some patriot writers had made precisely the same case before 1769. See, for example, William Hicks's claim that each of the colonies "has hitherto been considered as a particular plantation of the crown, and been governed by such loose, discretionary powers as were better calculated to support the *despotism* of a minister than the *liberties* of the settlers"; Hicks, *The Nature and Extent of Parliamentary Power Considered,* 5. Hicks notes in the preface that he composed this pamphlet before the repeal of the Stamp Act.

57 See, for example, Hopkins, *Rights of Colonies,* 511, 519. Hopkins is unusual in that he seems to have been developing something like this argument as early as 1757; see Jack P. Greene, *Peripheries and Center: Constitutional Development in the Extended Politics of the British Empire and the United States, 1607–1788* (Athens, GA, 1986), 58. See also "Britannus Americanus," *Boston Gazette,* March 17, 1766, in *American Political Writing during the Founding Era,* ed. Charles S. Hyneman and Donald S. Lutz, 2 vols. (Indianapolis, 1983), 1:88–91; Dickinson, *Letters from a Farmer,* 5; and [John Joachim Zubly], *A Humble Inquiry into the Nature of the Dependency of the American Colonies* ([Charleston], 1769), 10. Zubly argued for an analogy between the North American colonies and Ireland that would be much scrutinized during the subsequent debate. The problem with the comparison, from the patriot point of view, was that Coke's decision in *Calvin's Case*

(1608) seemed to hold that Christian lands conquered by the king (e.g., Ireland) were indeed subject to the jurisdiction of Parliament once the protections of English law had been extended to them; see, for example, Black, "Constitution of Empire," 1175–1184; and Mary Sarah Bilder, *The Transatlantic Constitution: Colonial Legal Culture and the Empire* (Cambridge, MA, 2008), 35–40. Zubly also made the important point that judicial appeals from British North America were heard not by the House of Lords but rather by the king-in-council. Compare Wilson, *Considerations*, 22. It is important to note, however, that at this stage none of these writers (with the possible exception of "Britannus Americanus") denied Parliament's jurisdiction over the external affairs of the colonies; see, for example, [Zubly], *A Humble Inquiry*, 6; and Hopkins, *Rights of Colonies*, 5, 11. All of this calls into question the reliability of Francis Bernard's famous report to the Board of Trade (November 30, 1765) that patriots were already claiming to "have no Superiors upon Earth but the King, and him only in the Person of the Governor, or according to the terms of the Charter"; Bernard Papers, IV, 203, Harvard College Library. Of course, quite a lot hangs on what precisely is meant by a "superior" in this context.

58 [William Knox], *The Controversy between Great Britain and Her Colonies, Reviewed* (London, 1769), 7–8.

59 He appears, for example, as "the Popish Secretary *Calvert*" in John Oldmixon's whig account of the 1621 Parliament. See Oldmixon, *The History of England, during the Reigns of the Royal House of Stuart* (London, 1730), 55.

60 [Knox], *Controversy between Great Britain and Her Colonies*, [146].

61 Ibid., [150–151]. This version of events was adopted by several administration spokesmen; see, for example, [John Lind], *An Englishman's Answer, to the Address, from the Delegates, to the People of Great-Britain* (New York, 1775), 10. It was also adopted by Lord Mansfield in his speech to the House of Lords of February 10, 1766. There he raised the issue of the debate over the fishery bill; admitted that "a doubt was thrown out, whether parliament had any thing to do in America"; and then pointedly observed that "this doubt was immediately answered, I believe by Coke." See *Parliamentary History of England*, 16:176. Compare Sir William Blackstone's speech to the House of Commons on February 3, 1766, in *Proceedings and Debates*, ed. Stock, 2:148.

62 [Knox], *Controversy between Great Britain and Her Colonies*, 156.

63 Ibid., 201.

64 Ibid., 137.

65 Ibid., 138.

66 For context of this pamphlet, see Thomas J. Schaeper, *Edward Bancroft: Scientist, Author, Spy* (New Haven, 2011), esp. 14–29. Schaeper is rightly dubious about earlier claims that Franklin may have co-written the *Remarks*. Evidence of Bancroft's espionage was not discovered until 1889. Schaeper also offers a powerful refutation of the long-standing charge that Bancroft poisoned Silas Deane in order to prevent the latter from unmasking him as a British agent (207–215).

67 This might seem a surprising claim. Bancroft, who lived mainly in London from 1767 to 1777, is usually regarded as a marginal and conflicted figure in the revolutionary crisis, and his pamphlet was only published once in North America. But as I demonstrate below, he was read by almost every patriot pamphleteer of the early 1770s, and his analysis, more than any other, gave shape to their arguments.

68 [Edward Bancroft], *Remarks on the Review of the Controversy between Great Britain and Her Colonies* (New London, CT, 1771), 49.

69 Ibid., 19.

70 Compare [Gervase Parker Bushe], *The Case of Great-Britain and America, Addressed to the King and Both Houses of Parliament*, 3rd ed. (Dublin, 1769), 3. Bushe, an Irishman who wrote in defense of the patriot position, likewise claimed that "from the earliest times, down to the present, the disposition of foreign territory belonging to Great-Britain, has always been vested in the Executive. It is a power which the Restoration and the [Glorious] Revolution have left unshaken." Bushe did not, however, make any use of the Stuart precedents. See also [Anon.], *A Letter to the Right Honourable the Earl of Hillsborough, on the Present Situation of Affairs in America* (London, 1769), 4.

71 On this, see the insightful discussions in Michael Kammen, "The Meaning of Colonization in American Revolutionary Thought," *Journal of the History of Ideas* 31 (1970): 337–358, esp. 343–344. Bancroft does not address the implications of his constitutional theory for colonies that did not possess charters, a point raised by his loyalist interlocutors; see, for example, [Lind], *An Englishman's Answer*, 6. Franklin likewise took this view: see ["Benevolus"], "On the Propriety of Taxing America," April 9–11, 1767, in *PBF*, 14:111.

72 On this, see Bilder, *Transatlantic Constitution*, 40–46.

73 [Bancroft], *Remarks on the Review*, 28.

74 In the 1629 Parliament, it failed to achieve even a first reading. See Conrad Russell, *Parliaments and English Politics, 1621–1629* (Oxford, 1979), 234, 276, 406. The statement attributed to Charles by Bancroft seems to be a paraphrase of James's message to the House of Commons of April 29, 1624 (referred to by Pownall above). As we shall see, Bancroft passed this error along to his various readers. For a more predictable (and far less incendiary) response to Knox's invocation of the Stuarts, see Arthur Lee, *Observations on the Review of the Controversy between Great-Britain and Her Colonies* (London, 1769), 24–26. Lee at this point was still willing to acknowledge Parliament's jurisdiction over American commerce as a matter of right.

75 [Bancroft], *Remarks on the Review*, 57.

76 Ibid., 29.

77 Ibid., 43. Note how far we have come here from the patriot position during the Stamp Act debate. In *The Colonel Dismounted* (1764), Richard Bland had utterly dismissed the view that "the King by his prerogative can establish any form of government he pleases in the colony [Virginia]," attributing it sarcastically to "Sir Robert Filmer's disciples"; *Pamphlets of the American Revolution*, 321.

78 [Bancroft], *Remarks on the Review*, 44–45. This discussion of the succession strikingly echoes arguments put forward by advocates of Irish legislative autonomy in the 1690s. See, for example, William Molyneux, *The Case of Ireland's Being Bound by Acts of Parliament, Stated* (1698; repr., Belfast, 1776), 25, 71–72. I am grateful to Noah McCormack for prompting me to focus on this comparison.

79 [Anon.], *A Letter to the Right Honourable the Earl of Hillsborough, on the Present Situation of Affairs in America* (London, 1769), 15. The MHS possesses a copy of the Boston edition of this text annotated by Harbottle Dorr, the title page of which features the following attribution: "Supposed to be wrote By D^r. Bancroft Native of N. England." However, the pamphlet is usually attributed to George Canning, Sr.

80 Franklin was responding to the Scottish artist Allan Ramsay. He went on to explain that the settlers "went to a Country where neither the Power of Parliament nor of Prerogative had any Existence, and where the King, on the Condition they would continue to own him as their Sovereign, was contented to limit the Pretensions of his Prerogative by solemn Charters"; "Marginalia in a Pamphlet by Allan Ramsey" (1769?), in *PBF*, 16:318–319.

81 James Lovell, "Oration, Delivered at Boston" (April 2, 1771), in *Principles and Acts of the Revolution in America*, ed. H. Niles (Baltimore, 1822), 3. For a lucid comparison of the view that the king was in fact the feudal lord of America and the rival view that the land had been acquired by settlers directly from the natives, see Yuhtaro Ohmori, "The Artillery of Mr. Locke: The Use of Locke's *Second Treatise* in Pre-Revolutionary America" (PhD diss., Johns Hopkins University, 1988), 119–136.

82 Lovell, "Oration, Delivered at Boston," 3.

83 For the context of the debate, consult Reid's commentary in *Briefs of the American Revolution*. See also Clark, *Language of Liberty*, 93–110, and Bernard Bailyn, *The Ordeal of Thomas Hutchinson* (Cambridge, MA, 1976), 196–220.

84 Years later, Adams recorded in his autobiography that an initial answer "was drawn prettily written, I never knew by whom, whether Mr. Samuel Adams or Dr. Joseph Warren <or both together> or Dr. [Benjamin] Church, or all three together." This "Draught of a report," he continued, "was full of very popular Talk and with those democratical Principles which have done so much mischief in this Country. I objected to them all and got them all expunged which I thought exceptionable, and furnished the committee with the Law Authorities, and the legal and constitutional Reasonings that are to be seen on the part of the House in that Controversy"; *Diary and Autobiography of John Adams*, ed. L. H. Butterfield, 3 vols. (Cambridge, MA, 1961), 3:305.

85 *Briefs of the American Revolution*, 58.

86 It is for this reason that I cannot accept Reid's assertion that Adams and his colleagues would have been "embarrassed" had Hutchinson replied by reminding them that the House of Commons had rejected James's view of the matter; Reid, *Constitutional History of the American Revolution: The Authority to Legislate*,

165. As we have seen, Bancroft and his readers knew this full well. They focused on this episode precisely because, in their view, it marked the beginning of Parliament's illicit campaign to deprive the crown of its prerogative rights in America—one that the Stuarts valiantly resisted until the regicide, at which point an unchecked and tyrannical Parliament finally managed to get its hands on the colonies. Unless we recognize this fact, we will fail to register the ideological stakes involved in the deployment of this precedent. Thus, Reid makes it his central claim that the patriots were "looking back to the constitution of Sir Edward Coke, to the constitution that beheaded Charles I"; Reid, *Constitutional History of the American Revolution: The Authority of Law*, 5; compare Reid, *Constitutional History of the American Revolution: The Authority to Legislate*, 60. In fact, as we have seen, patriots in the early 1770s were explicitly *rejecting* that understanding of the constitution; they were instead defending the constitution on behalf of which Charles had gone to the scaffold. Recall that it was Coke himself who led the opposition to James's assertions of prerogative in the 1621 and 1624 parliaments (most famously in his response to Calvert about the fishery bill). That is, the notion that the patriots were simply defending the "seventeenth-century" constitution (which emphasized checks on arbitrary power) against the "eighteenth-century" constitution (which assumed parliamentary supremacy) understates the radicalism of their position. The patriots were not merely rejecting the eighteenth-century understanding of the English constitution; they were championing *one particular interpretation* of the seventeenth-century English constitution against all of its rivals. In endorsing a revival of the royal veto in Britain and insisting that the Stuarts had been correct to assert a prerogative right to regulate imperial commerce without Parliament, the patriots were not taking a generic "seventeenth-century" view of the English constitution, but rather a Royalist one. On this theme, compare Adams's insistence that it remained a prerogative of the Crown to dismiss judges at pleasure; *WJA*, 3:548–556.

87 *Monthly Review* 51 (November 1774): 390. Bancroft is here reviewing John Dickinson's *Essay on the Constitutional Power of Great Britain over the Colonies* (1774). The *Monthly Review* published its reviews anonymously, but the magazine's records identify the authors of each essay. For a list of Bancroft's contributions, see Benjamin Christie Nangle, *The Monthly Review, First Series, 1749–1789; Indexes of Contributors and Articles* (Oxford, 1934), 3. Franklin recommended Bancroft to Ralph Griffiths, the owner of the *Monthly Review*, early in 1774. Over the next two years, Bancroft contributed over thirty reviews to the magazine, many relating to the American crisis. See Schaeper, *Edward Bancroft*, 42–43.

88 *Monthly Review* 51 (November 1774): 390–391.

89 *Briefs of the American Revolution*, 88.

90 Ibid., 90–91.

91 Hutchinson also quotes Sandys's rejoinder in the 1621 debate: "Sir Edwin Sandys, who was one of the Virginia Company and an eminent Lawyer, de-

clared that he knew Virginia had been annexed and *was held of the Crown as of the Manor of East Greenwich* and he believed New-England was so also"; ibid., 90.

92 Ibid., 99. The house replied exactly as Bancroft had; see 139.

93 Thomas Hutchinson, "A Dialogue between an American and a European Englishman," in *Perspectives in American History,* ed. Bernard Bailyn and Donald Fleming, vol. 9 (Cambridge, MA, 1975), 343–410. Indeed, the precision with which Hutchinson recapitulates and then refutes the patriot defense of Stuart constitutionalism in the "Dialogue" suggests that the dating of this manuscript should be reconsidered. Following Malcolm Freiburg, Bailyn assumed that the manuscript was composed during the summer of 1768 (Hutchinson, "Dialogue between an American and a European Englishman," 350; Bailyn, *Ordeal of Thomas Hutchinson,* 100n39) and that it was intended to answer Dickinson's *Letters from a Farmer.* However, Dickinson made no use at all of Stuart precedents in his pamphlet, and I am unaware of any patriot who did so prior to Bancroft in 1769 (as we have seen, although the pamphlet was not printed in British America until 1771, colonists plainly had access to the London edition). Since Hutchinson took himself to be summarizing the patriot position in the "Dialogue," it therefore seems likely that it was in fact composed no earlier than 1769. More work would of course need to be done in order to confirm this conjecture, but the evidence for a 1768 composition date has always been quite slim. As Bailyn pointed out, the "Dialogue" is not mentioned in any of Hutchinson's papers or in those of his close friends.

94 Hutchinson, "Dialogue between an American and a European Englishman," 374.

95 Ibid.

96 Ibid.

97 Ibid., 376. It is thus particularly ironic that, five years earlier, it had been Hutchinson who tried in vain to prevent the removal of Charles I's portrait from the Massachusetts Council chamber. Hutchinson opposed the gesture, not because he had any sympathy for the Stuarts but rather on the grounds that all English kings were entitled to have their portraits displayed in a chamber of state; see Bailyn, *Ordeal of Thomas Hutchinson,* 138. The radicals who demanded the removal of the portrait, on the other hand, would shortly find themselves defending Charles I.

98 Hutchinson, "Dialogue between an American and a European Englishman," 376.

99 Compare Lord Lyttleton's comment in the Lords debate on repeal of the Stamp Act (February 10, 1766): "[The colonists] went out subjects of Great Britain, and unless they can shew a new compact made between them and the parliament of Great Britain (for the king alone could not make a new compact with them) they are still subjects to all intents and purposes whatsoever"; *Parliamentary History of England,* 16:167. See also [Anon.], *Colonising, or a Plain Investigation of*

That Subject; with a Legislative, Political, and Commercial View of Our Colonies (London, 1774), 8–11.

100 [John Gray], *The Right of the British Legislature to Tax the American Colonies Vindicated* (London, 1774), 36. Compare [Anon.], "The Address of the People of Great Britain to the Inhabitants of America" (1774), in *Archives*, 1:1429.

101 [Gray], *Right of the British Legislature*, 37. It is worth noting the historical conflation that is occurring here: the charters of Virginia, Plymouth, and Massachusetts Bay were all granted before 1629 (the beginning of the Personal Rule).

102 Scholars have occasionally taken the same view. Robert Schuyler, for example, argued in his reply to McIlwain that "it may be that the first two Stuart sovereigns, with their lofty conceptions of royal prerogative and their numerous controversies with the House of Commons, convinced themselves that the American colonies did not lie within the range of parliamentary authority," but this, on Schuyler's account, was merely an absolutist delusion. See Schuyler, *Parliament and the British Empire* (New York, 1929), 22. Schuyler added in a footnote that "on the eve of the American Revolution it was urged by Americans who disputed Parliament's right to interfere in colonial affairs that James I and Charles I had held this opinion" (229n78). His reference is to the debate between Hutchinson and the Massachusetts house.

103 [Jonathan Boucher], *A Letter from a Virginian* (Boston, 1774), 13.

104 Ibid.

105 [John Lind], *Remarks on the Principal Acts of the Thirteenth Parliament of Great Britain* (London, 1775), 38–39. Compare [Anon.], *American Resistance Indefensible* (London, 1776), 18–19. See also Richard Hussey's remarks in the Commons debate on repeal of the Stamp Act (February 3, 1766): "The Fact was K.J.I. [King James I] assumed all Sovereign Power. The Lawyers then thought he might give them what Laws he pleased. It was said so in this house by the Secy of State. The Charters gave powers a King of Engd cannot. Hence arises the obscurity about the Constitution of the Colonies. The mistake was that no part can delegate its Supremacy without Consent of the others"; H. W. V. Temperley, "Debates on the Declaratory Act and the Repeal of the Stamp Act, 1766," *American Historical Review* 17 (1912): 563–586, esp. 569–570.

106 [Lind], *Remarks on the Principal Acts of the Thirteenth Parliament of Great Britain*, 174–184, 192–193. Compare William Knox, *The Claim of the Colonies to an Exemption from Internal Taxes Imposed by Authority of Parliament* (London, 1765), 8: "The question then will be, Can the crown grant an exemption to any subject of Great Britain, from the jurisdiction of parliament? Will any descendent of the associates of Pym or Hamden [sic], avow it for his opinion that the crown can do so? If he acknowledges a right in the crown to exempt the subject from the jurisdiction of parliament in the case of taxation, can he deny its power to dispense with acts of parliament, or to deprive the same subject of the benefits of the common law? And then, what becomes of the colonies birth-right as Englishmen, and the glorious securities for their persons and properties which

their forefathers obtained and handed down to them? Thank God, the constitution of Great Britain admits of no such power in the crown." See also [Anon.],
*A Letter to the Right Honourable the Earl of Hillsborough, on the Connection between
Great Britain and her American Colonies* (London, 1768), 31–37; and [Allan Ramsay,] *Thoughts on the Origin and Nature of Government, Occasioned by the Late Disputes between Great Britain and Her American Colonies: Written in the Year 1766*
(London, 1769), 5.

107 Thomas Hutchinson, *Strictures upon the Declaration of the Congress at Philadelphia* (London, 1776), 23.

108 See Jean-Louis Delolme, *The Constitution of England, or An Account of the English
Government*, 2nd ed., 2 vols. (London, 1778), 1:32n. This passage is not present in
the first edition of 1775. Delolme added a more substantial defense of his position to the third edition, which was then preserved in subsequent editions; see
Delolme, *The Constitution of England*, 4th ed. (London, 1784), 522–527. In a footnote, Delolme explains that he personally confronted Franklin with his objection that "the claim of the American Colonies directly clashed with one of the
vital principles of the English Constitution" (524n). It is of no small importance
that Delolme, despite his enthusiasm for monarchy and his anxiety about unchecked legislatures, should have regarded the American position as unacceptable—as more dangerously Royalist than his own. For an excellent recent
discussion of Delolme's view of monarchy, see Iain McDaniel, "Jean-Louis
Delolme and the Political Science of the English Empire," *Historical Journal*
55 (2012): 21–44, esp. 34–38. For a similar claim, see [Anon.], "Extract of a Letter
from London, to a Gentleman in New York, Dated Dec. 10, 1774," in *Archives*,
1:1037.

109 [Knox], *Controversy between Great Britain and Her Colonies*, 150–151. One defender
of the patriot position suggested a remedy for this perceived danger: "Your apprehensions that the Colonies might by Provincial grants render the Crown
independant, unless Parliament had a right to interpose, is only a pretence?
Why have you ever let them make grants then? And is not your complaint that
they have granted too little, not too much? But if that be your real fear, you can
remedy it without a civil war. Pass an Act of Parliament, declaring that it shall
not be lawful for the Crown to give the royal assent to any provincial grant
without the approbation of Parliament. America will not refuse you a negative
on her grants, but she will not relinquish a negative on your demands"; [Anon.],
*An Answer to a Pamphlet, Entitled Taxation No Tyranny, Addressed to the Author,
and to Persons in Power* (London, 1775), 33. Franklin addressed the issue in his
testimony before the House of Commons on February 13, 1766: "Q. Suppose
the King should require the Colonies to grant a revenue, and the parliament
should be against their doing it, do they think they can grant a revenue to the
King, without the consent of the parliament of G. Britain? A. That is a deep
question. As to my own opinion, I should think myself at liberty to do it, and
should do it, if I liked the occasion"; *PBF*, 13:153. As of June 1770, he was still

insisting that "our Parliaments have Right to grant [the King] Aids without the Consent of this Parliament [of Great Britain]"; Franklin to Samuel Cooper, June 18, 1770, in *PBF*, 17:163. But Franklin eventually seems to have arrived at precisely the same position as the author of *An Answer,* namely that "in time of War on Requisition made by the King with Consent of Parliament, every Colony shall raise money"; "Franklin's 'Hints' or Terms for a Durable Union," December 4/6, 1774, in *PBF*, 21:367. See also Willoughby Bertie, Lord Abingdon, *Thoughts on Mr. Burke's Letter to the Sheriffs of Bristol on the Affairs of America* (Dublin, 1777), 47.

110 *Boswell's Life of Johnson,* ed. George Birkbeck Hill and L. F. Powell, 2nd ed., 6 vols. (Oxford, 1964–1971), 3:221. The letter is dated February 28, 1778.

111 *Life and Correspondence of James Iredell, One of the Associate Justices of the Supreme Court of the United States,* ed. Griffith John McRee, 2 vols. (New York, 1857–1858), 1:213. Iredell had emigrated from England in 1767 at the age of seventeen.

112 Ibid., 213–214, Iredell's italics. Iredell makes a striking move in the passage that immediately follows this one. Having established that jurisdiction over North America is limited to the Crown, he next addresses the question of whether Parliament could legitimately interfere in colony matters provided it had the king's permission to do so. His answer is "no," on the grounds that the terms of any given charter are binding on *both* the colony and the chartering monarch (along with the latter's successors). But did James and Charles agree? "In the case of James and Charles," Iredell writes, "it may be said those kings perhaps thought that *they,* in the plenitude of their power, had authority to revoke the charters, if necessary, or to make any other regulations for us they might think proper. They were indeed sufficiently arbitrary in their tempers to form an idea of that sort; but it does not appear that *they did,* and our ancestors were certainly not fools enough to consider the only foundation of their security as alterable at pleasure by one of the contracting parties" (214). Here, having just cited James and Charles as his constitutional authorities, Iredell feels called upon to concede that they were "sufficiently arbitrary in their tempers" to have supposed that the charters might be altered at their whim—only to insist in the next breath that the Stuarts did not in fact take this "arbitrary" view.

113 Ibid., 214.

114 "Edmund Burke" [pseud.], "To the Right Honourable Lord North," in *Archives,* 1:338.

115 Ibid.

116 Ibid.

117 Ibid.

118 Ibid., 339. The author then adds an interesting twist to the argument: he suggests that after subduing the southern colonies that had "held out for the King," the Commonwealth Parliament settled for only a "nominal" degree of "supremacy" over them. On the author's account, this fact demonstrates' that "even those who had brought a Monarch to the scaffold, had the moderation

and justice to *respect,* and preserve those rights" that the colonies had been given by the Crown in their charters. There is some truth to this claim: in the 1640s and 1650s, the overwhelmingly anti-Royalist General Court of Massachusetts Bay continued to insist upon the importance of their charter despite the fact that it had been issued by Charles I, whom they roundly despised. But at no point during this period did the General Court deny Parliament's jurisdiction over the colonies, and Parliament unambiguously asserted its jurisdiction, at least in relation to trade. On this, see Mark Peterson, *The City-State of Boston: The Rise and Fall of an Atlantic World, 1630–1865* (New Haven, forthcoming), chapter 1. See also John Donoghue, *Fire under the Ashes: An Atlantic History of the English Revolution* (Chicago, 2013), 125–128.

119 See also ["A Philadelphian"], "To the Freemen of America," *Pennsylvania Gazette,* May 18, 1774: "Remember, my dear Countrymen, we are contending for the Crown and Prerogative of our King, as well as for Liberty—Property and Life.—The British Parliament have violated the Constitution, in usurping his *supreme* Jurisdiction over us" (3).

120 [Moses Mather], *America's Appeal to the Impartial World* (Hartford, 1775), 45.

121 Ibid., 31.

122 Ibid., 46. Franklin, for one, entertained doubts on this point; see Franklin, "Observations upon [Thomas Pownall], *State of the Constitution of the Colonies* [London, 1769?]," in *PBF,* 16:300.

123 The pamphlet had been loaned to him by Alexander McDougall, to whom he wrote as follows: "It is with the utmost chagrin I am obliged to inform you, that I am not able to return you all your pamph[l]ets; and what is still worse the most valuable of them is missing. I beg you will not impute it to carelessness; for I assure you upon my honor the true state of the case is this—I put your pamphlets in the case with my other books; and some person about the College got into my room through the window, broke open my case, & took out The friendly address, Bankrofts treatise, Two volumes of natural philosophy and a latin author. I have procured another Friendly address to replace the one lost; and have taken all possible pains to recover Bankroft's treatise or to get another in its stead; but my endeavors have heretofore been fruitless. Mr. Abram Livingston thinks he can get one for me, and has promised, if possible, to do it. . . . Be pleased to let me know the proper title of Bankrofts pamphlet (which I have forgotten) and I will publish it with the offer of a reward to any person that will restore it." See Alexander Hamilton to Alexander McDougall, [1774–1776], in *PAH,* 26:353–354. See also Schaeper, *Edward Bancroft,* 21–22. I am grateful to Daniel Hulsebosch for alerting me to the existence of Hamilton's letter.

124 [Samuel Seabury], *A View of the Controversy between Great Britain and Her Colonies* (New York, 1774), 10.

125 *Farmer Refuted,* 16. Compare "Marginalia in *An Inquiry,* an Anonymous Pamphlet" in *PBF,* 17:345 ("the King . . . alone is the Sovereign").

126 *Farmer Refuted*, 25. Compare John Cartwright, *American Independence the Interest and Glory of Great Britain* (London, 1774), 10. The colonists settled "in those regions, which, by the prerogative, were the property of the crown, and which the King, by the same prerogative, had the power of alienating without the consent of the people of England, particularly when such alienation was made to a part of his own subjects." See also Abingdon, *Thoughts on Mr. Burke's Letter*, 13.

127 Hamilton likewise confronts the charge of Jacobitism, which Seabury had raised: "Admitting, that the King of Great Britain was enthroned by virtue of an act of parliament, and that he is King of America, because he is King of Great-Britain, yet the act of parliament is not the *efficient cause* of his being the King of America: It is only the *occasion* of it. He is King of America, by virtue of a compact between us and the Kings of Great-Britain"; *Farmer Refuted*, 9.

128 Ibid., 30–31.

129 Ibid., 31. It is worth underlining that this is a virtual quotation from Bancroft's essay. Hamilton had certainly read it, as had Mather, the author(s) of the House's "Answer" (a point that Hutchinson recognized, as we have seen), the author of the "Edmund Burke" letter, and (quite probably) Iredell. This is a striking fact, given that recent scholarship has stressed the degree to which patriots were often not able to consult each other's pamphlets. See, for example, Trish Loughran, *The Republic in Print: Print Culture in the Age of U.S. Nation Building, 1770–1870* (New York, 2007).

130 For a fascinatingly different use of the Stuart precedent, see Joseph Hawley's March 1775 essay "To the Inhabitants of Massachusetts-Bay. No. V" (*Archives*, 2:18–24). Here Hawley (who, we should recall, is thought to have contributed to the House's "Answer") likewise cites the debate over the fishery bill and other precedents to show that "*Charles* the First [who granted the first Massachusetts charter] viewed the colonies as independent of the Empire, and exempt from the authority of Parliament, even in the matter of regulating trade" (23). But unlike the writers we have been considering, he follows the loyalists in attributing this attitude on the part of the Stuarts to their tyrannical cast of mind. For Hawley, it is precisely because James and Charles attempted to "govern the Nation by the terrors of Royalty" (21) and by loathsome "prerogatives" (23) that it is so implausible to assume that they intended to grant Parliament any jurisdiction over America in the charters. As to the loyalist riposte that this construction of the charters would leave America wholly at the mercy of an unencumbered Crown, Hawley answers coyly that "the present question is not what is best, but what is in reality the fact" (22). And anyway, "it is infinitely better to have but one tyrant than a million" (22).

131 *Farmer Refuted*, 32.

132 This is the view most recently advanced by Jack P. Greene in *Constitutional Origins of the American Revolution*, esp. 134–139. Greene is echoing Barbara Black's claim that "the [patriot] desire for sole external authority in the king (and Privy

Council) resulted from the perception that under those conditions there would shortly be no external authority with any force whatsoever"; Black, "Constitution of Empire," 1193. See also Adams, *Political Ideas of the American Revolution,* 49–56; Ernest Barker, "Natural Law and the American Revolution," in Barker, *Traditions of Civility: Eight Essays* (Cambridge, 1948), 263–355, esp. 305; and Bushman, *King and People in Provincial Massachusetts,* 251. Bushman notes that this characterization seems to have originated with Lord Mansfield. For an eloquent critique of this view, see Reid, *Constitutional History of the American Revolution: The Authority of Law,* 152–156.

133 See [Bancroft], *Remarks on the Review,* 118–128. Bancroft proposes that (as a necessary evil) the colonies should "submit their Trade to the absolute Government of the *British* Parliament, (without desiring a Representation therein,) to be restrained and directed by its Laws for the general Good" (122). And although he allows the king a veto over the acts of his proposed pan-colonial "Assembly," he does not directly propose reviving the veto in Britain and he suggests that judicial appeals should no longer be heard by the king-in-council, but rather by the colonial legislatures (although the king-in-council would continue to judge in cases of "any Differences between the Colonies and any other of his Majesty's Subjects, or Allies") (126).

134 Wilson's view on this subject was endorsed by several others. See, e.g., Hicks, *The Nature and Extent of Parliamentary Power Considered,* 8, 22; and [Wells], *A Few Political Reflections.* Rejecting the view that Parliament should be accorded the right to pass *"acts for regulating of trade"* (on the grounds that "I could never be convinced . . . of the practicability of drawing a line so near the borders of *taxation,* as not to encroach upon that ground"), Wells argues as follows: "Let it be remembered that the King has a negative upon all our bills, which ought to be deemed a sufficient check upon our conduct" (17). In other words, the royal veto is to replace parliamentary legislation as the "harmonizing force" in imperial commerce. Wells also reproduces Wilson's expansive account of the royal prerogative (40–41).

135 Thus, William Markham, archbishop of York, argued that the patriots "have maintained, that a charter which issues from the king's sole pleasure, is valid against an act of parliament. They have maintained, that a king of England has the power to discharge any number of his subjects that he pleases, from the allegiance that is due to the state. They used their best endeavours, to throw the whole weight and power of the colonies into the scale of the crown"—and that they therefore rejected the results of "the glorious revolution." See Markham, *A Sermon Preached before the Incorporated Society for the Propagation of the Gospel in Foreign Parts* (London, 1777), 22–23. See also [Anon.], "The Address of the People of Great Britain to the Inhabitants of America" (1774), in *Archives,* 1:1429–1430; [Anon.], *Answer to a Pamphlet,* 32–33; "Address of . . . the City of Oxford," *London Gazette,* November 11–14, 1775, 4; and [Anon.], *American Resistance Indefensible* (London, 1776). The author of the first of these pamphlets accuses

the colonists of attempting "to pay compliments to the King's personal power at the expense of his authority, and to mark his reign with the loss of Dominions, which with so much glory he extended"; the author of the second (a pro-American response to Johnson) acknowledges that the British concern is that "the Colonies might, by Provincial grants, render the Crown independent."

136 [Wells], *A Few Political Reflections*, 31.

137 *Farmer Refuted*, 16.

138 Franklin to Samuel Cooper, June 8, 1770, in *PBF*, 17:163. Compare also Franklin's defense of the patriot constitutional position in his apologia for his role in the dissemination of the Hutchinson letters: "From a thorough inquiry (on occasion of the Stamp Act) into the nature of the connexion between Britain and the colonies, I became convinced, that the bond of their union is not the Parliament, but the King. . . . At the same time, I considered the King's supreme authority over all the colonies as of the greatest importance to them, affording a *dernier resort* for settling all their disputes, a means of preserving peace among them with each other, and a centre in which their common force might be united against a common enemy"; *Works of Benjamin Franklin*, 4:408.

139 "Marginalia in a Pamphlet by Josiah Tucker," in *PBF*, 17:354. Franklin was commenting on a passage in Tucker's *A Letter from a Merchant in London to His Nephew in North America* (London, 1766), 7–8.

140 [Thomson Mason], "The British American" (1774), Letter 6, in *Archives*, 1:519.

141 It is striking that patriots interpreted even the Quebec Act as a reflection of parliamentarian rather than royal tyranny. Hamilton, for example, argued that while the measure seemed to ensure that "the whole Legislative, Executive, and Judiciary powers [in British Canada], are ultimately and effectually, though not immediately, lodged in the King," it should nonetheless be blamed on "the corruption of the british Parliament," not the king. See Hamilton, "Remarks on the Quebec Bill," in *The Works of Alexander Hamilton*, ed. John C. Hamilton, 7 vols. (New York, 1850), 2:131, 137. For the context of the act, see Philip Lawson, *The Imperial Challenge: Quebec and Britain in the Age of the American Revolution* (Montreal and Kingston, 1989), esp. 127–145.

142 "The British American," Letter 6, in *Archives*, 1:521.

143 "The British American," Letter 7, in ibid., 1:543. Note that Mason fully endorses the neo-Stuart account of American settlement and the charters and approvingly cites the "Edmund Burke" letter (522). Compare [Anon.], *Answer to a Pamphlet*, 45–47.

144 *Journals of the Continental Congress: 1774–1789*, 1:119.

145 Reid, *Constitutional History of the American Revolution: The Authority of Law*, 153.

146 A second possibility was to attempt to create a grand new imperial constitution along the lines proposed by Joseph Galloway that would entrust the regulation of American affairs to a new legislative body, but this approach failed to gain traction. See Lacroix, *Ideological Origins of American Federalism*, 105–131.

147 *Farmer Refuted*, 16. See also Hicks, *The Nature and Extent of Parliamentary Power Considered*, 8.

148 See McIlwain, *The American Revolution*, 159; and G. H. Guttridge, *English Whiggism and the American Revolution* (Berkeley, 1966), 61–63. For a similar development among English "radicals" at roughly the same time, see Reid, *Constitutional History of the American Revolution: The Authority of Law*, 156–162. As Reid points out, however, English reformers of the period sought to balance the royal prerogative by lobbying the House of Commons to resume its power of impeaching royal officials. No such balance existed in the patriot position.

149 It is worth noting, however, that the list of authors just discussed is quite diverse. A number are New Englanders (Adams, Hawley, Lovell, Mather, and Bancroft), but an even greater number (Franklin, Hamilton, Iredell, Mason, Wells, Wilson, and, presumably, the author of the anonymous Virginia letter to Lord North) are not. It is a point of interest that Hamilton, Iredell, and Wilson were all born outside of North America (and Bancroft spent several years in British Guiana), but they came from very different places. In short, the phenomenon of patriot Royalism does not seem to have been confined to a particular region of the country or to those of a specific background.

150 See Clark, *Language of Liberty*, 108; Kammen, "Meaning of Colonization," 349; McConville, *King's Three Faces*, 261. As we shall see, Clark's claim that by invoking the dominion theory, "Americans accepted the monarchical tie only in order to exploit its apparent weakness, and open the way for a natural-law rejection of the common-law sovereign" (108) is a perfectly good characterization of Jefferson's tactic in the *Summary View*, but Jefferson's posture in this respect was deeply uncharacteristic of contemporary defenses of the dominion theory.

151 *Summary View*, 7. For a cogent discussion of the pamphlet's argument, see LaCroix, *Ideological Origins of American Federalism*, 113–120. See also W. H. Bennett, "Early American Theories of Federalism," *The Journal of Politics* 4 (1942): 383–395; H. Trevor Colbourn, "Thomas Jefferson's Use of the Past," *WMQ* 15 (1958): 56–70; Anthony M. Lewis, "Jefferson's Summary View as a Chart of Political Union," *WMQ* 5 (1948): 34–51; Peter S. Onuf, *Jefferson's Empire: The Language of American Nationhood* (Charlottesville, VA, 2000), 61–65; and Garrett Ward Sheldon, *The Political Philosophy of Thomas Jefferson* (Baltimore, 1991), 19–40.

152 *Summary View*, 16.

153 Ibid.

154 Ibid.

155 Ibid, 22.

156 Franklin had been equally explicit on this point: "By our Constitution [the King] is, with [his] Plantation Parliaments, the sole Legislator of his American Subjects, and in that Capacity is and ought to be free to exercise his own Judgment, unrestrain'd and unlimited by his Parliament [in Great Britain]"; Franklin to

Samuel Cooper, June 18, 1770, in *PBF,* 17:163. Franklin in this letter offers a full endorsement of the patriot Royalist position in all of its particulars: "That the Colonies originally were constituted distinct States, and intended to be continued such, is clear to me from a thorough Consideration of their original Charters, and the whole Conduct of the Crown and Nation towards them until the Restoration. Since that Period, the Parliament here has usurp'd an Authority of making Laws for them, which before it had not. We have for some time submitted to that Usurpation, partly thro' Ignorance and Inattention, and partly from our Weakness and Inability to contend."

157 *Summary View,* 7.

158 Ibid., 8.

159 Ibid., 6. For an earlier statement of this position, see [John Allen], *The American Alarm, or the Bostonian Plea* (Boston, 1773), 22–23.

160 *Summary View,* 7.

161 For an endorsement of Jefferson's position, see Joseph Warren's "Oration" on the fifth anniversary of the Boston Massacre (March 5, 1775), in *Archives,* 2:38.

162 *Summary View,* 17.

163 Ibid., 18–19. To take just one example, patriots had decried the 1765 suspension of the New York legislature in part on the grounds that Parliament rather than the king had ordered it. As Dickinson summarized the complaint: "The crown might have restrained the governor of *New-York,* even from calling the assembly together, by its prerogative in the royal governments. This step, I suppose, would have been taken, if the conduct of the assembly of *New-York* had been regarded as an act of disobedience *to the crown alone*; but it is regarded as an act of 'disobedience to the authority of the British Legislature.' This gives the suspension a consequence vastly more affecting. It is a parliamentary assertion of the *supreme authority* of the *British* legislature over these colonies"; *Letters from a Farmer,* 5. Compare Mason, "The British American," Letter 9, in *Archives,* 1:652. Mason goes so far as to defend the king's prerogative "to remove the seat of Government of any particular Colony, to whatever place the King pleases within that Colony; and though this prerogative may be exercised oppressively, still the subject must submit. He may petition, but Majesty only can redress the grievance."

164 *Summary View,* 18. On this aspect of Jefferson's position, see the wise remark in Greene, *Constitutional Origins of the American Revolution,* 176.

165 Another pamphlet of the 1770s that attacked the Stuarts—although remained intriguingly silent on the dominion theory—was Josiah Quincy, *Observations on the Act of Parliament Commonly Called the Boston Port-Bill* (Boston, 1774), esp. 48, 59, 70. Indeed, Quincy, like Jefferson, flirted with overt anti-monarchism (70).

166 See David L. Jacobson, "John Dickinson's Fight against Royal Government, 1764," *WMQ* 19 (1962): 64–85; Fiala, "George III in the Pennsylvania Press," 99–104; Milton E. Fowler, *John Dickinson: Conservative Revolutionary* (Charlottes-

ville, VA, 1983), 35–47; and Jane Calvert, *Quaker Constitutionalism and the Political Thought of John Dickinson* (Cambridge, 2009), 195–203.

167 John Dickinson, "Speech on a Petition for a Change of Government of the Colony of Pennsylvania, May 24, 1764," in *The Writings of John Dickinson*, ed. Paul Leicester Ford (Philadelphia, 1895), 1:23, 28, 33.

168 Ibid., 1:40.

169 John Dickinson, *Essay on the Constitutional Power of Great Britain over the Colonies* (Philadelphia, 1774), 70–72. Compare Arthur Lee, *An Appeal to the Justice and Interests of the People of Great Britain, in the Present Dispute with America* (London, 1774), 15. For a direct reply to Dickinson on this point, see [John Gray], *Remarks on the New Essay of the Pennsylvania Farmer* (London, 1775), 41–42.

170 Dickinson, *Essay on the Constitutional Power of Great Britain over the Colonies*, 72.

171 Ibid., 108.

172 Ibid., 111.

173 Although it is noteworthy that, at one point, even Dickinson flirts with the notion of assigning the regulation of trade to the royal prerogative: "Time forbids a more exact enquiry into this point [i.e., where the constitutional authority to regulate commerce resides]; but such it is apprehended, will on enquiry be found to have been the power of the crown, that our argument may gain, but not lose. We will proceed on a concession that the power of regulating trade is vested in parliament"; ibid., 116–118.

174 Ibid., 117.

175 Ibid., 117–118.

176 The claim that Parliament possesses complete jurisdiction over North America, Dickinson informs us, was first made by the "illegal" Commonwealth Parliament; ibid., 108.

177 George III to Lord North, September 10, 1775, in *The Correspondence of King George the Third*, ed. Sir John Fortescue, 6 vols. (London, 1927), 3:256.

178 *The Grenville Papers*, ed. William James Smith, 4 vols. (London, 1852–1853), 3:215. See also John Brooke, *George III: A Biography of America's Last Monarch* (New York, 1972), 171.

179 George III, "Opening of Parliament" (November 30, 1774), in *Parliamentary History of England*, 18:34.

180 Ibid., 695.

181 "Address of . . . the City of Oxford," *London Gazette*, November 11–14, 1775, 4.

182 "Address of . . . the Corporation of Maidenhead in the County of Berks," *London Gazette*, November 21–25, 1775, 1.

183 [Anon.], *American Resistance Indefensible* (London, 1776), 18–19. This is the printed version of a sermon preached "by a Country Curate" on December 13, 1776.

184 Markham, *A Sermon Preached before the Incorporated Society for the Propagation of the Gospel*, 22–23. For a pro-American response to Markham (and to John

Stuart, 1st Marquess of Bute, who had made the same argument), see Abingdon, *Thoughts on Mr. Burke's Letter*, 46–47.

185 On this theme, see G. H. Guttridge, *English Whiggism and the American Revolution* (Berkeley, 1966), esp. 61–63; and Paul Langford, "New Whigs, Old Tories, and the American Revolution," *Journal of Imperial and Commonwealth History* 8 (1980): 106–130, see esp. 110–112.

186 See, for example, Bushman, *King and People in Provincial Massachusetts*, 212–226; William Liddle, "'A Patriot King, or None': American Public Attitudes towards George III and the British Monarchy, 1754–1776" (PhD diss., Claremont Graduate School, 1970), 379–383; Maier, *From Resistance to Revolution*, 198–208; McConville, *King's Three Faces*, 250–261; Andrew Jackson O'Shaughnessy, "'If Others Will Not be Active, I Must Drive': George III and the American Revolution," *Early American Studies* 2 (2004): 1–46, esp. 9–16; and O'Shaughnessy, *The Men Who Lost America: British Leadership, the American Revolution, and the Fate of the Empire* (New Haven, 2013), 17–28.

187 As early as the spring of 1775, John Adams, who had enthusiastically contributed to the defense of the Stuarts in the "Answer" of the Massachusetts House, declared himself in the "Novanglus" letters to be a defender instead of the "revolution principles" of "Sidney, Harrington, and Locke"—the same principles that had animated the struggle "against the Stuarts, the Charleses, and the Jameses, in support of the Reformation and the Protestant religion; and against the worst tyranny that the genius of toryism has ever yet invented; I mean the Roman superstition"; *Political Writings of John Adams*, 26–28. Compare [Matthew Robinson-Morris, Lord Rokeby], *Considerations on the Measures Carrying on with Respect to the British Colonies in North America* (London, 1774), 10; Drayton, *Letter from a Freeman*, 3–5, 13, 24–25; and Samuel Sherwood, *The Church's Flight into the Wilderness* (New York, 1776), 16.

188 David Armitage, *The Declaration of Independence: A Global History* (Cambridge, MA, 2007), 168. This was not, of course, the only charge directed against the king. The declaration was designed to appeal to several different constituencies, and, since its primary author was Jefferson, it unsurprisingly reprised his attack on the use of the royal negative in the colonies from the *Summary View* ("He has refused his Assent to Laws, the most wholesome and necessary for the public Good" [166]). I mean only to point out that even at this definitive moment of rupture, the patriot Royalist vision had not been set aside. For the highly political genesis of the list of charges against the king, see the excellent account in Pauline Maier, *American Scripture: Making the Declaration of Independence* (New York, 1998), 105–123.

189 This point is nicely made in Carl Becker, *The Declaration of Independence: A Study in the History of Political Ideas* (New York, 1922), 19–20. The text of the declaration likewise reminded "our British Brethren" that "we have warned them from Time to Time of Attempts by their Legislature to extend an un-

warrantable Jurisdiction over us"; quoted in Armitage, *Declaration of Independence,* 170.

2. "One Step Farther, and We Are Got Back to Where We Set Out From"

1 Adams published volume 1 of the *Defence* in 1787; volumes 2 and 3 followed in 1788. He then issued a considerably revised second edition in 1794.

2 Turgot, "Lettre au Docteur Price sur les constitutions américaines" (Mar. 28, 1778), in *Oeuvres de Turgot et documents le concernant,* ed. Gustave Schele, 5 vols. (Paris, 1913–1923), 5:534; quoted in English translation in *Defence,* 1:1–2. The letter was posthumously published in 1784. For the French context of Adams's intervention—and its French reception—see C. Bradley Thompson, "John Adams and the Coming of the French Revolution," *Journal of the Early Republic* 16 (1996): 361–387. For the complex publication and translation history of Turgot's letter and the difficulties involved in characterizing his position, see Will Slauter, "Constructive Misreadings: Adams, Turgot, and the American State Constitutions," *Papers of the Bibliographic Society of America* 105 (2011): 33–67.

3 *Defence,* 3:212. Compare Adams's later expression of contempt for the "enmity to monarchy and hierarchy" evinced by the "republicans who beheaded Charles I." Adams, annotations to Mary Wollstonecraft, *Historical and Moral View of the Origin and Progress of the French Revolution* (1796), reprinted in Zoltán Haraszti, *John Adams & the Prophets of Progress* (Cambridge, MA, 1952), 224.

4 *Defence,* 3:213. For Adams's reading of Nedham, see Haraszti, *John Adams,* 162–164.

5 *Defence,* 3:366.

6 Ibid., 366–367.

7 Ibid., 367.

8 Ibid., 367–368. It is noteworthy that Jean-Louis Delolme, who is often taken to be a source of the "late" Adams's political views, energetically denied this crucial claim about representation. Only the members of the House of Commons, for Delolme, could be styled "the Representatives of the Nation, and of the whole Nation." The "Royal authority" was rather to be regarded as a "counterpoise" to the "power of the People" (i.e., not as an agency of that power). See Jean Louis Delolme, *The Constitution of England,* 4th ed. (London, 1784), 33, 41, 202. I cite the 4th edition in this context because it was almost certainly the edition Adams consulted.

9 John Taylor, *An Inquiry into the Principles and Policy of the Government of the United States* (Fredericksburg, VA, 1814), 110–111. Hanna Pitkin includes an astute footnote about this exchange in her classic work, *The Concept of Representation* (Berkeley, 1964), 262.

10 Taylor, *Inquiry into the Principles and Policy of the Government of the United States,* 146.

11 Taylor accuses Adams of assailing "all our constitutions, under which the people, by representation, possess an uncontrolled legislative and executive power" (ibid., 431).

12 For a very different interpretation of the exchange between Adams and Taylor, see Gordon Wood, *The Creation of the American Republic, 1776–1787,* rev. ed. (Chapel Hill, 1998), 567–592, originally published 1969.

13 Adams also unsurprisingly regarded Franklin as "the weak disciple of Nedham." See, for example, Adams, annotations to Abbé de Maby, *De la législation* (1791), reprinted in Haraszti, *John Adams,* 203, 214; and annotations to Wollstonecraft, *Historical and Moral View,* reprinted in Haraszti, *John Adams,* 125.

14 Adams further developed this position in his lengthy response to Taylor: "All government, except the simplest and most perfect democracy, is REPRESENTATIVE GOVERNMENT. The simplest despotism, monarchy, or aristocracy, and all the most complicated mixtures of them that ever existed or can be imagined, are mere representatives of the people, and can exist no longer than the people will to support them"; *WJA,* 6:469.

15 *Digest of Justinian,* 4 vols., ed. Alan Watson (Philadelphia, 1985), 1:5 ("De statu hominis"); *Institutes of Gaius,* ed. Francis de Zulueta, 2 vols. (Oxford, 1953), 1:8. For the classic discussion in English law, see Henry de Bracton, *De legibus et consuetudinibus Angliae,* ed. George E. Woodbine and Samuel E. Thorne, 4 vols. (Cambridge, MA, 1968–1977), 2:30.

16 As one pamphleteer put the matter, if the king's negative voice were to be maintained, "the last Appeale must be to his discretion and understanding, and consequently, the Legislative power His alone"—from which it followed that the people would find themselves in the condition of slavery. See [Anon.], *Reasons Why This Kingdome Ought to Adhere to the Parliament* ([London], 1642), 11, 14.

17 [Henry Parker], *Observations upon Some of His Majesties Late Answers and Expresses* (London, 1642), 5. My discussion of the 1640s debate over representation is deeply indebted to Quentin Skinner, "Hobbes on Representation," *European Journal of Philosophy* 13 (2005): 155–184. For an astute early study of Parker's theory, see Margaret Atwood Judson, "Henry Parker and the Theory of Parliamentary Sovereignty," in *Essays in History and Political Theory: In Honor of Charles Howard McIlwain,* ed. Carl Wittke (Cambridge, MA, 1936), 138–167.

18 [Parker], *Observations upon Some of His Majesties Late Answers and Expresses,* 15.

19 [Henry Parker], *Some Few Observations upon His Majesties Late Answer to the Declaration or Remonstrance of the Lords and Commons of the 19th of May, 1642* (London, 1642), 4; [Parker], *Observations upon Some of His Majesties Late Answers and Expresses,* 28.

20 [Parker], *Observations upon Some of His Majesties Late Answers and Expresses,* 5.

21 [Henry Parker], *Ius Populi* (London, 1644), 18.

22 [Parker], *Observations upon Some of His Majesties Late Answers and Expresses,* 23.

23 [Parker], *Some Few Observations,* 9.

24 [Henry Parker], *The Contra-Replicant, His Complaint to His Maiestie* (London, 1643), 16.

25 [Parker], *Observations upon Some of His Majesties Late Answers and Expresses*, 9, 34.

26 [Parker], *Ius Populi*, 19.

27 [John Goodwin], *Anti-Cavalierisme* (London, 1642), 2.

28 [John Herle], *A Fuller Ansvver to A Treatise Written by Doctor Ferne* (London, 1642), 7.

29 Ibid., 4–5.

30 Ibid., 12.

31 Ibid., 6.

32 [Anon.], *A Soveraigne Salve to Cure the Blind; or, A Vindication of the Power and Priviledges Claim'd or Executed by the Lords and Commons in Parliament* (London, 1643), 22, 28.

33 Ibid., 8.

34 Richard Overton, *An Appeale from the Degenerate Representative Body of the Commons of England* (London, 1647), 12.

35 Overton, *An Appeale*, 12.

36 [Parker], *Ius Populi*, 18.

37 [Parker], *Contra-Replicant*, 16.

38 [John Herle], *An Answer to Doctor Ferne's Reply, Entitled Conscience Satisfied* (London, 1643), 12.

39 [Anon.], *Soveraigne Salve*, 8.

40 [Sir John Spelman], *A View of a Printed Book Intituled Observations upon His Majesties Late Answers and Expresses* (London, 1643), 7.

41 Ibid., 25. "25 H.8.21" refers to the 21st act passed in the 25th year of the reign of Henry VIII.

42 Ibid.

43 Compare William Prynne, *A Plea for the Lords* (London, 1648), 6–10. Prynne (writing in his later, anti-parliamentarian phase) drew the natural conclusion: "if the Lawes and Customes of the Realme were, that the King himselfe might call two Knights, Citizens and Burgesses to Parliament, such as himselfe should nominate in his writ out of every County, City and Burrough, without the Freeholders, Citizens, and Burgesses election of them by a common agreement and consent to such a Law and usage made by their Ancestors, and submitted and consented to for some ages without repeale, this Law and Custome were sufficient to make such Knights, Citizens and Burgesses lawfull Members of Parliament, and to represent the Commons of England without any election of the people" (8–9).

44 Dudley Digges, *The Unlawfulness of Subjects Taking up Arms* (London, 1643), 143.

45 [Charles I], *His Maiesties Ansvver to the XIX Propositions of Both Houses of Parliament* (London, 1642), 28. James I too had deployed this argument. Speaking to his first Parliament, he declared, "If you bee rich I cannot bee poore, if you bee happy I cannot but bee fortunate, and I protest that your welfare shall ever be

my greatest care and contentment"; *The Political Works of James I*, ed. Charles Howard McIlwain (Cambridge, 1918), 278.

46 Digges, *Unlawfulness of Subjects Taking Up Arms*, 33.

47 Digges's objection to this use of the term reflects his conviction that the two houses sitting without the participation and approval of the sovereign do not constitute a parliament.

48 Digges, *Unlawfulness of Subjects Taking Up Arms*, 67.

49 Ibid., 151.

50 Ibid., 152.

51 Thomas Hobbes, *Leviathan*, ed. Noel Malcolm, 3 vols. (Oxford, 2013), 2:288.

52 Digges had almost certainly read Hobbes's *Elements of Law* (1640), which circulated widely in manuscript. However, this first version of Hobbes's civil science did not contain the material on "personation" that is present in *Leviathan*.

53 Hobbes, *Leviathan*, 2:244.

54 Ibid., 2:260.

55 Indeed, Hobbes takes considerable pains to insist that there is simply no such thing as the "body of the people" before the creation of the sovereign representative. In the state of nature, there is merely a "multitude" of individuals; they become a "people" only in virtue of sharing a common representative.

56 Hobbes took the view that *any* action of the sovereign must count as the subject's action, such that it is incoherent to say that a subject may be "injured" by his sovereign (ibid., 2:270). But it was entirely possible to accept Hobbes's theory of representation while still rejecting his view about the open-endedness and unconditionality of the original grant of authority: that is, one could argue that a king should be authorized to act as my representative in some respects but not in others or that his authorization should be conditional on good behavior. This is an important point to bear in mind as we turn to the American material. Indeed, it is worth noting that Adams, when discussing the theory of representation in the *Defence*, referred to Hobbes as "a man, however unhappy in his temper, or detestable for his principles, equal in genius and learning to any of his contemporaries"; *Defence*, 3:211. He likewise listed "Hobbs" along with Harrington, Sydney, Nedham and Locke, as the authors on politics whom he had chiefly consulted before 1776; *Diary and Autobiography of John Adams*, 3 vols., ed. L. H. Butterfield (Cambridge, MA, 1961), 3:359. Hobbes had preached the cause of "simple monarchy and absolute power," but Adams saw that his theory of representation could be detached from these commitments.

57 See, for example, Jack P. Greene, *The Constitutional Origins of the American Revolution* (Cambridge, 2010), 69–71. Greene argues that it was Thomas Whately who "ingeniously developed the doctrine of virtual representation." The error seems to have originated with Alfred De Grazia, who claimed that the term "virtual representation . . . came into use in the late eighteenth century to justify the acts of a House of Commons, elections to which were controlled by a

few men"; see De Grazia, *Public and Republic: Political Representation in America* (New York, 1951), 14. The literature on the revolutionary debate over representation is vast. Important contributions include Bernard Bailyn, *The Ideological Origins of the American Revolution* (Cambridge, 1967), esp. 161–175; Bailyn, *The Origins of American Politics* (New York, 1968); Edmund S. Morgan, *Inventing the People: The Rise of Popular Sovereignty in England and America* (New York, 1988); J. R. Pole, *Political Representation in England & the Origins of the American Republic* (Berkeley, 1966); John Phillip Reid, *The Concept of Representation in the Age of the American Revolution* (Chicago, 1989); Gordon S. Wood, *Representation in the American Revolution,* rev. ed. (Charlottesville, VA, 2008), originally published 1969; and Wood, *The Creation of the American Republic,* esp. 162–202.

58 Soame Jenyns, *The Objections to the Taxation of Our American Colonies . . . Examined* (London, 1765), 8. Jenyns served on the Board of Trade during the imperial crisis.

59 Letter to Governor Thomas Finch, Feb. 11, 1765, in "A Selection from the Correspondence and Miscellaneous Papers of Jared Ingersoll," ed. Franklin B. Dexter, in *Papers of the New Haven Colony Historical Society* (New Haven, 1918), 307.

60 Burke to Sir Hercules Langrishe, Jan. 3, 1792, in *The Writings and Speeches of Edmund Burke,* ed. Paul Langford, 9 vols. (Oxford, 1981–2000), 9:629. Burke's remarks on the theory of representation are notoriously inconsistent. In his "Thoughts on the Cause of the Present Discontents" (1770), he offered a seemingly straightforward endorsement of the "authorization" theory (according to which "the King is the representative of the people; so are the Lords; so are the Judges. They are all trustees for the people, as well as the Commons"), but only a month earlier, in his speech on the London Livery's remonstrance, he had baldly stated that "in a legal, and technical sense of reasoning, the house of Commons in the only representative of the people." *Writings and Speeches of Edmund Burke,* 2:239, 292. I am grateful to Greg Conti for encouraging me to focus on this issue.

61 Burke's final point makes clear why the "authorization" and "resemblance" theories are so difficult to combine in any coherent fashion. Suppose one wanted to argue that authorization is necessary but not sufficient to establish a legitimate representative—i.e., that a people must indeed authorize its representative but that the representative in question must *also* constitute a good image of the people (such that any other choice of representative will be deemed "contrary to reason" and hence illicit). The problem is that on this view, the people cease to have any real choice in the matter and their "authorization" becomes purely formal. If reason tells us that only a popular assembly constituted along specific lines may legitimately govern a people—and if any desire on the part of the people to be governed in some other manner is simply to be regarded as "mistaken" (i.e., not what the people would *really* desire if they were thinking rationally) and therefore to be set aside, then we are really

no longer interested in what the people *actually* decide to authorize. We are interested, rather, in what they *should* authorize, which is to say that we are inferring their consent, not asking for it.

62 Contemporaries understood that *this* was the novel move in the 1760s; the doctrine of virtual representation within Britain itself had been attested for more than a century. See, for example, [Anon.], *The Crisis, Or, a Full Defence of the Colonies* (London, 1766), 4–6; Maurice Moore, *The Justice and Policy of Taxing the American Colonies, in Great Britain, Considered* (Wilmington, NC, 1765), 12.

63 [Martin Howard Jr.], *A Letter from a Gentleman at Halifax* (Newport, RI, 1765), 11.

64 Ibid., 13.

65 Jenyns, *Objections to the Taxation of Our American Colonies,* 7. Compare [Spelman], *View of . . . Observations upon His Majesties Late Answers and Expresses,* 25; [Samuel Seabury], *A View of the Controversy between Great Britain and Her Colonies* (New York, 1774), 10. The pro-American response was straightforward: "But even admitting that Birmingham and the other towns were actually without representatives, in the strictest sense of the expression, would that be a proper argument for taxing the Colonies without their own consent? Would it be a necessary consequence, because part of the British subjects were unfortunate enough to be in a state of slavery, that a yoke should be laid on the necks of the Americans?"; [Anon.], *Crisis,* 16. Compare [William Hicks], *Considerations upon the Rights of the Colonists to the Privileges of British Subjects* (New York, 1766), 18–19; and [Matthew Robinson-Morris, Lord Rokeby], *Considerations on the Measures Carrying on with Respect to the British Colonies in North America* (London, 1774), 30.

66 [Howard], *Letter from a Gentleman at Halifax,* 12.

67 Jenyns, *Objections to the Taxation of Our American Colonies,* 8.

68 John Gray, *The Right of the British Legislature to Tax the American Colonies Vindicated* (London, 1774), 4.

69 Ibid., 3, 12.

70 [Thomas Whately], *The Regulations Lately Made Concerning the Colonies and the Taxes Imposed upon Them, Considered* (London, 1765), 108–109. Whately was Grenville's secretary, so this pamphlet clearly embodied a statement of the latter's own view. Note that Whately's position differs from Gray's in one subtle but important respect: for Gray, members of Parliament should be regarded as "direct representatives of their own constituents, and the virtual representatives of every British commoner wherever he inhabits," whereas, for Whately, "all *British* Subjects are really in the same [situation]; none are actually, all are virtually represented in Parliament." Whately, in other words, endorses the orthodox parliamentarian theory according to which we are represented ("virtually present") so long as we are adequately "displayed" in a popular assembly; there is, on his account, no other sense in which individuals can be represented (the idea of an "actual," or "nonvirtual" kind of representation is

incoherent). Gray, in contrast, endorses a distinction between "real" and "virtual" representation, according to which electors are both "actually" and "virtually" represented, whereas non-electors are only "virtually" represented. To be sure, Gray agrees that the latter sort of representation is the only one that matters, but his argument plainly suggests that electors were represented to a different and greater degree than non-electors, a thought that the parliamentarian theory could not make sense of. Some contemporaries recognized that the distinction was newfangled: see, for example, [Anon.], *An Answer to a Pamphlet, Entitled Taxation No Tyranny, Addressed to the Author, and to Persons in Power* (London, 1775), 15. The author accuses his opponents of picking up "an idea that this controversy has created. It is that there are *two kinds* of representatives, one actual, and the other virtual; that those who have votes are actually represented; and those who have not votes are virtually represented."

71 [John Lind], *Remarks on the Principal Acts of the Thirteenth Parliament of Great Britain* (London, 1775), 66.

72 Ibid., 70–71, 84.

73 Ibid., 73–74.

74 [Daniel Dulany], *Considerations on the Propriety of Imposing Taxes in the British Colonies* (Annapolis, 1765), 6. On Dulany's argument and its influence, see Edmund S. Morgan and Helen M. Morgan, *The Stamp Act Crisis: Prologue to Revolution*, rev. ed. (Chapel Hill, 1995), 80–91, originally published 1953.

75 [Dulany], *Considerations on the Propriety of Imposing Taxes*, 6.

76 Ibid., 7–8.

77 Ibid., 10. This argument would continue to be made, even by those who, unlike Dulany, fundamentally rejected the parliamentarian theory. See, for example, James Iredell, *To the Inhabitants of Great Britain* (1774): "You have another very strong security against very atrocious designs in your Parliament; *that their own freedom and happiness, and that of their posterity, are inseparably connected with yours, and that they can make no partial regulations from which themselves are exempted.* But how does the case stand with us? We have no connection with them that secures their *affection*; we have no interest so attached to theirs as to secure their *caution*; they have no such merit as to obtain our *confidence*; and they may have an inseparably strong temptation to ease their *own* burdens by throwing them upon *us*. Let Reason and Justice attend to these things, and then let some narrow-minded advocate for Power and Oppression talk of *virtual representation*"; *Life and Correspondence of James Iredell, One of the Associate Justices of the Supreme Court of the United States*, ed. Griffith John McRee, 2 vols. (New York, 1857–1858), 1:211.

78 [Dulany], *Considerations on the Propriety of Imposing Taxes*, 11.

79 [Anon.], *American Resistance Indefensible* (London, 1776), 19.

80 For the manner in which "virtual representation" presupposes the idea of the "unity" of the people, see Wood, *Creation of the American Republic*, 174–175.

81 For precisely this critique, see [Anon.], *A Letter to the Right Honourable the Earl of Hillsborough, on the Connection between Great Britain and Her American Colonies* (London, 1768), 9–10.

82 See, for example, John Adams's claim that, if the British position were to prevail, "the People here will have no Influence, no Check, no Power, no Controul, no Negative"; Adams, "Notes for an Oration at Braintree, Spring 1772," in *WJA*, 4:101–102.

83 William Drayton, *A Letter from a Freeman of South-Carolina, to the Deputies of North-America, Assembled in the High Court of Congress at Philadelphia* (Charleston, SC, 1774) 17–18.

84 For the way in which the neo-Roman language of liberty could be turned against parliamentarians, see David Wootton, "Liberty, Metaphor, and Mechanism: 'Checks and Balances,'" in *Liberty and American Experience in the Eighteenth Century*, ed. David Womersley (Indianapolis, 2006), 209–274.

85 Stephen Hopkins, *The Rights of Colonies Examined* (Providence, 1765), 4.

86 Ibid., 4.

87 Ibid., 16.

88 Ibid., 11.

89 The Stamp Act Congress itself declared that "the only Representatives of the People of these Colonies, are persons chosen therein by themselves." See *Proceedings of the Congress at New-York* (Annapolis, 1766). See also John Dickinson, *Letters from a Farmer in Pennsylvania to the Inhabitants of the British Colonies* (Boston, 1768), 21–23.

90 James Otis, *A Vindication of the British Colonies, against the Aspersions of the Halifax Gentleman* (1765), in *Pamphlets of the American Revolution, 1750–1776*, ed. Bernard Bailyn, vol. 1 (Cambridge, MA, 1965), 567. Compare [Hicks], *Considerations upon the Rights of the Colonists*, 20: "The Members of the British Parliament can only be consider'd as Trustees for the Care and Direction of the Liberty and Property of their Constituents; and of that They may at Discretion legally and constitutionally dispose: But, with what Appearance of Reason, do They claim the Disposal of Property with which They were never entrusted, or arrogate to Themselves a Power to determine upon that Liberty which was never committed to their Care?"

91 Otis, *Vindication*, 566–567.

92 *The Political Writings of John Adams*, ed. George W. Carey (Washington, DC, 2000), 13. See also Adams, "The Earl of Clarendon to William Pym," Letter 3, *Boston Gazette*, Jan. 27, 1766. Compare Benjamin Church, "Oration, Delivered at Boston, Mar. 5, 1773," in *Principles and Acts of the Revolution in America*, ed. H. Niles (Baltimore, 1822), 11: "That the members of the British parliament are the representatives of the whole British empire, expressly militates with their avowed principles: property and residence within the island, alone constituting the right of election; and surely he is not my delegate in whose nomination or appointment I have no choice." Church rejects "the futile and absurd claim of virtual representation."

93 *Political Writings of John Adams,* 40 (these passages are from Adams's second "No-vanglus" letter). Pitkin notes that in a 1776 letter to John Penn of North Carolina, Adams argued that "the representative assembly should be an exact portrait, in miniature, of the people at large, as it should think, feel, reason, and act like them"; *WJA,* 4:205. In light of this claim, she characterizes Adams's later assertion in the *Defence* that a hereditary monarch might represent the people as a "more conserva-tive" view that he adopted after the Revolution. But nowhere in the Penn letter does Adams assert that the people may only be represented by a "representative" assembly; he simply claims that assemblies, to the extent that they exist, should be representative. He goes on in the letter to insist upon the creation of an indepen-dent council and a strong executive (with a "negative upon the legislature," al-though, interestingly, without "most of those badges of slavery called preroga-tives" [*PJA,* 4:80]), and makes it perfectly clear that he regards these agents too as proper representatives of the people (to the extent that they have been authorized). Indeed, Adams's fundamental point in the letter is that the people must under no circumstances be represented by an assembly alone (however "representative"), for an unchecked assembly will simply become "the Long Parliament" (*PJA,* 4:82).

94 Moore, *Justice and Policy,* 6.

95 Ibid., 7.

96 Ibid. Moore also rehearses the internal critique of the British argument, ac-cepting arguendo that virtual representation might explain why Parliament represents the people of Great Britain, even though most Britons lack the fran-chise (9–10). Even if this were true, he concludes, Parliament is not an adequate image of the colonies.

97 *Life and Correspondence of James Iredell,* 1:211.

98 [Thomas Fitch et al.], *Reasons Why the British Colonies in America, Should Not Be Charged with Internal Taxes, by Authority of Parliament* (1764) in *Pamphlets of the American Revolution,* 386. Bailyn argued long ago that various facts of colonial political life—widespread suffrage, the practice of giving voting instructions to deputies, residency requirements for representatives, and the constant need to dispatch agents to speak for the colonies in London—may well have predis-posed patriots to gravitate toward what I am calling the "election theory of authorization'"; Bailyn, *Ideological Origins of the American Revolution,* 164–166. On this, see also Pole, *Political Representation.*

99 *Pamphlets of the American Revolution,* 391.

100 [Joachim Zubly], *An Humble Enquiry into the Nature of the Dependency of the American Colonies upon the Parliament of Great-Britain, and the Right of Parliament to Lay Taxes upon the Said Colonies* ([Charleston], 1769), 21.

101 [Zubly], *Humble Enquiry,* 17–18. Compare William Drayton, who argued that the consent of "American Freeholders . . . is not signified in Parliament, by *a Representation of their own election*"; Drayton, *Letter from a Freeman,* 12.

102 Likewise, it is essential to recognize that one could reach the conclusion that every Member of Parliament is legitimately to be regarded as a representative

of the entire nation rather than only of his own particular constituency, while starting from *either* the theory of virtual representation or the authorization theory. That is, one could believe that this is the case because each member of the House of Commons resembles each commoner (virtual representation) or because each member has been *authorized* by every citizen (however tacitly) to act on his behalf, in the sense that every member of society has agreed to be bound by the determinations of the legislature, the composition of which is determined by a series of elections in which each member may or may not participate. For an explicit endorsement of the latter view, see [Anon.], *The People the Best Governors: or A Plan of Government Founded on Just Principles of Natural Freedom* ([United States], 1776), 9.

103 For an authorization theorist, the question of whether representatives should conduct themselves as "delegates" or as "trustees" is a question about the nature and extent of the authorization they receive (or ought to receive) from their constituents. Just as an individual might authorize someone to act on his behalf without placing that agent under any sort of obligation to honor his own preferences or dispositions (say, by conveying to the agent a "power of attorney"), so too might a people. And just as an individual might instead authorize someone to act on his behalf in a much more restricted manner (say, in the manner of a stockbroker, who must get permission from those he represents for each trade), a people might likewise choose to place its representatives under "delegate-style" restrictions; see Pitkin, *Concept of Representation*, 38–39. In the case of "virtual representation," a theorist could argue that the "representativeness" of the image constituted by an assembly depends on each member acting and speaking as an emissary of his own particular region or guild (i.e., an East Anglian farmer should speak and act like an East Anglian farmer so that his particular slice of the kingdom is duly "displayed" in Parliament). But a theorist of virtual representation could just as easily argue the contrary position: that while the representative assembly derives from its legitimacy from the fact that it constitutes a good image in miniature of the "natural body of the people," each member of that assembly should seek the good of the nation as a whole (as he sees it), rather than the interests of his own sort.

104 The elision of these two very different questions has introduced a good deal of confusion into the historiography. See, for example, Terence Ball, " 'A Republic—If You Can Keep It,' " in *Conceptual Change and the Constitution*, ed. Terence Ball and J. G. A. Pocock (Lawrence, KS, 1988), 137–164, esp. 145–150. Ball equates the "trusteeship" understanding of authorization with the theory of "virtual representation."

105 The pamphlet was written in 1768 but was not published until 1774.

106 James Wilson, *Considerations on the Nature and the Extent of the Legislative Authority of the British Parliament* (Philadelphia, 1774), 5.

107 Ibid., 15.

108 Ibid., 17–18.

109 Several pages later, Wilson states explicitly that the Irish, and by analogy the Americans, are not "represented" in Parliament because they do not "send Members to Parliament"; ibid., 21.

110 Ibid., 21–22.

111 Compare *Pennsylvania Gazette*, Mar. 8, 1775. The anonymous author of this essay argues, in a Wilsonian vein, that "the whole body of the [English] people" is "represented by the House of Commons" because "there is scarce a free agent in *England* who has not a vote" (*Archives*, 1:89).

112 *The Works of the Honourable James Wilson, L.L.D.*, ed. Bird Wilson, 3 vols. (Philadelphia, 1804), 1:430.

113 Ibid.

114 Ibid., 2:57. Wilson had made the same argument the previous year in his speech to the Pennsylvania convention on the mode of electing senators. Rejecting the view that senators should be elected by an intermediate body rather than by the people at large, he argued that "before the revolution . . . the exercise of authority by representation was confined in Pennsylvania, as in England, to one branch of one of the great powers, into which we have seen government divided: and over even that branch a double negative was held suspended by two powers, neither of them professing to derive their authority from the people." The problem with such a model, on Wilson's account, is that the people cannot say to those whom they do not directly elect that "you are our trustee, for you are the object of our choice." "The principles of representation," rightly understood, demand direct election of magistrates by the entire population of free men. See Wilson, "Speech on Choosing the Members of the Senate by Electors; Delivered, on the 31st December, 1789, in the Convention of Pennsylvania," in *Works of the Honourable James Wilson*, 3:319, 324, 333. See also Stephen A. Conrad, "James Wilson's Assimilation of the Common-Law Mind," *Northwestern University Law Review* 84 (1989): 186–219, esp. 209–211.

115 *Works of the Honourable James Wilson*, 1:445.

116 [Howard], *Letter from a Gentleman at Halifax*, 12–13.

117 Whately, *Regulations*, 109.

118 [Lind], *Remarks on the Principal Acts of the Thirteenth Parliament of Great Britain*, 66–67.

119 For precisely the same argument, see Josiah Tucker, *A Letter from a Merchant in London to His Nephew in North America* (London, 1766), 20–22. Note that Franklin's response to Tucker on this point begs the question; "Marginalia in a Pamphlet by Josiah Tucker," in *PBF*, 17:363.

120 [William Knox], *The Controversy between Great Britain and Her Colonies, Reviewed* (London, 1769), 88–90.

121 Jenyns, *Objections to the Taxation of Our American Colonies*, 5.

122 Tucker, for one, argued straightforwardly that if those for whom I never voted can count as my representatives "by implication," it follows that the theory of virtual representation is correct; Tucker, *Letter from a Merchant in London*, 21–22.

123 [Knox], *Controversy between Great Britain and Her Colonies*, 67. Note that Knox's wording here is almost identical to Spelman's from the 1640s; see [Spelman], *View of . . . Observations upon His Majesties Late Answers and Expresses*, 25. Knox's view is reproduced verbatim in Henry Goodricke, *Observations on Dr. Price's Theory of Government and Civil Liberty* (York, 1776), 8.

124 For another prominent English endorsement of this position, see Samuel Johnson, *Taxation No Tyranny: An Answer to the Resolutions and Addresses of the American Congress* (London, 1775), 33–35.

125 See my discussion in Chapter 1.

126 [Seabury], *View of the Controversy between Great Britain and Her Colonies*, 10.

127 Wilson, *Considerations*, 22.

128 Ibid., 31.

129 Hobbes, *Leviathan*, 3:1141.

130 On this, see the wise remark in Wood, *Creation of the American Republic*, 279.

131 Peter Whitney, *The Transgression of a Land Punished by a Multitude of Rulers* (Boston, 1774), 20. Compare Dan Foster, *A Short Essay on Civil Government* (Hartford, 1775), esp. 23–25; and [James Cannon], "Cassandra to Cato," Letter 3, in *Archives*, 5:1094. On this line of argument, see Jerrilyn Greene Marston, *King and Congress: The Transfer of Political Legitimacy, 1774–1776* (Princeton, 1987), 334n53. The classic work on this discourse remains J. G. A. Pocock, *The Ancient Constitution and the Feudal Law* (Cambridge, 1957).

132 One deep problem with this argument, frequently pointed out by opponents, was that most American colonies did not have charters. Note that while charters were framed as grants from the sovereign as "grantor"—not as "compacts" or "covenants" with the people—British North Americans had long been in the habit of regarding their charters as effective contracts by means of which the people had ratified and accepted the terms of the initial grant. See, for example, Donald S. Lutz, *The Origins of American Constitutionalism* (Baton Rouge, 1988), 20–21, 35–49.

133 It is important to distinguish this position from the far more orthodox view that the king could be regarded as the "representative" of the "the collective executive power of the whole realm" (see, e.g., Thomas Pownall, *The Administration of the Colonies*, 4th ed. [London, 1768], 134), or that the king, as executive, might be thought of as the "representative" of the legislative power of Great Britain (see, e.g., *Pennsylvania Gazette*, Mar. 8, 1775, in *Archives*, 1:89; and [Joseph Galloway], *A Candid Examination of the Mutual Claims of Great-Britain, and the Colonies* [New York, 1775], 7–8).

134 James Otis, *The Rights of the British Colonies, Asserted and Proved* (1764), in *Pamphlets of the American Revolution*, 427.

135 Ibid., 427–428.

136 Ibid., 428.

137 Otis, *A Vindication of the British Colonies, against the Aspersions of the Halifax Gentleman* (1765), in ibid., 565.

138 [Edward Bancroft], *Remarks on the Review of the Controversy between Great Britain and Her Colonies* (New London, CT, 1771), 21.

139 Ibid., 19, 42.

140 Ibid., 45.

141 See, for example, ibid., 46–47. Compare Arthur Lee, *Observations on the Review of the Controversy between Great-Britain and Her Colonies* (London, 1769), 22–23. Lee writes that he requires only an *"implied* consent by representatives unequally and partially chosen," not that "the people should give their actual consent by deputies equally elected" (as he thinks Locke proposes).

142 *The Briefs of the American Revolution: Constitutional Arguments between Thomas Hutchinson, Governor of Massachusetts Bay, and James Bowdoin for the Council and John Adams for the House of Representatives*, ed. John Phillip Reid (New York and London, 1981), 73.

143 Ibid., 60.

144 Ibid., 58–59.

145 Compare "To the Inhabitants of New York" (Oct. 6, 1774): "Let that august Assembly [Parliament] only relinquish all pretence of right to govern the *British* Colonies in *America,* and leave that to whom it solely and exclusively belongs, namely the King, our lawful Sovereign, with his Parliament in the respective Colonies, and the *Americans* have a Constitution without seeking further"; *Archives,* 1:826.

146 [Moses Mather], *America's Appeal to The Impartial World* (Hartford, 1775), 39. It followed that the colonists could "submit" themselves voluntarily to certain acts of parliamentary regulation without depriving themselves of the status of freemen. This was the logic behind the patriot claim that Parliament might be "conceded" a right to regulate American trade. As John Adams put it in the seventh "Novanglus" letter, "America has all along consented, still consents, and ever will consent, that parliament being the most powerful legislature in the dominions, should regulate the trade of the dominions. This is founding the authority of parliament to regulate our trade, upon compact and consent of the colonies, not upon any principle of common or statute law, not upon any original principle of the English constitution, not upon the principle that parliament is the supream and sovereign legislature over them in all cases whatsoever" (*PJA,* 3:307). In the same letter, Adams refers to this authorization as a "treaty of commerce, by which those distinct states are cemented together, in perpetual league and amity. And if any further ratifications of this pact or treaty are necessary, the colonies would readily enter into them, provided their other liberties were inviolate" (*PJA,* 3:320).

147 *Life and Correspondence of James Iredell,* 1:213.

148 Ibid., 214.

149 "Edmund Burke" [pseud.], "To the Right Honourable Lord North," in *Archives*, 1:338. Compare [Thomson Mason], "The British American," Letter 6 (Jul. 7, 1774), in *Archives*, 1:522.

150 Compare "Novanglus" [John Adams], Letter 8. Defenders of the patriot position who resisted the Royalist turn predictably found it important to deny this claim (i.e., that Parliament would have been the legitimate representative of the Americans if it had been authorized to act as such in the various charters). The radical English pamphleteer John Cartwright, for example, insisted that even "had the original charters to the American settlers been granted on the express and sole condition of acknowledging the sovereignty of parliament, even all that would not have bettered our present title one jot; for freedom, notwithstanding all that sophistry may say to the contrary, cannot be alienated by any human creature; much less may he enslave his posterity"; John Cartwright, *American Independence the Interest and Glory of Great Britain* (London, 1774), 22. This argument rests on the premise that a legislature to which a given people does not elect members cannot be regarded as the representative of that people (i.e., cannot be said to speak and act in their name), even if "authorized." Indeed, Cartwright more or less accepts the parliamentarian theory (see, e.g., 42). Compare Lord Rokeby, *Considerations*, 17; and Samuel West, *A Sermon Preached Before the Honorable Council, and the Honorable House of Representatives of the Colony of Massachusetts-Bay, in New-England, May 29th, 1776* (Boston, 1776), 20.

151 Oliver North, *Some Strictures upon the Sacred Story Recorded in the Book of Esther* (Newburyport, MA, 1775), 22.

152 *Farmer Refuted*, 9.

153 Ibid., 7. Hamilton had made precisely the same argument in a pamphlet published the previous year: "No reason can be assigned why one man should exercise any power, or pre-eminence over his fellow creatures more than another; unless they have voluntarily vested him with it. Since then, Americans have not by any act of their's impowered the British Parliament to make laws for them, it follows they can have no just authority to do it." See [Alexander Hamilton], *A Full Vindication of the Measures of the Congress* (New York, 1774), 5.

154 *Farmer Refuted*, 18. Gerald Stourzh insightfully notes that Hobbes made precisely the same argument, but we should resist Stourzh's suggestion that the claim in question is distinctively "Hobbesian"; Stourzh, *Alexander Hamilton and the Idea of Republican Government* (Stanford, 1970), 108–109. As we have seen, this argument about the unique symmetry of interests between king and people was a staple of Royalist polemic during the 1640s. It is a claim to which Hamilton would frequently return in his writings from the 1780s.

155 [Parker], *Observations upon Some of His Majesties Late Answers and Expresses*, 22.

156 *Farmer Refuted*, 21.

157 *Federalist 71*, 433. John Adams likewise rejected this conceit with great energy in his letters of reply to Taylor: "What shall I say of the 'resemblance of our

house of representatives to a legislating nation?' It is perhaps a miniature which resembles the original, as much as a larger picture would or could. But, sir, let me say, once and for all, that as no picture, great or small, no statue, no bust in brass or marble, gold or silver, every yet perfectly resembled the original, so no representative government ever perfectly represented or resembled the original nation of people"; Adams, *WJA*, 6:462.

158 Compare *Defence*, 3:214: "An excellent writer had said, somewhat incautiously, that 'a people will never oppress themselves, or invade their own rights.' This compliment, if applied to human nature, or to mankind, or to any nation or people in being or in memory, is more than has been merited. If it should be admitted, that a people will not unanimously agree to oppress themselves, it is as much as is ever, and more than is always true." See also Franklin, "Marginalia in *An Inquiry,* an Anonymous Pamphlet" in *PBF*, 17:323–324.

159 [Hicks], *Considerations upon the Rights of the Colonists*, 21. Compare [Anon.], *An Answer to a Pamphlet, Entitled Taxation No Tyranny*, 46; Benjamin Franklin to Samuel Cooper, June 8, 1770, in *PBF*, 17:163–164; and James Madison, "Vices of the Political System of the United States," in *The Papers of James Madison*, Congressional Series, ed. William T. Hutchinson and William M. E. Rachal, 17 vols. (Chicago and Charlottesville, 1962–1991), 9:357.

160 *Farmer Refuted*, 7.

161 Compare "Novanglus" [John Adams], Letter 7, 308–311.

162 See, for example, [Bancroft], *Remarks on the Review*, 19, 90–91. Bancroft, unlike his followers, even goes so far as to question whether the king has a true negative (i.e., whether he "represents" the people in any legislative capacity): "How far the Sovereign is, by *the British* Constitution, vested with the Legislative Authority, let others determine; his Assent is, indeed, necessary to give Validity to Laws, yet by his Coronation Oath he is obliged to assent to '*such Laws as the People choose.*' (*Quas Vulgus elegerit.*)" (90–91). See also the "Resolutions Adopted by the House of Representatives of the English Colony of Connecticut" of May 1774 in *Archives*, 1:356.

163 [Anon.], *American Resistance Indefensible*, 20.

164 A number of theorists acknowledged this point after the imperial crisis had passed. See, for example, Zabdiel Adams, "An Election Sermon" (Boston, 1782), in *American Political Writing during the Founding Era, 1760–1805*, ed. Charles S. Hyneman and Donald S. Lutz, 2 vols. (Indianapolis, 1983), 1:543–545. Adams agrees that "to be deprived of the power of chusing our rulers is to be deprived of self dominion," but he likewise insists that the people may choose a hereditary monarch as their "representative."

165 It had not lacked for defenders in the late 1770s and early 1780s. In 1778, for example, the Essex County convention responded to the proposed Massachusetts constitution of 1778 by stating that "the representatives should have the same views, and interests with the people at large. They should think, feel, and act like them, and, in fine, should be an exact miniature of their constituents.

They should be (if we may use the expression) the whole body politic, with all it's property, rights, and priviledges, reduced to a smaller scale, every part being diminished in just proportion"; "The Essex Result," in *The Popular Sources of Political Authority: Documents on the Massachusetts Constitution of 1780*, ed. Oscar and Mary F. Handlin (Cambridge, MA, 1966), 341.

166 "Brutus," Letter 3, in *The Complete Anti-Federalist*, ed. Herbert J. Storing, 7 vols. (Chicago, 1981), 2:9:42.

167 *Observations of the System of Government Proposed by the Late Convention. By a Federal Farmer*, in *Pamphlets on the Constitution of the United States*, ed. Paul Leicester Ford (New York, 1968), 303 (Letter 3).

168 Ibid., 288–289 (Letter 2).

169 *PAH*, 2:654; *The Debates in the Several State Conventions on the Adoption of the Federal Constitution*, 5 vols., ed. Jonathan Elliot (Washington, DC, 1836), 2:253.

170 Nathanial Chipman, *Sketches of the Principles of Government* (Rutland, MA, 1793), 150.

171 *Connecticut Courant and Weekly Intelligencer*, Apr. 2, 1787. This claim had likewise been made by the Massachusetts convention in 1780: "The Governor is emphatically the Representative of the whole People, being chosen not by one Town or County, but by the People at large. We have therefore thought it safest to rest this power [the negative voice] in his hands"; "The Address of the Convention, March 1780," in *Popular Sources of Political Authority*, 437.

172 [Thomas Tudor Tucker], *Conciliatory Hints, Attempting by a Fair State of Matters to Remove Party Prejudice* (Charleston, 1784), 25.

173 It is noteworthy that, during the Constitutional Convention, Wilson proposed the direct election of both the senate and the president "by the people at large." He also favored giving the executive an "absolute negative" over acts of the legislature. See Chapter 5.

3. "The Lord Alone Shall Be King of America"

1 William Henry Drayton, *A Charge, on the Rise of the American Empire* (Charleston, 1776), 3. For evidence in favor of Drayton's claim, see Robert Dennis Fiala, "George III in the Pennsylvania Press: A Study in Changing Opinions, 1760–1776" (PhD diss., Wayne State University, 1967), 74–80.

2 [Thomson Mason], "The British American" (1774), Letter 6, in *Archives*, 1:522; [Anon.], "The Address of the People of Great Britain to the Inhabitants of America" (1774), in *Archives*, 1:1429.

3 James Lovell, "Oration, Delivered at Boston" (Apr. 2, 1771), in *Principles and Acts of the Revolution in America*, ed. H. Niles (Baltimore, 1822), 2.

4 Ibid., 3.

5 For the abrupt end of the "flight to the king," see, for example, Richard Bushman, *King and People in Provincial Massachusetts* (Chapel Hill, 1985), 212–226; William Liddle, "A Patriot King, or None: American Public Attitudes towards

George III and the British Monarchy" (PhD diss., Claremont Graduate School, 1970), 379–383; Pauline Maier, *From Resistance to Revolution: Colonial Radicals and the Development of American Opposition to Britain, 1775–1776* (New York, 1972), 198–208; Brendan McConville, *The King's Three Faces: The Rise and Fall of Royal America, 1688–1776* (Chapel Hill, 2006), 250–261; and Andrew Jackson O'Shaughnessy, "'If Others Will Not Be Active, I Must Drive': George III and the American Revolution," *Early American Studies* 2 (2004): 1–46, esp. 9–16.

6 David Ramsay, *The History of the American Revolution*, 2 vols. (Philadelphia, 1789), 1:340.

7 Ibid., 336–337.

8 Drayton, *Charge*, 8.

9 Ibid., 4.

10 Ibid. Compare Thomas Jefferson, *Notes on the State of Virginia* (London, 1787), 247: "It is well known, that in July 1775, a separation from Great-Britain and establishment of Republican government had never yet entered into any person's mind."

11 "Johannes in Eremo" [John Cleaveland], "To the Publick" (Jan. 1776), in *Archives*, 4:527. Compare "Monitor," Letter 12, *The New-York Journal, or, The General Advertiser*, Jan. 25, 1776: "If he [the king] has been the author of those mischiefs, which the whole empire is tottering under, he must be a *despot*; and if he has simply been the dupe of a designing ministry, he must certainly be a very *weak* man. In either case, he is no good King."

12 Lovell, "Oration, Delivered at Boston," 3.

13 *Farmer Refuted*, 16.

14 George III to Lord North, Sept. 10, 1775, in *The Correspondence of King George the Third*, ed. Sir John Fortescue, 6 vols. (London, 1927), 3:256; "Novanglus" [John Adams], Letter 7 (Mar. 6, 1775), in *PJA*, 2:314.

15 Washington to Joseph Reed, Apr. 1, 1776, in *The Papers of George Washington, Revolutionary War Series*, ed. W. W. Abbot and Dorothy Twohig, 20 vols. (Charlottesville, 1985–), 4:11. Washington reiterated this point in a 1784 letter to Richard Henry Lee: "[Paine's] Common Sense, and many of his Crises, were well-timed and had a happy effect upon the public mind"; in *Memoir of the Life of Richard Henry Lee and His Correspondence*, ed. Richard H. Lee, 2 vols. (Philadelphia, 1825), 2:25. John Adams noted in an Apr. 20 letter to Joseph Warren that "Mr. John Penn, one of the Delegates from North Carolina, lately returned home to attend the Convention of that Colony, in which he informs, that he heard nothing praised in the Course of his Journey, but Common sense and Independence. This was his Cry, throughout Virginia"; Adams to Joseph Warren, Apr. 20, 1776, in *PJA*, 4:130–131. See also Benjamin Franklin to Charles Lee, Feb. 19, 1776, in *PBF*, 22:357; Fielding Lewis to George Washington, Mar. 6, 1776, in *Papers of George Washington*, 3:419; and *Dunlap's Pennsylvania Packet, or, The General Advertiser* (Philadelphia), Mar. 23, 1776.

16 William Franklin to Lord George Germain, Mar. 28, 1776, in *Documents of the American Revolution, 1770–1783*, Colonial Office Series, ed. K. G. Davies, 21 vols. (Dublin, 1976), 12:99–100. Franklin also enclosed a copy of one of the most important responses to Paine, "Candidus" [James Chalmers], *Plain Truth; Addressed to the Inhabitants of America* (Philadelphia, 1776). Compare "A Letter from Philadelphia to a Gentleman in England," Mar. 12, 1776, in *Archives*, 5:187–188.

17 Ramsay, *History of the American Revolution*, 1:338–339.

18 Ibid., 338. For a virtually identical account of the pamphlet's influence and the distinctive character of its antimonarchism, see William Gordon, *The History of the Rise, Progress, and Establishment, of the Independence of the United States of America*, 4 vols. (London, 1788), 2:275.

19 Richard Parker to Richard Henry Lee, Apr. 27, 1776, in Lee Family Papers, MSS 38-112, Box 6 (Jan.–Nov. 1776), Albert and Shirley Small Special Collections Library, University of Virginia, Charlottesville, VA. This passage appears on 1r. For a full transcription of this letter and a discussion of its contents and significance, see Eric Nelson, "Hebraism and the Republican Turn of 1776: A Contemporary Account of the Debate over *Common Sense*," *WMQ* 70 (2013): 781–812. Parker was Lee's neighbor in Westmoreland County and often served as his trusted agent in both financial and political matters. Originally employed as king's attorney, he joined the patriot movement quite early on and became a member of the county's Committee of Safety in 1775–1776. He was appointed a judge of the General Court in 1788 and, later, of the first Court of Appeals. For Parker's friendship with Lee, see, e.g., *The Diary of Colonel Landon Carter of Sabine Hall, 1752–1778*, 2 vols., ed. Jack P. Greene (Charlottesville, VA, 1965), 2:1006–1007; John Carter Matthews and Sarah deGraffenreid Robertson, eds.,"The Leedstown Resolutions," *Northern Neck of Virginia Historical Magazine* 16 (1966): 1491–1506; and *The Letters of Richard Henry Lee*, ed. James Curtis Ballagh, 2 vols. (New York, 1911), 1:32–34, 42, 127, 297n11, 299.

20 Parker to Lee, Apr. 27, 1776, 1^r, 2^r.

21 Parker rather surprisingly writes that "the present contest between Cato & Cassandra should be of the Expediency or Inexpediency of Independence" rather than about the divine permissibility of monarchy. In fact, while "Cato" (William Smith) did indeed focus on refuting Paine's scriptural argument, "Cassandra" (James Cannon) spent no time at all attacking the institution of monarchy per se. Unlike Paine, the latter argued simply that America ought not to be governed by a *British* monarch. See "Cassandra to Cato," in *Archives*, 5:41–43, 431–434, 921–926.

22 Peter Whitney, *American Independence Vindicated: A Sermon Delivered September 12, 1776* (Boston, 1777), 45.

23 Adams to William Tudor, Apr. 12, 1776, in *PJA*, 4:118. Adams was particularly anxious to dispel the rumor that he himself was the author of *Common Sense*: "You talk about Common sense, and Say it has been attributed to me. But I am

innocent of it as a Babe. The most atrocious literary sins, have been imputed to me these last twelve years. . . . I could not reach the Strength and Brevity of his style, nor his elegant Simplicity, nor his piercing Pathos. But I really think in other Respects, the Pamphlet would do no Honour even to me. The old Testament Reasoning against Monarchy would never have come from me. The Attempt to frame a Continental Constitution, is feeble indeed. It is poor, and despicable. Yet this is a very meritorious Production."

24 *Diary and Autobiography of John Adams,* ed. L.H. Butterfield, 3 vols. (Cambridge, MA, 1961), 3:330–331.

25 Carter to Washington, May 9, 1776, in *Papers of George Washington,* 4:238. Compare *Diary of Colonel Landon Carter,* 2:986–987, 999, 1016, 1046.

26 [Anon.], *Reason in Answer to a Pamphlet Entituled, Common Sense* (Dublin, 1776), 7.

27 The epigraph reads in full: " 'Mark ye this, / The Devil can cite Scripture for his purpose, / An evil soul, producing holy witness, / Is like a villain with a smiling cheek, / A goody apple rotten at the Heart'. Shakesp." Compare Shakespeare, *Merchant of Venice* I.3. The verse is based on the temptation of Jesus, as recounted in Matt. 4:5–10 and Luke 4:9–13.

28 Sir Brooke Boothby, *Observations on the Appeal from the New to the Old Whigs, and on Mr. Paine's Rights of Man* (London, 1792), 99. Boothby characterizes Paine's scriptural argument against monarchy as "such monstrous nonsense as might, for what I know, be suited to the fanatics of Boston, where witchcraft was in great vogue in the beginning of this century, but here will excite nothing but contempt." After challenging Paine's reading of I Sam. 8, Boothby then adds that "in truth, such stuff is no otherwise worthy of notice, except to shew the low arts to which this mountebank has recourse, to adapt his drugs to people of all sorts. Provided he can *overturn,* he cares not whether it be by the hand of philosophy or superstition, and it is nothing to him which of the two possess themselves of the ruined edifice" (100).

29 "Cato" [Rev. William Smith], "To the People of Pennsylvania," Letter 6 (Apr. 10, 1776), in *Archives* 5:843.

30 Ibid., 841.

31 [Anon.], *Reason in Answer,* 20.

32 Ibid., 9.

33 *Diary and Autobiography of John Adams,* 3:333. A supporter of Paine likewise agreed that "in the celebrated writings of Thomas Paine, there is not a political maxim which is not to be found in the works of Sydney, Harrington, Milton and Buchanan"; Henry Yorke, *These Are the Times That Try Men's Souls! A Letter to John Frost* (London, 1793), 34.

34 See Eric Nelson, *The Hebrew Republic: Jewish Sources and the Transformation of European Political Thought* (Cambridge, MA, 2010), 23–56; and Nelson, " 'Talmudical Commonwealthsmen' and the Rise of Republican Exclusivism," *The Historical Journal* 50 (2007): 809–835. My argument that Paine was reviving a

seventeenth-century, Hebraizing form of "exclusivist" republican theory has since been taken up by Nathan Perl-Rosenthal, who has applied it to the newspaper debate about *Common Sense*. I am deeply indebted to his essay. See Nathan Perl-Rosenthal, "'The 'Divine Right of Republics': Hebraic Republicanism and the Legitimization of Kingless Government in America," *WMQ* 66 (2009): 535–564. For Paine's use of the Israelite example in his polemical writings, see also Maria Teresa Pichetto, "La 'respublica Hebraeorum' nella rivoluzione Americana," *Il pensiero politico* 35 (2002): 497–500; and David Wootton, "Introduction," in *Republicanism, Liberty, and Commercial Society, 1649–1776*, ed. David Wootton (Stanford, 1994), esp. 26–41. Aldridge's skepticism about Paine's claim to have taken his argument from Milton strikes me as unfounded, not least because he maintains (incorrectly) that Milton never composed a "complete version of the episode" (i.e., of "the appointing of a king over the Israelites"). As we shall see, Milton did indeed provide such an account. See A. Owen Aldridge, *Thomas Paine's American Ideology* (Newark and London, 1984), 98. Winthrop D. Jordan, in contrast, finds the attribution entirely plausible. See Jordan, "Familial Politics: Thomas Paine and the Killing of the King, 1776," *Journal of American History* 60 (1973): 294–308, esp. 302.

35 The classic discussion of this discourse remains Quentin Skinner, *Liberty before Liberalism* (Cambridge, 1998). See also Skinner, *Hobbes and Republican Liberty* (Cambridge, 2008); and Philip Pettit, *Republicanism: A Theory of Freedom and Government* (Oxford, 1997).

36 *The Essential Thomas Paine*, ed. Sidney Hook (Harmondsworth, UK, 1984), 30.

37 See James Hankins, "Exclusivist Republicanism and the Non-Monarchical Republic," *Political Theory* 38 (2010): 452–482.

38 Machiavelli, *Il principe*, ed. Piero Melograni (Milan, 1998), 48 (chap. 1): "*Tutti gli stati, tutti e' dominii che hanno avuto e hanno imperio sopra gli uomini, sono stati e sono o republiche o principati.*"

39 *His Maiesties Ansvver to the XIX Propositions of Both Houses of Parliament* (London, 1642), 9. The king's "Answer" was most probably drafted by Viscount Falkland and Sir John Culpepper. See Michael Mendle, *Dangerous Positions: Mixed Government, the Estates of the Realm, and the Making of the Answer to the XIX Propositions* (Alabama, 1985); and Corinne Comstock Weston, "The Theory of Mixed Monarchy under Charles I and After," *English Historical Review* 75 (1960): 426–443.

40 Philip Livingston, *The Other Side of the Question* (New York, 1774), 25. See also Alexander Hamilton's claim that a proper examination of the early history of the colonies "ought to silence the infamous calumnies of those, who represent the first settlers in New-England, as enemies to kingly government; and who are in their own opinions, wondrous witty, by retailing the idle and malicious stories that have been propagated concerning them; such as their having erased the words *King, Kingdom,* and the like, out of their bibles, and inserted in their stead, civil magistrate, parliament, and republic"; *Farmer Refuted*, 32n.

41 John Trenchard and Thomas Gordon, *Cato's Letters, or Essays on Liberty, Civil and Religious, and Other Important Subjects,* ed. Ronald Hamowy, 2 vols. (Indianapolis, 1995), 1:262–263. John Locke had likewise freely referred to the king as "the head of the Republick"; John Locke, *Two Treatises of Government,* ed. Peter Laslett, rev. ed. (Cambridge, 1967), 420.

42 "Novanglus," Letter 7, in *PJA,* 2:314. Adams insisted upon this claim both before and after the Revolution. In a 1788 letter to Roger Sherman, for example, he wrote that "England is a republic, a monarchical republic it is true, but a republic still"; *WJA,* 6:428. For the use of the terms "republic," "republican," and "republicanism" in British North America in the decades before the Revolution, see W. Paul Adams, "Republicanism in Political Rhetoric before 1776," *Political Science Quarterly* 85 (1970): 397–421. W. Paul Adams might have placed greater emphasis on the colonists' willingness to use the term "republic" in this older, broader sense.

43 See Roger Sherman to John Adams, July 20, 1789, in *WJA,* 6:437. Sherman points out that the term is so defined in "[John] Entick's Dictionary." Compare John Entick, *A School Dictionary; or, Entick's English Dictionary, Abridged and Adapted to the Use of Schools* (London, 1821), 153.

44 Machiavelli, *Discourses on Livy,* II.2: *"Non il bene particulare ma il bene commune è quello che fa grandi le città. E senza dubbio questo bene commune non è osservato se non nelle republiche."* See Machiavelli, *Discorsi sopra la prima deca di Tito Livio,* ed. Giorgio Inglese (Milan, 1984), 297.

45 Marchamont Nedham, *The Case of the Commonwealth of England, Stated,* ed. Philip Knachel (Charlottesville, VA, 1969), 116.

46 For a very different early-modern defense of republican government, see Eric Nelson, *The Greek Tradition in Republican Thought* (Cambridge, 2004).

47 Classic statements of this view include Cicero, *De officiis,* I.64–65; Sallust, *Bellum Catilinae,* 6–7; Tacitus, *Historiae,* I.1; and Tacitus, *Annales,* I.1–3. It is important to note, however, that the Roman authors themselves did not use the term *respublica* to mean "kingless regime" or to distinguish government by senate and consuls from the principate. Tacitus, *Annales,* I.3 offers a borderline case of such a usage: after Actium, he asks, *"quotus quisque reliquus, qui rem publicam vidisset?"* (compare *Historiae,* I.50). But it is more likely that he is using the term in its traditional sense to mean "good, properly functioning government," and even Tacitus continues to speak of the "respublica Romana" after Augustus. See Hankins, "Exclusivist Republicanism," 458, 460.

48 "An Act for the Abolishing of the Kingly Office in England and Ireland, and the Dominions Thereunto Belonging," in *Acts and Ordinances of the Interregnum, 1642–1660,* ed. C. H. Firth and R. S. Rait (London, 1911), 18–20.

49 See, for example, [Anon.], *Reasons Why This Kingdome Ought to Adhere to the Parliament* ([London], 1642), 11, 14.

50 The analysis contained in the next several pages is drawn substantially from Nelson, *Hebrew Republic,* 23–56.

51 All biblical quotations are taken from the King James Version.

52 Prominent examples of this reading can be found in the *glossa ordinaria*, John
    of Salisbury, *Policraticus*, VIII.18, in John of Salisbury, *Policraticus*, ed. and trans.
    Cary Nederman [Cambridge, 1990], 201–202; Aquinas [?], *De reg.*, 1.5–6, in *On the
    Government of Rulers: De Regimine Principum*, ed. and trans. James M. Blythe
    (Philadelphia, 1997); Aquinas, *Summa theologiae*, 1a 2ae, q. 105 a.1; and Erasmus,
    Institutio principis christiani (1516), in A. H. T. Levi, ed., *Collected Works of Eras-
    mus*, 86 vols. (Toronto, 1986), 27:226–227.

53 See, for example, Jean Calvin, *Institutes of the Christian Religion*, 2 vols., trans.
    John Allen (Philadelphia, 1955), 2:IV.7. But see also Jean Bodin, *Les six livres de la
    république*, ed. Christiane Frémont, Marie-Dominique Couzinet, and Henri
    Rochais, 6 vols. (Paris, 1986), 1:10; and, earlier, Ptolemy of Lucca (*On the Govern-
    ment of Rulers*, 139–140).

54 Josephus, *Contra Apionem*, 2:163–8, in Josephus, *The Life: Against Apion*, ed. and
    trans. H. St. J. Thackeray (Cambridge, MA, 1926).

55 Josephus, *De antiquitate Iudaeorum*, 6:60. See Josephus, *Jewish Antiquities*, ed.
    and trans. H. St. J. Thackeray and Louis H. Feldman, 8 vols. (Cambridge,
    MA, 1930–1965). Josephus was, in effect, reading I Sam. 8:7 in light of I Sam.
    12:12.

56 It would be more precise to say that Christian exegetes understood Josephus's
    position in this manner; Josephus himself may well have regarded Israel as a
    model for other nations to emulate (although he does not seem to have re-
    garded monarchy as illicit). See, for example, *De antiquitate Iudaeorum*, 14:38;
    18:6; *De bello iudaico*, 2:2.

57 See, for example, Theodore Beza, *De iure magistratum* (1574), in *Constitutional-
    ism and Resistance in the Sixteenth Century: Three Treatises by Hotman, Beza, &
    Mornay*, ed. Julian Franklin (New York, 1969), 116.

58 Here it is important to note the central rabbinic distinction between *pshat* (the
    literal meaning of the biblical text) and *drash* (interpretive exegesis). This gloss
    is clearly an instance of the latter.

59 This is, importantly, how the Vulgate renders the line: *"cum ingressus fueris ter-
    ram quam Dominus Deus tuus dabit tibi et possederis eam habitaverisque in illa et
    dixeris constituam super me regem sicut habent omnes per circuitum nationes."*

60 I have drawn from two English translations of this discussion. The first is that
    of Jacob Shachter in the *Soncino Hebrew-English Edition of the Babylonian Talmud*
    (London, 1994); the second is that provided in volume 1 of *The Jewish Political
    Tradition*, ed. Michael Walzer and Menachem Lorberbaum (New Haven, 2000),
    141–142. For the rabbinic debate over monarchy, see Gerald Blidstein, "The
    Monarchic Imperative in Rabbinic Perspective," *Association for Jewish Studies
    Review* 7–8 (1982–1983), 15–39.

61 *"Observarunt Hebraei tria praecepta fuisse Israelitis cum ingressuri essent Terram
    promissionis, nempe ut super se constituerent Regem, exterminarent semen Amalec,
    & exstruerent Domino Templum"*; *Critici sacri, sive, Doctissimorum virorum in ss.*

Biblia annotationes (London, 1660), 1:1247. This nine-volume work is a compendium of famous biblical commentaries.

62 *"Tradunt Iudaeorum magistri, tria injuncta fuisse Israelitis quae facere eos oporteret postquam introducti essent in terram sanctam,* regem sibi constituere, exscindere Amalechitas, templum exstruere"; Claude de Saumaise [Salmasius], *C. L. Salmasii Defensio pro Carolo I* (Cambridge, 1684), 63. This work was originally published in November 1649. Maimonides also repeats this dictum in his *Mishneh Torah*; as a result, various Christian authors attributed it to him. See, for example, Peter van der Cun (Cunaeus), *Petrus Cunaeus of the Commonwealth of the Hebrews,* trans. Clement Barksdale (London, 1653), 124.

63 *"Leges autem de Rege, de Templo, & excidio Amalecitarum pertinent ad tempora possessae Terrae"; Critici sacri,* 1:1253. For a general account of Grotius's use of rabbinica in his *Annnotationes,* see Peter T. van Rooden, *Theology, Biblical Scholarship and Rabbinical Studies in the Seventeenth Century: Constantijn L'Empereur (1591–1648) Professor of Hebrew and Theology at Leiden* (Leiden, 1989), 142–148.

64 See Locke, *Two Treatises,* 361.

65 Once again, I have drawn together elements from two different translations of this text. The first is that of Rabbi J. Rabbinowitz in *Midrash rabbah,* 10 vols., ed. Rabbi H. Freedman and Maurice Simon (London, 1939), 7:109–13. The second is the excerpted version found in *Jewish Political Tradition,* 148–149. The Hebrew text is taken from *Midrash debarim rabbah,* ed. S. Lieberman (Jerusalem, 1940). The Lieberman version reproduces a different recension of the text (although with no significant differences for our purposes). I should also note that in the penultimate paragraph, the phrase translated as "idolatry" is *avodat kokhavim,* which literally means "worship of the stars." It is a later formulation that often stands in for the more conventional term for idolatry: *avodah zarah* (lit. "strange worship"). Early-modern readers were well aware of this fact. See, for example, John Selden, *De synedriis & praefecturis iuridicis veterum Ebraeorum,* vol. 1 (London, 1650), 9. For Selden's Hebrew scholarship, see Jason Rosenblatt, *Renaissance England's Chief Rabbi: John Selden* (Oxford, 2006).

66 It is important to note that the rabbis of the Midrash never explicitly state that, as a juridical matter, monarchy is equivalent to idolatry; that would have committed them to the view that defenders of monarchy had to be put to death.

67 John Milton, *The Tenure of Kings and Magistrates* (1649), in *Complete Prose Works of John Milton,* ed. Merritt Hughes, 8 vols. (New Haven, 1962), 3:208.

68 *"Deo irato, non solum quod regem vellent ad exemplum gentium, et non suae legis, sed plane quod vellent regem"*; Milton, *Pro populo anglicano defensio* (London, 1651), 43. The remaining English translations from Milton's *Defensio* are taken from *Complete Prose Works of John Milton,* vol. 4, ed. Don Wolfe (New Haven, 1966). In this instance, however, I have had to replace Donald Mackenzie's translation with my own. His version is found on page 347.

69 *"Ut omnes autem videant te nullo modo ex Hebraeorum scriptis id probare, quod pro-*
    bandum hoc capite susceperas, esse ex magistris tua sponte confiteris, qui negant
    alium suis majoribus regem agnoscendum fuisse praeter Deum, datum autem in poe-
    nam fuisse. Quorum ego in sententiam pedibus eo"; Milton, *Defensio*, 62, in *Complete*
    Prose Works of John Milton, vol. 4, ed. Don Wolfe, 366. The third and fourth lines
    reproduce Salmasius's words almost verbatim.

70 Milton had excerpted this text in the Commonplace Book. See *Complete Prose*
    Works, vol. 1, ed. Don Wolfe (New Haven, 1953), 460. Interestingly, the one
    paragraph of the long midrashic commentary which Schickard does *not* repro-
    duce is the one that most explicitly draws the connection between monarchy
    and idolatry: "Whosoever puts his trust in flesh and blood passes away and his
    dignity also passes away, as it is said, 'Nor in the son of man in whom there is
    no help' (Ps. 146:3)." But Milton had no trouble drawing the appropriate conclu-
    sion, either by inference or, just as likely, because he had encountered the rest
    of the Midrash elsewhere. The *editio princeps* of *Devarim Rabbah* dates to 1512
    (Constantinople), and it was frequently reprinted thereafter. An important edi-
    tion for our purposes is the one printed in Amsterdam in 1640, which employed
    standard Hebrew lettering rather than italic script: *Sefer Rabot:. . . midrashot 'al*
    Hamishah Humshe Torah, 2 vols. (Amsterdam, 1640). There is also uniform
    agreement that Milton knew the Midrash to Genesis (*Bereshith Rabbah*), which
    echoes the relevant paragraph in the Midrash to Deut. 17:14 quite clearly in
    places. He also probably knew the midrashic *Pirkei de Rabbi Eliezer,* translated
    into Latin by G. H. Vorstius in 1644 (*Chronologia sacra-profana . . . Cui addita*
    sunt Pirke vel Capitula R. Elieser [Leiden]), which echoes it as well. On Milton's
    midrashic materials, see Golda Werman, *Milton and Midrash* (Washington,
    DC, 1995), 27–92.

71 The closest thing to a precedent I have been able to find is John Lilburne's *Re-*
    gall Tyrannie Discovered (London, 1647), 11–14. Lilburne does not, however, actu-
    ally refer to monarchy as a form of "idolatry." See also John Goodwin, *Anti-*
    cavalierisme (London, 1642), esp. 4–5; and (after the release of Milton's *Defensio*)
    John Cook, *Monarchy, No Creature of Gods Making* (London, 1652), esp. 29, 42, 47,
    93. All of these texts (including Lilburne's) distinguish sharply between abso-
    lute monarchs who rule according to their will and legitimate monarchs who
    rule by law.

72 *"Passim enim testatur Deus valde sibi displicuisse quod regem petissent. ver. 7. Non te*
    sed me spreverunt ne regnem super ipsos, secundum illa facta quibus dereli-
    querunt me & coluerunt Deos alienos: ac si species quaedam idololatriae videre-
    tur regem petere, qui adorari se, & honores prope divinos tribui sibi postulat. Sane qui
    supra omnes leges terrenum sibi dominum imponit, prope est ut sibi Deum statuat ali-
    enum; Deum utique haud saepe rationabilem, sed profligata saepius ratione brutum
    & belluinum. Sic I Sam. 10.19. Vos sprevistis Deum vestrum qui ipse servat vos ab om-
    nibus malis, & angustiis vestris, cum dixistis ei, regem praeponens nobis . . . plane ac

si simul docuisset, non hominis esse dominari in homines, sed solius Dei"; Milton, *Defensio,* 66–67.

73 *"Populus denique resipiscens apud Isaiam 26.13. calamitosum hoc sibi fuisse queritur, quod alios praeter Deum dominos habuerat. Indicio sunt haec omnia regem irato Deo Israelitis fuisse datum"*; ibid., 67. I have altered the translation here. This concluding passage constitutes good evidence that Milton was familiar with sections of the Midrash *not* excerpted by Schickard. The verse from Isaiah to which he refers appears as part of the "song" that will greet the dawn of the Messianic age and simply reads: "O LORD our God, other lords beside thee have had dominion over us: but by thee only will we make mention of thy name" (Isa. 26:13). There is nothing at all in this verse to suggest that the Israelites came to recognize that they had made an egregious error in asking for a king in I Sam. 8; Isaiah is plainly talking about something completely different. Milton's analysis does, however, precisely mirror the reading offered in the last paragraph of the Midrash: "When Israel saw what befell them on account of their kings they all began to cry out: 'We do not desire a king, we desire our first king' [as it is said], For the Lord is our Judge, the Lord is our Lawgiver, the Lord is our King; He will save us (Isa. 33:22)." The Midrash attaches its reading to a different verse from Isaiah but was almost certainly responsible for suggesting to Milton the notion that, at a certain point, the Israelites "came to their senses" and regretted their request for a mortal king.

74 Milton, *Defensio,* 374.

75 Cook, *Monarchy, No Creature of God's Making,* 29.

76 Ibid., 42.

77 Ibid., 47.

78 Ibid., 93. It is important to recognize that, like Milton before him, Cook was not always consistent on this point. Just a few pages after his unqualified endorsement of the view that monarchy per se is idolatry, he writes instead that "it is not the name of a King but the boundlesse power which I argue against (though the Romans for the insolence of *Tarquin* would not endure the name) if any people shall place the Legislative power in Parliamentary authority and give unto one man the Title of King for their better correspondency with foraigne Kingdomes, with no more power to hurt the people, then the Duke of *Venice* or the Duke of *Genoa* have; such a government may be Iust and Rationall, but domination is a sweet morsel" (53). For a similar inconsistency in Milton's later pamphlets, see, e.g., *Complete Prose Works of John Milton,* vol. 7, ed. Robert W. Ayers (New Haven, 1980), 377–378. The point is not that these authors were always perfectly consistent, but rather that each of them formulated an extensive, detailed defense of the exclusivist position—one that eighteenth-century Americans would rediscover in 1776.

79 Algernon Sidney, *Court Maxims,* ed. Hans Blom et al. (Cambridge, 1996), 65. Even Sidney, however, was not always consistent. Earlier in the same treatise

he writes: "Let us have such kings [as described in Deut. 17:14] and we will not complain; and that we may have none but such, let us have means of punishing them if they be not so and I am content with that government" (49). An earlier endorsement of the Miltonic reading, this time by a Digger, can be found in Gerrard Winstanley, *The Law of Freedom in a Platform, or, True Magistracy Restored* (London, 1652), 28–9. See also Marchamont Nedham, *Mercurius Politicus* 56 (June 26–July 3, 1651), 885–887.

80 Sidney, *Court Maxims*, 48. Note the echo of Cook ("kings are the peoples Idols, creatures of their own making").

81 Algernon Sidney, *Discourses Concerning Government*, ed. Thomas G. West (Indianapolis, 1996), 338. Interestingly, Sidney cites Abravanel to defend this view (124). Abravanel tended not to be invoked in this context, simply because Schickard had not excerpted him.

82 Milton, *Complete Prose Works of John Milton*, vol. 7, ed. Robert W. Ayers (New Haven, 1980): 360–361.

83 See my discussion in Chapter 2.

84 See Blair Worden, *Literature and Politics in Cromwellian England: John Milton, Andrew Marvell, Marchamont Nedham* (Oxford, 2007), 256–288. The phrase "single person" derives from the text of the "Act for the Abolishing the Kingly Office," cited above, and was famously used in the Declaration of Parliament of May 6, 1659, announcing the end of the protectorate. England was there said to be a "Commonwealth . . . without a single Person, Kingship, or House of Peers." See *Journal of the House of Commons*, 85 vols. (London, 1802–1830), 7:644–646.

85 [Anon.], *The Judgment of Whole Kingdoms and Nations, Concerning the Rights, Power, and Prerogative of Kings, and the Rights, Priviledges, and Properties of the People* (London, 1710), 7. This text (which appeared in two earlier incarnations) has traditionally been attributed either to Lord John Somers or Daniel Defoe, but recent scholars have rejected the former possibility and found only tenuous evidence in favor of the latter. See Richard Ashcraft and M. M. Goldsmith, "Locke, Revolution Principles and the Formation of Whig Ideology," *Historical Journal* 26 (1983): 773–800, esp. 796–799.

86 *Judgment of Whole Kingdoms and Nations*, 9.

87 Ibid., 14.

88 Roger Acherley, *The Britannic Constitution: or, the Fundamental Form of Government in Britain* (London, 1727), 6.

89 Ibid., 7.

90 Ibid., 7, 9.

91 Dan Foster, *A Short Essay on Civil Government* (Hartford, 1775), 71.

92 Ibid., 14.

93 Ibid., 16.

94 Ibid., 23.

95 Ibid., 24.

96 Ibid., 50.

97 Ibid., 70. This argument was a favorite of parliamentarian writers in the 1640s. They focused on the wording of the coronation oath sworn by Edward II (and allegedly sworn by Charles I) in which the king promised *"corroborare justas leges et consuetudines quas vulgus eligerit."* If one (mis)construed the final verb to express the future perfect indicative rather than the perfect subjunctive tense, it seemed to commit the monarch to give his assent to any laws that "the people shall choose"—meaning that although all bills formally had to receive the assent of the sovereign in order to become law, the king was in fact *required* to give his assent to all bills chosen by the people (which is to say, enacted by Parliament). There was thus no true negative voice. See, for example, [Henry Parker], *Observations upon Some of His Majesties Late Answers and Expresses* (London, 1642), 5; and William Prynne, *The Soveraigne Power of Parliaments and Kingdomes* (London, 1643), 65–68. Compare Conal Condren, *Argument and Authority in Early Modern England: The Presupposition of Oaths and Offices* (Cambridge, 2006), 254–268.

98 Foster, *A Short Essay*, 4.

99 See also the essay (repr. from the *London Evening Post* of June 30, 1774) in *The Connecticut Gazette and the Universal Intelligencer*, Oct. 7, 1774, 1: "Power long entrusted either to single persons, or to bodies of men, generally increases itself so greatly as to become subversive of the intentions, and dangerous to the rights of those who delegated it. Kings are but men, are subject to all the passions and frailties of human nature, and consequently are too prompt to grasp at arbitrary power, and to wish to make all things bend and submit to their will & pleasure."

100 Samuel Langdon, *Government Corrupted by Vice* (Watertown, MA, 1775), 11–12. For a discussion of Langdon's sermon in the context of a broader turn to the "Jewish republic" among New England ministers, see Harry S. Stout, *The New England Soul: Preaching and Religious Culture in Colonial New England* (1986; repr., Oxford, 2012), 301–305.

101 Langdon, *Government Corrupted by Vice*, 12.

102 Ibid., 16.

103 Samuel Williams, *A Discourse on the Love of Our Country; Delivered on a Day of Thanksgiving, December 15, 1774* (Salem, 1775), 5–6.

104 Ibid., 6.

105 See also "Monitor," Letter 12, *The New-York Journal, or, The General Advertiser*, Jan. 25, 1776. The author goes so far as to attribute to loyalists "an idolatrous veneration for the king and parliament, more especially for the former," and laments that "the imaginations of men are exceedingly prone to deify and worship them [i.e., kings]; though, to the great misfortune of mankind, they are more commonly fiends, than angels." But he immediately adds that notwithstanding all of this, "it is noble and generous to love, to admire a virtuous

prince." Compare [Anon.], "Political Observations, without Order: Addressed to the People of America," *Pennsylvania Packet*, Nov. 14, 1774, 3; and "An Oration on Arbitrary Power, Delivered by One of the Candidates for a Second Degree at the Late Commencement Held at Princeton, in New-Jersey, September 27, 1775," *The Connecticut Gazette and the Universal Intelligencer* (New London), Dec. 22, 1775.

106 Important discussions of Paine and his pamphlet include Bernard Bailyn, "The Most Uncommon Pamphlet of the American Revolution: *Common Sense*," *Magazine of History* 25 (1973): 36–41; Jordan, "Familial Politics"; Aldridge, *Thomas Paine's American Ideology*; Eric Foner, *Tom Paine and Revolutionary America* (New York, 1976); Jack Fruchtman Jr., *Thomas Paine and the Religion of Nature* (Baltimore, 1993); Fruchtman, *Thomas Paine: Apostle of Freedom* (New York, 1994); Fruchtman, *The Political Philosophy of Thomas Paine* (Baltimore, 2009); Nichole Eustace, *Passion Is the Gale: Emotion, Power, and the Coming of the American Revolution* (Chapel Hill, 2008); and Edward Larkin, *Thomas Paine and the Literature of Revolution* (Cambridge, 2005). As Perl-Rosenthal points out in "The 'Divine Right of Republics,'" none of these sources addresses the Hebraic origins of Paine's argument.

107 *Essential Thomas Paine*, 29–30.

108 Ibid., 30–31. For an antecedent to Paine, see "A Republican," *The Massachusetts Spy*, Apr. 8, 1773. The author acknowledges the legitimacy of limited kingly government (in this he is unlike Paine) but nonetheless cites Milton in attacking the "trappings of monarchy" and claims that "every man of sense and independency must give the preference to a well constructed REPUBLIC." He continues: "I am not peculiar in my notion of Kings or monarchical governments; besides all the antients who adjudged them tyrants; besides the Jewish people whom God, in his wrath plagued with a vengeance by giving them a King; besides these, moderns innumerable are on my side" (1).

109 *Essential Thomas Paine*, 35–36. Paine adds that "in England a king hath little more to do than to make war and give away places; which in plain terms, is to impoverish the nation and set it together by the ears. A pretty business indeed for a man to be allowed eight hundred thousand sterling a year for, and worshipped into the bargain!" But Paine then seems to reverse himself by stressing the dangers of the royal negative (45).

110 [Anon.], *Reason in Answer*, 7–8.

111 Ibid., 8–9.

112 Ibid., 9.

113 Ibid., 13.

114 [Anon.], *The True Merits of a Late Treatise, Printed in America, Intitled Common Sense . . . by a Late Member of the Continental Congress, a Native of a Republican State* (London, 1776), 11. For Rutledge's possible authorship of the pamphlet, see Aldridge, *Thomas Paine's American Ideology*, 206–207.

115 [Anon.], *The True Merits of a Late Treatise*, 14.

116 Ibid., 15–16.

117 Note that the author is referring here to the biblical judges.

118 For a detailed discussion of the chronology and context of this debate, see Aldridge, *Thomas Paine's American Ideology*, 158–198.

119 "Candidus" [James Chalmers], *Plain Truth; Addressed to the Inhabitants of America* (Philadelphia, 1776), 5. The letters were republished in book form.

120 Ibid., 5–6.

121 Ibid., 72. The letters of "Rationalis" were appended to Chalmers's "Candidus" letters when the latter were published in volume form as *Plain Truth*.

122 Ibid., 75.

123 "An American" [Charles Inglis], *The True Interest of America Impartially Stated* (Philadelphia, 1776), 23.

124 Ibid., 25.

125 Ibid., 25–26.

126 Ibid., 27.

127 Ibid.

128 Ibid., 28.

129 "Cato" [Rev. William Smith], "To the People of Pennsylvania," Letter 6 (Apr. 13, 1776), in *Archives*, 5:839. "Cato's" letters were reprinted in Connecticut, Virginia, and New York, among other places. See Perl-Rosenthal, "'Divine Right of Republics,'" 557.

130 *Archives*, 5:839.

131 Ibid., 840.

132 Ibid.

133 Ibid.

134 Paine responded to "Cato" directly on this point in his third "Forester" letter, also printed in the *Pennsylvania Gazette*, Apr. 24, 1776: "The Scripture institutes no particular form of Government, but it enters a protest against the Monarchal form; and a negation on one thing, where two only are offered, and one must be chosen, amounts to an affirmative on the other. Monarchal Government was first set up by the Heathens, and the Almighty permitted it to the Jews as a punishment. "'I gave them a King in mine anger.'"—Hosea xiii, 11"; *Archives*, 5:1018.

135 *Archives*, 5:840.

136 Ibid., 841. See *Hugonis Grotii Annotationes in Vetus Testamentum*, ed. Georg Johann Ludwig Vogel, 2 vols. (Halle, 1775), 1:215; and Grotius, *De iure belli ac pacis libri tres* (Amsterdam, 1626), I.4.7.

137 *Archives*, 5:841.

138 "Cato" [Rev. William Smith], "To the People of Pennsylvania," Letter 8, in *Archives*, 5:1050.

139 Ibid.

140 Ibid.

141 Relevant literature on the diffusion of *Common Sense* includes Richard Gimbel, *Thomas Paine: A Bibliographical Check List of Common Sense with an Account of Its*

Publication (New Haven, 1956); Aldridge, *Thomas Paine's American Ideology,* 43–46; and Trish Loughran, "Disseminating Common Sense: Thomas Paine and the Problem of the Early National Bestseller," *American Literature* 78 (2006): 1–28.

142 *Connecticut Courant and Weekly Intelligencer,* Feb. 19, 1776.

143 Ramsay, *History of the American Revolution,* 1:338.

144 *Diary of Colonel Landon Carter,* 2:1007, 1049–1050. Lee himself appears to have been thinking about the analogy between monarchy and idolatry as early as November 1775. In a letter to Catherine Macaulay he wrote that "as a good *Christian* properly attached to your native Country, I am sure you must be pleased to hear, that North America is not fallen, nor likely to fall down before the *Images* that the King hath set up"; Lee to Macaulay, Nov. 29, 1775, in *Letters of Richard Henry Lee,* 1:160. Lee's admiration for *Common Sense* did not, however, extend to its proposal for a new unicameral continental legislature. Indeed, it was Lee to whom John Adams had sent his draft of a "sketch" on government in November 1775 and who, in the wake of the release of *Common Sense,* arranged for Adams's completed essay (which rejected Paine's view) to be published as *Thoughts on Government* in both New York and Virginia. See *Diary and Autobiography of John Adams,* 3:333; John Adams to Richard Henry Lee, Nov. 15, 1775, in *PJA,* 3:307–308; Richard Henry Lee to Patrick Henry, Apr. 20, 1776, in *Letters of Richard Henry Lee,* 1:179–180; Oliver Perry Chitwood, *Richard Henry Lee: Statesman of the Revolution* (Morgantown, WV, 1967), 94–95; and Paul Chadwick Bowers, "Richard Henry Lee and the Continental Congress: 1774–1779 (PhD diss., Duke University, 1965), 168–173. Note that Lee's letter to Henry about *Thoughts on Government* was written in the same week that he would have received Parker's letter about biblical monarchy.

145 Parker to Lee, Apr. 27, 1776, 1^r.

146 Ibid., 2^r.

147 Parker interestingly rejected the Josephan account of Israelite theocracy: "As to calling [Israelite government before Saul] a Theocracy it is talking Nonsense because every State in the Universe is equally a Theocracy[.] Whoever believes in a particular Providence must acknowledge that the Events of States are governed by the Almighty and I am sure the Hand of God has been with us[.] It is true as the Jews were in such a state of Ignorance as to be unable to make any Laws for themselves God did prescribe a Set of Laws for them such as would be sufficient for their Government; that his wise purposes in bringing abt. the Redemption of man by his Son Jesus Christ might be fully answered but he left the Execution of these laws to the people themselves (ibid., 1^r).

148 Ibid., 4. For a detailed analysis of Parker's intervention that emphasizes the degree to which it vacillated between the Hebraizing and the neo-Roman readings of the biblical text, see Nelson, "Hebraism and the Republican Turn of 1776," 799–803.

149 Scholars have usually located the scriptural case against monarchy exclusively in a set of sermons delivered by New England ministers. See, for example,

Eran Shalev, *American Zion: The Old Testament as a Political Text from the Revolution to the Civil War* (New Haven, 2013), 57–69; Stout, *New England Soul*, 301–305; and Perl-Rosenthal, "'Divine Right of Republics,'" 553–554, 560. Perl-Rosenthal rightly doubts that, in light of Ramsay's testimony, it is plausible to suppose that this discourse was confined to a group of New England ministers, but he is unable to offer examples of its use elsewhere.

150 One anonymous writer, in contrast, attempted to defend Paine by softening his position. See [Anon.], "Reply to the Remarks of Rationalis on Common Sense," in *Archives*, 5:974–977. See also [John Jay], "Address of the Convention of the Representatives of the State of New York to their Constituents," in *The Correspondence and Public Papers of John Jay*, ed. Henry P. Johnston, 3 vols. (New York, 1890), 1:118.

151 [John Leacock], *The Fall of British Tyranny, or, American Liberty Triumphant. The First Campaign. A Tragi-Comedy of Five Acts . . .* (Philadelphia, 1776), 66.

152 Samuel West, *A Sermon Preached Before the Honorable Council, and the Honourable House of Representatives, of the Colony of Massachusetts Bay, in New-England. May 29th, 1776* (Boston, 1776).

153 Ibid., 22.

154 Ibid., 62–63.

155 This last passage is a virtual quotation from Paine's pamphlet. See also "A Letter from Philadelphia to a Gentleman in England" (Mar. 12, 1776): "'*Common Sense*,' which I herewith send you, is read by all ranks; and, as many as read, so many become converted; though, perhaps, the 'hour before were most violent against the least idea of independence.' This summer's campaign will, I make no doubt, set 'us free from the shackles of education;' and the King of *Britain*, instead of being the idol of *Americans*, will be of little more importance here than to frighten little children"; *Archives*, 5:187–188; and [Anon.], *The People the Best Governors: or A Plan of Government Founded on the Just Principles of Natural Freedom* (n.p., 1776): "GOD gave mankind freedom by nature, made every man equal to his neighbour, and has virtually enjoined them, to govern themselves by their own laws. The government, which he introduced among his people, the *Jews*, abundantly proves it, and they might have continued in that state of liberty, had they not desired a King" (Preface).

156 Whitney, *American Independence Vindicated*, 11.

157 Ibid., 43–44.

158 Ibid., 44.

159 Ibid., 44–45.

160 "Salus Populi" [Anon.], "To the People of North-America on the Different Forms of Government" (1776), in *Archives*, 5:182.

161 Ibid.

162 "Instructions to Delegates for Charlotte County, Virginia" (Apr. 23, 1776), in *Archives*, 5:1035.

163 Benjamin Hichborn, "Oration, Delivered at Boston, March 5, 1777," in Niles, *Principles and Acts of the Revolution in America*, 27. Compare [Anon.], "Cosmo-

politan," Letter 10, in *Archives*, 5:1172. Even John Adams seems to have been swept up momentarily in this discourse; see, for example, Adams to William Tudor, Feb. 27, 1777, in *PJA*, 4:94: "I hope We shall e'er long renounce some of our Monarchical Corruptions, and become Republicans in Principle in Sentiment, in feeling and in Practice. . . .   In Republican Governments the Majesty is all in the Laws. They only are to be adored." Compare Adams to Congress, July 23, 1780, in *PJA*, 10:27: "The total and absolute suppression of the Tumults in London . . . has now given them [the Ministry] such Exultation and Confidence, that the People of America will dethrone the Congress and like the Israelites demand a King."

164   Philip Freneau, "America Independent; And Her Everlasting Deliverance from British Tyranny and Oppression," in Philip Morin Freneau, *Poems Written and Published during the American Revolutionary War*, 2 vols. (Philadelphia, 1809), 1:241. Compare Benjamin Rush, writing to John Adams while the latter was posted to the French court: "While you are *gazed* at for your American-manufactured principles, and *gazing* at the folly and pageantry of animals in the shape of men cringing at the feet of an animal called a king, I shall be secluded from the noise and corruption of the times"; Benjamin Rush to John Adams, Jan. 22, 1778, in *Letters of Benjamin Rush,* ed. L. H. Butterfield, 2 vols. (Princeton, 1951), 1:192.

165   Samuel Cooper, *A Sermon Preached Before His Excellency John Hancock, Esq. . . . October 25, 1780. Being the Day of the Commencement of the Constitution and Inauguration of the New Government* (Boston, 1780), 1. For a similar use of the same biblical text, see William Drayton, "Charge to the Grand Jury of Charleston, South Carolina" (Apr. 23, 1776), in *Archives*, 5:1031.

166   Cooper, *Sermon Preached Before His Excellency John Hancock,* 7.

167   Ibid., 8.

168   Ibid., 14.

169   Joseph Huntington, *A Discourse, Adapted to the Present Day, on the Health and Happiness, or Misery and Ruin, of the Body Politic, in Similitude to That of the Natural Body* (Hartford, 1781), 8.

170   Ibid., 9.

171   Ibid. For the Hebrew republic as a constitutional model in revolutionary America, see Eran Shalev, "'A Perfect Republic'': The Mosaic Constitution in Revolutionary New England, 1775–1788," *New England Quarterly* 82 (2009): 235–263. See also Eric Slauter, *The State as a Work of Art: The Cultural Origins of the Constitution* (Chicago, 2009), 43–46.

172   Huntington, *Discourse,* 10.

173   Ibid., 11.

174   John Murray, *Jerubbaal, Or Tyranny's Grove Destroyed, and the Altar of Liberty Finished . . . December 11, 1783, on the Occasion of the Public Thanksgiving for Peace* (Newburyport, 1784), 7. This is a direct echo of Paine; see *The Essential Thomas Paine,* 48–49.

175 Ibid., 21.

176 Ibid., 32.

177 Ibid., 43.

178 Ibid., 44. This language continued to appear during the debates over ratification. See, for example, "Camillus" in *The Pennsylvania Packet, and Daily Advertiser* (Philadelphia), June 13, 1787; orig. in *The Independent Chronicle* (Boston). The author attacks proponents of the new constitution as those who "raved about monarchy, as if we were ripe for it; and as if we were willing to take from the plough-tail or dram shop, some vociferous committee-man, and to array him in royal purple, with all the splendor of a King of the Gypsies . . . our king, whenever Providence in its wrath shall send us one, will be a blockhead or a rascal" (2; note the use of Hosea). Compare Mercy Otis Warren's characterization of the Constitution's opponents: "They deprecate discord and civil convulsions, but they are not yet generally prepared, with the ungrateful Israelites, to ask a King, nor are their spirits sufficiently broken to yield the best of their olive grounds to his servants, and to see their sons appointed to run before his chariots"; Warren, *Observations on the New Constitution, and on the Federal and State Conventions* (Boston, 1788), 18, in *Pamphlets on the Constitution of the United States,* ed. Paul Leicester Ford (New York, 1968). Compare speeches by Robert Livingston and Melanchthon Smith to the New York ratifying convention in *The Debates in the Several State Conventions on the Adoption of the Federal Constitution,* ed. Jonathan Elliot, 5 vols. (Washington, DC, 1836), 2:210; 225–226; and "Agrippa," Letter 17, in *Essays on the Constitution of the United States,* ed. Paul Leicester Ford (New York, 1892), 79. See also Thomas Jefferson to James Madison, Mar. 15, 1789, in *The Papers of Thomas Jefferson,* ed. Julian P. Boyd et al., 40 vols. (Princeton, 1950–), 14:661: "I know there are some among us who would now establish a monarchy. But they are inconsiderable I number and weight of character. The rising race are all republicans. We were educated in royalism: no wonder if some of us retain that idolatry still. Our young people are educated in republicanism. An apostacy from that to royalism is unprecedented and impossible."

179 "Moderator," *Pennsylvania Ledger,* Apr. 27, 1776, 2–3.

180 *Pennsylvania Ledger,* Apr. 27, 1776. For a lucid discussion of this essay's place in a broader turn toward "republican" astronomy, see Eran Shalev, "'A Republic amidst the Stars': Political Astronomy and the Intellectual Origins of the Stars and Stripes," *Journal of the Early Republic* 31 (2011): 39–73.

181 For a judicious exploration of the myth that Washington was "offered a crown" in 1782, see Robert Haggard, "The Nicola Affair: Lewis Nicola, George Washington, and American Military Discontent during the Revolutionary War," *Proceedings of the American Philosophical Society* 146 (2002): 139–169. For the uncertain evidence surrounding the charge that Nathanial Gorham of Massachusetts, while serving as president of the Continental Congress in 1786, attempted to persuade Prince Henry of Prussia to consider accepting an American crown,

see Louise Burnham Dunbar, *A Study of "Monarchical" Tendencies in the United States: From 1776 to 1801* (1920; repr., Urbana, 1923), 54–75.

182 Paine remained a committed opponent of prerogative power in a "single person" throughout his life, and justified his opposition on thoroughly whig grounds. As he put the point in 1805, in the midst of an attack on Pennsylvania's revised constitution, "this negativing power in the hands of an individual ["by whatever name or official title he may be called"] ought to be constitutionally abolished. It is a dangerous power. There is no prescribing rules for the use of it. It is discretionary and arbitrary, and the will and temper of the person at any time possessing it, is its only rule. There must have been a great want of reflection in the Convention that admitted it into the Constitution." See Paine, "Constitutional Reform" (Aug. 1805), in *The Writings of Thomas Paine*, ed. Moncure Daniel Conway, 4 vols. (New York, 1894), 4:457–458.

183 Thomas Jefferson to Samuel Kercheval, Jan. 22, 1816, in *The Works of Thomas Jefferson*, ed. Paul Leicester Ford, 12 vols. (New York, 1904–1905), 12:1.

184 John Adams to John Taylor, Apr. 15, 1814, in *WJA*, 6:470.

185 Adams to Sherman, July 17, 1789, in *WJA*, 6:428.

186 Ibid., 430. Adams likewise wrote to Taylor in 1814 that "the general sense of mankind clearly sees, and fully believes, that our president's office has 'some resemblance of monarchy,' and God forbid that it should ever be diminished" (ibid., 470). Compare Mercy Otis Warren's claim that the constitution created a "Republican *form* of government, founded on the principles of monarchy"; Warren, *Observations on the New Constitution*, 14.

187 Montesquieu, *De l'ésprit des lois*, V.19, in Montesquieu, *Oeuvres Complètes*, ed. Daniel Oster (Paris, 1964), 555, my translation.

4. "The Old Government, as Near as Possible"

 1 *The Federal and State Constitutions, Colonial Charters, and Other Organic Laws of the States, Territories, and Colonies Now or Heretofore Forming the United States of America*, ed. Francis Newton Thorpe, 7 vols. (Washington, DC, 1909), 6:3241–3248. See esp. Article VII. New Hampshire, Virginia, New Jersey, Delaware, Pennsylvania, Maryland, and North Carolina also adopted new state constitutions in 1776. See Charles C. Thach Jr., *The Creation of the Presidency, 1775–1789: A Study in Constitutional History* (1922; repr., Indianapolis, 2007), 13–23; Marc W. Kruman, *Between Authority and Liberty: State Constitution Making in Revolutionary America* (Chapel Hill, 1997), esp. 123–126; and Willi Paul Adams, *The First American Constitutions: Republican Ideology and the Making of the State Constitutions in the Revolutionary Era* (New York, 2001), 66–80. The classic account of the ideology of the first state constitutions remains Gordon S. Wood, *The Creation of the American Republic, 1776–1787* (Chapel Hill, 1969), 127–255. Wood empha-

sizes the "whig" character of the weak executives created in 1776, and to this extent, he and I are in agreement. Our disagreement concerns the degree to which this whig agenda was continuous with the dominant patriot ideology of the imperial crisis. When Wood writes that the repudiation of executive power in 1776 reflected a revolutionary "radical Whig" consensus that "George III was only a transmigrated Stuart bent on tyranny" (136), the distance between our respective views becomes clear. I have been emphasizing the degree to which patriots instead *faulted* George III for refusing to augment the royal prerogative and, in so doing, to vindicate a neo-Stuart conception of monarchy.

2 David Ramsay, *History of the Revolution of South Carolina, from a British Province to an Independent State,* 2 vols. (Trenton, 1785), 1:132. See also Christopher F. Lee, "The Transformation of the Executive in Post-Revolutionary South Carolina," *South Carolina Historical Magazine* 93 (1992): 85–100; and Jerome J. Nadelhaft, *The Disorders of War: The Revolution in South Carolina* (Orono, ME, 1981), 27–43. Rutledge had outlined his "regal" conception of the chief magistrate's office in a speech to the legislature on Apr. 11, 1776: "On my part, a most solemn oath has been taken for the faithful discharge of my duty. On yours, a solemn assurance has been given to support me therein. Thus a public compact between us stands recorded. You may rest assured that I shall keep this oath ever in mind. The Constitution shall be the invariable rule of my conduct. My ears shall always be open to the complaints of the injured. Justice in mercy shall neither be denied or delayed. Our laws and religion and the liberties of America shall be maintained and defended to the utmost of my power. I repose the most perfect confidence in your engagement"; William Edwin Hemphill et al., eds., *Journals of the General Assembly and House of Representatives, 1776–1780* (Columbia, SC, 1970), 52–53.

3 Ramsay, *History of the Revolution,* 1:132–133.

4 Ibid., 133–134. Rutledge goes on to offer several other examples of parliamentary usurpation, including the Septennial Act and more recent measures delegating parliamentary powers to the Crown.

5 *The Colonial Records of North Carolina,* ed. William L. Saunders, 10 vols. (Raleigh, 1886–1890), 10:868.

6 *PJI,* 1:367.

7 Ibid., 2:17.

8 Ibid., 20.

9 Ibid., 19.

10 Ibid.

11 Ibid., 17–18.

12 Ibid., 1:384.

13 Ibid., 389.

14 Ibid., 390.

15 That is, in *To the Inhabitants of Great Britain* (1774), discussed in Chapter 1. Quoted in *The Life and Correspondence of James Iredell, One of the Associate Justices*

of the Supreme Court of the United States, ed. Griffith John McRee, 2 vols. (New York, 1857–1858), 1:213–214.

16 *PJI,* 1:391.

17 Ibid., 390–391n.

18 "To His Majesty George The Third, King of Great Britain, etc.," in ibid., 438.

19 Ibid., 438–439.

20 Ibid., 435.

21 Ibid., 439. For further endorsements of the "patriot Royalist" position in Iredell's papers, see ibid., 331 ("Principles of an American Whig") and ibid., 2:17–19. Iredell also received an important letter from Archibald Neilson in August 1774 that summarized the two major positions on the imperial constitution. See Neilson to Iredell, Aug. 20, 1774, in ibid., 1:248.

22 James Iredell to Thomas Iredell Sr., Feb. 23, 1786 in ibid., 3:202.

23 Ibid. It is striking to note the similarities between Iredell's formulation here and that of Lord North in his address to the Commons of May 7, 1783. See *The Parliamentary History of England: From the Earliest Period to the Year 1803,* ed. Thomas C. Hansard, 36 vols. (London, 1806–1820), 23:849.

24 For the relationship between the two, see Hampton L. Carson, "James Wilson and James Iredell: A Parallel and a Contrast," *Pennsylvania Magazine of History and Biography* 45 (1921): 1–33. Iredell took Wilson in at the end of his life, and the latter was originally buried at Iredell's Edenton estate in North Carolina.

25 *Journals of the Continental Congress, 1774–1789,* ed. Worthington Chauncey Ford et al., 34 vols. (Washington, DC, 1904–1937), 4:135. On this address, see also Geoffrey Seed, *James Wilson* (New York, 1978), 11–12.

26 *Journals of the Continental Congress,* 4:145.

27 Ibid.

28 Ibid., 144.

29 Ibid., 8:398.

30 Ibid.

31 Ibid., 400.

32 *The Works of James Wilson,* ed. Robert Green McCloskey, 2 vols. (Cambridge, MA, 1967), 1:364–368. The passage cited appears on 364.

33 *Summary View,* 16–17.

34 Ibid., 6–8.

35 *The Papers of Thomas Jefferson,* ed. Julian P. Boyd et al., 40 vols. (Princeton, 1950–), 1:339, 342.

36 Ibid., 340.

37 *Summary View,* 16.

38 David Armitage, *The Declaration of Independence: A Global History* (Cambridge, MA, 2007), 168.

39 Thomas Jefferson, *Notes on the State of Virginia,* ed. Frank Shuffelton (New York and London, 1999), 119.

40 Ibid.

41 In *The Works of Thomas Jefferson*, ed. Paul Leicester Ford, 12 vols. (New York, 1904–1905), 1:14.

42 Ibid. Jefferson's claim that he "had never been able to get any one to agree with me but Mr. [George] Wythe" about this theory of the imperial constitution, as we saw in Chapter 1, massively overstates the originality and idiosyncrasy of his view. For a less skeptical analysis of Jefferson's assertion, see Randolph Green-field Adams, *Political Ideas of the American Revolution* (Durham, 1922), 55–56.

43 It is no accident that Jefferson wrote to his grandson in the very same year that Bolingbroke—the great advocate of the Patriot King—"was called indeed a tory; but his writings prove him a stronger advocate for liberty than any of his countrymen, the whigs of the present day"; Jefferson to Francis Eppes, Jan. 19, 1821, in *Works of Thomas Jefferson*, 10:183.

44 "Marginalia in Protests of the Lords against Repeal of the Stamp Act, 1766," in *PBF*, 13:212, 214–215.

45 John Adams expressed his disappointment and surprise at this fact in a letter to Francis Dana (Aug. 16, 1776): "The Convention of Pennsylvania has voted for a single Assembly, such is the Force of Habit, and what Surprizes me not a little is, that the American Philosopher [Franklin], should have So far accommodated himself to the Customs of his Countrymen as to be a zealous Advocate for it. No Country, ever will be long happy, or ever entirely Safe and free, which is thus governed"; *PJA*, 4:466. See also Gordon Wood, *The Americanization of Benjamin Franklin* (New York, 2004), 164–165.

46 "Novanglus," Letter VII, *PJA*, 2:314. The classic analysis of the "Novanglus" letters remains R. G. Adams, *Political Ideas of the American Revolution*, 99–108. See also C. Bradley Thompson, *John Adams and the Spirit of Liberty* (Lawrence, KS, 1998), 66–87. Several scholars have argued that Adams's political thought underwent a fundamental shift in the 1780s. On this view, the later Adams jettisoned the orthodox republicanism of the early 1770s in favor of a reactionary and idiosyncratic sort of conservatism. As will become clear from what follows, I am unpersuaded by this argument. See, chiefly, John R. Howe, *The Changing Political Thought of John Adams* (Princeton, 1966); Wood, *Creation of the American Republic*, 567–592; and Joyce Appleby, "The New Republican Synthesis and the Changing Political Thought of John Adams," *American Quarterly* 25 (1973): 578–595. Mercy Otis Warren offered an early version of this charge when she stated in 1805 that, while Adams was abroad serving as ambassador to Great Britain, "he became so enamored with the British constitution, and the government, manners, and laws of the nation, that a partiality for monarchy appeared, which was inconsistent with his former professions of republicanism"; Mercy Otis Warren, *History of the Rise, Progress, and Termination of the American Revolution*, 3 vols. (Boston, 1805), 3:392. Adams himself vehemently denied that his political and constitutional theory—particularly his views on monarchy—had changed in any appreciable way during the 1770s and 1780s. See John Adams to Mercy Otis Warren, July 11, 1807, in *Correspondence between*

John Adams and Mercy Otis Warren Relating to Her History of the American Revolution, ed. Charles Francis Adams (1878; repr., New York, 1972), 324–326.

47 "Novanglus," Letter IV, in *PJA*, 2:260.

48 "Novanglus," Letter VII, in ibid., 320.

49 "Novanglus," Letter XII, in ibid., 379.

50 Ibid.

51 "Novanglus," Letter VII, in ibid., 320.

52 Ibid.

53 *Diary and Autobiography of John Adams,* ed. L. H. Butterfield, 3 vols. (Cambridge, MA, 1961), 3:354. Adams repeated this view during a subsequent debate in the Continental Congress: asked "what Plan of a Government" he would advise for the new American states, he replied "A Plan as nearly resembling the Governments under which We were born and have lived as the Circumstances of the Country will admit. Kings We never had among Us, Nobles We never had. Nothing hereditary ever existed in the Country: Nor will the Country require or admit of any such Thing: but Governors, and Councils We have always had as Well as Representatives. A Legislature in three Branches ought to be preserved, and independent Judges"; (3:356).

54 *PJA*, 4:74. Adams claimed that he had been "convinced" of this view by reading "the Works of Sidney, Harrington, Lock, Milton, Nedham, Burnet, Hoadly," which had been "put into my Hands" in "early Youth." As T. H. Breen pointed out long ago, however, it is exceedingly unlikely that Adams had in fact read Nedham, Milton, or Sidney at all carefully at this stage. Adams himself admitted in his *Autobiography* that before the late 1770s, "I had read Harrington, Sydney, Hobbs, Nedham and Lock, but with very little Application to any particular Views"; *Diary and Autobiography of John Adams,* 3:358. He would have occasion to delve into the writings of Nedham and Milton in particular in the 1780s and would be appalled by what he found there. See Timothy H. Breen, "John Adams' Fight against Innovation in the New England Constitution: 1776," *The New England Quarterly* 40 (1967): 501–520; see esp. 509–510n.

55 *PJA*, 4:74.

56 Ibid., 80.

57 An appreciation of this distinction would have improved Eric Slauter's otherwise illuminating discussion of the language of "portrait," "miniature," and "transcription" in the debate over representation in the 1780s. See Slauter, *The State as a Work of Art: The Cultural Origins of the Constitution* (Chicago, 2009), 123–166. Slauter discusses Adams's *Thoughts on Government* on 130–132.

58 *PJA*, 4:75.

59 Ibid., 81.

60 Ibid., 76.

61 Ibid.

62 Ibid.

63 Ibid., 87.

64 Writing as "The Earl of Clarendon," Adams had described "the two branches of popular power"—the House of Commons and trial by jury—as "the heart and lungs, the mainspring and central wheel" of the English Constitution, in which "consist wholly the liberty and security of the people"; *Boston Gazette*, Jan. 27, 1766. It is possible that he was reverting to this earlier analysis. Indeed, Adams did occasionally juxtapose the terms "monarchy" and "republic" during this period—usually when he was writing in a nontechnical vein. See, for example, Adams to Mercy Otis Warren, Jan. 8, 1776, in *PJA*, 3:397 ("Pray Madam, are you for an American Monarchy or a Republic?").

65 *PJA*, 4:89.

66 Ibid., 182.

67 Ibid., 466.

68 Ibid. At the same time, Adams was writing to southern correspondents to reassure them that they were, from his point of view, at perfect liberty to dilute some of the more "popular" elements of his proposal that had been conceived with New England in mind: "Whether the Plan of the Pamphlet, is not too popular, whether the Elections are not too frequent, for your Colony I know not. The Usages and Genius and Manners of the People must be consulted. And if Annual Elections of the Representatives of the People, are Sacredly preserved, those Elections by Ballott, and none permitted to be chosen but Inhabitants, Residents, as well as qualified Freeholders of the City, County, Parish, Town, or Burrough for which they are to serve, three essential Prerequisites of free Government; the Council or middle Branch of the Legislature may be triennial, or even Septennial without much Inconvenience"; Adams to Patrick Henry, June 3, 1776, in ibid., 234. For the degree to which Adams intended *Thoughts on Government* to speak primarily to southern and mid-Atlantic readers, see Thompson, *John Adams and the Spirit of Liberty*, 236–238.

69 *Federal and State Constitutions*, 6:3081, Art. II, Sec. 2.

70 Charles P. Smith, *James Wilson: Founding Father, 1742–1798* (Chapel Hill, 1956), 110. See also McCloskey's important introduction to *The Works of James Wilson*, 1:19–27.

71 "Resolutions Passed at a Meeting in the State House Yard, Philadelphia," in *American Archives: Fifth Series*, ed. Peter Force, 3 vols. (Washington, DC, 1837), 2:1149.

72 "Associator," *The Pennsylvania Journal; and the Weekly Advertiser*, May 21, 1777, 2. Benjamin Rush would use virtually identical language in a letter written the following year: "Nothing more was necessary to have made us a free and happy people than to abolish the royal and proprietary power of the state. A *single* legislature is big with tyranny. I had rather live under the government of one man than 72. They will soon become like the 3[0 tyrants of] Athens"; Rush to Anthony Wayne, May 19, 1777, in *Letters of Benjamin Rush*, ed. L. H. Butterfield, 2 vols. (Princeton, 1951), 1:148.

73 This, of course, was the language of the Declaratory Act.

74 Force, *American Archives: Fifth Series*, 2:1150.

75 Ibid.

76 Rush to Ebenezer Howard, Oct. 22, 1768, in *Letters of Benjamin Rush*, 1:68.

77 "Ludlow," Letter 2, in *Pennsylvania Journal*, May 28, 1777, 1. Rush's opposition to the Pennsylvania constitution provoked the assembly to remove him from Congress in 1777; see Rush to Anthony Wayne, Apr. 2, 1777, in *Letters of Benjamin Rush*, 1:137.

78 *Pennsylvania Journal*, May 28, 1777, 1.

79 Adams wrote to Abigail on June 4, 1777 unhappily that "you will see by the same Papers too, that the Writers here in Opposition to the Constitution of Pensilvania, are making a factious Use of my Name and Lucubrations. Much against my Will, I assure you, for altho I am no Admirer of the Form of this Government, yet I think it is agreeable to the Body of the People, and if they please themselves they will please me. And I would not choose to be impressed into the service of one Party, or the other—and I am determined I will not inlist. Besides it is not very genteel in these Writers, to put my Name to a Letter, from which I cautiously withheld it myself"; John Adams to Abigail Adams, 4 June 1777 (electronic edition), *Adams Family Papers: An Electronic Archive*, MHS, http://www.masshist.org/digitaladams/.

80 "Ludlow," Letter 3, in *Pennsylvania Journal*, June 4, 1777, 1. Rush had endorsed the same position in a private letter to Anthony Wayne several months earlier: "A convention have at last formed a government for our state. . . . It is thought by many people to be rather too much upon the democratical order, for liberty is as apt to degenerate into licentiousness as power is to become arbitrary. Restraints are therefore as necessary in the former as the latter case. Had the governor and council in the new Constitution of Pennsylvania possessed a negative upon the proceedings of the assembly, the government would have derived safety, wisdom, and dignity from it. But we hope the council of censors will remedy this defect at the expiration of seven years"; Rush to Wayne, Sept. 24, 1776, in *Letters of Benjamin Rush*, 1:114.

81 *Pennsylvania Journal*, June 4, 1777, 1.

82 Benjamin Rush, *Observations upon the Present Government of Pennsylvania* (Philadelphia, 1777), 5.

83 Ibid. This pamphlet carried as its epigraph a slightly altered quotation from Adams's *Thoughts on Government*: "A republic is the best of governments, so that particular arrangement of the powers of society, or, in other words, that form of government which is best contrived to secure an impartial and exact execution of the laws, is the best of republics." Rush likewise reproduced Adams's attack on the Long Parliament (6).

84 See Daniel Hulsebosch, *Constituting Empire: New York and the Transformation of Constitutionalism in the Atlantic World, 1664–1830* (Chapel Hill, 2005), esp. 170–180.

85 *Journals of the Provincial Congress, Provincial Convention, Committee of Safety and Council of Safety of the State of New York, 1775–1776–1778*, 2 vols. (Albany, 1842),

1:860–862. On the council of appointment, see *Federal and State Constitutions*, 5:2633.

86 Hamilton to the New York Committee of Correspondence, May 7, 1777, in *PAH*, 1:248.

87 Hamilton's views in this respect were very similar to those expressed by William Duer of New York in a letter to John Jay: "I congratulate you on the completion of the task of forming and organizing our new Government. I think it upon the maturest reflection the best system which has as yet been adopted, and possibly as good as the temper of the times would admit of"; Duer to Jay, May 28, 1777, in *The Correspondence and Public Papers of John Jay*, ed. Henry P. Johnston, 3 vols. (New York, 1890), 1:138.

88 Hamilton to Gouverneur Morris, May 16, 1777, in *PAH*, 1:253–254. Given the vastness of the literature on Hamilton, it is somewhat surprising that so little has been written about the development of his political theory during the war years. The topic is not mentioned at all in the one book-length study of Hamilton's career during this period (see Broadus Mitchell, *Alexander Hamilton: The Revolutionary War Years* [New York, 1970]); and it is discussed only briefly in Ron Chernow's recent biography (see Chernow, *Alexander Hamilton* [New York, 2004], 110–112, 170–172). See also Michael P. Federici, *The Political Philosophy of Alexander Hamilton* (Baltimore, 2012).

89 *PAH*, 1:255. This letter has been cited periodically as evidence that Hamilton, in the full flush of independence, briefly "abandoned his faith in balanced government" in favor of "democratic" principles—only to revert to form a year or two later; see Gerald Stourzh, *Alexander Hamilton and the Idea of Republican Government* (Stanford, 1970), 67–68, 180. It is undoubtedly true that the letter is unique in Hamilton's oeuvre, in that it counsels against a bicameral, "compound legislature" and argues that "the danger of an abuse of power from a simple legislative would not be very great, in a government where the equality and fulness of popular representation is so wisely provided for as in yours [i.e., that of New York]" (255). But Hamilton writes only several lines earlier that "to determine the qualifications proper for the chief executive Magistrate requires the deliberate wisdom of a select assembly, and cannot be safely lodged with the people at large." In short, while Hamilton (along with many) found himself questioning in 1776–1777 whether an "aristocratical" upper house of the legislature was necessary or salutary in a country without an established aristocracy, his commitment to the prerogatives of the executive remained intact—as did his broader suspicion of "democratical" principles.

90 For a cogent analysis of Hamilton's notes, see Philip Stadter, "Alexander Hamilton's Notes on Plutarch in His Pay Book," *Review of Politics* 73 (2011): 199–217. This analysis does not, however, address the centrality of the term "prerogative" in the passages from Dryden's Plutarch that Hamilton chooses to comment upon. See also E. P. Panagopoulos, "Hamilton's Notes in his Pay Book of the New York State Artillery Company," *American Historical Review* 62 (1957):

310–325 (Hamilton's notes on Plutarch are briefly cataloged on 317–318); and Stourzh, *Alexander Hamilton*, 179–180.

91 The text is found in *Plutarch's Lives, in Six Volumes. Translated from the Greek*, trans. John Dryden (London, 1758).

92 Plutarch (correctly) cites Plato, not Aristotle. See Plato, *Laws*, 692a.

93 For a provocative analysis of the role of this text in the emerging eighteenth-century discourse of "checks and balances," see David Wootton, "Liberty, Metaphor, and Mechanism: 'Checks and Balances' and the Origins of Modern Constitutionalism" in *Liberty and American Experience in the Eighteenth Century*, ed. David Womersley (Indianapolis, 2006), 209–274.

94 *PAH*, 1:397.

95 *PAH*, 1:398. Dryden actually has: "Although *Lycurgus* had in this manner regulated and tempered the constitution of the republick, yet those who succeeded him found that too much power was allowed to the kings and senate, in consequence of which they grew imperious and oppressive; and therefore, as *Plato* says, a bridle was put upon them, which was the power of the *Ephori*, established 130 years after the death of *Lycurgus*. *Elatus* was the first who had this dignity conferred upon him, in the reign of *Theopompus*, who when his Queen upbraided him one day, that he would leave the regal power to his children less than himself had received it from his ancestors, replied, that he should leave it greater because more durable. For the prerogative being thus kept within reasonable bounds, the Kings of *Sparta* were secured both from envy and dangers"; *Plutarch's Lives*, 1:112–113. Compare Plutarch, *Lycurgus*, VII.

96 Plutarch, *Lycurgus*, VII.

97 Here Hamilton quotes Dryden verbatim. Compare *PAH*, 1:396; *Plutarch's Lives*, 1:96. See Plutarch, *Comparison of Theseus and Romulus.*, II.1–2.

98 *PAH*, 1:396. Stadter (like Stourzh before him) sees in this comment an attack on the "arbitrary rule" of "the 'tyrant' George III"; Stadter, "Alexander Hamilton's Notes," 205; Stourzh, *Alexander Hamilton*, 180. But we should recall that Hamilton's complaint about George III was that he had *neglected* to exercise his (hibernating) prerogative powers, not that he had impermissibly augmented them. Hamilton's comment seems perfectly continuous with his position in *The Farmer Refuted*.

99 This, for example, was the basis of his critique of the Quebec Act. By this measure, on his account, "the whole Legislative, Executive, and Judiciary powers, are ultimately and effectually, though not immediately, lodged in the King." See Hamilton, "Remarks on the Quebec Bill," in *The Works of Alexander Hamilton*, ed. John C. Hamilton, 7 vols. (New York, 1850), 2:131. Hamilton, however, characteristically blamed the measure on "the corruption of the british Parliament," not the king (137).

100 *Plutarch's Lives*, 1:96.

101 Hamilton to James Duane, Sept. 3, 1780, in *PAH*, 2:404.

102 Ibid.

103 See Hamilton to the Marquis de Barbé-Marbois, Feb. 7, 1781, in *PAH*, 2:554. This
was the very day that Congress voted to adopt the proposal to create three executive departments (Finance, Marine, and War—the department of Foreign
Affairs had been created a month earlier). On this development, see Jack Rakove, *The Beginnings of National Politics: An Interpretive History of the Continental
Congress* (New York, 1979), 282–296. See also Hamilton to Robert Morris, Apr.
30, 1781, in *PAH*, 3:604. James Wilson likewise welcomed the move. See Wilson
to Robert Morris, Jan. 14, 1777, in "The Life and Writings of James Wilson," ed.
Burton Alva Konkle, unpublished MS (1946), Box 2, Folder 1, Letter 82, Manuscript Division, Department of Rare Books and Special Collections, Princeton
University Library.

104 "The Continentalist," Letter 2, in *PAH*, 2:654.

105 Compare ["Publius"], *Federalist* 18.

106 *PAH*, 2:657. Compare ["Publius"], *Federalist* 20.

107 *Farmer Refuted*, 16; *Summary View*, 7. See also Franklin, "Marginalia in a Pamphlet by Josiah Tucker," in *PBF*, 17:393: "There is no such *Dependence* [of America on Great Britain]. There is only a *Connection*, of which the King is the common
Link."

108 See *The Popular Sources of Political Authority: Documents on the Massachusetts Constitution of 1780*, ed. Oscar and Mary F. Handlin (Cambridge, MA, 1966), 293.

109 Ibid.

110 Quoted in *PJA*, 4:71.

111 *Popular Sources of Political Authority*, 343.

112 Ibid., 351, 344.

113 This provision was only meant to be activated in the event that no candidate
secured an outright majority on the first (and only) ballot. See "The Rejected
Constitution of 1778," in ibid., 195.

114 Ibid., 346.

115 Ibid., 360.

116 Ibid., 361.

117 Adams to Elbridge Gerry, Aug. 27, 1779, in *PJA*, 8:127.

118 Elbridge Gerry to John Adams, Oct. 12, 1779, in ibid., 198.

119 Ibid.

120 Adams to Elbridge Gerry, Nov. 4, 1779, in ibid., 8:276. For an excellent discussion of the place of this passage in Adams's broader oeuvre, see Richard Alan
Ryerson, "'Like a Hare before the Hunters': John Adams and the Idea of Republican Monarchy," *Proceedings of the Massachusetts Historical Society*, 3rd series, 107 (1995): 16–29.

121 It is striking that only several months later, Adams was driven to write a series
of angry letters to correspondents, adopting (for the first time since his Royalist turn in the late 1760s) an unambiguously "Country" whig perspective on
Britain's constitutional predicament and its failure to seek peace with America. For example, he announced to Edmund Jenings that "all Endeavours in

parliament to reform, will be ineffectual. Reformation must be made in a Congress if any Way. Corruption has too many hereditary, and legal Supporters in Parliament. . . . either the remaining Virtue in the Nation must overcome the Corruption, or the Corruption will wholly exterminate the remaining Virtue. I see but one Alternative and no middle Way. Either Absolute Monarchy, or a Republic and Congress"; Adams to Jenings, Apr. 29, 1780, in *PJA*, 9:251. See also Adams to William Lee, Oct. 7, 1780, and Adams to Congress, Oct. 14, 1780, in *PJA*, 9:258, 269. Adams would not write in these terms again.

122 "The Report of a Constitution of Form of Government for the Commonwealth of Massachusetts," in *PJA*, 8:242.

123 Adams to Benjamin Rush, Nov. 4, 1779, in ibid., 279.

124 Ibid., 242; "The Constitution of 1780," in *Popular Sources of Political Authority*, 448–449.

125 Adams to Jonathan Jackson, Oct. 2, 1780, in *PJA*, 10:192.

126 *Popular Sources of Political Authority*, 437–438.

127 Adams to William Gordon, May 26, 1780, in *PJA*, 9:343.

128 *Popular Sources of Political Authority*, 648.

129 Ibid.

130 For a rare (and very different) discussion of this document, see Edmund Morgan, *Inventing the People: The Rise of Popular Sovereignty in England and America* (New York, 1988), 259–260.

131 *Popular Sources of Political Authority*, 735.

132 Ibid.

133 Ibid.

134 Ibid., 735–736.

135 Ibid., 736–737.

136 Ibid.

137 *Farmer Refuted*, 18.

138 [William Hicks], *Considerations upon the Rights of the Colonists to the Privileges of British Subjects* (New York, 1766), 21. Compare [Anon.], *An Answer to a Pamphlet, Entitled Taxation No Tyranny, Addressed to the Author, and to Persons in Power* (London, 1775), 46; Benjamin Franklin to Samuel Cooper, June 8, 1770, in *PBF*, 17:163–164; and James Madison, "Vices of the Political System of the United States," in *The Papers of James Madison*, ed. William T. Hutchinson, Robert Rutland, et al. (Chicago, 1962–), 9:357.

139 Doc. no. PJA09d128, Adams Papers, MHS.

140 Doc. no. PJA09d321, Adams Papers, MHS.

141 Smith, *James Wilson*, 296–304.

142 "A Peace Maker," *Pennsylvania Journal*, June 30, 1784, 2.

143 Proponents of the revised frame of government likewise stressed the degree to which it was indebted to Adams's brand of constitutionalism: Benjamin Rush wrote to Adams in 1790 that "you were my first preceptor in the science of government. From you I learned to discover the danger of the Constitution of

Pennsylvania, and if I had any merit or guilt in keeping the public mind awake to its folly or danger for 13 years, you alone should have the credit for the former and be made responsible for the latter. . . . The reformation of our state government has completed my last political wish"; Rush to Adams, Feb. 12, 1790, in *Letters of Benjamin Rush*, 1:530–531.

144 "A Peace Maker," *Pennsylvania Journal*, June 30, 1784, 2.

145 *The Proceedings Relative to Calling the Conventions of 1776 and 1790* (Harrisburg, 1825), 79.

146 "Address of the Minority of the Council of Censors," *Pennsylvania Gazette*, Jan. 28, 1784, 1.

147 Ibid.

148 "Draft of a Constitution for Virginia," in *Papers of Thomas Jefferson*, 6:298–299.

149 Ibid., 302–303.

150 Jefferson, *Notes on the State of Virginia*, 126. Madison would quote this passage in ["Publius"], *Federalist* 48.

151 Jefferson to James Madison, Mar. 15, 1789, in *Papers of Thomas Jefferson*, 14:661.

152 Adams to Jefferson, Oct. 28, 1787, in *The Adams-Jefferson Letters*, ed. Lester J. Cappon (Chapel Hill, 1987 [orig. 1959]), 204.

153 Doc. no. 369, Adams Papers, MHS. In an 1807 letter to Mercy Otis Warren, Adams himself retrospectively characterized his position as of 1787 in the very same manner. Responding to Warren's charge that he had exclaimed in private conversation, "For my part, I want King, Lords, and Commons," he answered that he had meant only "such a balance of power as the Constitution we had been talking of contained, which is a miniature resemblance of kings, lords, and commons, though without the names, and without the permanent qualities of the two former"; John Adams to Mercy Otis Warren, July 11, 1807, in *Correspondence between John Adams and Mercy Otis Warren*, 327).

154 *The Records of the Federal Convention of 1787*, ed. Max Ferrand, 3 vols. (New Haven, 1911), 1:71 (June 1, 1787).

155 *Diary and Autobiography of John Adams*, 3:354, 356. See also "The Essex Result," in *Popular Sources of Political Authority*, 330.

156 Adams to Mercy Otis Warren, Jan. 8, 1776, in *PJA*, 3:398.

157 Adams to William Tudor, Feb. 27, 1777, in *PJA*, 5:94.

158 Adams was unusual in that he later made his peace with pageantry and monarchical pomp. See, for example, Adams to Benjamin Rush, June 9, 1789, in *Old Family Letters: Copied from the Originals for Alexander Biddle*, 2 vols. (Philadelphia, 1892), 1:37.

159 Benjamin Rush to John Adams, Jan. 22, 1778, in *Letters of Benjamin Rush*, 1:192. Compare John Jay to Robert Morris, Apr. 25, 1782, in *Correspondence and Public Papers of John Jay*, 2:195–199.

160 See Rush to Ebenezer Howard, Oct. 22, 1768, in *Letters of Benjamin Rush*, 1:68.

161 Jefferson to James Madison, Mar. 15, 1789, in *Papers of Thomas Jefferson*, 14:661.

162 Mercy Otis Warren, *Observations on the New Constitution, and on the Federal and State Conventions* (Boston, 1788), in *Pamphlets on the Constitution of the United States,* ed. Paul Leicester Ford (New York, 1968), 7.

5. "All Know That a Single Magistrate Is Not a King"

1 The classic statement of this view is to be found in Charles Beard, *Economic Interpretation of the Constitution* (New York, 1913). It was later developed by Merrill Jensen and his students; see Jensen, *The Articles of Confederation: An Interpretation of the Social-Constitutional History of the American Revolution, 1774–1781* (1940; repr., Madison, 1976); and Jensen, *The New Nation: A History of the United States during the Confederation, 1781–1789* (New York, 1950). It has reappeared with remarkable exactitude in the "ideological" historiography that supplanted Beard's reductionist approach in the 1960s and 1970s. See, for example, Gordon Wood, *The Creation of the American Republic, 1776–1787* (Chapel Hill, 1969), esp. 483–499; and Wood, *The Radicalism of the American Revolution* (New York, 1992), 229–270. Wood himself acknowledges the basic continuity; see Wood, *Creation of the American Republic,* 626. For two significant restatements, see Terence Ball, "'A Republic—If You Can Keep It,'" in *Conceptual Change and the Constitution,* ed. Terence Ball and J. G. A. Pocock (Lawrence, KS, 1988), 137–164, esp. 138–140; and John Murrin, "The Great Inversion, or Court Versus Country?: A Comparison of the Revolution Settlements in England (1688–1721) and America (1776–1816)," in *Three British Revolutions: 1641, 1688, 1776,* ed. J. G. A. Pocock (Princeton, 1980), 368–453, esp. 401–404. This view has also been defended in recent years by a number of "neo-progressive" historians. See, for example, Alfred F. Young, "The Framers of the Constitution and the 'Genius of the People,'" *Radical History Review* 42 (1988), 8–18; and Terry Bouton, *Taming Democracy: "The People," the Founders, and the Troubled Ending of the American Revolution* (Oxford, 2007). For two important dissents, see Bernard Bailyn, *The Ideological Origins of the American Revolution,* rev. ed. (Cambridge, MA, 1992), 321–379; and Jack Rakove, *Original Meanings: Politics and Ideas in the Making of the Constitution* (New York, 1996).

2 Thus, Max Edling, who offers a penetrating critique of the progressive narrative—and of the tendency to see the ratification debates as a controversy between "republican" Antifederalists and "liberal" Federalists—nonetheless concludes that the Antideferalists were unambiguously defending the principles of the Revolution against a Federalist counterrevolution "in favor of government." On his account, Antifederalists kept faith with the "Country" ideology that had provoked the rupture with Britain, whereas Federalists, in pursuing their dream of a "fiscal-military state," adopted several crucial commitments of the English "Court" party. See Edling, *A Revolution in Favor of Government: Origins of the U.S. Constitution and the Making of the American State* (Oxford, 2003), esp. 31–46, 219–229.

3 Donald Robinson quite rightly calls these men "radicals" but then distinguishes them from the "Old Republicans" who "espoused the faith of the Revolution." What is missed here is that his "radicals" were themselves speaking for "Revolution principles"—their position was not "starkly new in the American context." See Donald L. Robinson, "The Inventors of the Presidency," *Presidential Studies Quarterly* 13 (1983), 8–25, esp. 8, 12–13. George M. Dennison, in contrast, regards Wilson and his allies as "moderates"; see Dennison, "The 'Revolution Principle': Ideology and Constitutionalism in the Thought of James Wilson," *Review of Politics* 157 (1977): 157–191. For a recent statement of the view that these men should be regarded as "conservatives," see David Lefer, *The Founding Conservatives: How a Group of Unsung Heroes Saved the American Revolution* (New York, 2013). Having characterized them in this fashion, Lefer regards it as "curious" that Wilson, Morris, and their allies—those "on the right"—should have defended "greater democracy" and "increased political participation" against those on "the left" (Roger Sherman et al.); see 318.

4 In a sense, I am taking up a challenge laid down obliquely by John Phillip Reid: "Perhaps it cannot be attributed to the revolutionary controversy, but the fact is striking that American constitution drafters adopted from the old constitution of tripartite balances a major institution of prerogativism then virtually discarded by British constitutionalism [i.e., the veto]"; Reid, *The Constitutional History of the American Revolution*, abridged ed. (Madison, 1995), 104. My argument is that this development can and must be attributed to the "revolutionary controversy" and that the very same figures who had developed the patriot Royalist position in 1770s championed it once again in the 1780s. Moreover, as we shall see, they themselves highlighted the continuity in their thought.

5 Our sources for the debates in Philadelphia include the official journal of proceedings kept by William Jackson, secretary of the convention, along with the surviving sets of notes taken by James Madison, Robert Yates, Rufus King, John Lansing, and James McHenry. Of these, Madison's notes are much the most important. Yates's, while more extensive, were heavily redacted by "Citizen Gênet" for publication in 1821. Only two pages of the original manuscript survive, and they differ greatly from Gênet's published text. But Madison's notes are far from unproblematic. Mary Sarah Bilder's recent work demonstrates that Madison subsequently revised his own notes far more extensively than was previously supposed (see Bilder, *Madison's Hand: Revising the Constitutional Convention*, forthcoming from Harvard University Press), and his style of note-taking lent itself to summary rather than precise transcription. King's notes are occasionally quite useful, in that they appear to preserve statements that are elided in Madison's account of the debates. But any claim about what a given delegate said during the convention must be regarded, at least to some degree, as conjecture. When I write that "Delegate X argued Y," the reader should take this as shorthand for "So far as we can tell, Delegate X argued Y." For a lucid and careful analysis of the documentary evidence, see James

H. Hutson, "The Creation of the Constitution: The Integrity of the Documentary Record," *Texas Law Review* 65 (1986): 1–39. Bilder has recently offered an important amendment to this standard account, stressing the value of Jackson's official *Journal* as a source; see Mary Sarah Bilder, "How Bad Were the Official Records of the Federal Convention?," *George Washington Law Review* 80 (2012): 1620–1682.

6 *Records*, 1:65. All references to statements in the convention are drawn from Madison's notes unless otherwise specified. The most sophisticated account of Wilson's role in the convention is to be found in William Ewald, "James Wilson and the Drafting of the Constitution," *University of Pennsylvania Journal of Constitutional Law* 10 (2008): 901–1009. See also Nicholas Pederson, "The Lost Founder: James Wilson in American Memory," *Yale Journal of Law and Humanities* 22 (2010): 257–337; George W. Carey, "James Wilson's Political Thought and the Constitutional Convention," *Political Science Reviewer* 17 (1987): 49–107, esp. 76–103; and Charles Page Smith, *James Wilson: Founding Father, 1742–1798* (Chapel Hill, 1956), 215–261.

7 To my knowledge, the origins and resonance of this phrase have not been noticed before. The closest thing to such an acknowledgement is to be found in some characteristically shrewd remarks by J. G. A. Pocock; see Pocock, "States, Republics, and Empires: The American Founding in Early Modern Perspective," in Ball and Pocock, *Conceptual Change and the Constitution*, 55–77, esp. 62–64. Pocock is not, however, discussing Wilson's motion.

8 "An Act for the Abolishing of the Kingly Office in England and Ireland, and the Dominions thereunto Belonging," in *Acts and Ordinances of the Interregnum, 1642–1660*, ed. C. H. Firth and R. S. Rait (London, 1911), 18–20; *Journals of the House of Commons* (London, 1802–), 7:843.

9 *The Memoirs of Edmund Ludlow*, ed. C. H. Firth, 2 vols. (Oxford, 1894), 2:173n.

10 *Defence*, 3:461.

11 *Records*, 1:66. The most sensitive analysis of the debate that follows remains Louise Burnham Dunbar, *A Study of "Monarchical" Tendencies in the United States: from 1776 to 1801* (1920; repr., Urbana, 1923), 76–98.

12 *Records*, 1:71 (King). See my discussion of the reliability of King's report in note 3 to the Introduction.

13 Ibid., 65–66.

14 Recall that such a council had been attached to the chief magistracy in all of the state constitutions, with the exception of those of New Hampshire and New York. (In the latter, however, the governor could only wield his veto in conjunction with a "council of revision.") Even Massachusetts had "shackled" its governor with such a council, as Adams later complained; *WJA*, 6:461. Charles Pinckney aptly summarized the Royalist objection to this model during the convention debates: "His own idea was that the President shd. be authorized to call for advice or not as he might chuse. Give him an able Council and it will thwart him; a weak one and he will shelter himself under their sanction"; *Rec-*

ords, 2:329. This critique was of course a direct inheritance of the imperial crisis; patriots had initially lamented that the king was in thrall to his parliamentary ministers. After he declared the colonists in rebellion, however, he was denounced for hiding behind them.

15 *Records,* 1:98; 2:73–74.

16 Wilson fiercely opposed the single seven-year term that the convention initially considered.

17 *Records,* 1:119; 2:185; 2:426; 2:538; 2:626.

18 Ibid., 1:68–69. The "Virginia Plan," in contrast, had proposed that the chief magistrate be elected for a single, fixed term by the new federal legislature and assigned him only a qualified negative voice (to be wielded jointly with "a council of revision"). See ibid., 1:21. For Wilson's view of the presidency, see Robert E. DiClerico, "James Wilson's Presidency," *Presidential Studies Quarterly* 17 (1987): 301–317; and Daniel J. McCarthy, "James Wilson and the Creation of the Presidency," *Presidential Studies Quarterly* 17 (1987): 689–696.

19 *Records,* 1:68.

20 Ibid., 69.

21 This is the line of argument that explains Wilson's celebrated insistence that it was only in the new United States that "the supreme, absolute, and uncontrollable power remains in the people"; "Speech Delivered on 26th November, 1787, in the Convention of Pennsylvania," in *Works of James Wilson,* ed. Robert Green McCloskey, 2 vols. (Cambridge, MA, 1967), 2:770. The people of Great Britain, on his account, cannot be regarded as sovereign because only one-third of their supreme legislature can claim to represent them. Because a hereditary monarch cannot represent the people, any "original contract" between king and nation must be taken to "exclude, rather than to imply delegated power." In other words, some share of political authority is *transferred* from the people to the king in Britain, whereas the totality of it is *derived* from them in the United State; see "Lectures on Law," (1790) in *Works of James Wilson,* 1:311, 317.

22 *Records,* 1:151.

23 Ibid., 132–133. Compare "Lectures on Law," in *Works of James Wilson,* 1:400–405. This view seems to sit uneasily alongside Wilson's remarks in the *Lectures* on the nature of customary law: "In the introduction, in the extension, in the continuance of customary law, we find the operation of consent universally predominant" (1:122). If the people can be said to have consented tacitly to customary law (i.e., law for which neither they nor their elected representatives have voted), why cannot they be said to have tacitly authorized unelected magistrates to govern them? And, if they can, why should such magistrates not be regarded as "representatives" of the people? For a comparison of Wilson and Blackstone on the issue of customary law, see John V. Jezierski, "Parliament or People: James Wilson and Blackstone on the Nature and Location of Sovereignty," *Journal of the History of Ideas* 32 (1971): 95–106, esp. 99–100.

24 *Records*, 1:359. It is, therefore, incorrect to claim that Wilson proposed the popular election of the president and senators only because "he sensed that democratic concessions would be necessary in order to win popular approval for the proposed expansion and relocation of power"; see Russell L. Hanson, "'Commons' and 'Commonwealth' at the American Founding: Democratic Republicanism as the New American Hybrid," in Ball and Pocock, *Conceptual Change and the Constitution*, 165–193, esp. 177.

25 See Wilson, "Speech on Choosing the Members of the Senate by Electors; Delivered, on the 31st December, 1789, in the Convention of Pennsylvania," in *Works of James Wilson*, 2:781–793; "Lectures on Law," in *Works of James Wilson*, 1:411.

26 *Records*, 1:71 (King).

27 Ibid., 2:48–9. See the Constitution of the United States, Article IV.4.

28 *Records*, 1:87. Note that Dickinson represented Delaware rather than Pennsylvania in the convention.

29 Ibid., 86, 90 (King).

30 Ibid., 83. During the convention, Franklin was in the midst of a term as "president" of Pennsylvania's plural executive, a post that Dickinson had held as well.

31 See my discussion in Chapter 1.

32 *Records*, 1:65–66.

33 It is also worth pointing out that while the Constitution would divide what remained the formal "federative" powers of the Crown between the president and Congress in various ways, the share of these powers it would assign to the president alone was far greater than the share wielded *in fact* by any British monarch of the eighteenth century. This issue is explored in detail below. On this set of questions, see the insightful remarks in Daniel Hulsebosch, "The Plural Prerogative," *WMQ* 68 (2011): 583–587. For my response, see Eric Nelson, "Taking Them Seriously: Patriots, Prerogative, and the English Seventeenth Century," *WMQ* 68 (2011): 588–596, esp. 595–596.

34 *Records*, 2:300–301.

35 Ibid., 30–31. Morris added that he supported "the expedient of an absolute negative in the Executive" on the grounds that the "encroachments of the popular branch of the Government ought to be guarded agst." His chief example, once again, was the Long Parliament: "If the Executive be overturned by the popular branch, as happened in England the tyranny of one man will ensue"; ibid., 299–300.

36 Ibid., 1:96.

37 Wilson subsequently flirted with a somewhat different view, quite similar to the one Hamilton defended (as we shall see). In the Pennsylvania ratifying convention, he defined "a republick or democracy" as a state in which "the people at large retain the supreme power, and act either collectively or by representation"; *Works of James Wilson*, 2:771. On this account, monarchy is defined by its

hereditary character (recall that Wilson denied that hereditary magistrates could represent the people). Both views converge in denying that monarchical power in a "single person" is incompatible with republican government.

38 "Lectures on Law," in *Works of James Wilson*, 1:316. Compare Blackstone, *Commentaries*, 1:234.

39 *Works of James Wilson*, 1:316.

40 *Records*, 1:96.

41 Ibid., 98. Hamilton is mistaken here. Queen Anne refused her assent to the Scottish Militia Bill in 1707. As we have seen, many of Hamilton's contemporaries were similarly unaware of this fact.

42 Gerald Stourzh deserves great credit for having registered that Hamilton's mature constitutional thought "was influenced by the peculiar predicament of the final stage of the British-American contest before independence, from 1774 to 1775 . . . the period when leading colonial advocates like John Adams, Thomas Jefferson, James Wilson, and Alexander Hamilton himself espoused a dominion theory of the British Empire. While they now denied the supremacy of the British Parliament . . . they continued to see in the king of England their sovereign ruler." Stourzh refers to this period as "an Indian summer of virtual Tory philosophy"; Stourzh, *Alexander Hamilton and the Idea of Republican Government* (Stanford, 1970), 26, 43.

43 *Records*, 1:288. Hamilton is referring to Jacques Necker, finance minister to Louis XVI. The obvious point to make is that Hamilton would hardly have endorsed the model of the British Constitution if he regarded hereditary power as "non-representative"—and therefore enslaving. Indeed, he stated explicitly later in the convention that "real liberty" is enjoyed in all "moderate governments" (i.e., those avoiding both absolute monarchy and "the extremes of democracy"); *Records*, 1:432. For a similar insistence that the British Constitution "as it stood on paper, was one of the freest, at that time, in the world," see Tench Coxe, "An Examination of the Constitution for the United States of America," in *Essays on the Constitution of the United States*, ed. Paul Leicester Ford (Brooklyn, 1892), 135.

44 *Records*, 1:424.

45 Ibid., 289.

46 Ibid., 289, 299 (Yates). On this theme, see also Clement Fatovic, *Outside the Law: Emergency and Executive Power* (Baltimore, 2009), 238–239.

47 Ibid., 289.

48 Ibid., 291–293. Revealingly, Charles Pinckney supported this proposal.

49 Compare ibid., 290. Here Madison reports Hamilton as arguing that "as long as offices are open to all men, and no constitutional rank is established, it is pure republicanism."

50 The central difference is that Madison restricted the class of "republics" to include *only* such regimes, whereas Hamilton insisted that regimes in which the people themselves rule directly (i.e., without the device of representation)

were likewise to be classified as "republics." On this disagreement, see Stourzh, *Alexander Hamilton*, 55.

51 *Records*, 1:290.

52 Ibid.

53 See *Federalist* 37, 227; *Federalist* 39, 240–246. See also Madison on elective monarchy in *Records*, 1:70 (King).

54 For example, Yates has Hamilton claim that "by making the executive subject to impeachment, the term monarchy cannot apply," but this thought is wholly absent from the accounts of Madison and King—and from Hamilton's own notes. See *Records*, 1:330. Hamilton does not clarify the issue in his "Syllabus" of *The Federalist*. In that context, he identifies "various senses" in which contemporaries used the term "republic" but does not endorse one of these, despite the fact that he offers definitions of monarchy, aristocracy, democracy, and mixed government "in my sense." See *The Federalist*, ed. Paul Leicester Ford (New York, 1898), xliii.

55 *Records*, 1:308–313.

56 Hamilton claimed years later that he had jettisoned the notion of a life term for the president in the convention itself, eventually proposing a "plan of a Constitution" in which "the Office of President has no greater duration than for three years"; Hamilton to Thomas Pickering, Sept. 16, 1803, in *PAH*, 26:148. The claim is false, but Hamilton's reasoning is striking: he came to reject the life term, on this account, because he eventually recognized "1 That the political principles of the people of this country would endure nothing but republican Government. 2 That in the actual situation of the Country, it was in itself right and proper that the republican theory should have a fair and full trial—3 That to such a trial it was essential that the Government should be so constructed as to give it all the energy and stability reconcilable with the principles of that theory. These were the genuine sentiments of my heart, and upon them I acted." Hamilton, in other words, attributed to his younger self the view that a chief magistrate elected for life would not be consistent with "republican theory" in its "full" form.

57 *Records*, 2:33–36 (King). Madison wrote to Jefferson that "as to the duration in office [of the president], a few would have preferred a tenure during good behaviour—a considerable number would have done so, in case an easy & effectual removal by impeachment could be settled"; Madison to Jefferson, Oct. 24, 1787, in *The Papers of James Madison*, Congressional Series, ed. William T. Hutchinson and William M. E. Rachal, 17 vols. (Chicago and Charlottesville, 1962–1991), 10:207–215. This statement seemingly contradicts a footnote later added by Madison to the final text of his convention notes in which he cautions the reader that "this vote [in favor of a presidential life term 'during good behavior'] is not to be considered as any certain index of opinion, as a number in the affirmative probably had it chiefly in view to alarm those attached to a dependence of the Executive on the Legislature, & thereby facilitate some final

arrangement of a contrary tendency. ⟨The avowed friends of an Executive, 'during good behaviour' were not more than three or four nor is it certain they would finally have adhered to such a tenure . . . ⟩"; *Records,* 2:36n. Madison had obvious reasons for wishing to downplay both his own support for the measure and its favorable reception among his fellow delegates. For the dating of this page and the footnotes, see Bilder, *Madison's Hand.*

58 *Records,* 2:36. See also Glenn A. Phelps, *George Washington and American Constitutionalism* (Lawrence, KS, 1993), 105. Hamilton later emphasized the fact that "the highest toned propositions, which I made in the Convention, were for a President, Senate and Judges during good behaviour—a house of representatives for three years . . . A vote was taken on the proposition respecting the Executive. Five states were in favour of it; among those Virginia; and though from the manner of voting, by delegations, individuals were not distinguished, it was morally certain, from the known situation of the Virginia members (six in number, two of them Mason and Randolph possessing popular doctrines) that Madison must have concurred in the vote of Virginia. Thus, if I sinned against Republicanism, Mr. Madison was not less guilty"; Hamilton to Thomas Pickering, Sept. 16, 1803, in *PAH,* 26:148. (Note that, in fact, only four state delegations supported a presidential term "during good behavior.") This passage is important evidence in favor of the view that Hamilton's June 18 speech in the convention was not merely strategic, designed to draw fire away from the proposals of Madison and Wilson by making them look tame in comparison to his own. Had this been the case, Hamilton would presumably have been happy to say so in this context.

59 Adams to Thomas Jefferson, Dec. 6, 1787, in *The Adams-Jefferson Letters,* ed. Lester J. Cappon (1959; repr., Chapel Hill, 1987), 213. Although Wilson favored a short presidential term, he too plainly hoped that the president would simply be reelected "voluntarily, and cheerfully" until the end of his life; see "Lectures on Law," in *Works of James Wilson,* 1:319.

60 Adams to Rush, June 9, 1789, in *Old Family Letters: Copied from the Originals for Alexander Biddle,* 2 vols. (Philadelphia, 1892), 1:37–38.

61 Washington to Madison, Mar. 31, 1787, in *Papers of George Washington,* Confederation Series, ed. W. W. Abbot and Dorothy Twohig, 6 vols. (Charlottesville and London, 1992–), 5:114–117.

62 See my discussion in Chapter 2;, and *Defence,* 1:4.

63 For a quantitative analysis of the activity and voting behavior of Sherman and his allies, see David Brian Robertson, "Madison's Opponents and Constitutional Design," *American Political Science Review* 99 (2005): 225–243, esp. 231. Sherman himself spoke, made motions, or seconded motions 177 times (roughly the same number as Madison).

64 *Records,* 1:65.

65 Wilson, like Adams, was happy to concede that "the Legislature ought to be the most exact transcript of the whole Society" (*Records,* 1:132), but he never

supposed that *only* an assembly embodying an "exact transcript" of society could count as the "representative" of the people. His point was simply that an assembly would not be able to play its proper institutional role within a mixed constitutional scheme unless it reflected the composition of the body of the people. His claim, in other words, was about what makes popular assemblies *effective,* not about what entitles them to claim that they represent the people. He never endorsed the "imaging" theory. On the eighteenth-century discourse of "transcription," see Eric Slauter, *The State as a Work of Art: The Cultural Origins of the Constitution* (Chicago, 2009), 148–164.

66 *Records,* 1:48.

67 Ibid., 85.

68 Compare Elbridge Gerry's claim that "the primary object of the revisionary check in the President is not to protect the general interest, but to defend his own department"; ibid., 2:586. For Gerry, who refused to sign the Constitution, the chief magistrate could not be regarded as the representative of the people.

69 Ibid., 1:100–101, 68.

70 Ibid., 2:52. Morris had wholeheartedly endorsed the patriot Royalist position during the imperial crisis, insisting even in 1776 that "we have no business with the King. We did not quarrel with him"; see Morris, "Oration on the Necessity for Declaring Independence from Britain," in *To Secure the True Blessings of Liberty: Selected Writings of Gouverneur Morris,* ed. J. Jackson Barlow (Indianapolis, 2012), 15, 24.

71 A recognition of this tradition's prominence within American political and constitutional thought in the 1780s would have improved Lance Banning's otherwise excellent analysis. See, for example, Banning, "Republican Ideology and the Triumph of the Constitution, 1783–1793," *WMQ* 31 (1974): 167–188, esp. 177–179. Forrest McDonald comes much closer to the mark when he identifies Wilson, Hamilton, Morris, Pinckney, et al., as "'court-party' nationalists"— although only Hamilton in fact offered an affirmative defense of "influence"; see McDonald, *Novus Ordo Seclorum: The Intellectual Origins of the Constitution* (Lawrence, KS, 1985), 187–189.

72 *Records,* 1:66, 144 (King). Wilson added that "the proper cure . . . for corruption in the Legislature was to take from it the power of appointing to offices," thus directly rejecting the view that the source of legislative corruption was to be found in the appointment power of the *executive.* See *Records,* 1:387. Wilson also received a letter from Silas Deane in April 1783 that offered a strikingly similar account of Britain's constitutional woes. See Silas Deane to James Wilson, Apr. 1, 1783, in "The Life and Writings of James Wilson," ed. Burton Alva Konkle, unpublished MS (1946), Box 1, Folder 7, Letter 173, Department of Rare Books and Special Collections, Princeton University Library. Madison offered a glancing endorsement of this sort of view when he observed that "the King of G[reat]. B[ritain]. with all his splendid attributes would not be able to withstand ye. unanimous and eager wishes of both houses of Parliament" (*Records,*

1:100). Adams would defend this understanding of the English constitutional dilemma for the rest of his life. In a set of 1804 annotations, glossing Bolingbroke's claim that "in a monarchy like ours liberty would be safer, perhaps, if we inclined a little more than we do to the popular side," Adams retorts: "This is very questionable in England." Adams, annotations to Bolingbroke, *Remarks on the History of England* (1804), reprinted in Zoltán Haraszti, *John Adams & the Prophets of Progress* (Cambridge, MA, 1952), 56. Compare Adams, annotations to Abbé de Mably, *De la législation* (1791), reprinted in Haraszti, *John Adams*, 132.

73 *Records*, 1:376. On Hamilton's use of Hume, see Paul Rahe, *Republics Ancient and Modern*, 3 vols. (Chapel Hill, 1994), 3:115–116; Forrest McDonald, *The American Presidency: An Intellectual History* (Lawrence, KS, 1994), 94–97; and Stourzh, *Alexander Hamilton*, 70–87. This was the aspect of Hamilton's thought that Jefferson would later bowdlerize for polemical purposes; see Jefferson, "The Anas, 1791–1806," in *The Works of Thomas Jefferson*, ed. Paul Leicester Ford (New York, 1901), 1:167–180. "Hamilton," Jefferson announced, "was not only a monarchist, but for a monarchy bottomed on corruption" (179). For a discussion of Jefferson's use of "political gossip" in constructing this account of Hamilton's constitutionalism, see Joanne B. Freeman, "Poison, Whispers, and Fame: Jefferson's 'Anas' and Political Gossip in the Early Republic," *Journal of the Early Republic* 15 (1995): 25–57, esp. 36–39, 55. Wilson likewise came quite close to endorsing Hume's position in remarks to the Pennsylvania ratifying convention: "The reason why it is necessary in England to continue such influence [i.e the king's patronage power], is, that the crown, in order to secure its own influence against two other branches of the legislature, must continue to bestow places; but those places produce the opposition which frequently runs so strong in the British Parliament"; *The Debates in the Several States Conventions, on the Adoption of the Federal Constitution*, 5 vols., ed. Jonathan Elliot (Philadelphia, 1907), 2:484.

74 David Hume, "Of the Independency of Parliament," in *Political Essays*, ed. Knud Haakonssen (Cambridge, 1994), 25.

75 *Debates in the Several States Conventions*, 2:265. Interestingly, Gouverneur Morris is quoted as observing on July 21 that "the influence the English Judges may have . . . in strengthening the Executive check can not be ascertained, as the King by his influence in a manner dictates the laws"; *Records*, 2:75–76. Assuming that Madison reported Morris's words correctly, this is a surprising and uncharacteristic remark. For a full-throated endorsement of the view that Britain was a parliamentary "aristocracy" masquerading as a monarchy, see Morris, "Notes on the United States of America" (1806), in Barlow, *To Secure the True Blessings of Liberty*, 420–421. Morris observed in the convention itself that "the Minister" was "the real King" of England; *Records* 2:104.

76 *Records*, 1:362. Wilson dissented on this point; see *Works of James Wilson*, 1:313.

77 *Records*, 3:113. Compare the version reported in Madison's notes: "under the British Govt. the negative of the Crown had been found beneficial"; *Records*, 1:164. Pinckney likewise agreed with Hamilton that "the Constitution of

G[reat]. Britain" was "the best constitution in existence"; *Records*, 1:398. See also Edward Carrington to Thomas Jefferson, June 9, 1787, in *Records*, 3:39: "the negative which the King of England had upon our Laws was never found to be materially inconvenient." Pinckney, born in 1757, had been too young to participate in the imperial debate. For a general study, see Marty D. Matthews, *Forgotten Founder: The Life and Times of Charles Pinckney* (Columbia, SC, 2004).

78 *Records*, 1:100. Compare Butler's reported remarks in *Records*, 1:391 (Yates). Two years later, Sherman would assail the proposal to assign the president "the sole appointment of all office" on the grounds that "the Crown of Great Britain, by having that prerogative has been enabled to swallow up the whole administration; the influence of the Crown upon the Legislature subjects both Houses to its will and pleasure"; *Records*, 3:357.

79 *Records*, 1:101. Compare Mason as reported by Yates: "I admire many parts of the British constitution and government, but I detest their corruption. Why has the power of the crown so remarkably increased the last century? A stranger, by reading their laws, would suppose it considerably diminished; and yet, by the sole power of appointing the increased officers of government, corruption pervades every town and village in the kingdom"; *Records*, 1:380–381.

80 It is striking that, in the vast literature on the convention, so little has been written on the degree to which the debate over the Constitution took the form of a debate over the character and meaning of the Revolution. For a valiant exception, see Frederick C. Black, "The American Revolution as 'Yardstick' in the Debates on the Constitution, 1787–1788," *Proceedings of the American Philosophical Society* 117 (1973): 162–185. Black notes Wilson's remark on page 169. He does not, however, reconstruct the other side of the debate, nor does he relate it to the larger controversy over the nature of the English Constitution.

81 *Records*, 1:83. See Genesis 47:13–26.

82 *Records*, 1:99.

83 Ibid.

84 Franklin to Samuel Cooper, June 8, 1770, in *PBF*, 17:163.

85 See also Franklin, "Queries and Remarks Respecting Alterations in the Constitution of Pennsylvania" (1789), in *Franklin: The Autobiography and Other Writings on Politics, Economics, and Virtue*, ed. Alan Houston (Cambridge, 2004), 364–365. Franklin's account of his own position on the imperial constitution in Part Four of the *Autobiography* (written at the very end of his life) also substantially effaces his early Royalism. See, e.g., 139–140.

86 Madison was at least publicly agnostic in the debate on June 1 as between "a unity and a plurality in the Executive"; *Records*, 1:66–67. Indeed, to the extent that he took an emphatic position of any kind on this interlocking set of questions, it was in favor of a "council of revision"; see, for example, *Records*, 1:138, 2:298. For a cogent analysis of Madison's role in the convention debates over executive power (albeit one that, in my view, overstates its scope), see Jack Rakove and Susan Zlomke, "James Madison and the Independent Executive,"

Presidential Studies Quarterly 17 (1987): 293–300. See also Charles C. Thach Jr., *The Creation of the Presidency, 1775–1789: A Study in Constitutional History* (1922; repr., Indianapolis, 2007), 70–73.

87 Madison to Randolph, Apr. 8, 1787, in *Papers of James Madison,* 9:370. Compare Madison to Caleb Wallace, Aug. 23, 1785, in *Papers of James Madison,* 8:352: "I have made up no final opinion whether the first Magistrate should be chosen by the Legislature or the people at large or whether the power should be vested in one man assisted by a council or in a council of which the President shall be only primus inter pares."

88 Madison to Jefferson, Oct. 24, 1787, in *Papers of James Madison,* 10:208.

89 For Madison's investment in this device, see, e.g., Charles F. Hobson, "The Negative on State Laws: James Madison, the Constitution, and the Crisis of Republican Government," *WMQ* 36 (1979): 215–235; and Alison LaCroix, *The Ideological Origins of American Federalism* (Cambridge, MA, 2010), 136–174.

90 Madison to Washington, Apr. 16, 1787, in *Papers of James Madison,* 9:383–384.

91 Not only did Madison publish no intervention in the imperial debate but, as Jack Rakove reminds us, his few surviving letters from the early 1770s indicate a complete lack of interest in the details of the controversy. See Rakove, *James Madison and the Creation of the American Republic,* 3rd ed. (New York, 2007), 6.

92 Madison reused the phrase in *Federalist* 43; see 272.

93 *Records,* 2:30.

94 See, for example, ibid., 1:165–166, 291–293, 2:27–28.

95 Wilson, Hamilton, and their allies did not, however, propose to assign the president the sort of negative on state laws that Madison wished to assign Congress, although, as we have seen, Hamilton and Pinckney proposed that such a negative should be wielded by governors appointed by the federal government.

96 As Madison put the point in the convention, there would have been no objection to the royal negative prior to the Revolution, if it "had been faithful to the American interest, and had possessed the necessary information"—it had not, on Madison's account, in part because it was wielded by a monarch; see *Records,* 1:168; compare *Records,* 2:28.

97 Edmund Burke, though a friend of the American cause, had offered a canonical statement of this orthodoxy in his speech of Apr. 19, 1774 on American taxation. See *The Writings and Speeches of Edmund Burke,* ed. Paul Langford, 9 vols. (Oxford, 1981–2000), 2:459–460. Madison wrote to Jefferson that "if the supremacy of the British Parliament is not necessary as has been contended, for the harmony of that Empire; it is evident I think that without the royal negative or some equivalent controul, the unity of the system would be destroyed"; Madison to Jefferson, Oct. 24, 1787, in *Papers of James Madison,* 10:210. Madison, unlike his patriot Royalist colleagues, plainly believed that "some equivalent control," rather than the royal prerogative itself, had been necessary to resolve the imperial crisis. In this respect, his view resembled that of Joseph Galloway,

who had proposed the creation of a new imperial legislature in order to serve as the "superintending" power of the British dominions; see LaCroix, *Ideological Origins of American Federalism,* 111–113.

98 For Madison's use of the Royalist language of "superintending" and "pervading" power, as well as that of "interposition," in relation to the federal legislature, see, e.g., *Records,* 1:165; and *Federalist 43,* 275–276.

99 See, for example, Richard A. Watson, "Origins and Early Development of the Veto Power," *Presidential Studies Quarterly* 17 (1987): 401–412, esp. 407–408. The important exception is the 1815 national bank bill, which Madison vetoed on the grounds that it would fail to achieve its fiscal objectives. See James A. Richardson, *A Compilation of the Messages and Papers of the Presidents, 1789–1897* (Washington, DC, 1900), 1:555.

100 [James Madison], *Letters of Helvidius; Written in Reply to Pacificus* (1793; repr., Philadelphia, 1796), 6. At issue was Washington's authority to "proclaim" American neutrality in the conflict between France and Britain.

101 Ibid., 6n.

102 [William Knox], *The Controversy between Great Britain and Her Colonies, Reviewed* (London, 1769), 78–80. On this point, see Yuhtaro Ohmori, "The Artillery of Mr. Locke: The Use of Locke's *Second Treatise* in Pre-Revolutionary America" (PhD diss., Johns Hopkins University, 1988), 125–126.

103 Elliot, *Debates in the Several States Conventions,* 3:501. Compare George Mason's remarkable statement on the same subject; ibid., 508. Madison was likely following the opinion of Burlamaqui, whom he had read as a Princeton undergraduate; see Jean-Jacques Burlamaqui, *The Principles of Natural and Politic Law,* 2 vols. (London, 1763), 2:215–219; and Dennis Thompson, "The Education of a Founding Father: The Reading List for John Witherspoon's Course in Political Theory, as Taken by James Madison," *Political Theory* 4 (1976): 523–529. Vattel agreed with Burlamaqui on this point; see Emer de Vattel, *Le Droit des gens* (Amsterdam, 1775), I.iii.117. The issue had reemerged quite prominently at the conclusion of the Revolutionary War, when the British administration determined that Parliament would be required to ratify any treaty ceding the American colonies. Patriots mocked this notion to the very end, insisting that America had always remained "outside the realm" of Great Britain and that Parliament accordingly was in no legal position to "cede" it. See, for example, Adams's plainly sarcastic report of Thomas Pownall's comment in 1780 that "he was perfectly clear, that it was not in the Royal Prerogative to make any peace, by which the dominions of the Crown might be alienated"; Adams to Unknown, June 9, 1780, in *PJA,* 9:401. There were, thus, two different questions at stake in this debate: (1) whether it remained a prerogative of the Crown to alienate territories from the realm "at pleasure"; and (2) whether it remained a prerogative of the Crown to cede territories from the realm in the context of a peace treaty. The latter was a more delicate question, in that the making of war and peace remained (as a legal matter) an acknowledged royal prerogative.

See C. G. Gibbs, "Laying Treaties Before Parliament in the Eighteenth Century," in *Studies in Diplomatic History: Essays in Memory of David Bayne Horn*, ed. R. M. Hatton and M. S. Anderson (Harlow, UK, 1970), 124; and, more generally, David Armitage, *Foundations of Modern International Thought* (Cambridge, 2013), 148–150.

104 *Farmer Refuted,* 25. Compare John Cartwright, *American Independence the Interest and Glory of Great Britain* (London, 1774), 10.

105 [Edward Bancroft], *Remarks on the Review of the Controversy between Great Britain and Her Colonies* (New London, CT, 1771), 19. See also [Anon.], *A Letter to the Right Honourable the Earl of Hillsborough, on the Present Situation of Affairs in America* (London, 1769), 4: "The king of this realm has, by his prerogative, a constitutional right to alienate all acquisitions of territory, not previously annexed to this kingdom, and emancipate any part of his subjects from their allegiance to himself, and (as a necessary consequence) from the authority of parliament."

106 See, for example, Thomas Hutchinson, "A Dialogue between an American and a European Englishman" in *Perspectives in American History,* ed. Donald Fleming and Bernard Bailyn, vol. 9 (Cambridge, MA, 1974), 374–376; and [John Lind], *Remarks on the Principal Acts of the Thirteenth Parliament of Great Britain* (London, 1775), 38–39. Compare Anon., *American Resistance Indefensible* (London, 1776), 18–19.

107 Edling, *A Revolution in Favor of Government,* 3.

108 See Rakove, *Original Meanings,* 23–93.

109 See, for example, Ewald, "James Wilson and the Drafting of the Constitution," 915–929; and McDonald, *Novus Ordo Seclorum,* 205–209.

110 For the data, see Robertson, "Madison's Opponents and Constitutional Design."

111 See Ewald, "James Wilson and the Drafting of the Constitution," 946.

112 The details of the article were finalized in the Committee of Detail (or, as it was technically known, the committee "for the purpose of reporting a Constitution conformably to the Proceedings"), which met from July 27 to Aug. 6. Wilson was among its members and the final draft of the committee's report is in his hand. See *Documentary History of the Constitution of the United States of America,* 5 vols. (Washington, DC, 1894–1905), 1:107; Ewald, "James Wilson and the Drafting of the Constitution," 983.

113 See Ewald, "James Wilson and the Drafting of the Constitution," 983–993. Wilson was joined on the committee by his houseguest John Rutledge, who, as we have seen, had been a strident defender of prerogative power in the executive since 1776. It was Rutledge who first endorsed Wilson's motion that the executive should consist of "a single person;" *Records,* 1:65. Wilson's ideas also clearly guided the deliberations of the Committee of Eleven, established by the convention on August 31 to finalize the details of the presidency. Gouverneur Morris and John Dickinson (under whom Wilson had studied as a legal apprentice in 1766) were both members, and, while the latter harbored grave doubts as to the wisdom of the powerful executive championed by Wilson, he believed that

only some form of popular election would reconcile the people to the sweeping prerogatives of the office. See John Dickinson to George Logan, Jan. 16, 1802, in *Supplement to Max Farrand's Records of the Federal Convention of 1787*, ed. James H. Hutson (New Haven, 1987), 300–302.

114 Several other delegates had departed the convention early. A standard Royalist verdict on the Constitution was rendered by Charles Pinckney in the South Carolina House of Representatives: "And the executive, he said, though not constructed upon those firm and permanent principles which he confessed would have been pleasing to him, is still as much so as the present temper and genius of the people will admit. . . . He had been opposed to connecting the executive and the Senate in the discharge of those duties, because their union, in his opinion, destroyed that responsibility which the Constitution should, in this respect, have been careful to establish; but he had no apprehensions of an aristocracy"; *Records*, 3:249–250.

115 See *Records*, 2:68–69. See also Madison's similar remark in *Records*, 2:66. Rufus King argued the reverse, namely that only a chief magistrate serving "during good behavior" should be subject to removal by impeachment. A president elected for a short, renewable term would instead be "tried for his behaviour by his electors." See *Records*, 2:67.

116 See *Records*, 2:585–587.

117 On this subject, see the wise remarks in Pauline Maier, *Ratification: The People Debate the Constitution, 1787–1788* (New York, 2010), xiv–xv, 92–95.

118 Elliott, *Debates in the Several States Conventions*, 2:510.

119 "Centinel," Letter 2, in *The Complete Anti-Federalist*, ed. Herbert J. Storing, 7 vols. (Chicago, 1981), 2:7:49.

120 Ibid., 3:11:45; Compare *Federalist* 38, 236.

121 "Cincinnatus," Letter 4, in *The Complete Anti-Federalist*, 3:6:21–22. Compare Jean-Louis Delolme, *The Constitution of England*, 4th ed. (London, 1784), 215–218. The North Carolina Antifederalist Samuel Spencer likewise lamented in his state's ratifying convention that "on the present plan, from the necessary connection of the President's office with that of the Senate, I have little ground to hope that his firmness will long prevail against the overbearing power and influence of the Senate." The result, Spencer had no doubt, would be a "despotic aristocracy." See Elliot, *Debates in the Several States Conventions*, 4:116.

122 Elliot, *Debates in the Several States Conventions*, 3:279.

123 Even Patrick Henry flirted with the claim that the Article II presidency did not sufficiently resemble the British monarchy. See ibid., 387–388.

124 [Roger Sherman], "Observations on the New Federal Constitution," in Ford, *Essays on the Constitution of the United States*, 159. Many Antifederalists had, of course, rejected even the qualified negative on the grounds that "to give the executive a control over the legislative" would affirm "the doctrine of prerogative and other peculiar properties of the royal character" that are "incompatible with the view of these states when they are settling the form of a republi-

can government"; [Anon.], "The Impartial Examiner," Letter 4, *Virginia Independent Chronicle*, June 11, 1788.

125   The notion that Adams's argument was outside the mainstream of contemporary American constitutional thought, and was accordingly greeted with a combination of mystification and hostility by his peers, has by now been put to rest. See C. Bradley Thompson, *John Adams and the Spirit of Liberty* (Lawrence, KS, 1998), esp. 251–258. Tench Coxe, for one, wrote from Philadelphia that the *Defence* was "much and justly admired here" and had "come out very opportunely for the convention"; Coxe to John Brown Cutting, May 19, 1787, in *The Documentary History of the Ratification of the Constitution*, ed. John P. Kaminiski and Gaspare Saldino (Madison, 1976–), 16:83. Benjamin Rush similarly enthused that Adams's text had "diffused such excellent principles among us, that there is little doubt of our adopting a vigorous and compounded federal legislature. Our illustrious minister [to Great Britain] in this gift to his country has done us more service than if he had obtained alliances for us with all nations in Europe"; Rush to Richard Price, June 2, 1787, in *Letters of Benjamin Rush*, ed. L. H. Butterfield, 2 vols. (Princeton, 1951), 1:418. On the eve of the convention, even Franklin informed Adams that his book was "in such Request here, that it is already put to Press, and a numerous Edition will speadily be abroad"; Franklin to Adams, May 18, 1787, in *The Writings of Benjamin Franklin*, ed. Albert Henry Smyth, 10 vols. (New York, 1907), 9:585. Perhaps most revealingly, "Centinel," an opponent of the Constitution, observed that "I am fearful that the principles of government inculcated in Mr. Adams's treatise, and enforced in the numerous essays and paragraphs in the newspapers, have misled some well designing members of the late Convention"; *The Complete Anti-Federalist*, 2:2:138. Some Antifederalists were, however, prepared to endorse Adams's ideas; see, for example, "Agrippa," Letter 18, in Ford, *Essays on the Constitution of the United States*, 82. Other noteworthy responses include Jefferson to Adams, Feb. 23, 1787, in *Adams-Jefferson Letters*, 174; and John Jay to Adams, May 12, 1787, in *The Correspondence and Public Papers of John Jay*, ed. Henry P. Johnston, 3 vols. (New York, 1890), 3:247 (Jay writes that he had read the book "with pleasure and profit" and noted that "a new edition of your book is printing in this city [New York]"). Adams himself worried that "it is a hazardous Enterprize, and will be an unpopular Work in America for a long time," although he later opined that "the Constitution of U.S. of 1787 was concluded . . . by the arrival of a ship with the first volume of the Defence"; see Adams to Jefferson, Mar. 1, 1787, in *Adams-Jefferson Letters*, 176; Adams to Mercy Otis Warren, July 20, 1807, in *Correspondence between John Adams and Mercy Otis Warren Relating to Her History of the American Revolution*, ed. Charles Francis Adams (1878; repr., New York, 1972), 332–334; and Adams, annotations to [Alexandre Hauterive], *L'État de la France à la fin de l'an VIII* (1801), reprinted in Haraszti, *John Adams*, 267. The myth that the *Defence* was received negatively in the United States derives almost entirely from a single snide remark offered by Madison: "Men of learning

find nothing new in it; men of taste many things to criticize; and men without either, not a few things which they will not understand"; Madison to Jefferson, June 6, 1787, in *Papers of James Madison*, 10:29. Even Madison, however, went on in the same letter to acknowledge the book's considerable influence on the convention: "Mr Adams' book, which has been in your hands, of course has excited a good deal of attention. An edition has come out here, and another is in the press at N. York. It will probably be much read, particularly in the Eastern States, and contribute, with other circumstances, to revive the predelictions of this country for the British Constitution. . . . It will, nevertheless, be read and praised, and become a powerful engine in forming the public opinion. The name and character of the author, with the critical situation of our affairs, naturally account for such an effect. The book also has merit, and I wish many of the remarks in it which are unfriendly to republicanism may not receive fresh weight from the operations of our governments."

126 *Defence*, 1:70.
127 Adams always retained his pre-revolutionary conviction that "if [the negative voice] has not been used in England for a long time past, it by no means follows that there have not been occasions when it might have been employed with propriety." See ibid., 3:294.
128 Adams to Sherman, July 17, 1789, in *WJA*, 6:428.
129 Adams to Sherman, July 18, 1789, in ibid., 429.
130 As Adams put the point in the *Defence*, "the people must be taught to be governed more by reason, and less by sounds. The word king, like magic, excites the adoration of some, and the execration of others: some, who would obey the lawful orders of a king, would rebel against the same orders, given by the same authority under the name of governors or president; others would cheerfully submit to a governor or president, but think rebellion against a king, with only the same authority, virtue and merit, and obedience to God"; *Defence*, 3:435.
131 Adams to Sherman, July 18, 1789, in *WJA*, 6:429.
132 *Defence*, 3:367–368.
133 Adams to Thomas Jefferson, Dec. 6, 1787, in *Adams-Jefferson Letters*, 214.
134 This was precisely the issue at stake in Paine's famous debate with the Abbé Sieyès in 1791. The latter offered a somewhat muddled defense of Adams's position. See *Sieyès: Political Writings, Including the Debate between Sieyès and Tom Paine in 1791*, ed. Michael Sonenscher (Indianapolis, 2003), 165–173. For Adams's role in French constitutional debate from 1789 to 1791, see C. Bradley Thompson, "John Adams and the Coming of the French Revolution," *Journal of the Early Republic* 16 (1996): 361–387, esp. 383–385.
135 Adams to Sherman, July 18, 1789, in *WJA*, 6:430.
136 Ibid.
137 Ibid., 430–431.
138 Ibid., 428.
139 "Brutus," Letter 3, in *The Complete Anti-Federalist*, 2:9:42.

140 "The Federal Farmer," Letters II and III, in *The Complete Anti-Federalist*, 2:8:38, 2:8:15.

141 Elliot, *Debates in the Several States Conventions*, 3:245–248.

142 Sherman to Adams, July 20, 1788, in *WJA*, 6:438–439.

143 Ibid.

144 "Lectures on Law," in *Works of James Wilson*, 1:322. Strikingly, it is on the very same page that Wilson offers his one and only endorsement of the whig explanation for the decline of the royal negative: "Indeed, this influence [of the Crown] has been so great and so uniform that for more than a century past, it has been found, that reliance could be placed on it implicitly. Accordingly, during that whole period, the king has never once been under the disagreeable necessity of interposing his negative to prevent the passing of an obnoxious law. It has been discovered to be a less ungracious, though not a less efficacious method, to stop its progress in one of the two houses of parliament."

145 See *Federalist* 73, 442–446. This essay initially appeared in print on Mar. 21, 1788, and was then republished when *The Federalist* emerged in volume form (volume 2 was published in May 1788). Federalists eagerly distributed copies of the text to delegates in the various ratifying conventions. For the logistics, see Maier, *Ratification*, 257.

146 Sherman to Adams, July 20, 1788, in *WJA*, 6:439.

147 Ibid., 437. Sherman was referring here specifically to the definition offered in John Enticks' *New Spelling Dictionary* (1765).

148 *Federalist* 39, 241.

149 *Federalist* 10, 81–82. For Madison, the ancient Greek city-states were therefore not "republics," properly speaking, but rather "democracies"—in that the people ruled collectively, and not by means of representation. Hamilton noticeably refused to follow Madison's terminology in this respect; see *Federalist* 9, 71–72.

150 It would be more precise to say that Sherman seems to have adopted a "modified" Wilsonian view, in that he appears (like Madison) to regard indirect election as a valid mechanism of authorization.

151 Elliot, *Debates in the Several States Conventions*, 2:253. Compare Wilson, "Lectures on Law," in *Works of James Wilson*, 1:293.

152 Elliot, *Debates in the Several States Conventions*, 2:254. Hamilton observed that "in Rome, the people were represented by three tribunes."

153 Tucker composed this account in 1784. [Thomas Tudor Tucker], *Conciliatory Hints, Attempting by a Fair State of Matters to Remove Party Prejudice* (Charleston, 1784), 25.

154 *Defence*, 1:7; *WJA*, 6:462.

155 Elliot, *Debates in the Several States Conventions*, 2:257–258.

156 We might say that Hamilton is arguing "internally" here: that is, he is assuming for the sake of argument that "authorization" requires voting. His own view, of course, is that the people can be said to have authorized hereditary

powers as well. As Charles Tillinghast reported from the convention to John Lamb, "You would be surprised did you not know the Man, what an *amazing Republican* Hamilton wishes to make himself be considered. But he is known"; Tillinghast to Lamb, June 21, 1788, John Lamb Papers, New-York Historical Society.

157 *Federalist* 35, 214.

158 Mercy Otis Warren, *Observations on the New Constitution, and on the Federal and State Conventions* (Boston, 1788), in *Pamphlets on the Constitution of the United States*, ed. Paul Leicester Ford (New York, 1968), 7, 15. Compare Grayson's comment in the Virginia ratifying convention: "What, sir, is the present Constitution? A republican government founded on the principles of monarchy, with the three estates. Is it like the model of Tacitus or Montesquieu? Are there checks in it, as in the British monarchy? There is an executive fetter in some parts, and as unlimited in others as a Roman dictator"; Elliot, *Debates in the Several States Conventions*, 3:280.

159 Ford, *Pamphlets on the Constitution of the United States*, 17.

160 Luther Martin, "Mr. Martin's Information to the General Assembly of the States of Maryland," in *The Complete Anti-Federalist*, 2:4:86.

161 "Letter from Montezuma," *Independent Gazetteer* (Philadelphia), Oct. 17, 1787. The author continues by attributing to the president all of the prerogatives of the Crown, as ennumerated by Blackstone.

162 Elliot, *Debates in the Several States Conventions*, 3:56.

163 Ibid., 59.

164 "Tamony," *Virginia Independent Chronicle*, Dec. 20, 1787, repr. *Independent Gazetteer* (Philadelphia).

165 Benjamin Rush, "Address to the People of the United States" (Jan. 1787), in *Principles and Acts of the Revolution in America*, ed. H. Niles (Baltimore, 1822), 402.

166 Ibid. Compare Wilson, "Lectures on Law," in *Works of James Wilson*, 1:292–293.

167 *Records*, 2:36.

168 [James Iredell], "Answers to Mr. Mason's Objections to the New Constitution," in Ford, *Pamphlets on the Constitution of the United States*, 351n. Iredell is specifically discussing the prerogative of clemency in this passage.

169 It is important to note, however, that Iredell occasionally voiced doubts in the mid-1780s as to the wisdom of expanding the prerogatives of the executive; he was more interested at that time in the notion of a judicial check on legislative power. See, for example, Iredell, "To the Public" (1786), in *PJI*, 3:229.

170 Tench Coxe, "An Examination of the Constitution for the United States of America" in Ford, *Pamphlets on the Constitution of the United States*, 135.

171 Ibid., 136.

172 "Ludlow," Letter 2, *Pennsylvania Journal*, May 28, 1777, 1.

173 Adams to Elbridge Gerry, Nov. 4, 1779, in *PJA*, 8:276.

174 Adams to Jefferson, Dec. 6, 1787, in *Adams-Jefferson Letters*, 213. Compare Adams's later claim that "cities have advanced liberty and knowledge by setting

up kings to control nobles. . . . Since the existence of courts, the barons have been humbled and the people liberated from villainage." Adams, annotations to Mary Wollstonecraft, *Historical and Moral View of the Origin and Progress of the French Revolution* (1796), reprinted in Haraszti, *John Adams*, 232–233.

175 *Defence*, 3:299. Compare Delolme, *The Constitution of England*, 210–211.

176 *Defence*, 3:460.

177 *Records*, 1:523. For Wilson's impassioned rejection of hereditary aristocracy, see "Lectures on Law," in *The Works of James Wilson*, esp. 314–315.

178 Elliot, *Debates in the Several States Conventions*, 2:353–354.

179 Ibid., 354. Compare *Federalist 17*, 120–121.

180 Abigail Adams to John Quincy Adams, Mar. 20, 1787, #369, Adams Papers, MHS.

181 See the wise remark on this subject in Frank Prochaska, *The Eagle & the Crown: Americans and the British Monarchy* (New Haven, 2008), 14. See also Ray Raphael, *Mr. President: How and Why the Founders Created a Chief Executive* (New York, 2012), 151; and Josep M. Colomer, "Elected Kings with the Name of Presidents. On the origins of Presidentialism in the United States and Latin America," in *Revista Latinoamericana de Política Comparada* 7 (2013): 79–97.

182 Scholars have tended to take Hamilton's description of the powers of the Crown at face value. See, most recently, Michael P. Federici, *The Political Philosophy of Alexander Hamilton* (Baltimore, 2012), 135. The Royalism of Hamilton's account of the English constitution is rivaled in the eighteenth century only by that on display in Timothy Brecknock, *Droit le Roy. Or a Digest of the Rights and Prerogatives of the Imperial Crown of Great Britain* (London, 1764). Parliament ordered Brecknock's book publicly burnt.

183 *Federalist 67*, 407.

184 Ibid., 407–408.

185 *John Milton*, ed. Stephen Orgel and Jonathan Goldberg (Oxford, 1991), 376.

186 Hamilton also compares both to the governor of New York, with the aim of demonstrating that the president is far more similar to him than to the king.

187 *Federalist 69*, 416.

188 Ibid.

189 Ibid., 421.

190 Ibid., 420–421.

191 I say "relatively" because even here Hamilton's account is significantly exaggerated. As a legal matter, all appointments to office were indeed a matter of the royal prerogative—and eighteenth-century monarchs did retain the discretionary power to create peers and bishops—but in practice, the king was not at liberty to select ministers at pleasure (any minister was required to command the support of the House of Commons). Moreover, it was an accepted norm that he would not dictate appointments to executive departments below the ministerial level. On this, see John Brooke, *George III: A Biography of America's Last Monarch* (New York, 1972), 241; and John Brewer, "Ministerial

Responsibility and the Powers of the Crown," in Brewer, *Party Ideology and Popular Politics at the Accession of George III* (Cambridge, 1976), 112–136.

192 *Federalist* 69, 416.

193 Compare *Federalist* 73, 444.

194 "Centinel," Letter 2, in *Antifederalist*, 2:7:49. On this issue, see the wise remarks in William E. Scheuerman, "American Kingship? Monarchical Origins of Modern Presidentialism," *Polity* 37 (2005): 24–53, esp. 41.

195 *Federalist* 73, 446.

196 "Philadelphiensis" [Benjamin Workman], Letter 12, in *The Complete Anti-Federalist*, 3:9:96–97.

197 *Federalist* 69, 417. Compare "Philadelphiensis," Letter 10, in *The Complete Anti-Federalist*, 3:9:76.

198 See, in general, Jeremy Black, *Parliament and Foreign Policy in the Eighteenth Century* (Cambridge, 2004), 1–12.

199 On this, see Andrew Jackson O'Shaughnessy, "'If Others Will Not be Active, I Must Drive': George III and the American Revolution," *Early American Studies* 2 (2004): 1–46, esp. 33. When forced to accept the principle of American independence in 1782, George went so far as to draft a letter of abdication, lamenting that "one Branch of the legislature" had "totally incapacitated Him" from "conducting the War with effect"; quoted in O'Shaughnessy, *The Men Who Lost America: British Leadership, the American Revolution, and the Fate of the Empire* (New Haven, 2013), 42–43. For a more general account, see Brewer, *Party Ideology and Popular Politics*, 112–136.

200 The Act of Settlement had likewise imposed a requirement of parliamentary consent for any war fought for non-British interests, although this limitation was not invoked during the eighteenth century. See Jeremy Black, *A System of Ambition? British Foreign Policy 1660–1793*, 2nd ed. (Sutton, UK, 2000), 14; and Jack Rakove, "Taking the Prerogative out of the Presidency: An Originalist Perspective," *Presidential Studies Quarterly* 37 (2007): 85–100, esp. 88–91. As his title makes clear, however, Rakove's perspective on the broader question of the "prerogativism" of the Constitution is quite different from mine; see, in particular, his remarks on 89–90.

201 "Cato" [George Mason], Letter 4, in Ford, *Essays on the Constitution of the United States*, 174.

202 *Records*, 3:348.

203 Elliot, *Debates in the Several States Conventions*, 4:214. Iredell, for one, acknowledged this fact; Ford, *Pamphlets on the Constitution of the United States*, 363.

204 "Tamony," *Virginia Independent Chronicle*, Dec. 20, 1787. Madison conceded this point; see *Federalist* 41, 259.

205 *Federalist* 69, 418n.

206 See William Blackstone, *Commentaries on the Laws of England*, 4 vols. (London, 1765–1769), 1:254.

207 *Federalist* 69, 419.

208 Elliot, *Debates in the Several States Conventions*, 3:503–504.

209 Ibid., 359. Roger Sherman likewise conceded that "the king of Great Britain has by the constitution a power to make treaties, yet in matters of great importance he consults the parliament"; Ford, *Essays on the Constitution of the United States*, 155.

210 Elliot, *Debates in the Several States Conventions*, 3:510.

211 See, for example, Patrick Henry's remarks in ibid., 513.

212 *Federalist* 69, 419–420. It is worth noting that even at the level of pure theory, the Crown was required to seek parliamentary approval for any treaty requiring expenditures of money or changes to British law. See Black, *Parliament and Foreign Policy*, 2, 10, 102. This point was raised in the convention; see *Records*, 2:395 (McHenry).

213 Elliot, *Debates in the Several States Conventions*, 4:128. Iredell heaped praise on *The Federalist* in his response to Mason's objections, calling it "a work which I hope will soon be in every body's hands"; Ford, *Pamphlets on the Constitution of the United States*, 363. Hamilton's analysis is similarly repeated in Tench Coxe's "Examination"; see Ford, *Pamphlets on the Constitution of the United States*, 3:301–304.

214 *Federalist* 69, 422.

215 *Federalist* 70, 429.

216 *Summary View*, 22.

217 George III vehemently opposed this bill (drafted by Edmund Burke), which would have nationalized the East India Company. It passed the House of Commons, raising the prospect that the king might be left with the unpalatable choice of either accepting the bill or attempting to revive the defunct royal negative. Instead, when the bill reached the House of Lords, the king let it be known that "whoever voted for the India Bill were not only not his friends, but he should consider as his enemies." The bill was defeated on Dec. 17, 1783. Hamilton is stressing the fact that the king was afraid to wield his negative power. For this episode, see Brooke, *George III*, 250–255.

218 *Federalist* 71, 435. Compare Hamilton's remarks in the New York ratifying convention (Elliott, *Debates in the Several States Conventions*, 2:265).

219 Elliot, *Debates in the Several States Conventions*, 4:39–40.

220 Ibid., 3:16.

221 Ibid., 13.

222 *Blackstone's Commentaries: with Notes of Reference to the Constitution and Laws of the Federal Government of the United States*, ed. St. George Tucker, 5 vols. (Philadelphia, 1803), 1:349. Tucker was particularly worried about the president's power of appointment to offices: "The influence which this power gives him, personally, is one of those parts of the constitution, which assimilates the government, in its administration, infinitely more nearly to that of Great Britain,

than seems to consist with those republican principles, which ought to pervade every part of the federal constitution" (321).

223   To take one important example, although Blackstone agreed that the Crown is empowered to act on behalf of the nation "in foreign concerns," he never supposed that this category embraced "imperial" concerns. It was for this reason that he utterly rejected the patriot Royalist position during the 1760s and 1770s. In the Commons debate over repeal of the Stamp Act on Feb. 3, 1766, Blackstone insisted that "all the Dominions of G[reat].B[ritain]. are bound by Acts of Parl[iamen]t"—not dependent only on the Crown. See *Proceedings and Debates of the British Parliaments Respecting North America,* ed. Leo Francis Stock (Washington, DC, 1924), 2:148. He likewise readily conceded that although the king retained a legal prerogative to raise and equip armies, such forces were in fact now "kept on foot it is true only from year to year, and that by the power of parliament"; Blackstone, *Commentaries,* 1:325. Many other examples could be offered.

224   Blackstone, *Commentaries,* 1:323.

225   Blackstone notes approvingly that "when the fiscal/military state is properly restrained, this adventitious power of the crown will slowly and imperceptibly diminish, as it slowly and imperceptibly rose"; ibid., 326.

226   Ibid., 324–326. Tucker's comments on this section of Blackstone make clear that he regarded this as a profoundly unwelcome development; see Tucker, *Blackstone's Commentaries,* 2:335n, 337.

227   Tucker, *Blackstone's Commentaries,* 2:280n. One important example of such a "transfer" is the fact that the Article IV, Section 3 of Constitution assigns Congress the right to dispose of territories "belonging to the United States," thus detaching from the executive the crucial power of alienation that had undergirded the dominion theory—a development that ought to remind us of how easily theories can become detached from the concerns that initially motivated them. But the issue is also a bit tricky. Patriot Royalists, after all, had never denied Parliament's right to dispose of territories "belonging to Great Britain"; instead, they denied that overseas possessions did in fact belong to Great Britain.

228   Tucker, *Blackstone's Commentaries,* 1:316–317. Tucker may well have drawn this argument from Wilson. The latter had made precisely the same observation in his "Lectures on Law," in *Works of James Wilson,* 1:318–319.

229   In relation to treaties, Tucker points out that while the Crown possesses "plenitude of authority in this respect," Blackstone had laid considerable stress on the fact that "the constitution hath interposed a check by means of parliamentary impeachment, for the punishment of such members as from criminal motives advise or conclude any treaty, which shall afterwards be judged to derogate from the honor and interest of the nation"; Tucker, *Blackstone's Commentaries,* 1:335.

230   Ibid., 319.

231 Ibid., 318–319.

232 Consider Willi Paul Adams's claim that "the presidential system did not develop in America because Americans wanted a substitute for the king. If that is what they had wanted, a more exact copy of the British system with a prime minister, a cabinet responsible to the legislature, and a head of state elected for life would have served them much better"; Adams, *The First American Constitutions: Republican Ideology and the Making of the State Constitutions in the Revolutionary Era* (New York, 2001), 289. But patriot Royalists had never wanted a king-in-parliament of this kind; they had instead desired the sort of independent monarchy Charles I had defended, and it is this that they tried to recreate in 1787.

233 Tucker, *Blackstone's Commentaries*, 1:323.

234 *Records*, 1:96.

Conclusion

1 *Journal of William Maclay: United States Senator from Pennsylvania, 1789–1791* (New York, 1890), 10. Maclay's journal contains the only surviving record of the Senate's first session.

2 Ibid., 11.

3 Ibid., 10, Maclay's italics.

4 Ibid., 12.

5 Ibid.

6 For a wonderful sketch of his character, see Philip Shriver Klein, "Senator William Maclay," *Pennsylvania History* 10 (1943): 83–93.

7 Adams, "The Vice-President's Answer" (May 17, 1789), in *WJA*, 8:493.

8 Adams's argument here possibly reflects his encounter with Delolme. See Jean-Louis Delolme, *The Constitution of England*, 4th ed. (London, 1784), 203–204. Note that Adams defended the converse of this argument as well, viz., that "if power is not in proportion to dignity, dignity is only a snare to prince and people." Adams, annotations to Abbé de Mably, *De la législation* (1791), reprinted in Zoltán Haraszti, *John Adams & the Prophets of Progress* (Cambridge, MA, 1952), 128.

9 On this, see the valuable account in Gordon Wood, *Empire of Liberty: A History of the Early Republic, 1789–1815* (Oxford, 2009), 72–85. See also Wood, *Monarchism and Republicanism in the Early United States* (Melbourne, 2002).

10 *Journal of William Maclay*, 11.

11 Paine, "Common Sense," in *The Essential Thomas Paine*, ed. Sidney Hook (Harmondsworth, UK, 1984), 30.

12 Washington Irving, *The Legend of Sleepy Hollow and Other Stories*, ed. Janet Baine Kopito (New York, 2008), 35.

13 The Parliament Act of 1911 deprived the lords of the power to veto legislation but preserved their ability to delay most bills.

14 For a fascinating, if highly polemical, discussion of this point, see William Godwin, *An Enquiry Concerning Political Justice, and Its Influence on General Virtue and Happiness,* 2 vols. (London, 1793), 2:13–17. The chapter in question is entitled "Of a President with Regal Powers." America, Godwin lamented, was the last "refuge" of monarchy (13). Godwin's account was read out on the floor of the Pennsylvania House during a debate over the president's treaty power. See Speech of Dr. Leib, Pennsylvania Legislature, House of Representatives, Feb. 24, 1796 (repr. in *Aurora General Advertiser* [Feb. 29, 1796]). I am grateful to Adam Lebovitz for calling this source to my attention. Compare Walter Bagehot, *The English Constitution* (London, 1867), 83–84, 262–263, 270, 315–316. Quintin Hogg, Lord Hailsham, reportedly told an American audience in 1963 that "your system of government is an elective monarchy with a king who rules with a splendid court and even—it is rumored on my side of the Atlantic—a royal family [the Kennedys], but does not reign. Ours in Britain is a republic with a hereditary life president, who, being a queen, reigns but does not rule." "Kennedys and Coronets," *Chicago Daily Tribune,* Jan. 29, 1963.

Bibliography

Manuscripts

Harvard College Library
   Bernard Papers

Massachusetts Historical Society
   Adams Papers

New-York Historical Society
   Lamb Papers

Historical Society of Pennsylvania
   Penn Family Papers

Princeton University Library, Department of Rare Books and Special
Collections
   "The Life and Writings of James Wilson." Ed. Burton Alva Konkle. Unpublished MS (1946)

University of Virginia (Charlottesville, VA), Albert and Shirley Small Special
Collections Library
   Lee Family Papers

Periodicals

Aurora General Advertiser

Boston Gazette

Chicago Daily Tribune

Connecticut Courant and Weekly Intelligencer

Connecticut Gazette and the Universal Intelligencer, The

Dunlap's Pennsylvania Packet, or, The General Advertiser

Independent Gazetteer

London Gazette

Massachusetts Spy, The

Monthly Review

New-York Gazette

New-York Journal, or, The General Advertiser, The

Pennsylvania Evening Post

Pennsylvania Gazette, The

Pennsylvania Journal; and the Weekly Advertiser, The

Pennsylvania Ledger, The

Pennsylvania Packet, and Daily Advertiser, The

Providence Gazette

Public Advertiser, The

Scots Magazine

Virginia Independent Chronicle

Primary Sources

Acherley, Roger. *The Britannic Constitution: or, the Fundamental Form of Government in Britain.* London, 1727.

Acts and Ordinances of the Interregnum, 1642–1660. Ed. C. H. Firth and R. S. Rait. 3 vols. London, 1911.

Adams, John. *The Political Writings of John Adams.* Ed. George W. Carey. Washington, DC, 2000.

———. *Papers of John Adams.* Series Three. Ed. Robert J. Taylor, Mary-Jo Kline, and Gregg L. Lint, 15 vols. Cambridge, MA, 1977.

———. *Diary and Autobiography of John Adams.* Ed. L. H. Butterfield. 3 vols. Cambridge, MA, 1961.

———. *The Works of John Adams, Second President of the United States.* Ed. Charles Francis Adams. 10 vols. Boston, 1850–1856.

———. *A Defence of the Constitutions of Government of the United States of America.* 3 vols. London, 1787–1788.

Adams, John, and Mercy Otis Warren. *Correspondence between John Adams and Mercy Otis Warren Relating to Her* History of the American Revolution. Ed. Charles Francis Adams. 1878; repr., New York, 1972.

Adams, John, and Thomas Jefferson. *The Adams-Jefferson Letters.* Ed. Lester J. Cappon. Chapel Hill, 1987.

[Allen, John]. *The American Alarm, or the Bostonian Plea.* Boston, 1773.

American Archives: Fifth Series. Ed. Peter Force. 3 vols. Washington, DC, 1837.

American Archives: Fourth Series. Ed. Peter Force. 6 vols. Washington, DC, 1837.

American Political Writing during the Founding Era. Ed. Charles S. Hyneman and Donald S. Lutz. 2 vols. Indianapolis, 1983.

[Anon.]. *American Resistance Indefensible.* London, 1776.

[Anon.]. *An Answer to a Pamphlet, Entitled Taxation No Tyranny, Addressed to the Author, and to Persons in Power.* London, 1775.

[Anon.]. *Colonising, or A Plain Investigation of That Subject; with a Legislative, Political, and Commercial View of Our Colonies.* London, 1774.

[Anon.]. *The Crisis, Or, a Full Defence of the Colonies.* London, 1766.

[Anon.]. *The Judgment of Whole Kingdoms and Nations, Concerning the Rights, Power, and Prerogative of Kings, and the Rights, Priviledges, and Properties of the People.* London, 1710.

[Anon.]. *A Letter to the Right Honourable the Earl of Hillsborough, on the Present Situation of Affairs in America.* London, 1769.

[Anon.]. *A Letter to the Right Honourable the Earl of Hillsborough, on the Connection between Great Britain and Her American Colonies.* London, 1768.

[Anon.]. *People the Best Governors: or A Plan of Government Founded on the Just Principles of Natural Freedom, The.* N.p., 1776.

[Anon.]. *Reason in Answer to a Pamphlet Entitled, Common Sense.* Dublin, 1776.

[Anon.]. *Reasons Why This Kingdome Ought to Adhere to the Parliament.* [London], 1642.

[Anon.]. *A Soveraigne Salve to Cure the Blind. Or, A Vindication of the Power and Priviledges Claim'd or Executed by the Lords and Commons in Parliament.* London, 1643.

[Anon.]. *A Speech, in Behalf of the Constitution, Against the Suspending and Dispensing Prerogative, &c.* London, 1767.

[Anon.]. *True Merits of a Late Treatise, printed in America, Intitled Common Sense . . . by a Late Member of the Continental Congress, a Native of a Republican State, The.* London, 1776.

Aquinas, Thomas. *Summa Theologiae.* 5 vols. Ed. Institutum Studiorum Mediavalium Ottaviensis. Ottawa, 1941–1945.

Bagehot, Walter. *The English Constitution.* London, 1867.

[Bancroft, Edward]. *Remarks on the Review of the Controversy between Great Britain and Her Colonies.* New London, CT, 1771.

Barker, John. *The British in Boston: Being the Diary of Lieutenant John Barker of the King's Own Regiment from November 15, 1774 to May 31, 1776*. Ed. Elizabeth Ellery Dana. Cambridge, MA, 1924.

Baxter, Richard. *A Holy Commonwealth*. London, 1659.

Benton, Thomas Hart. *Thirty Years' View, Or a History of the Working of the American Government for Thirty Years, from 1820–1850*. 2 vols. New York, 1858.

Bertie, Willoughby, Lord Abingdon. *Thoughts on Mr. Burke's Letter to the Sheriffs of Bristol on the Affairs of America*. Dublin, 1777.

Beza, Theodore. *De iure magistratum* (1574). In *Constitutionalism and Resistance in the Sixteenth Century: Three Treatises by Hotman, Beza, & Mornay*, ed. Julian Franklin. New York, 1969.

Blackstone, Sir William. *Blackstone's Commentaries: With Notes of Reference to the Constitution and Laws of the Federal Government of the United States*. Ed. St. George Tucker. 5 vols. Philadelphia, 1803.

———. *Commentaries on the Laws of England*. 4 vols. London, 1765–1769.

Bland, Richard. *The Colonel Dismounted*. Williamsburg, 1764.

Bodin, Jean. *Les six livres de la république*. Ed. Christiane Frémont, Marie-Dominique Couzinet, and Henri Rochais. 6 vols. Paris, 1986.

Bolingbroke, Henry St. John, Viscount. *Political Writings*. Ed. David Armitage. Cambridge, 1997.

Boothby, Sir Brooke. *Observations on the Appeal from the New to the Old Whigs, and on Mr. Paine's Rights of Man*. London, 1792.

Boswell, James. *Boswell's Life of Johnson*. Ed. George Birkbeck Hill and L. F. Powell. 2nd ed. 6 vols. Oxford, 1964–1971.

[Boucher, Jonathan]. *A Letter from a Virginian*. Boston, 1774.

Bracton, Henry de. *De legibus et consuetudinibus Angliae*. Ed. George E. Woodbine and Samuel E. Thorne. 4 vols. Cambridge, MA, 1968–1977.

Brecknock, Timothy. *Droit le Roy. Or a Digest of the Rights and Prerogatives of the Imperial Crown of Great Britain*. London, 1764.

Briefs of the American Revolution: Constitutional Arguments between Thomas Hutchinson, Governor of Massachusetts Bay, and James Bowdoin for the Council and John Adams for the House of Representatives, The. Ed. John Phillip Reid. New York and London, 1981.

Burgh, James. *Political Disquisitions: Or, An Enquiry into Public Errors, Defects, and Abuses*. 3 vols. London, 1774.

Burke, Edmund. *Pre-Revolutionary Writings.* Ed. Ian Harris. Cambridge, 1993.

———. *The Writings and Speeches of Edmund Burke.* Ed. Paul Langford. 9 vols. Oxford, 1981–2000.

Burlamaqui, Jean-Jacques. *The Principles of Natural and Politic Law.* 2 vols. London, 1763.

[Bushe, Gervase Parker]. *The Case of Great-Britain and America, Addressed to the King and Both Houses of Parliament.* 3rd ed. Dublin, 1769.

Calvin, Jean. *Institutes of the Christian Religion.* Trans. John Allen. 2 vols. Philadelphia, 1955.

Carter, Landon. *The Diary of Colonel Landon Carter of Sabine Hall, 1752–1778.* Ed. Jack P. Greene. 2 vols. Richmond, VA, 1987.

Cartwright, John. *American Independence the Interest and Glory of Great Britain.* London, 1774.

[Chalmers, James]. "Candidus." *Plain Truth; Addressed to the Inhabitants of America.* Philadelphia, 1776.

[Charles I]. *King Charls His Speech Made upon the Scaffold at Whitehall-Gate.* London, 1649.

———. *His Maiesties Ansvver to the XIX Propositions of Both Houses of Parliament.* London, 1642.

Cicero. *De officiis.* Ed. and trans. Walter Miller. Cambridge, MA, 1913.

Colonial Records of North Carolina, The. Ed. William L. Saunders. 10 vols. Raleigh, 1886–1890.

Commons Debates 1621. Ed. Wallace Notestein, Frances Relf, and Hartley Simpson. 7 vols. New Haven, 1935.

Compilation of the Messages and Papers of the Presidents, 1789–1897, A. Ed. James A. Richardson. Washington, DC, 1900.

Complete Anti-Federalist, The. Ed. Herbert J. Storing. 7 vols. Chicago, 1981.

Cook, John. *Monarchy No Creature of Gods Making.* Waterford, Ireland, 1652.

Cooper, Samuel. *A Sermon Preached Before His Excellency John Hancock, Esq. . . . October 25, 1780. Being the Day of the Commencement of the Constitution and Inauguration of the New Government.* Boston, 1780.

Critici sacri, sive, Doctissimorum virorum in ss. Biblia annotationes. London, 1660.

Cun, Peter van der [Cunaeus]. *Petrus Cunaeus of the Commonwealth of the Hebrews.* Trans. Clement Barksdale. London, 1653.

Debates in the Several State Conventions on the Adoption of the Federal Constitution, The. Ed. Jonathan Elliot. 5 vols. Washington, DC, 1836.

Delolme, Jean-Louis. *The Constitution of England.* 4th ed. London, 1784.

———. *The Constitution of England, or An Account of the English Government.* 2nd ed. 2 vols. London, 1778.

———. *The Constitution of England.* London, 1775.

Dickinson, John. *The Writings of John Dickinson.* Ed. Paul Leicester Ford. Philadelphia, 1895.

———. *Essay on the Constitutional Power of Great Britain over the Colonies.* Philadelphia, 1774.

———. *Letters from a Farmer in Pennsylvania to the Inhabitants of the British Colonies.* Boston, 1768.

Digges, Dudley. *The Unlawfulness of Subjects Taking Up Arms.* London, 1643.

Documentary History of the Constitution of the United States of America. 5 vols. Washington, DC, 1894–1905.

Documentary History of the Ratification of the Constitution, The. Ed. John P. Kaminiski and Gaspare Saldino. 16 vols. to date. Madison, 1976–.

Documents of the American Revolution, 1770–1783. Colonial Office Series. Ed. K. G. Davies. 21 vols. Dublin, 1976.

Downer, Silas. *A Discourse, Delivered in Providence . . . at the Dedication of the Tree of Liberty.* Providence, 1768.

Drayton, William. *A Charge, on the Rise of the American Empire.* Charleston, 1776.

———. *A Letter from a Freeman of South-Carolina, to the Deputies of North-America, Assembled in the High Court of Congress at Philadelphia.* Charleston, 1774.

[Dulany, Daniel]. *Considerations on the Propriety of Imposing Taxes in the British Colonies.* Annapolis, 1765.

Echard, Laurence. *History of England from Julius Caesar to 1689.* 3 vols. London, 1707–1718.

Entick, John. *A School Dictionary; or Entick's English Dictionary, Abridged and Adapted to the Use of Schools.* London, 1821.

Erasmus. *Collected Works of Erasmus* Ed. A. H. T. Levi. 86 vols. Toronto, 1986.

Federal and State Constitutions, Colonial Charters, and Other Organic Laws of the States, Territories, and Colonies Now or Heretofore Forming the United States of America, The. Ed. Francis Newton Thorpe. 7 vols. Washington, DC, 1909.

Federalist Papers, The. Ed. Clinton Rossiter. New York, 1961.

Ferne, Henry. *Conscience Satisfied*. London, 1643.

Filmer, Robert. *Filmer: Patriarcha and Other Writings*. Ed. Johann P. Sommerville. Cambridge, 1991.

Ford, Paul Leicester, ed. *Essays on the Constitution of the United* States. New York, 1892.

Foster, Dan. *A Short Essay on Civil Government*. Hartford, 1775.

Franklin, Benjamin. *Franklin:* The Autobiography *and Other Writings on Politics, Economics, and Virtue*. Ed. Alan Houston. Cambridge, 2004.

———. *The Papers of Benjamin Franklin*. Ed. William B. Willcox et al. 39 vols. New Haven, 1977–2008.

———. *Benjamin Franklin's Letters to the Press, 1758–1775*. Ed. Verner W. Crane. Williamsburg, 1950.

———. *The Writings of Benjamin Franklin*. Ed. Albert Henry Smyth. 10 vols. London, 1907.

———. *The Works of Benjamin Franklin*. Ed. Jared Sparks. 10 vols. Boston, 1856.

———. *Cool Thoughts on the Present Situation of Our Public Affairs*. Philadelphia, 1764.

Freneau, Philip. *Poems Written and Published during the American Revolutionary War*. 2 vols. Philadelphia, 1809.

Gaius. *Institutes of Gaius*. Ed. Francis de Zulueta. 2 vols. Oxford, 1953.

[Galloway, Joseph]. *A Candid Examination of the Mutual Claims of Great-Britain, and the Colonies*. New York, 1775.

George III. *The Correspondence of King George the Third*. Ed. Sir John Fortescue. 6 vols. London, 1927.

Godwin, William. *An Enquiry Concerning Political Justice, and Its Influence on General Virtue and Happiness*. 2 vols. London, 1793.

Goodricke, Henry. *Observations on Dr. Price's Theory of Government and Civil Liberty*. York, 1776.

Goodwin, John. *Anti-cavalierisme*. London, 1642.

Gordon, William. *The History of the Rise, Progress, and Establishment, of the Independence of the United States of America*. 4 vols. London, 1788.

[Gray, John]. *Remarks on the New Essay of the Pennsylvania Farmer*. London, 1775.

———. *The Right of the British Legislature to Tax the American Colonies Vindicated*. London, 1774.

Grenville, George. *The Grenville Papers.* Ed. William James Smith. 4 vols. London, 1852–1853.

Grotius, Hugo. *Hugonis Grotii Annotationes in Vetus Testamentum.* Ed. Georg Johann Ludwig Vogel. 2 vols. Halle, 1775.

———. *De iure belli ac pacis libri tres.* Amsterdam, 1626.

Hamilton, Alexander. *The Papers of Alexander Hamilton.* Ed. Harold C. Syrett et al. 27 vols. New York, 1961–1979.

———. *The Works of Alexander Hamilton.* Ed. John C. Hamilton. 7 vols. New York, 1850.

[Hamilton, Alexander]. *The Farmer Refuted: or, A More Impartial and Comprehensive View of the Dispute between Great-Britain and the Colonies.* New York, 1775.

———. *A Full Vindication of the Measures of the Congress.* New York, 1774.

Harrington, James. *The Political Works of James Harrington.* Ed. J. G. A. Pocock. Cambridge, 1977.

[Herle, John]. *An Answer to Doctor Ferne's Reply, Entitled Conscience Satisfied.* London, 1643.

———. *A Fuller Ansvver to a Treatise Written by Doctor Ferne.* London, 1642.

Hicks, William. *The Nature and Extent of Parliamentary Power Considered.* New York, 1768.

[Hicks, William]. *Considerations upon the Rights of the Colonists to the Privileges of British Subjects.* New York, 1766.

Hobbes, Thomas. *Leviathan.* Ed. Noel Malcolm. 3 vols. Oxford, 2013.

Hopkins, Stephen. *The Rights of Colonies Examined.* Providence, 1765.

[Howard, Martin, Jr.]. *A Letter from a Gentleman at Halifax.* Newport, RI, 1765.

Hume, David. *Political Essays.* Ed. Knud Haakonssen. Cambridge, 1994.

———. *The History of England from the Invasion of Julius Caesar to the Revolution in 1688.* Ed. William B. Todd. 6 vols. Indianapolis, 1983.

Huntington, Joseph. *A Discourse, Adapted to the Present Day, on the Health and Happiness, or Misery and Ruin, of the Body Politic, in Similitude to That of the Natural Body.* Hartford, 1781.

Hutchinson, Thomas. "A Dialogue between an American and a European Englishman." In *Perspectives in American History,* ed. Bernard Bailyn and Donald Fleming. Vol. 9, 343–410. Cambridge, MA, 1975.

————. *Strictures upon the Declaration of the Congress at Philadelphia*. London, 1776.

Ingersoll, Jared. "A Selection from the Correspondence and Miscellaneous Papers of Jared Ingersoll." In 9 *Papers of the New Haven Colony Historical Society*, ed. Franklin B. Dexter, 201–472. New Haven, 1918.

[Inglis, Charles] "An American" *The True Interest of America Impartially Stated*. Philadelphia, 1776.

Iredell, James. *The Papers of James Iredell*. Ed. Don Higginbotham. 3 vols. Raleigh, NC, 1976.

————. *Life and Correspondence of James Iredell, One of the Associate Justices of the Supreme Court of the United States*. Ed. Griffith John McRee. 2 vols. New York, 1857–1858.

Irving, Washington. *The Legend of Sleepy Hollow and Other Stories*. Ed. Janet Baine Kopito. New York, 2008.

James I. *The Political Works of James I*. Ed. Charles Howard McIlwain. Cambridge, 1918.

Jay, John. *The Correspondence and Public Papers of John Jay*. Ed. Henry P. Johnston. 3 vols. New York, 1890.

Jefferson, Thomas. *Notes on the State of Virginia*. Ed. Frank Shuffelton. New York and London, 1999.

————. *The Papers of Thomas Jefferson*. Ed. Julian P. Boyd, et al. 40 vols. Princeton, 1950–.

————. *The Works of Thomas Jefferson*. Ed. Paul Leicester Ford. 12 vols. New York, 1904–1905.

————. *Notes on the State of Virginia*. London, 1787.

[Jefferson, Thomas]. *A Summary View of the Rights of British America*. Williamsburg, 1774.

Jenyns, Soame. *The Objections to the Taxation of Our American Colonies . . . Examined*. London, 1765.

Jewish Political Tradition, The. Ed. Michael Walzer and Menachem Lorberbaum. New Haven and London, 2000.

John of Salisbury. *Policraticus*. Ed. and trans. Cary Nederman. Cambridge, 1990.

Johnson, Samuel. *Taxation No Tyranny: An Answer to the Resolutions and Addresses of the American Congress*. London, 1775.

[Jones, John]. *Christus Dei, The Lords Annoynted*. London, 1643.

Josephus. *Jewish Antiquities*. Ed. and trans. H. St. J. Thackeray and Louis H. Feldman. 8 vols. Cambridge, MA, 1930–1965.

———. *The Life. Against Apion.* Ed. and trans. H. St. J. Thackeray. Cambridge, MA, 1926.

Journal of the House of Commons. 85 vols. London, 1802–1830.

Journals of the Continental Congress: 1774–1789. Ed. Worthington Chauncey Ford et al. 34 vols. Washington, DC, 1904–1937.

Journals of the General Assembly and House of Representatives, 1776–1780. Ed. William Edwin Hemphill et al. Columbia, SC, 1970.

Journals of the House of Commons. From November the 8th 1547 . . . to March the 2d 1628 . . . [London, 1742].

Journals of the Provincial Congress, Provincial Convention, Committee of Safety and Council of Safety of the State of New York, 1775–1776–1778. 2 vols. Albany, 1842.

Justinian. *Digest of Justinian.* 4 vols. Ed. Alan Watson. Philadelphia, 1985.

[Knox, William]. *The Controversy between Great Britain and Her Colonies, Reviewed.* London, 1769.

Knox, William. *The Claim of the Colonies to an Exemption from Internal Taxes Imposed by Authority of Parliament.* London, 1765.

Langdon, Samuel. *Government Corrupted by Vice.* Watertown, MA, 1775.

[Leacock, John]. *The Fall of British Tyranny, or, American Liberty Triumphant. The First Campaign. A Tragi-Comedy of Five Acts. . . .* Philadelphia, 1776.

Lee, Arthur. *An Appeal to the Justice and Interests of the People of Great Britain, in the Present Dispute with America.* London, 1774.

———. *Observations on the Review of the Controversy between Great-Britain and her Colonies.* London, 1769.

Lee, Richard Henry. *The Letters of Richard Henry Lee.* Ed. James Curtis Ballagh. 2 vols. New York, 1911.

———. *Memoir of the Life of Richard Henry Lee and His Correspondence.* Ed. Richard H. Lee. 2 vols. Philadelphia, 1825.

"Leedstown Resolutions, The." Ed. John Carter Matthews and Sarah deGraffen-reid Robertson. *Northern Neck of Virginia Historical Magazine* 16 (1966): 1491–1506.

[Leonard, Daniel] "Massachusettensis." *The Origin of the American Contest with Great Britain.* New York, 1775.

Lilburne, John. *Regall tyrannie discovered.* London, 1647.

[Lind, John]. *An Answer to the Declaration of the American Congress.* London, 1776.

———. *An Englishman's Answer, to the Address, from the Delegates, to the People of Great-Britain.* New York, 1775.

———. *Remarks on the Principal Acts of the Thirteenth Parliament of Great Britain.* London, 1775.

Livingston, Philip. *The Other Side of the Question.* New York, 1774.

Locke, John. *Two Treatises of Government.* Ed. Peter Laslett. Rev. ed. Cambridge, 1967.

Lost War: Letters from British Officers during the American Revolution, The. Ed. Marion Balderston and David Syrett. New York, 1975.

Lovell, James. "Oration, Delivered at Boston" (Apr. 2, 1771). In *Principles and Acts of the Revolution in America,* ed. H. Niles. Baltimore, 1822.

Ludlow, Edmund. *The Memoirs of Edmund Ludlow.* Ed. C. H. Firth. 2 vols. Oxford, 1894.

Machiavelli. *Il principe.* Ed. Piero Melograni. Milan, 1998.

———. *Discorsi sopra la prima deca di Tito Livio.* Ed. Giorgio Inglese. Milan, 1984.

Maclay, William. *Journal of William Maclay: United States Senator from Pennsylvania, 1789–1791.* Ed. E. S. Maclay. New York, 1890.

Madison, James. *The Papers of James Madison.* Congressional Series. Ed. William T. Hutchinson and William M. E. Rachal. 17 vols. Chicago and Charlottesville, 1962–1991.

———. *The Writings of James Madison.* Ed. Gaillard Hunt. 9 vols. New York, 1900–1910.

[Madison, James]. *Letters of Helvidius; Written in Reply to Pacificus.* 1793; repr., Philadelphia, 1796.

Markham, William. *A Sermon Preached before the Incorporated Society for the Propagation of the Gospel in Foreign Parts.* London, 1777.

Marx, Karl. *Karl Marx: Selected Writings.* Ed. Lawrence K. Simon. Indianapolis, 1994.

[Mather, Moses]. *America's Appeal to The Impartial World.* Hartford, 1775.

Mayhew, Jonathan. *The Snare Broken.* Boston, 1766.

———. *Observations on the Charter and Conduct of the Society for the Propagation of the Gospel in Foreign Parts.* Boston, 1763.

Midrash debarim rabbah. Ed. S. Lieberman. Jerusalem, 1940.

Midrash rabbah. Ed. Rabbi H. Freedman and Maurice Simon. 10 vols. London, 1939.

Milton, John. *John Milton*. Ed. Stephen Orgel and Jonathan Goldberg. Oxford, 1991.

———. *Complete Prose Works of John Milton*. Ed. Merritt Hughes. 8 vols. New Haven, 1953–82.

———. *Pro populo anglicano defensio*. London, 1651.

Molesworth, Robert. *An Account of Denmark, with Francogalia and Some Considerations for the Promoting of Agriculture and Employing the Poor*. Ed. Justin Champion. Indianapolis, 2011.

Molyneux, William. *The Case of Ireland's Being Bound by Acts of Parliament, Stated*. 1698; repr., Belfast, 1776.

Montesquieu. *The Spirit of the Laws*. Ed. and trans. Anne M. Cohler, Basia Carolyn Miller, and Harold Samuel Stone. Cambridge, 1989.

———. *Oeuvres Complètes*. Ed. Daniel Oster. Paris, 1964.

Moore, Maurice. *The Justice and Policy of Taxing the American Colonies, in Great Britain, Considered*. Wilmington, NC, 1765.

Morris, Gouverneur. *To Secure the True Blessings of Liberty: Selected Writings of Gouverneur Morris*. Ed. J. Jackson Barlow. Indianapolis, 2012.

Murray, John. *Jerubbaal, Or Tyranny's Grove Destroyed, and the Altar of Liberty Finished . . . December 11, 1783, On the Occasion of the Public Thanksgiving for Peace*. Newburyport, 1784.

Nedham, Marchamont. *The Case of the Commonwealth of England, Stated*. Ed. Philip Knachel. Charlottesville, VA, 1969.

———. *Mercurius Politicus* 56 (June 26–July 3, 1651): 885–887.

Nineteen Propositions Made by Both Houses of Parliament to the Kings Maiestie. London, 1642.

North, Oliver. *Some Strictures upon the Sacred Story Recorded in the Book of Esther*. Newburyport, MA, 1775.

Oldmixon, John. *The History of England, During the Reigns of the Royal House of Stuart*. London, 1730.

Overton, Richard. "An Arrow against All Tyrants." In *The English Levellers*, ed. Andrew Sharp. Cambridge, 1988.

———. *An Appeale from the Degenerate Representative Body of the Commons of England*. London, 1647.

Paine, Thomas. *The Essential Thomas Paine*. Ed. Sidney Hook. Harmondsworth, UK, 1984.

————. *The Writings of Thomas Paine*. Ed. Moncure Daniel Conway. 4 vols. New York, 1894.

Pamphlets of the American Revolution, 1750–1776. Vol. 1. Ed. Bernard Bailyn. Cambridge, MA, 1965.

Pamphlets on the Constitution of the United States. Ed. Paul Leicester Ford. New York, 1968.

[Parker, Henry]. *The Contra-Replicant, His Complaint to His Maiestie*. London, 1644.

————. *Ius Populi*. London, 1644.

————. *Observations upon Some of His Majesties Late Answers and Expresses*. London, 1642.

————. *Some Few Observations upon His Majesties Late Answer to the Declaration or Remonstrance of the Lords and Commons of the 19th of May, 1642*. London, 1642.

Parliamentary History of England: From the Earliest Period to the Year 1803, The. Ed. Thomas C. Hansard. 36 vols. London, 1806–1820.

Plato. *The Collected Dialogues of Plato, Including the Letters*. Ed. Edith Hamilton and Huntington Cairns. Princeton, NJ, 1961.

Plutarch. *Lives*. 11 vols. Ed. and trans. Harold North Fowler. Cambridge, MA, 1936.

————. *Plutarch's Lives, in Six Volumes. Translated from the Greek*. Trans. John Dryden. London, 1758.

Popular Sources of Political Authority: Documents on the Massachusetts Constitution of 1780, The. Ed. Oscar and Mary F. Handlin. Cambridge, MA, 1966.

Pownall, Thomas. *The Administration of the Colonies*. 4th ed. London, 1768.

Principles and Acts of the Revolution in America. Ed. H. Niles. Baltimore, 1822.

Proceedings and Debates of the British Parliaments respecting North America. Ed. Leo Francis Stock. 5 vols. Washington, DC, 1924.

Proceedings and Debates of the House of Commons, in 1620 and 1621. Comp. Edward Nicholas. 2 vols. Oxford, 1766.

Proceedings of the Congress at New York. Annapolis, 1766.

Proceedings Relative to Calling the Conventions of 1776 and 1790, The. Harrisburg, 1825.

Prologue to Revolution: Sources and Documents on the Stamp Act Crisis, 1764–1766. Ed. Edmund S. Morgan. Chapel Hill, 1959.

Prynne, William. *A Plea for the Lords*. London, 1648.

————. *The Soveraigne Power of Parliament and Kingdomes*. London, 1643.

Ptolemy of Lucca. *On the Government of Rulers: De Regimine Principum.* Ed. and trans. James M. Blythe. Philadelphia, 1997.

Quincy, Josiah. *Observations on the Act of Parliament Commonly Called the Boston Port-Bill.* Boston, 1774.

[Ramsay, Allan]. *Thoughts on the Origin and Nature of Government, Occasioned by the Late Disputes between Great Britain and Her American Colonies: Written in the Year 1766.* London, 1769.

Ramsay, David. *The History of the American Revolution.* 2 vols. Philadelphia, 1789.

———. *History of the Revolution of South Carolina, from a British Province to an Independent State.* 2 vols. Trenton, 1785.

Records of the Federal Convention of 1787, The. Ed. Max Farrand. 3 vols. New Haven, 1911.

[Robinson-Morris, Matthew, Lord Rokeby]. *Considerations on the Measures Carrying on with Respect to the British Colonies in North America.* London, 1774.

Rush, Benjamin. *Letters of Benjamin Rush.* Ed. L. H. Butterfield. 2 vols. Princeton, 1951.

———, et al. *Old Family Letters: Copied from the Originals for Alexander Biddle.* 2 vols. Philadelphia, 1892.

———. *Observations upon the Present Government of Pennsylvania.* Philadelphia, 1777.

Sallust. *Sallust.* Ed. and trans. J. C. Rolfe, Cambridge, MA, 1921.

Saumaise, Claude de [Salmasius]. *C. L. Salmasii Defensio pro Carolo I.* Cambridge, 1684.

[Seabury, Samuel]. *A View of the Controversy between Great Britain and Her Colonies.* New York, 1774.

Selden, John. *De synedriis & praefecturis iuridicis veterum Ebraeorum.* Vol. 1. London, 1650.

Shakespeare, William. *The Norton Shakespeare: Based on the Oxford Edition,* ed. Stephen Greenblatt, et al. New York, 1997.

Sherwood, Samuel. *The Church's Flight into the Wilderness.* New York, 1776.

Sidney, Algernon. *Court Maxims.* Ed. Hans Blom et al. Cambridge, 1996.

———. *Discourses Concerning Government.* Ed. Thomas G. West. Indianapolis, 1996.

Sieyès, Emmanuel Joseph. *Sieyès: Political Writings, including the Debate between Sieyès and Tom Paine in 1791.* Ed. Michael Sonenscher. Indianapolis, 2003.

Soncino Hebrew-English Edition of the Babylonian Talmud. Ed. Jacob Shachter. London, 1994.

[Spelman, Sir John]. *A View of a Printed Book Intituled Observations upon His Majesties Late Answers and Expresses.* London, 1643.

Strahan, William, and David Hall. "Correspondence between William Strahan and David Hall, 1763–1777." *Pennsylvania Magazine of History and Biography* 10 (1886): 86–99.

Supplement to Max Farrand's Records of the Federal Convention of 1787. Ed. James H. Hutson. New Haven, 1987.

Tacitus. *Annals.* 3 vols. Ed. and trans. John Jackson. Cambridge, MA, 1931–1937.

———. *Histories.* 2 vols. Ed. and trans. C. H. Moore. Cambridge, MA, 1925–1931.

Taylor, John. *An Inquiry into the Principles and Policy of the Government of the United States.* Fredericksburg, VA, 1814.

Trenchard, John, and Thomas Gordon. *Cato's Letters, or Essays on Liberty, Civil, and Religious, and Other Important Subjects.* Ed. Ronald Hamowy. 2 vols. Indianapolis, 1995.

Tucker, Josiah. *A Letter from a Merchant in London to His Nephew in North America.* London, 1766.

[Tucker, Thomas Tudor]. *Conciliatory Hints, Attempting by a Fair State of Matters to Remove Party Prejudice.* Charleston, 1784.

Turgot, Anne-Robert-Jacques. *Oeuvres de Turgot et Documents le concernant.* Ed. Gustave Schele. 5 vols. Paris, 1913–1923.

Turner, Baptist Noel. *The True Alarm.* London, 1783.

Vattel, Emer de. *Le Droit des gens.* Amsterdam, 1775.

Warren, Mercy Otis. *History of the Rise, Progress, and Termination of the American Revolution.* 3 vols. Boston, 1805.

———. *Observations on the New Constitution, and on the Federal and State Conventions.* Boston, 1788. In *Pamphlets on the Constitution of the United States,* ed. Paul Leicester Ford. New York, 1968.

Washington, George. *The Papers of George Washington.* Revolutionary War Series. Ed. W. W. Abbot and Dorothy Twohig. 20 vols. Charlottesville and London, 1985–.

[Wells, Richard]. *A Few Political Reflections Submitted to the Consideration of the British Colonies, by a Citizen of Philadelphia.* Philadelphia, 1774.

West, Samuel. *A Sermon Preached Before the Honorable Council, and the Honourable House of Representatives, of the Colony of Massachusetts Bay, in New-England, May 29th, 1776.* Boston, 1776.

[Whately, Thomas]. *The Regulations Lately Made Concerning the Colonies and the Taxes Imposed upon Them, Considered.* London, 1765.

Whitney, Peter. *American Independence Vindicated.* Boston, 1777.

———. *The Transgression of a Land Punished by a Multitude of Rulers.* Boston, 1774.

Williams, Samuel. *A Discourse on the Love of Our Country; Delivered on a Day of Thanksgiving, December 15, 1774.* Salem, 1775.

Wilson, James. *The Works of James Wilson.* Ed. Robert Green McCloskey. 2 vols. Cambridge, MA, 1967.

———. *The Works of the Honourable James Wilson, L.L.D.* Ed. Bird Wilson. 3 vols. Philadelphia, 1804.

———. *Considerations on the Nature and the Extent of the Legislative Authority of the British Parliament.* Philadelphia, 1774.

Yorke, Henry. *These Are the Times That Try Men's Souls! A Letter to John Frost.* London, 1793.

[Zubly, Joachim]. *An Humble Inquiry into the Nature of the Dependency of the American Colonies.* [Charleston], 1769.

Secondary Sources

Adams, Randolph Greenfield. *Political Ideas of the American Revolution: Britannic-American Contributions to the Problem of Imperial Organization, 1765–1775.* Durham, 1922.

Adams, Willi Paul. *The First American Constitutions: Republican Ideology and the Making of the State Constitutions in the Revolutionary Era.* New York, 2001.

———. "Republicanism in Political Rhetoric before 1776." *Political Science Quarterly* 85 (1970): 397–421.

Aldridge, A. Owen. *Thomas Paine's American Ideology.* Newark and London, 1984.

Andrews, Charles M. "The Royal Disallowance." *Proceedings of the American Antiquarian Society* 24 (1914): 342–362.

Appleby, Joyce. "The New Republican Synthesis and the Changing Political Thought of John Adams." *American Quarterly* 25 (1973): 578–595.

Armitage, David. *Foundations of Modern International Thought.* Cambridge, 2013.

———. *The Declaration of Independence: A Global History.* Cambridge, MA, 2007.

———. "A Patriot for Whom? The Afterlives of Bolingbroke's Patriot King." *Journal of British Studies* 36 (1997): 397–418.

Ashcraft, Richard, and M. M. Goldsmith. "Locke, Revolution Principles and the Formation of Whig Ideology." *The Historical Journal* 26 (1983): 773–800.

Bailyn, Bernard. *The Ideological Origins of the American Revolution.* Rev. ed. Cambridge, MA, 1992.

———. *The Ordeal of Thomas Hutchinson.* Cambridge, MA, 1976.

———. "The Most Uncommon Pamphlet of the Revolution: *Common Sense.*" *Magazine of History* 25 (1973: 36–41).

———. *The Origins of American Politics.* New York, 1965.

Ball, Terence, and J. G. A. Pocock, eds. *Conceptual Change and the Constitution.* Lawrence, KS, 1988.

Banning, Lance. "Republican Ideology and the Triumph of the Constitution, 1783–1793." *William and Mary Quarterly* 31 (1974): 167–188.

Barker, Ernest. "Natural Law and the American Revolution." In *Traditions of Civility: Eight Essays,* 263–355. Cambridge, 1948.

Beard, Charles. *Economic Interpretation of the Constitution.* New York, 1913.

Becker, Carl. *The Declaration of Independence: A Study in the History of Political Ideas.* New York, 1922.

Bennett, W. H. "Early American Theories of Federalism." *The Journal of Politics* 4 (1942): 383–395.

Berkowitz, David. *John Selden's Formative Years: Politics and Society in Early Seventeenth-Century England.* Washington, DC, 1988.

Bilder, Mary Sarah. *Madison's Hand: Revising the Constitutional Convention.* Cambridge, MA, forthcoming.

———. "How Bad Were the Official Records of the Federal Convention?" *The George Washington Law Review* 80 (2012): 1620–1682.

———. *The Transatlantic Constitution: Colonial Legal Culture and the Empire.* Cambridge, MA, 2008.

Black, Barbara A. "The Constitution of Empire: The Case for the Colonists." *University of Pennsylvania Law Review* 124 (1976): 1157–1211.

Black, Frederick C. "The American Revolution as 'Yardstick' in the Debates on the Constitution, 1787–1788." *Proceedings of the American Philosophical Society* 117 (1973): 162–185.

Black, Jeremy. *Parliament and Foreign Policy in the Eighteenth Century.* Cambridge, 2004.

————. *A System of Ambition? British Foreign Policy 1660–1793.* 2nd ed. Sutton, UK, 2000.

Blidstein, Gerald. "The Monarchic Imperative in Rabbinic Perspective." *Association for Jewish Studies Review* 7–8 (1982–3): 15–39.

Bliss, R. M. *Revolution and Empire: English Politics and the American Colonies in the Seventeenth Century.* Manchester, 1990.

Bouton, Terry. *Taming Democracy: "The People," the Founders, and the Troubled Ending of the American Revolution.* Oxford, 2007.

Bowers, Paul Chadwick. "Richard Henry Lee and the Continental Congress: 1774–1779. PhD diss, Duke University, 1965.

Breen, T. H. "Ideology and Nationalism on the Eve of the American Revolution: Revisions *Once More* in Need of Revising." *Journal of American History* 84 (1997): 13–39.

————. "John Adams' Fight against Innovation in the New England Constitution: 1776." *New England Quarterly* 40 (1967): 501–520.

Brewer, John. *Party Ideology and Popular Politics at the Accession of George III.* Cambridge, 1976.

Brooke, John. *George III: A Biography of America's Last Monarch.* New York, 1972.

Burgess, Glenn. *Absolute Monarchy and the Stuart Constitution.* New Haven, 1996.

Bushman, Richard. *King and People in Provincial Massachusetts.* Chapel Hill, 1985.

Butterfield, Herbert. *George III and the Historians.* London, 1957.

Calvert, Jane. *Quaker Constitutionalism and the Political Thought of John Dickinson.* Cambridge, 2009.

Carey, George W. "James Wilson's Political Thought and the Constitutional Convention." *Political Science Reviewer* 17 (1987): 49–107.

Carson, Hampton L. "James Wilson and James Iredell. A Parallel and a Contrast." *Pennsylvania Magazine of History and Biography* 45 (1921): 1–33.

Chernow, Ron. *Alexander Hamilton.* New York, 2004.

Chitwood, Oliver Perry. *Richard Henry Lee: Statesman of the Revolution.* Morgantown, WV, 1967.

Clark, J. C. D. *The Language of Liberty, 1660–1832: Political Discourse and Social Dynamics in the Anglo-American World.* Cambridge, 1994.

Cohen, G. A. *Karl Marx's Theory of History: A Defence.* Oxford, 1978.

Colbourn, Trevor. *The Lamp of Experience: Whig History and the Intellectual Origins of the American Revolution.* 3rd ed. Indianapolis, 1998.

———. "Thomas Jefferson's Use of the Past." *William and Mary Quarterly* 15 (1958): 56–70.

Colomer, Josep M. "Elected Kings with the Name of Presidents. On the Origins of Presidentialism in the United States and Latin America." *Revista Latinoamericana de Política Comparada* 7 (2013): 79–97.

Compton, John, and Karen Orren. "Political Theory in Institutional Contex: The Case of Patriot Royalism." *American Political Thought* 3 (2014): 1–31.

Condren, Conal. *Argument and Authority in Early Modern England: The Presupposition of Oaths and Offices.* Cambridge, 2006.

Conrad, Stephen A. "James Wilson's Assimilation of the Common-Law Mind." *Northwestern University Law Review* 84 (1989): 186–219.

Dalberg, John Emerich, Lord Acton. "Inaugural Lecture on the Study of History." In *Lectures on Modern History,* ed. J. N. Figgis and R. V. Laurence, 1–30. London, 1906.

De Grazia, Alfred. *Public and Republic: Political Representation in America.* New York, 1951.

Dennison, George M. "The 'Revolution Principle': Ideology and Constitutionalism in the Thought of James Wilson." *Review of Politics* 157 (1977): 157–191.

DiClerico, Robert E. "James Wilson's Presidency." *Presidential Studies Quarterly* 17 (1987): 301–317.

Donoghue, John. *Fire Under the Ashes: An Atlantic History of the English Revolution.* Chicago, 2013.

Dunbar, Louise Burnham. *A Study of "Monarchical" Tendencies in the United States: From 1776 to 1801.* 1920; repr., Urbana, 1923.

Dunn, John. *The Political Thought of John Locke: An Historical Account of the Argument of the 'Two Treatises of Government'.* Cambridge, 1969.

———. "The Politics of Locke in England and America in the Eighteenth-Century." In *John Locke: Problems and Perspectives, A Collection of New Essays,* ed. John W. Yolton. Cambridge, 1969.

Edling, Max. *A Revolution in Favor of Government: Origins of the U.S. Constitution and the Making of the American State.* Oxford, 2003.

Egnal, Marc, and Joseph A. Ernst. "An Economic Interpretation of the American Revolution." *William and Mary Quarterly* 29 (1972): 3–32.

Eustace, Nichole. *Passion is the Gale: Emotion, Power, and the Coming of the American Revolution.* Chapel Hill, 2008.

Ewald, William. "James Wilson and the Drafting of the Constitution." *The University of Pennsylvania Journal of Constitutional Law* 10 (2008): 901–1009.

Fatovic, Clement. *Outside the Law: Emergency and Executive Power.* Baltimore, 2009.

Federici, Michael P. *The Political Philosophy of Alexander Hamilton.* Baltimore, 2012.

Fiala, Robert Dennis. "George III in the Pennsylvania Press: A Study in Changing Opinions, 1760–1776." PhD diss., Wayne State University, 1967.

Flaherty, Martin S. "More Apparent than Real: The Revolutionary Commitment to Constitutional Federalism." *Kansas Law Review* 45 (1996–1997): 993–1014.

Foner, Eric. *Tom Paine and Revolutionary America.* New York, 1976.

Fowler, Milton E. *John Dickinson: Conservative Revolutionary.* Charlottesville, VA, 1983.

Freeman, Joanne B. "Poison, Whispers, and Fame: Jefferson's 'Anas' and Political Gossip in the Early Republic." *Journal of the Early Republic* 15 (1995): 25–57.

Fruchtman Jr., Jack. *The Political Philosophy of Thomas Paine.* Baltimore, 2009.

———. *Thomas Paine: Apostle of Freedom.* New York, 1994.

———. *Thomas Paine and the Religion of Nature.* Baltimore, 1993.

Gibbs, C. G. "Laying Treaties before Parliament in the Eighteenth Century." In *Studies in Diplomatic History: Essays in Memory of David Bayne Horn,* ed. R. M. Hatton and M. S. Anderson, 116–137. Harlow, UK, 1970.

Gimbel, Richard. *Thomas Paine: A Bibliographical Check List of Common Sense with an Account of Its Publication.* New Haven, 1956.

Goldie, Mark. "The English System of Liberty." In *The Cambridge History of Eighteenth-Century Political Thought,* ed. Mark Goldie and Robert Wokler, 40–78. Cambridge, 2006.

———. "Introduction." In *The Reception of Locke's Politics,* ed. Mark Goldie, vol. 1, xlix–lix. London, 1999.

Greene, Jack P. *The Constitutional Origins of the American Revolution.* Cambridge, 2010.

———. *Peripheries and Center: Constitutional Development in the Extended Politics of the British Empire and the United States, 1607–1788.* Athens, GA, 1986.

Guttridge, G. H. *English Whiggism and the American Revolution.* Berkeley, 1966.

Haggard, Robert. "The Nicola Affair: Lewis Nicola, George Washington, and American Military Discontent during the Revolutionary War." *Proceedings of the American Philosophical Society* 146 (2002): 139–169.

Hankins, James. "Exclusivist Republicanism and the Non-Monarchical Republic." *Political Theory* 38 (2010): 452–482.

Haraszti, Zoltán. *John Adams & the Prophets of Progress.* Cambridge, MA, 1952.

Hartz, Louis. *The Liberal Tradition in America: An Interpretation of American Political Thought since the Revolution.* New York, 1955.

Hobson, Charles F. "The Negative on State Laws: James Madison, the Constitution, and the Crisis of Republican Government." *William and Mary Quarterly* 36 (1979): 215–235.

Howe, John R. *The Changing Political Thought of John Adams.* Princeton, 1966.

Hulsebosch, Daniel J. "The Plural Prerogative." *William and Mary Quarterly* 68 (2011): 583–587.

———. *Constituting Empire: New York and the Transformation of Constitutionalism in the Atlantic World, 1664–1830.* Chapel Hill, 2005.

———. "*Imperia in Imperio*: The Multiple Constitutions of Empire in New York, 1750–1777." *Law and History Review* 16 (1998): 319–379.

Hutson, James H. "The Creation of the Constitution: The Integrity of the Documentary Record." *Texas Law Review* 65 (1986): 1–39.

Jacobson, David L. *John Dickinson and the Revolution in Pennsylvania, 1764–1776.* Berkeley, 1965.

———. "John Dickinson's Fight against Royal Government, 1764." *William and Mary Quarterly* 19 (1962): 64–85.

Jensen, Merrill. *The Articles of Confederation: An Interpretation of the Social-Constitutional History of the American Revolution, 1774–1781.* 1940; repr., Madison, 1976.

———. *The New Nation: A History of the United States during the Confederation 1781–1789.* New York, 1950.

Jezierski, John V. "Parliament or People: James Wilson and Blackstone on the Nature and Location of Sovereignty." *Journal of the History of Ideas* 32 (1971): 95–106.

Johnson, Richard R. "'Parliamentary Egotisms': The Clash of the Legislatures in the Making of the American Revolution." *Journal of American History* 74 (1987): 338–362.

Jordan, Winthrop D. "Familial Politics: Thomas Paine and the Killing of the King, 1776." *Journal of American History* 60 (1973): 294–208.

Judson, Margaret Atwood. "Henry Parker and the Theory of Parliamentary Sovereignty." In *Essays in History and Political Theory: In Honor of Charles Howard McIlwain*, ed. Carl Wittke, 138–167. Cambridge, MA, 1936.

Juricek, John T. "English Claims in North America to 1660: A Study in Legal and Constitutional History." PhD diss., University of Chicago, 1970.

Kammen, Michael. "The Meaning of Colonization in American Revolutionary Thought." *Journal of the History of Ideas* 31 (1970): 337–358.

Klein, Philip Shriver. "Senator William Maclay." *Pennsylvania History* 10 (1943): 83–93.

Kruman, Marc W. *Between Authority and Liberty: State Constitution Making in Revolutionary America*. Chapel Hill, 1997.

LaCroix, Alison. *The Ideological Origins of American Federalism*. Cambridge, MA, 2010.

Lambert, Paul F. "Benjamin Rush and American Independence." *Pennsylvania History* 39 (1972): 443–454.

Langford, Paul. "New Whigs, Old Tories, and the American Revolution." *Journal of Imperial and Commonwealth History* 8 (1980): 106–130.

Larkin, Edward. *Thomas Paine and the Literature of Revolution*. Cambridge, 2005.

Lawson, Philip. *The Imperial Challenge: Quebec and Britain in the Age of the American Revolution*. Montreal and Kingston, 1989.

Lee, Christopher F. "The Transformation of the Executive in Post-Revolutionary South Carolina." *The South Carolina Historical Magazine* 93 (1992): 85–100.

Lefer, David. *The Founding Conservatives: How a Group of Unsung Heroes Saved the American Revolution*. New York, 2013.

Lewis, Anthony M. "Jefferson's Summary View as a Chart of Political Union." *William and Mary Quarterly* 5 (1948): 34–51.

Liddle, William D. "'A Patriot King, or None': Lord Bolingbroke and the American Renunciation of George III." *Journal of American History* 65 (1979): 951–970.

———. "A Patriot King, or None: American Public Attitudes towards George III and the British Monarchy, 1754–1776." PhD diss., Claremont Graduate School, 1970.

Loughran, Trish. *The Republic in Print: Print Culture in the Age of U.S. Nation Building, 1770–1870*. New York, 2007.

———. "Disseminating Common Sense: Thomas Paine and the Problem of the Early National Bestseller." *American Literature* 78 (2006): 1–28.

Lutz, Donald S. *The Origins of American Constitutionalism*. Baton Rouge, 1988.

Lynd, Staughton, and David Waldstreicher. "Free Trade, Sovereignty, and Slavery: Toward an Economic Interpretation of American Independence." *William and Mary Quarterly* 68 (2011): 597–630.

Maier, Pauline. "Whigs against Whigs against Whigs: The Imperial Debates of 1765–1776 Reconsidered." *William and Mary Quarterly* 68 (2011): 578–582.

———. *Ratification: The People Debate the Constitution, 1787–1788*. New York, 2010.

———. *American Scripture: Making the Declaration of Independence*. New York, 1998.

———. *From Resistance to Revolution: Colonial Radicals and the Development of American Opposition to Britain, 1775–1776*. New York and London, 1972.

———. "John Wilkes and American Disillusionment with Britain." *William and Mary Quarterly* 20 (1963): 373–395.

Mansfield, Harvey C. *Taming the Prince: The Ambivalence of Modern Executive Power*. New York, 1989.

Marston, Jerrilyn Greene. *King and Congress: The Transfer of Political Legitimacy, 1774–1776*. Princeton, 1987.

Matthews, Marty D. *Forgotten Founder: The Life and Times of Charles Pinckney*. Columbia, SC, 2004.

McCarthy, Daniel J. "James Wilson and the Creation of the Presidency." *Presidential Studies Quarterly* 17 (1987): 689–696.

McConville, Brendan. *The King's Three Faces: The Rise and Fall of Royal America, 1688–1776*. Chapel Hill, 2006.

McDaniel, Iain. "Jean-Louis Delolme and the Political Science of the English Empire." *The Historical Journal* 55 (2012): 21–44.

McDonald, Forrest. *The American Presidency: An Intellectual History*. Lawrence, KS, 1994.

———. *Novus Ordo Seclorum: The Intellectual Origins of the Constitution*. Lawrence, KS, 1985.

McIlwain, Charles Howard. *The American Revolution: A Constitutional Interpretation*. New York, 1923.

———. *The High Court of Parliament and Its Supremacy: An Historical Essay on the Boundaries between Legislation and Adjudication in England*. New Haven, 1910.

Mendle, Michael. *Dangerous Positions: Mixed Government, the Estates of the Realm, and the Making of the Answer to the XIX Propositions*. Tuscaloosa, 1985.

Mitchell, Broadus. *Alexander Hamilton: The Revolutionary War Years*. New York, 1970.

Morgan, Edmund S. *Inventing the People: The Rise of Popular Sovereignty in England and America*. New York, 1988.

———. "Colonial Ideas of Parliamentary Power." *William and Mary Quarterly* 5 (1948): 311–341.

Morgan, Edmund S., and Helen M. Morgan. *The Stamp Act Crisis: Prologue to Revolution*. Chapel Hill, 1953.

Nadelhaft, Jerome J. *The Disorders of War: The Revolution in South Carolina*. Orono, ME, 1981.

Namier, Sir Lewis. *The Structure of Politics at the Accession of George III*. 2nd ed. London, 1957.

———. *Personalities and Powers*. London, 1955.

———. *England in the Age of the American Revolution*. London, 1930.

Nangle, Benjamin Christie. *The Monthly Review, First Series, 1749–1789; Indexes of Contributors and Articles*. Oxford, 1934.

Nelson, Eric. "Hebraism and the Republican Turn of 1776: A Contemporary Account of the Debate over *Common Sense*." *William and Mary Quarterly* 70 (2013): 781–812.

———. "Patriot Royalism: The Stuart Monarchy in American Political Thought, 1769–75." *William and Mary Quarterly* 68 (2011): 533–577.

———. "Taking Them Seriously: Patriots, Prerogative, and the English Seventeenth Century." *William and Mary Quarterly* 68 (2011): 588–596.

———. *The Hebrew Republic: Jewish Sources and the Transformation of European Political Thought*. Cambridge, MA, 2010.

———. " 'Talmudical Commonwealthsmen' and the Rise of Republican Exclusivism." *The Historical Journal* 50 (2007): 809–835.

———. *The Greek Tradition in Republican Thought*. Cambridge, 2004.

O'Shaughnessy, Andrew Jackson. *The Men Who Lost America: British Leadership, the American Revolution, and the Fate of the Empire*. New Haven, 2013.

———. " 'If Others Will Not be Active, I Must Drive': George III and the American Revolution." *Early American Studies* 2 (2004): 1–46.

Ohmori, Yuhtaro. "The Artillery of Mr. Locke: The Use of Locke's *Second Treatise* in Pre-Revolutionary America." PhD diss., Johns Hopkins University, 1988.

Olson, Alison Gilbert. *Making the Empire Work: London and American Interest Groups, 1690–1790*. Cambridge, MA, 1992.

Onuf, Peter S. *Jefferson's Empire: The Language of American Nationhood*. Charlottesville, VA, 2000.

Palmer, R. R. *The Age of the Democratic Revolution: A Political History of Europe and America, 1760–1800: The Challenge*. Princeton, 1959.

Panagopoulos, E. P. "Hamilton's Notes in His Pay Book of the New York State Artillery Company." *American Historical Review* 62 (1957): 310–325.

Pederson, Nicholas. "The Lost Founder: James Wilson in American Memory." *Yale Journal of Law and Humanities* 22 (2010): 257–337.

Perl-Rosenthal, Nathan. " 'The Divine Right of Republics': Hebraic Republicanism and the Legitimization of Kingless Government in America." *William and Mary Quarterly* 66 (2009): 535–564.

Peterson, Mark. *The City-State of Boston: The Rise and Fall of an Atlantic World, 1630–1865*. New Haven, forthcoming.

Pettit, Philip. *Republicanism: A Theory of Freedom and Government*. Oxford, 1997.

Phelps, Glenn A. *George Washington and American Constitutionalism*. Lawrence, KS, 1993.

Pichetto, Maria Teresa. "La 'respublica Hebraeorum' nella rivoluzione Americana." *Il pensiero politico* 35 (2002): 481–500.

Pitkin, Hanna, *The Concept of Representation*. Berkeley, 1964.

Pocock, J. G. A. "Hume and the American Revolution: The dying thoughts of a North Briton." In *Virtue, Commerce, and History: Essays on Political Thought and History, Chiefly in the Eighteenth Century*, 125–141. Cambridge, 1985.

———. "1776: The Revolution against Parliament." In *Three British Revolutions: 1641, 1688, 1776*, ed. J. G. A. Pocock. Princeton, 1980.

———. *The Machiavellian Moment: Florentine Political Thought and the Atlantic Republican Tradition*. Princeton, 1975.

———. *The Ancient Constitution and the Feudal Law: A Study of English Historical Thought in the Seventeenth Century*. Cambridge, 1957.

Pole, J. R. *Political Representation in England & the Origins of the American Republic*. Berkeley, 1966.

Prochaska, Frank. *The Eagle & the Crown: Americans and the British Monarchy*. New Haven, 2008.

Rabb, Theodore K. *Jacobean Gentleman: Sir Edwin Sandys, 1561–1629.* Princeton, 1998.

Rahe, Paul. *Republics Ancient and Modern.* 3 vols. Chapel Hill, 1994.

Rakove, Jack. "Got Nexus?" *William and Mary Quarterly* 68 (2011): 635–638.

———. "Taking the Prerogative out of the Presidency: An Originalist Perspective." *Presidential Studies Quarterly* 37 (2007): 85–100.

———. *Original Meanings: Politics and Ideas in the Making of the Constitution.* New York, 1996.

———. *The Beginnings of National Politics: An Interpretive History of the Continental Congress.* New York, 1979.

Rakove, Jack, and Susan Zlomke. "James Madison and the Independent Executive." *Presidential Studies Quarterly* 17 (1987): 293–300.

Raphael, Ray. *Mr. President: How and Why the Founders Created a Chief Executive.* New York, 2012.

Reid, John Philip. *Constitutional History of the American Revolution.* Abridged ed. Madison, 1995.

———. *Constitutional History of the American Revolution: The Authority of Law.* Madison, 1993.

———. *Constitutional History of the American Revolution: The Authority to Legislate.* Madison, 1991.

———. *The Concept of Representation in the Age of the American Revolution.* Chicago, 1989.

Robbins, Caroline. *The Eighteenth-Century Commonwealthmen: Studies in the Transmission, Development, and Circumstance of English Liberal Thought from the Restoration of Charles II until the War with the Thirteen Colonies.* Cambridge, MA, 1959.

Robertson, David Brian. "Madison's Opponents and Constitutional Design." *American Political Science Review* 99 (2005): 225–243.

Robinson, Donald L. "The Inventors of the Presidency." *Presidential Studies Quarterly* 13 (1983): 8–25.

Rodgers, Daniel T. "Republicanism: The Career of a Concept." *Journal of American History* 79 (1992): 11–38.

Roper, L. H. *The English Empire in America, 1602–1658: Beyond Jamestown.* London, 2009.

Rose, Emily. "The Reluctant Imperialist: King James I and the Surrender of Virginia." Working Paper No. 07–02. International Seminar on the History of the Atlantic World, 1500–1825, 2007.

Rosenblatt, Jason. *Renaissance England's Chief Rabbi: John Selden.* Oxford, 2006.

Russell, Conrad. *Parliaments and English Politics, 1621–1629.* Oxford, 1979.

Ryerson, Richard Alan. "'Like a Hare before the Hunters': John Adams and the Idea of Republican Monarchy." *Proceedings of the Massachusetts Historical Society,* 3rd series, 107 (1995): 16–29.

Schaeper, Thomas J. *Edward Bancroft: Scientist, Author, Spy.* New Haven, 2011.

Scheuerman, William E. "American Kingship? Monarchical Origins of Modern Presidentialism." *Polity* 37 (2005): 24–53.

Schutz, John A. *Thomas Pownall, British Defender of American Liberty: A Study of Anglo-American Relations in the Eighteenth Century.* Glendale, CA, 1951.

Schuyler, Robert. *Parliament and the British Empire.* New York, 1929.

Seed, Geoffrey. *James Wilson.* New York, 1978.

Shackleton, Robert. "Montesquieu, Bolingbroke, and the Separation of Powers." *French Studies* 3 (1949): 25–38.

Shalev, Eran. *American Zion: The Old Testament as a Political Text from the Revolution to the Civil War.* New Haven, 2013.

———. "'A Republic amidst the Stars': Political Astronomy and the Intellectual Origins of the Stars and Stripes." *Journal of the Early Republic* 31 (2011): 39–73.

———. "'A Perfect Republic': The Mosaic Constitution in Revolutionary New England, 1775–1788." *The New England Quarterly* 82 (2009): 235–263.

Sharpe, Kevin. *The Personal Rule of Charles I.* New Haven, 1992.

Sheldon, Garrett Ward. *The Political Philosophy of Thomas Jefferson.* Baltimore, 1991.

Skinner, Quentin. "On Trusting the Judgment of Our Rulers." In *Political Judgment: Essays for John Dunn,* ed. Richard Bourke and Raymond Geuss, 113–130. Cambridge, 2009.

———. "Hobbes on Representation." *European Journal of Philosophy* 13 (2005): 155–184.

———. *Visions of Politics.* 3 vols. Cambridge, 2002.

———. *Liberty before Liberalism.* Cambridge, 1997.

———. *The Foundations of Modern Political Thought.* 2 vols. Cambridge, 1978.

———. "The Principles and Practice of Opposition: The Case of Bolingbroke versus Walpole." In *Historical Perspectives: Studies in English Thought and Society, in Honour of J. H. Plumb,* ed. Neil McKendrick, 93–128. London, 1974.

Slauter, Eric. *The State as a Work of Art: The Cultural Origins of the Constitution.* Chicago, 2009.

Slauter, Will. "Constructive Misreadings: Adams, Turgot, and the American State Constitutions." *Papers of the Bibliographic Society of America* 105 (2011): 33–67.

Smith, Charles P. *James Wilson: Founding Father, 1742–1798.* Chapel Hill, 1956.

Smith, David L. *Constitutional Royalism and the Search for Settlement, c. 1640–1649.* Cambridge, 1994.

Smith, Joseph Henry. *Appeals to the Privy Council from the American Plantations.* New York, 1950.

Southwick, Albert B. "The Molasses Act—Source of Precedents." *William and Mary Quarterly* 8 (1951): 389–405.

Spalding, James. "Loyalist as Royalist, Patriot as Puritan: The American Revolution as a Repetition of the English Civil Wars." *Church History* 45 (1976): 329–340.

Spencer, Mark G. *David Hume and Eighteenth-Century America.* Rochester, 2005.

Spitzer, Robert J. *The Presidential Veto: Touchstone of the American Presidency.* Albany, 1988.

Stadter, Philip. "Alexander Hamilton's Notes on Plutarch in His Pay Book." *Review of Politics* 73 (2011): 199–217.

Steele, Ian K. "The British Parliament and the Atlantic Colonies to 1760: New Approaches to Enduring Questions." *Parliamentary History* 14 (2005): 29–46.

Stourzh, Gerald. *Alexander Hamilton and the Idea of Republican Government.* Stanford, 1970.

Stout, Harry S. *The New England Soul: Preaching and Religious Culture in Colonial New England.* 1986; repr., Oxford, 2012.

Targett, Simon. "Government and Ideology during the Age of the Whig Supremacy: The Political Arguments of Sir Robert Walpole's Newspaper Propagandists." *The Historical Journal* 37 (1994): 289–317.

Temperley, H. W. V. "Debates on the Declaratory Act and the Repeal of the Stamp Act, 1766." *American Historical Review* 17 (1912): 563–586.

Thach, Jr., Charles C. *The Creation of the Presidency, 1775–1789: A Study in Constitutional History.* 1922; repr., Indianapolis, 2007.

Thompson, C. Bradley. *John Adams and the Spirit of Liberty.* Lawrence, KS, 1998.

———. "John Adams and the Coming of the French Revolution." *Journal of the Early Republic* 16 (1996): 361–387.

Thompson, Dennis. "The Education of a Founding Father: The Reading List for John Witherspoon's Course in Political Theory, as Taken by James Madison." *Political Theory* 4 (1976): 523–529.

van Rooden, Peter T. *Theology, Biblical Scholarship and Rabbinical Studies in the Seventeenth Century: Constantijn L'Empereur (1591–1648), Professor of Hebrew and Theology at Leiden.* Leiden, 1989.

Watson, Richard A. "Origins and Early Development of the Veto Power." *Presidential Studies Quarterly* 17 (1987): 401–412.

Werman, Golda. *Milton and Midrash.* Washington, DC, 1995.

Weston, Corinne Comstock. "The Theory of Mixed Monarchy under Charles I and After." *English Historical Review* 75 (1960): 426–443.

Wood, Gordon. "The Problem of Sovereignty." *William and Mary Quarterly* 68 (2011): 573–577.

———. *Empire of Liberty: A History of the Early Republic, 1789–1815.* Oxford, 2009.

———. *The Americanization of Benjamin Franklin.* New York and London, 2004.

———. *Monarchism and Republicanism in the Early United States.* Melbourne, 2002.

———. *The Creation of the American Republic, 1776–1787.* Rev. ed. Chapel Hill, 1998.

———. *The Radicalism of the American Revolution.* New York, 1991.

———. "Rhetoric and Reality in the American Revolution." *William and Mary Quarterly* 23 (1966): 3–32.

Wootton, David. "Liberty, Metaphor, and Mechanism: 'Checks and Balances.'" In *Liberty and American Experience in the Eighteenth Century,* ed. David Womersley, 209–274. Indianapolis, 2006.

———. "Introduction." In *Republicanism, Liberty, and Commercial Society, 1649–1776,* ed. David Wootton, 1–44. Stanford, 1994.

Worden, Blair. *Literature and Politics in Cromwellian England: John Milton, Andrew Marvell, Marchamont Nedham.* Oxford, 2007.

Yirush, Craig. *Settlers, Liberty, and Empire: The Roots of Early American Political Theory, 1675–1775*. Cambridge, 2011.

Young, Alfred F. "The Framers of the Constitution and the 'Genius of the People.'" *Radical History Review* 42 (1988): 8–18.

Zaller, Robert. *The Parliament of 1621: A Study in Constitutional Conflict*. Berkeley, 1971.

Acknowledgments

My first thanks must go to the extraordinary group of scholars who read and offered detailed comments on this book in manuscript: Daniel Aaron, David Armitage, Bernard Bailyn, Noah Feldman, Jonathan Gienapp, James Hankins, Mark Kishlansky, J. G. A. Pocock, Jack Rakove, Michael Rosen, Quentin Skinner, Shannon Stimson, and Richard Tuck. Each has improved my argument and presentation in extremely important ways. I shall find it difficult to repay their generosity.

To Bernard Bailyn, however, I owe a debt that is greater still. He has read at least three different drafts of the full manuscript, offering encouragement and unfailingly constructive criticism at every stage. His friendship and example have meant more to me than I can say.

For correspondence, references, and counsel about various aspects of the manuscript, I am indebted to Eric Beerbohm, Mary Bilder, Richard Bourke, Daniel Clinkman, Greg Conti, Bryan Garsten, John Goldberg, Philip Gorski, Chris Grasso, David Hall, Kinch Hoekstra, the late Istvan Hont, Jim Kloppenberg, Matthew Landauer, Adam Lebovitz, Rhodri Lewis, Karuna Mantena, the late Bayley Mason, Noah McCormack, John McCormick, Isaac Nakhimovsky, Mark Noll, Nancy Rosenblum, Nathan Perl-Rosenthal, Mark Peterson, Philip Pettit, Steve Pincus, Shirley Sarna, Tom Schaeper, Will Selinger, Amartya Sen, Bernard Septimus, Eran Shalev, Meir Soloveichik, Andrew Stern, Albert Tillson Jr., David Womersley, and Craig Yirush.

An invitation to lead a Late Spring Seminar at the Folger Institute in 2012 provided me with an invaluable opportunity to develop many of the arguments offered here. I am deeply grateful to the Steering Committee of the Institute's Center for the History of British Political Thought for proposing the seminar; to Owen Williams and the rest of the institute's staff for their warm hospitality during my five weeks in Washington, DC; and to the remarkable cohort of faculty colleagues and graduate students who attended. I learned a very great deal from each of them.

The Center for American Political Studies at Harvard University generously sponsored a daylong symposium on the book manuscript when it was in the final stages of preparation. I am exceedingly grateful to Dan Carpenter, the director of the center, for making the event possible and for offering characteristically incisive comments on the text, as well as to the intimidating group of discussants he managed to assemble for the occasion: David Armitage, Noah Feldman, Tara Helfman, Dan Hulsebosch, Sandy Levinson, and Emma Rothschild. Each of them offered valuable suggestions and warm encouragement at a critical moment in the life of this project.

Chapter 1 expands on and incorporates excerpts from "Patriot Royalism: The Stuart Monarchy in American Political Thought, 1769–75," in *The William and Mary Quarterly* 68 (2011). Chapter 3 expands on and incorporates excerpts from "Hebraism and the Republican Turn of 1776: A Contemporary Account of the Debate over *Common Sense*," in *The William and Mary Quarterly* 70 (2013). I am grateful to the editor of the *Quarterly* for permission to reproduce parts of both articles here. The *Quarterly* likewise published a Forum on my "Patriot Royalism" essay that featured generous and challenging responses from Dan Hulsebosch, Gordon Wood, and the late Pauline Maier. It is a pleasure to have the opportunity to renew my thanks to each of these scholars, the last of whom I dearly miss.

I was privileged to be invited to deliver the 2012 Laura Shannon Prize Lecture at the University of Notre Dame; the 2013 John Hamilton Fulton Lecture in the Liberal Arts at Middlebury College; and the 2013 Navin Narayan Memorial Lecture in Social Studies at Harvard University. Each of these occasions allowed me to refine various arguments from the book, and I am deeply grateful to my audiences for their energetic engagement. Material drawn from the manuscript was also presented to colloquia and conferences at Harvard Law School, Johns Hopkins University, the Newberry Library, UC Berkeley, UCLA, the University of London, and Yale University. My thanks go to each of these institutions for hosting me so graciously. I likewise owe a very great debt to the undergraduates and graduate students who took my course on the "Political Thought of the American Founding" at Harvard in the fall of 2009 and the spring of 2013. As always, I am certain that I learned at least as much from them as they did from me.

Much of my research was made possible by a John Simon Guggenheim Memorial Foundation Fellowship and a Frederick Burkhardt Residential Fellowship for Recently Tenured Scholars. I am deeply grateful to the Guggenheim Foundation and to the American Council of Learned Societies for their generous support of this project. I spent a year's sabbatical leave in 2011–2012 as a fellow at the Radcliffe Institute for Advanced Study, and I am delighted to be able to thank Judy Vichniac, the staff of the institute, and the other members of my fellowship cohort for making my term in residence so congenial and productive. Lastly, my continuing association with the Harvard Society of Fellows has enriched my work and thought in ways too numerous to mention.

I owe sincere thanks to the librarians and staff at Harvard's Houghton and Widener libraries, the Department of Rare Books and Special Collections at Princeton University, and the Albert and Shirley Small Special Collections Library at the University of Virginia. Like all students of the early modern period, I am exceedingly indebted to the array of digital resources that have recently transformed the practice of scholarship in the field: Early American Imprints, Early American Newspapers, Early English Books Online, Eighteenth-Century Collections Online, and numerous others. I am equally grateful to the legion of Americanists, past and present, who have seen to it that the correspondence and private papers of almost every major figure of the revolutionary period have been skillfully edited and published. In this area of inquiry, perhaps more than any other, one is constantly aware of the degree to which the scholarship of the past has made possible that of the present.

I have once again been very well served indeed by Harvard University Press. My superb editor, Ian Malcolm, has been a delight to work with and has offered crucial guidance throughout. I also remain indebted to my friend Lindsay Waters, who persuaded me that the Press was the right home for this project. Finally, I am eager to thank Joshua Ehrlich for providing expert editorial assistance with the manuscript and proofs, and for helping me prepare the bibliography.

When I arrived in the United Kingdom to begin graduate studies in October of 1999, I boarded a train from King's Cross to Cambridge and found myself sitting opposite a woman who had just recently completed her PhD. She asked what I planned to study and I replied, "the history of political thought." She then wished to know who would be supervising my research. I answered, "Quentin Skinner." At this point she smiled and asked, "Do you know how lucky you are?" If I didn't then, I certainly do now. This book is dedicated to him with gratitude and affection.

Index